Handbook of Management Skills

Handbook of Management Skills

Edited by
Dorothy M Stewart

A Gower Handbook

Published by
Gower Publishing Company Limited,
Gower House,
Croft Road,
Aldershot,
Hants GU11 3HR,
England

Gower Publishing Company,
Old Post Road,
Brookfield,
Vermont 05036,
U.S.A.

Reprinted 1989

British Library Cataloguing in Publication Data
Handbook of management skills.—(A Gower handbook)
   1. Management
   I. Stewart, Dorothy M.   II. Series
   658.4   HD31

ISBN 0 566 02635 X

Printed and bound in Great Britain by
Anchor Press Ltd, Tiptree, Essex

Contents

PART I   MANAGING YOURSELF

PART II MANAGING OTHER PEOPLE

Contents

Contents

Illustrations

List of illustrations

Preface

Management is a bit like wallpapering. Either you've lived with the old paper for a while but now you need something fresh, or you've moved house and your tastes don't coincide with those of the previous owners. Either way, it's time for new wallpaper. Similarly, you may be promoted into a managerial role or move to a new job in a new company. Either way, you've a management job to do.

The first thing you realise when you decide to do some wallpapering is the amount of kit you need. First the wallpaper. This requires serious consideration, examining samples, making a choice you're confident, for the moment, you will be able to live with. If you're lucky, the store will be able to provide your choice there and then; if not, you'll have to wait for delivery. In any case, it is as well to have done some arithmetic and careful budgeting.

The management equivalent is management itself. What is it? What are you meant to do? And how? What management style do you want? Do you have a choice? Unlike the selection of wallpaper, most people do not stop to consider these questions until they have been in the job for some time and disaster strikes. This is the 'when all else fails read the instructions' approach, and is as successful in management as it is in wallpapering or any other complex task.

A wiser course of action might be to try to find out as much as possible about management in general and the management task in particular which you are being asked to fulfil. The first can be achieved through books (see Further reading); the second requires that you ask questions. Don't be afraid you'll be revealing your lamentable ignorance. You won't! You'll be demonstrating that you have the courage to ask for the information you don't have, and getting that information at the same time.

The next task is to assess yourself and your skills against those involved in this business called management. You will find help on this in Chapter 1 of this Handbook. It is as well to make your first personal skills review totally private and ruthlessly honest. If you are interested in a more scientific and detailed approach, you may find it useful to consult a careers counsellor or industrial psychologist (someone in your own personnel department may be able to help, or advise) who will administer the Myers-Briggs Type Inventory for you. This will reveal your strengths as well as your weaknesses, and will provide a sound base for planning your growth as a manager.

What you are planning is your future. There are few things more important to you than this, so do allocate resources of time – and money – to this. You will find this effort repaid beyond measure in the future.

Just as with wallpaper, this assessment is only the start. For wallpapering, there is a great list of equipment to be found: paste bucket and brush, pasting table, plumb bob, spirit level, sponges, ladders, wallpaper shears, lining paper, etc. Some of these are essential, some are useful, and some are for the professional, or the gadget enthusiast, or those with special wall problems.

A comparison of your self-assessment against the requirements of your job will uncover a similar 'shopping list' of skills and knowledge. It may be a good idea to give this list careful thought, and then work out some priorities. Which skills and knowledge do you think are going to be most needed in your job? Which ones are likely to be needed soonest? Which are essential? Which are optional – great to have, when you have time?

You may find the contents list in this Handbook a useful starting point. I have tried to cover a very wide range of skills and knowledge for managers: Part I with personal skills for management, Part II with the skills for managing other people, and Part III with the skills and knowledge necessary for managing the business. Each chapter offers an introduction, how-to guidelines and, in most cases, a list of further reading to enable you to pursue the subject. You will notice cross-references between chapters, and some overlap and duplication where techniques apply in more than one area. I have tried to keep this to a minimum but since management skills tend to be multi-purpose some duplication has been unavoidable.

Although it is very pleasant to come home to a room that has been wallpapered by someone else, there is more satisfaction to be had from an attractive room that you have wallpapered yourself. Just so with management development. You can hand the task over to the experts in your organisation. You can rely on them to be efficient and professional. But for a really satisfying job, you need to take responsibility for your own development needs, and work *with* the experts, rather than playing a merely passive role.

One last thought. Remember the wallpaper you put on the sitting room four years ago? It was exactly what you wanted then and it has lasted very well. But now, you've been thinking the room could do with a facelift. Something a bit brighter, more modern. So too with management development. Today's plans and today's learning are fine for today, but remember that tomorrow needs tomorrow's skills. You can plan ahead to a considerable extent. But in an environment of constant change, your plans need to have flexibility built into them, to enable and encourage you to face tomorrow's challenges.

Dorothy M Stewart

FURTHER READING

Drucker, Peter F, *The Effective Executive,* Pan, 1970. This is the Drucker 'how to do it' book. A terrific starter for any manager.

Drucker, Peter F, *The Practice of Management*, Pan, 1968. All about management by Drucker at his most readable. Masses of anecdotes to help the medicine down. A great book.

Stewart, Rosemary, *The Reality of Management*, Pan, 1986. One of the classics, about what managers actually do.

Notes on contributors

John Adair *(Leadership and motivation* and *Managing communication)* ex-Professor in Leadership Studies at the University of Surrey, is no armchair theorist. He has served in the Arab Legion, been a deckhand on an Arctic trawler and worked as an orderly in a hospital. For seven years he was Senior Lecturer in Military History and Adviser on Leadership Training at the Royal Military Academy, Sandhurst. During this period he led a number of expeditions, including one across the Jordanian desert by camel. At one time Assistant Director of the Industrial Society, Professor Adair has written and lectured widely on both management and military history. *Effective Leadership* (Gower, 1983) is his fourteenth book.

Pauline Barrett *(Team building)* undertook her first team building exercise in 1970 with a group of youth and community workers, and district youth officers, who were having difficulty in reconciling their individual and group needs and responsibilities. It was in that exercise that her interest in working with managers focused on the effect of group working on the success of the enterprise. Later Pauline joined the staff at Slough College and worked on a wide variety of management development programmes for both private and public sector clients. In 1981 she left the College to work as a freelance consultant and finally had the opportunity to work with teams as she has always wished. Her other work interests are in orchestrating learning communities of managers, and running programmes on assertiveness, stress, and intensive interviewing skills for line managers, personnel officers and trainers.

John Courtis, FCA *(Interviewing)* has been in management search or selection for 20 years. He trained as a Chartered Accountant, was commissioned in the RAF and then spent five years in Ford Motor Co., before joining Reed Executive in 1967. He was then with EAL for a four-year period before setting up JC&P in 1974. He has been active in management education since 1972, for the Institute of Chartered Accountants in England and Wales and other bodies and is the author of ten books on management, profit improvement, public relations and recruitment. He is now chairman of JC&P Ltd, of Deeko plc and vice-chairman of the recruitment trade association, FRES. In his spare time he writes more books, searches for the ideal motor car of yesteryear and wonders why modern management techniques don't quite work in family life.

Corinne Devery *(Making the most of your support staff)* was, until recently, Head of Secretarial Development at the Industrial Society, where she and her team ran courses for secretaries at all levels (and also for managers) in how to use support staff, and in time management. Before joining the Society, Corinne worked as a secretary, in both the public sector and in private industry.

John Gregory *(Making meetings work)* is, in his early 50s, enjoying his fourth career – that of a management selection consultant. He joined the accountancy profession straight from school and later joined mechanical handling engineers, Lansing Bagnall Ltd, as a junior accountant. National Service led to a Short Service Commission in the Royal Army Pay Corps and this, indirectly, to a second career in management education because his three years in the army were spent in the RAPC Headquarter Training Unit. A developing interest in training led to John joining the Management School at Portsmouth Polytechnic where he stayed nine years taking leave in 1967 to study for an MSc in Management Control at Bath University. In 1972, he joined the Institute of Chartered Accountants in England and Wales as Assistant Director Post Qualifying Training, becoming Director, Professional Development Services in 1980. Five years later he became a partner in management selection consultants, John Courtis and Partners, where he is in charge of their Milton Keynes office. John retains a close interest in management education and is a visiting speaker at Cranfield School of Management.

Feona J Hamilton *(Managing information in the office)* has been a member of the information management profession for over 20 years. Starting as a junior library assistant at East Sussex County Library, she held progressively more senior positions in a wide variety of academic and learned society libraries. Her most recent post was as a Group Manager with Aslib. She left Aslib in April 1985, in order to complete research on which she had been working part-time since 1981. In 1985 she began operating as a freelance information consultant. Feona Hamilton is a member of the Library Association Council, a specialist adviser on information needs and access for the Recreation and Sports Studies Board of the Council for National Academic Awards, and a founder committee member of the Sport and Recreation Information Group (SPRIG). She has contributed widely to the literature of her profession, and is an experienced editor of directories, current awareness bulletins, and newsletters. Feona Hamilton has a BA in Humanities from the Open University, an MPhil in Librarianship, is a Chartered Librarian, and a Member of the British Institute of Management.

Valerie J. Hammond *(Skills for women managers)* is Director of Research at Ashridge Management College. She, together with a team of researchers, carries out studies about managers and the issues that concern them. The research is either requested directly by the College, sponsored by funding bodies or commissioned by individual companies. In the latter case, the work is often an attitude survey. By discipline she is a psychologist, and her particular research interests are the development of women, management futures, the implications of information technology for managers and organisations and the culture and value systems that exist in organisations. She has published many articles and reports out of her research. Before joining Ashridge in 1980 she was in line and training functions in the oil industry, initially with Mobil and then with the Petroleum ITB. In the 1960s she worked with an office equipment manufacturer (now part of ICL) introducing some of the earliest forms of electronic office equipment. (This is what triggered an interest in training and development and then in research.) Outside Ashridge, she is actively involved in European and national management development networks.

Roger Haywood *(Being an ambassador for your organisation)* has been marketing and public relations adviser to leading British and international companies in industries ranging from high technology to leisure and consumer products. He lectures, writes and broadcasts on marketing and communications and has presented papers at several conferences. Roger Haywood began his career as a copywriter in advertising agencies before moving on to hold marketing positions with Dunlop and Dexion International. He was European communications adviser to Air Products and Chemicals Incorporated, one of the largest American chemical corporations, before forming his own London consultancy. He has been a governor of the Communication, Advertising and Marketing Education Foundation (CAM), and is moderator of the CAM PR diploma, a member of the board of management and chairman of the education committee of the Public Relations Consultants' Association, a member of the national executive and past branch chairman of the Institute of Marketing. Haywood is also an accredited business communicator and one of the few practitioners in the UK to hold the CAM diploma qualification in both advertising and public relations. He wrote the standard guide to business communication *All About PR*.

Dr Peter Honey *(People skills)* has been a freelance psychologist and management consultant since 1969. He specialises in anything to do with people's behaviour and its consequences. He divides his work into designing and running courses on interactive skills, team building, creative thinking, problem solving and self-development; consultancy projects on such things as customer satisfaction, assessment centre criteria, management training needs, staff attitudes, behaviour in meetings and groups; researching and writing books and articles. Some major clients during the last two years have been the Atomic Energy Authority, the Bank of England, Fisons, Ford Motor Company, ICL, ICI, Kimberly-Clark and Thomas Cook. Peter Honey is a member of the British Psychological Society, the Institute of Management Consultants, the Association of Teachers of Management and a Fellow of the International Management Centre from Buckingham and the Institute of Training and Development.

P T Humphrey *(Recruitment and Selection)* is a managing consultant with Price Waterhouse Management Consultants. Previously he was managing director of Ashton Containers (Southern) and personnel director with the Mettoy Company Ltd. He is a Companion of The Institute of Personnel Management, a Fellow of the British Institute of Management, and Member of the Institute of Management Consultants. He is a contributor to *Administration of Personnel Policies* edited by Torrington and Naylor (Gower, 1974), *The Gower Handbook of Management* edited by Lock and Farrow (Gower, 1983) and author of *How to be Your Own Personnel Manager* (Institute of Personnel Management, 1981).

Andrew Kakabadse (*The politics of management*) is Professor of Management Development at Cranfield School of Management, and his current research interest is in leadership and politics in organisations. He is a director of two companies and has worked as a consultant to a wide range of organisations, including banks, motor manufacturers and multinational corporations. He is editor of the *Leadership and Organisation Development Journal* and co-editor of the *Journal of Managerial Psychology*. Professor Kakabadse has published numerous books and articles on various aspects of management and was recently elected a Fellow of the International Academy of Management. He is the principal author of *Working in Organisations* (Gower, 1987).

John Lewington *(Project management)* is Director, Management Studies Division at Harrow College of Higher Education. He originally trained as a Production Engineer with the Ever Ready Co. (GB) Ltd whilst completing his degree at City University. He spent three years working for General Motors Ltd (AC Delco) as Group Project Planning Engineer devising plans for new product proposals. In the 1970s he developed a number of short courses for executives in production planning and control techniques. His teaching experience spans the Open University, Middlesex Polytechnic and the Polytechnic of Central London undergraduate and postgraduate management programmes. In 1979 he gained an MSc in Business Administration from the City University Business School, where he specialised in operations research and corporate planning. His current post involves the design and development of management programmes to be conducted at Harrow College and on an in-plant basis. He has also worked as a consultant for a number of organisations in the UK. His current interest is the development of computer-based simulation models for management training in problem solving and decision making.

Bruce Lloyd *(Strategic planning)* has a degree in Chemical Engineering, a Masters Degree in Business Studies from the London Business School (1968) and a Diploma in International Affairs. He started work with the British Petroleum Company in 1964, before going to business school and joining Hoare & Co. as an investment analyst. From 1970 to 1978 he was an investment manager with the Commonwealth Development Finance Company, and from 1978 to 1983 he was a finance manager in the Merchant Banking Division of the Bank of Credit and Commerce International SA, concerned with venture capital investments for the bank and undertaking internal consulting activities. He then spent 18 months undertaking freelance consultancy, fund raising and writing and lecturing assignments, before joining ICI Agricultural Division in Billingham to assist with corporate venturing – organising existing ventures, identifying new projects, as well as attempting to change attitude in the core business. During this time he was also seconded to Northern Investors, a venture capital company based in Newcastle, and concerned with developing links with the venture capital industry as a whole. He has currently returned to freelance consultancy, writing and lecturing. Bruce Lloyd is a member of: Institution of Chemical Engineers (C.Eng); British Institute of Management (FBIM, member of council); Society of Investment Analysts; Institute of Directors; Strategic Planning Society (Executive Committee member and member of the editorial board of *Long Range Planning* journal); and Business Graduates' Association (Chairman 1985/7).

Pauric McGowan *(Creativity and innovation)* graduated in Economics in 1976 from the Polytechnic at Wolverhampton. He returned to his native Northern Ireland to follow a career in accountancy. In 1980, he returned to the West Midlands of England to undertake a Master in Business Administration degree at the Management Centre of the University of Aston in Birmingham. He first became interested in the subject of creativity and innovation while studying at Aston University, where a large part of the programme was dedicated to this important topic. He undertook a major project on the management of creativity, researching the great wealth of contributions of many writers in the area. He returned to Ireland after graduating in 1981 and took up a post at Ireland's premier Technological University at Limerick (the National Institute for Higher Education). He has recently joined the University of Ulster at Jordanstown lecturing in management and entrepreneurship, but continues his research into management and innovation through the network of the Association of Teachers of Management (Irish region).

Mike Megranahan *(Counselling in the work place)* completed his first degree in psychology and then worked in personnel for three years covering such aspects as recruitment and selection, psychometric testing, job evaluation and the development of survey materials. He then moved into lecturing before going to Henley – the Management College – to undertake PhD research into the psychological effects of redundancy with a particular focus on counselling strategies used to alleviate the impact of redundancy. After working as an occupational psychologist for the Manpower Services Commission in the area of employment rehabilitation, assessment and counselling he joined Control Data as a counsellor for their employee assistance program, the Employee Advisory Resource (EAR) before becoming the manager. EAR was the first in-house counselling programme of its kind in the UK and currently provides a range of counselling services to employees of Control Data as well as other organisations. He has also been involved in the development of a work counselling skills course for a leading consultancy; adapted and extended a computer interactive system to act as a basis for career change counselling for use in a large UK chemicals company; and acted as a counsellor, in a voluntary capacity, to several unemployment support groups. He has had several articles published on counselling and redundancy. He is also Chairman of the Counselling at Work Division of the British Association for Counselling and a member of the Occupational Psychology Division of the British Psychological Society.

William P Rees *(Accounting and business decisions)* is a lecturer in accounting in the Department of Economics at the University of Newcastle-upon-Tyne. His specialisms in lecturing, research and consultancy are centred on financial analysis and financial management. Before joining the University Bill lectured in the School of Business at Kingston Polytechnic and previously was a researcher in the Department of Industrial Relations at the University of Sydney. This research focused on the disclosure of information to employees. Before commencing his academic career Bill worked in the accounting profession for eight years, qualifying as a Chartered Accountant in 1975 whilst with Deloitte Haskins and Sells and gained his Master of Business Administration at the University of Liverpool in 1976.

John Rogers *(Manage your time)* obtained a research degree in Materials Science in 1972 and has spent most of his working time as a trainer. Currently he is setting up and managing an Information and Research Unit at the TSB Group Management College, Solihull. His work interests mostly involve technology and information in learning, facilitating the development of senior managers and helping others use the time of their life well. A major previous employer was the British Gas Corporation, Northern Region, John being primarily responsible for employee relations training and developing managers.

Brian Sanders *(Effective speaking)* trained as an actor and toured the British Isles, France, Belgium and Egypt with the Donald Wolfit Shakespeare Company. He left the theatre in 1954 to take up a career in education. He is a qualified teacher of speech, drama and English and for several years was head of the Speech and Drama Department of a constituent college of London University. He first broadcast in 1960 when he wrote and narrated programmes on acting, the theatre and Shakespeare. From 1970 to 1979 he wrote and presented a drama programme for BBC Schools Radio. Nowadays he broadcasts regularly on radio as an actor and narrator. He has extensive experience of teaching professional people in all aspects on communication and presentation. He runs courses on effective speaking and on speaking professionally through the media in which he deals in a practical way with interviews and talks on TV and radio, the phone-in, and discussions. He runs one-, two- and three-day practical workshop courses for the Industrial Society, the Institute of Accountants, Touche Ross, the Army School of Recruiting, the CEGB, the Electricity Council and firms of solicitors and actuaries. Since 1985 he has devised and run courses for several UK marketing companies. He lectures to large conferences and small groups.

Bill Scott *(Negotiating)* is an independent consultant working internationally and specialising in communication. His background comprises a rare mixture of industrial and academic achievement. He conducted business research from the University of Keele and later became project director of the Centre for Business Research and eventually assistant director of Manchester Business School. His experience in industry includes six years as group training manager with Wiggins Teape and six directing management development in the 22,000-strong Carrington and Dewhurst Group. Mr Scott has lectured for Management Centre Europe, the ILO and numerous other organisations, and runs seminars regularly, in the UK and overseas, on communication and negotiation skills. He is the author of *The Skills of Negotiating* (Gower, 1981).

Andrew M Stewart *(Coping with stress* and *Performance appraisal)* is managing director of Informed Choice Ltd, an organisation which applies psychology to business and industry. His activities range from diagnosing the characteristics of effective performance, conducting training needs analyses and employee attitude surveys, to personnel and management selection, performance appraisal, and the identification and development of potential managers and entrepreneurs. He also conducts stress management programmes and assists with the problems of team building. He uses many different techniques, but is probably best known for his work with repertory grid, psychological tests and, above all, assessment centres, which he has been designing and running since 1970. Andrew graduated in psychology from Aberdeen University. He lectured at Surrey University for two years, and then held personnel and management development posts with IBM. He was seconded to the Institute of Manpower Studies at Sussex University, where he remained until 1977, developing the research interests which underpin his current work. He was managing director of Macmillan Stewart Ltd until 1986. He has published over 40 papers, six chapters for various handbooks, and six books, covering assessment centres, performance appraisal, management development, poor performance, and repertory grid. He is a member of the British Psychological Society, a Fellow of the Royal Statistical Society, and an Associate of the Royal College of Psychiatrists.

Dorothy M Stewart *(Effective writing)* is a management consultant with special expertise and interest in written communication. Beginning as a journalist, she worked in every aspect of book publishing, on a wide range of subjects and levels. She spent five years in Northern Nigeria, where she was involved in teaching English to Eastern Europeans and pre-university students, and setting up Ahmadu Bello University Press, a scholarly publishing house. After five years running McGraw-Hill's UK management book publishing programme, she set up the Writing Consultancy. Her work now centres on a range of training and development programmes and consultancy projects on business and creative writing. The Writing Consultancy aims to enable people to achieve their objectives through writing, whether it is for publication, general business purposes, marketing or promotion. She has an MA from Aberdeen University, and an MBA (special subject, finance) from Middlesex Business School, which she did the hard way—part-time while continuing to work full-time. She is a member of the British Institute of Management and the Association of Teachers of Management.

Cathy Stoddart *(Developing your people)* graduated in economics and government but chose to go into industrial relations working for a major employers' association. After initially dealing with day-to-day queries arising from the intricacies of a 26-clause National Agreement, she was soon dealing with national officials of the major trade unions with which the association negotiated. In this period, she also developed an interest and skills in job evaluation. In 1978 she was appointed job evaluation co-ordinator (in addition to her IR responsibilities) with an independent seat on the National Joint Council for the Environmental Engineering Industry. In her next job as a personnel manager she became interested in training and development and later joined a relatively new consultancy company, the Prospect Centre, which specialises in developing strategic manpower development policies and practices for organisations. Finally, Cathy's personal experiences as a woman and now a mother of two small children who also wants to work have sparked an interest in the whole field of equal opportunities. This is another area in which she and the Prospect Centre are also working.

Peter Walker *(Decision making and problem solving)* is the European training and development manager for Texas Instruments, with the responsibility for helping develop effective training organisations. In addition he has a personal interest in developing training programmes which provide the vehicle for integrating individual skill development and cultural change within the organisation. He also lectures outside Texas Instruments and his training approach has proved successful in a number of organisations. Peter Walker has worked in management training and organisation development over the last ten years at Rank Xerox and now Texas Instruments. As a chartered engineer he brings management and business experience to the training function in fields such as technical sales, product support and services management. His experience of adult education and technical training goes back to his national service days as an instructor in the Royal Army Education Corps.

Michael Williams *(Management self-development* and *Career planning)* is senior partner of Michael Williams and Partners and director of Applied Skills for Management. He held posts in organisation development and management development in BL Cars following experience in personnel, marketing and production in a variety of major UK companies. In 1980 he set up his own consultancy specialising in organisation development, team building and individual development. Mr Williams has lectured extensively in the UK and Europe on various management topics – especially leadership and management style. His publications include *Human Relations* (Longmans, 1967), *Supervisory Management in the Office* (Heinemann, 1969) and *Performance Appraisal in Management* (Heinemann, 1972).

Peter Woodcock *(Marketing)* made his first career in the chemical industry where he worked for about 18 years. During this time, his experience was very varied, making heavy chemicals, recruiting graduates from universities (what is these days called 'the milk round'), selling speciality chemicals, and, finally, examining the marketing activities of potential acquisition candidates. His second career was with Middlesex Polytechnic where he was fortunate to have played a part in two 'firsts'. The Polytechnic was the first British academic institution to set up and run a joint degree programme with a French Grande Ecole – the Ecole Supérieure de Commerce at Reims. This course entailed students spending half their time in each country, including a period in industry in both countries, and Woodcock taught on that course from its inception until he retired in 1983. The course was extended to West Germany, in cooperation with the Fachhochschule at Reutlingen, and Woodcock was a member of the British and French team negotiating this development. He also helped to launch the first part-time Master of Business Administration degree in a Polytechnic. He continues to teach on this programme, and it is appropriate to note at this point that the editor of this Handbook gained her MBA on that very course. Peter Woodcock continues his interest in industry by acting as a consultant to a number of small and medium sized firms.

Dr H Beric Wright *(Managing your health)* qualified at University College and Hospital, after which he spent four years in the army doing operational research as an applied physiologist. Later he trained as a surgeon and worked overseas for an oil company in Sarawak and Trinidad where he started a birth control clinic in a Catholic island. In 1958 he joined the staff of the Institute of Directors under the enlightened leadership of the late Sir Richard Powell, to start a medical research unit looking at the occupational health problems of managers. In 1964 this became the IOD Executive Health Centre which merged with BUPA in 1970 to become the BUPA Medical Centre which now provides a countrywide health screening facility. Dr

Wright was a governor of BUPA and chairman of the BUPA Medical Centre and Hospital companies. He has also been involved in the growth of the Abbeyfield Society, providing homes for the lonely elderly, and is their national vice-chairman and medical adviser. He is past chairman and president of the Pre-Retirement Association and on the board of several companies and charities. Dr Wright thus has both medical and direct managerial experience which helps him to advise managers about maintaining a prudent lifestyle. He is interested in the development of holistic medicine. He writes, lectures and broadcasts on health topics and preventive medicine. His books include *Executive Ease and Disease* (Gower, 1976).

Part I
MANAGING YOURSELF

Introduction: Understanding yourself and your skills needs as a manager

Among the most bewildering causes of unemployment are shortages of skills. There are plenty of people who want to work and there are people who want to employ workers. But the posts and the people do not match – because the people do not have the skills the employers want.

As business moves on towards the twenty-first century, the skills that managers need are changing too. A mismatch between posts and people is increasingly likely, especially for people in a post which changes when they do not. In the all too common case of companies that offer no management training, your future is indeed in your own hands.

A personal inventory of your current skills, their strengths and weaknesses, and of the skills demanded currently by your job, will provide a start. But do look ahead to where you think you and your job may be going, and assess your skills needs for the future. Then it is time to get to work on plugging the gaps you see, and polishing up your poorer skills.

Part I of this Handbook focuses on your personal skills. Chapter 1 will help you plan your own course of management development, and contains suggestions for methods. The other chapters in Part I offer guidance on fundamental skills for the manager: managing your time, which provides a review of the main time management systems and methods; managing the information that threatens to overwhelm us all, with guidance on assessing your own information needs and how to control the information when you've got it – highlighted by Hamilton's wry 'laws'; and two chapters on the other side of the coin: managing the production of information – effective writing, which aims to help you save time and effort in producing effective written material, and effective speaking, which treats not only the planning and preparation of the material of your presentation but also the technical details of delivery and presentation.

Management is a demanding profession and many managers find that the lifestyle can be damaging in many ways. Dr Beric Wright in Chapter 6 maintains that it is not only possible but necessary that managers manage their own health to achieve a high level of wellbeing, and points out both the dangers and some ways to survive them. Dr Andrew Stewart in Chapter 7 focuses on the effects of stress, its various symptoms and causes, and provides guidelines for its management, both by the individual and by the organisation.

Part I concludes with a brief but useful chapter on career and life planning, and a chapter aimed specifically at the woman manager (which male managers will find contains much of interest). The number of female managers in industry is growing but for women there are as yet few of the role models, informal networks or assumptions about managing that men have always had. This chapter looks at skills that female managers may be weaker in than males and skills where they may be stronger, to enable female managers to identify their own management development needs. Male managers may find it a helpful review both for themselves and for their female subordinates. Many of the subjects touched on in this chapter are treated in detail elsewhere in this book.

1

Management self-development

Michael Williams

It is widely believed that management development = management training = 'send him on a course'. This view assumes that management development is 'done' by someone to someone else − applied, in other words, like an external treatment.

Management development planned in this spirit rarely involves the person who requires development in either the diagnosis of the problem or the formulation of the prescription and follow-up. Thus he tends to find himself playing a largely passive role in important activities concerned (as the case may be) with:

- his growth as a person;
- his development for future promotion or transfer;
- improving his current performance or increasing his contribution as a manager;
- helping him make the transition from specialist to managerial role;
- developing his skills in specific areas.

Traditional forms of management training, moreover, are more likely to be 'off the peg' than tailor-made, and may not always be the most suitable for the individual in question.

Perhaps most serious of all is the constant failure to recognise that ultimately the company, a boss, or the management development manager is not responsible for the development of the organisation's managers. The managers themselves are. The boss's responsibility is to encourage, support and 'facilitate' the process of his subordinates' self-development and therefore is principally one of helping them to help themselves to develop and become more effective.

At its most fundamental, management development means self-development – that is, a conscious response on the part of the individual to deal with what *he* recognises as his development needs. Real development takes place when the individual sees, for himself, the need to modify his behaviour, change his attitudes, develop new skills, improve his performance, or prepare himself for a different role. The rationale that 'only the learner will learn' is recognised in some organisations and by a growing number of management development specialists, tutors and trainers.

Because many of the barriers to self-development that exist in companies and within boss–subordinate relationships are self-imposed and psychological, the process needs stimulation, guidance and sensitive managing. The next level up in the management hierarchy often serves as the best excuse for not getting things done and provides a frequent let-out for the individual who chooses to deny his responsibility for his own development:

> 'I'm employed by the company; it's up to my boss to decide what my development needs are. I don't know which way my career is going to to go.'

Such self-imposed constraints are not strategies for success. They need to be recognised by managers as recipes for mediocrity. The evidence that such self-protective behaviour is prevalent at managerial and supervisory levels usually takes the form of:

- scepticism and a general 'don't want to know' attitude;
- unwillingness to take ownership of problems;
- reluctance to exercise initiative and authority;
- opting out and buck-passing;
- failure to take necessary risks leading to a record of lost opportunities;
- forfeiture of influence as a 'power-source' within the organisation.

The true basis of self-development – namely that the individual takes responsibility for his own learning – may be quite alien to some managers. Traditionally much education (schools, further education and training) has put the emphasis on teaching rather than on learning. That approach tends to create inappropriately high levels of student passivity towards developing new attitudes and behaviours ('It's up to *them* to teach *me*').

To some people the idea of taking responsibility for their own learning is even seen as threatening, because it involves a personal shift from a largely uncommitted or passively receptive state to one which demands the individual's commitment and action.

Others may be so disillusioned with their particular lot or with the company in general that they are demotivated and demoralised to the extent that they cease to care about self-development altogether. To people in such negative states of mind the process is likely to be seen at best as 'pie in the sky'.

More probably it will be viewed with suspicion as a management confidence trick, personnel department propaganda or (by the real cynics) as a 'do-it-yourself hangman's kit'.

Some managers may take a tougher, more calculative view and expect to see direct links between any effort on their part in self-development and the company's reward system.

Finally there will always be managers (usually senior executives) who assume inviolability. They claim, with or without coyness, that they have already 'arrived' and that 'this sort of thing is all right for other people'.

SELF-DEVELOPMENT IN THEORY AND PRACTICE

There are two aspects of the human personality which are relevant to the understanding of self-development. These are:

1 The 'self-image' (the 'me as I see myself') by which each individual identifies himself, his personal values, beliefs, knowledge, wants, needs and fears as well as his physical presence.
2 The 'ego ideal' (which amounts to the individual's 'me as I would really like to be'). In essence this consists of the attainable 'plus me' which exists in every individual in addition to the hopes, dreams and wishes which may make up the idealised or fantasy self.

Personal growth (which by definition is largely determined by self-development) is the linking route from the self-image to the ego ideal. This is illustrated in Figure 1.1.

Practical self-development in management, necessarily, is concerned with attainable realities – what has been termed the 'plus-me', rather than simply with the individual's fantasy world. The 'plus-me' represents the difference between what the individual currently does, how effectively he operates, what contributions he

7

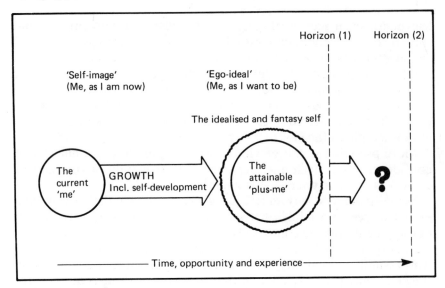

Figure 1.1   Personal growth

makes in his present role and what that person is realistically capable of doing and being, within *self-selected periods of time*. The concept of the 'plus-me', therefore, is related to a series of progressively emerging horizons – rather than to some ultimate limit which he or others have put on his potential. The horizons become more readily discernible as the individual consciously links his current behaviour and performance to what he feels are, for him, *requisite* standards, levels or modes of behaviour and which he judges are within his identifiable capacity. In practical terms the 'plus-me' can be related to and reinforced by what Hodgson and Myers refer to as the 'plus-job'. This is an attainable, realistic and viable role in which there are opportunities for increased satisfaction for the individual, coupled with increased contribution to the organisation in which he operates.

Identifying the 'plus-me' and the 'plus-job' involves the individual manager working through a series of key questions, preferably with his boss and (where available) a management development specialist. From the responses are built up pictures of how the individual wants to grow as a person and how his job, or role, might be realistically developed to cater for and capitalise on that person's growth. The next stage is to evolve appropriate action plans, principally within the scope of the manager's work environment. Exercises are given later in this chapter which illustrate the processes and show how more diagnostic information can be obtained in order for the prescriptive action plans to be evolved for individual managers and for managerial teams. The crucial following activities are monitoring, review and follow-through, without which there would only be action plans − not action.

SELF-DEVELOPMENT: DISCLOSURE AND FEEDBACK

The self-diagnosis described above represents a systematic analysis of a manager's performance, especially his behaviour in role and, therefore, his *management style*. The evidence of his immediate boss, his boss's superior, his peers and his subordinates represents crucial feedback to help him identify his real training and development needs for himself.

Informal performance reviews by his boss, periodic discussions with colleagues whose opinions and judgement he values, together with the data available to him from formal appraisal interviews all help him to place himself in relation to the demands of his job. Similarly, discussions with effective and experienced management development or training managers should provide valuable feedback and insights into how others see him and his contribution.

The process of feedback, however, is often best enhanced by *disclosure*, that is by disclosing expectations, needs or concerns which invite response and discussion. By specifically asking for information about personal effectiveness, management style, role as a colleague or boss, or contributions as a subordinate, a manager can build up a picture of both confirmatory and contradictory evidence about his perceived competence in his job. For example, he can turn what is so often the rather sterile ritual of the annual appraisal into a fruitful discussion by taking the initiative himself and encouraging his boss to ask the right questions. By using a simple self-appraisal instrument which more or less parallels the questions and areas of analysis of the company appraisal form he can prepare himself (and his reviewer) for a worthwhile and relevant diagnosis of his real performance improvement or development needs. One of the hallmarks of the really effective manager or specialist is his capacity to 'manage upwards'.

Influencing superiors is not the same as falling into the trap of self-weakening by *delegating* authority and responsibility upwards. Rather, it means letting a boss know exactly what you need from him, in order to do your own job more effectively. Equally, it means finding out from him where he needs you to change your behaviour in some way. The process is about helping a superior to act as a necessary and appropriately supportive source of organisational authority in order to open doors or give sanction to requisite innovation. Some managers may well feel vulnerable when the significance of their epaulets is drawn to their attention by a subordinate who is saying, in effect – 'Come on, you're the boss, so act like one and give me the authority to go and do what we need to get done.'

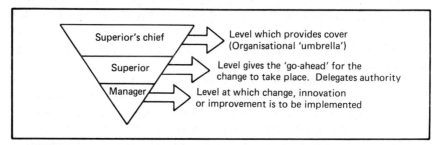

Figure 1.2   Hierarchical support needed for change to be implemented
This diagram shows the levels of support required to implement and sustain far-reaching change and improvement.

Generally most major or far-reaching changes require management at at least three levels within the organisation, as Figure 1.2 illustrates. First, there is the level at which the innovation or change is to be implemented. Immediately above that is the superior who may have to go out on a limb in order to give the necessary 'go-ahead' – hence the sense of vulnerability at this level. Then above him is the 'umbrella' often necessary to provide senior managerial or organisational cover for the venture, even though all the evidence suggests that the change will result in necessary performance improvement.

Much of the art of the process lies in the extent to which both joint and mutually exclusive areas of accountability are identified and spelled out. In this way, mutual perceptions and expectations about obstacles to effective results and about opportunities that should or should not be exploited can be clarified. Such disclosure and feedback need to be 'core' features of any boss–subordinate relationship in management, as a matter of course not just during periods of innovation and change. As an essential part of the personal (and hopefully mutual) stocktake which is what the annual performance appraisal should be, at least the following questions need to be raised and worked through from the subordinate's point of view:

- 'These are what I see as my current priorities.'
- 'This is what I believe(d) you (my boss) expect(ed) from me' or 'This is what I believe is/was expected of me in my job.'
- 'These are the results I believe I have achieved.'
- 'This is what I feel I have done well.'
- 'This is where I see I need to improve.'
- 'This is where/how I need you (my boss) to act on my behalf (or to give me support) in order for me to do my job more effectively.'
- 'These are the areas where I see our relationship as

  – good
  – less than satisfactory.'

- 'What do you need me to do differently in order for you to

  – act more effectively as my boss?
  – do your own job more effectively?'

- 'I see these as my main training development needs.'
- 'What training or development do you feel I need?'

THE 'FLY ON THE WALL'

A process which provides detailed minute-by-minute data about a manager's role and performance over several short periods of time is that of direct observation, accompanied by feedback and discussion. The purpose of the observation is to identify, record and review what a manager actually *does* in the course of several working days. Observation takes the form of a 'fly on the wall' technique, which involves the observer sitting in with the manager so that the latter's every work activity can be recorded under appropriate headings and subsequently fed back to him for review and analysis. As a tool for learning, self-development and performance improvement it is invaluable, given an observer who is a credible, competent and sensitive individual in whom the manager being observed has confidence. The observer therefore may be a management development or training manager, external consultant, colleague, superior, or in some cases a subordinate.

The process can be structured to suit the situation, status and role of the manager being observed and the relationship between the observer and the observed. A case study later in this chapter illustrates a structured observation over a period of several hours. The subject in this case was a typical middle manager at work. His activities have been recorded in detail, in this format, in order to provide him with accurate data about:

- How he spends his time in a variety of management situations, covering a range of managerial activities. In particular, where he needs to create periods of uninterrupted time for himself.
- Where he could or should delegate and make greater use of other people, especially his secretary.
- In which situations and with which people he needs to control his 'boundaries' more effectively by developing more assertive approaches.
- How he could acquire vital information from other functions in a more timely way, with less effort.
- Where he needs to develop a more effective 'eyes and ears', or 'field intelligence' service through other people to reduce the amount of time he personally spends seeking information.

The amount of time required and frequency of observation for a 'fly on the wall' exercise will vary, depending on:

- the purpose and intended outcomes of the observations;
- the role and nature of the activities of the manager under observation;
- whether or not remedial work is to begin after the first session or commence once all the observation is at an end and diagnostic feedback has been completed.

Generally the process takes place in four or five phases, which are described below.

Phase 1: Initial discussion and decision to mount the exercise

This includes:

- Agreement of the 'contract' between the observer and his client about mutual expectations and intended outcomes (N.B. the client may well not be the person to be observed; it could be his immediate superior, or other more senior executive).

- Ice-breaking and establishment of relationship between observer and observed.
- Agreement on whether to hold observation sessions on set dates, or turn up on a random basis.
- Confirmation of what are and are not legitimate activities for observation.

Phase 2: Observation

This phase may consist of any number of sessions but, typically, four or five half-days over a period of two weeks represents the minimum necessary. During those sessions the observer is virtually 'glued' to the manager so that he may record the latter's activities and *reactions* in adequate detail. Normally the observer will use a log with appropriate headings under which he can detail what he sees happening (or not happening, since part of the observer's role during later stages will be to talk through significant omissions in the observed manager's behaviour). A typical log is illustrated in the case study later in this chapter (see Figure 1.3). Codes used are also explained in the case study. Others may be added as necessary. This is largely a matter of matching the tool to the task and evolving a relevant shorthand vocabulary which is convenient and quick to use.

Phase 3: The feedback stage

At this stage copies of the log are given to the manager. This may be done either at the end of each observation session, when his memory is fresh, or as a complete 'package' at the end of the exercise.

To stimulate review and analysis and to help the manager draw out the necessary learning points the observer usually works through a series of relevant questions, typified by the following:

- How far do the observations match your understanding of what happened?
- Are there any surprises in the data contained in the log?
- Does time actually spent on some activities fit your recollections of the time you believed you spent?
- What can you learn about the way you analyse situations, make decisions and take action?
- When are you most effective? Which situations do you handle well?
- When are you least effective? Which situations could you handle better?

- What could and should you be delegating?
- How well do you plan against contingencies and cope with events that you could not plan for?
- How effective are you in obtaining the information you need to do your job?
- How well do you warn others of impending difficulties, or actions likely to affect them?
- What exactly do you need to do differently in order to be more effective at your job?
- From all the above data what skills do you need to improve in order to be more effective and how best can you develop them?

Phase 4: The action plan stage

Both the data presented and the manager's response to that feedback provide the basis for his personal development action plans. Where appropriate the action plans may well be discussed with the manager's superior and a specialist from the personnel department or an external consultant. The plans need to be implemented and followed through to ensure that the requisite changes in operation, management style and personal development *are* taking place.

Phase 5

As a variation on a theme, a team workshop consisting of all the managers who have been through a 'fly on the wall' exercise may be run to confirm development needs and action plans to meet the needs. Each manager (who is well known to the others) presents the essence of his feedback and the lessons drawn from it, together with his action plans for treatment. These are added to, modified and ratified by his colleagues or team mates on the basis of their knowledge of him. They are then implemented by the team on a mutually supportive basis which ensures a high level of monitoring, review and follow-through.

SELF-DEVELOPMENT – CASE STUDY IN ACTIVITY ANALYSIS

John Walton is a transport manager. In this exercise the procedure is described by which over three hours of his working day were recorded on an activity log in order to obtain an impression of his typical work pattern. The activity key looks fairly complicated, but it becomes relatively simple when considered under the four right hand columns, as described below.

Format of the activity log

A proforma is used to record the activities, with the layout shown in Figure 1.3.

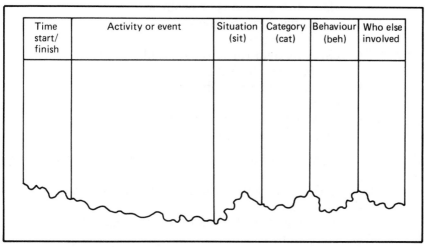

Time start/ finish	Activity or event	Situation (sit)	Category (cat)	Behaviour (beh)	Who else involved

Figure 1.3   Format for activity log

A shorthand key is used to speed up the entry process and condense data into the limited space available on the form. In this example, the shorthand codes used were as follows:

Under 'sit' (the situation in which the individual was observed):

AW	working alone
TI	making an incoming telephone call
TO	making an outgoing telephone call
D	discussion with one other person
MI	meeting − informal
MF	meeting − formal
O	outside own office

The above can be used in combination, and might have been supplemented by:

WSP	with superior
WSB	with subordinate
WSBS	with more than one subordinate
AD	dictating to secretary
AT	working alone − thinking

Under 'cat' (the category of managerial activity observed) the codes used were:

PA   establishing causes of problems
SA   clarifying situations or problems
GD   giving data/information
BV   briefing verbally
XCA   checking data for relevance and accuracy
SDI   seeking data/information
E   evaluating or reviewing progress
O   organising
OGI   organising and giving instructions
RH   requesting and requiring help

Other possibilities which might have been used under this heading are:

DA   making decisions (choosing between alternatives)
P   planning
PP   protecting the plan (contingency planning)
CO   controlling
S   social chat
A   arbitrating

The following codes were applied under the 'beh' column, where the behaviour of the observed individual was recorded:

PA   positive/assertive
LA   listening attentively
Q   questioning
D   disagreeing
X   confused
U   constructive
C   composed (when under stress)

To these codes might have been added:

UN   uncertain/indecisive
CR   critical
DI   dominant
DG   domineering
E   emotional
DF   defensive
SWO   switched off
DY   switched on (dynamo)

GA   playing psychological games
AG   aggression
 H   humour
NU   nurturing/building

Codes under 'who else'

are simply the initials of others involved in the observed situation

Activity log for Mr John Walton

The activity log compiled for John Walton is shown complete in Figure 1.4. The impression gained is that the period of observation involved activities and work patterns which were typical of John Walton's normal work load and working style. Assuming this to be so, then what emerges as a representative picture is the following:

- About 5 per cent of his time is free to work alone (thinking and planning time).
- 95 per cent of his time is spent face to face with someone, or on the telephone.
- 50 per cent of his time is spent seeking information and clarifying situations.
- 30 per cent of his time is spent giving instructions or briefing.
- The remainder is spent in arranging/organising transport, solving problems, etc.

Some questions raised by the analysis

Given that the above *is* typical of John's working day then some questions that need to be asked are:

- How could JW create more thinking and planning time for himself?
- How much of the time he personally spends chasing up data and information could be reduced by:
  - using other information sources (production planning and control)
  - delegating to his subordinates the task of securing much of the information
  - the introduction of an up-to-the-hour information service to JW from production (or production planning and control)?
- How much more, generally, could and should he use his

Manager observed: John Walton
Position: Transport Manager
Date(s) observed: 3 August 19XX
Times observed: 11.09am — 12.30pm and 1.45pm — 3.45pm

Time on/off	Subject / activity / event	sit	cat	beh	who else?
11.09		AW	PA	PA	
11.10	Arthur collects notes on transport routes	D	SA	LS	ART
11.11	Graphic statistics — analysing what, where and when	D	SA	Q	BRI
11.12	Checking details/facts/figures with supervisor	D	SA	Q	BRI
			PA	PA	BRI
11.13	J. goes out to collect outwork book, disagrees on section III; agrees on sections I and II	D	SA	D	BRI
			GDI	PA	BRI
			BV	Q	BRI
	J. seeking reliable accurate information		BV	X	BRI
	(given contradictory 'facts')			Q	
11.18			SA	U	
11.19	Telephone call to Transport Haulage Company	TO	SDI	PA	
	— seeking information on lorries and drivers		SDI	Q	
11.26	— ? work completion notes to clerk	D	E	PA	CLE
11.27	Recommences work with BRI	D	BV	PA	BRI
11.28	Query work in progress	AW	O	PA	NEV
11.28	Telephone call	TI	SDI	PA	
11.28	Second telephone rings (J. also takes this one over from secretary)	TI	SA	PA	
11.29	First call finished and first phone rings again	TI	SDI	PA	Visitor
11.31	Organising people to do things, including	D	SA	PA/Q	Secret
11.35	gathering information	D	OGI	PA	MIK
		D	OGI	PA	DON
11.38	Given more wrong data (goes out to TER next door)	MO	SA	X	TER
	Checks paperwork with loader (loader unhelpful)	MO	SDI	PA	LOA
11.39	Wrong feedback — visitor gets data/information mixed up	D	SA	XQ	DON
		D	SDI	Q	
11.40	Talks to driver	D	GI	PA	Driver
		D	SA	PA	
11.40	Clarifying delivery situation on goods	D	SA	PA/Q	MIK
11.42	Discussion with driver — gives more information	D	GI	PA	Driver
11.46	Reaffirms delivery date on goods	D	SA	PA	MIK
11.47	MIK returns regarding possible shortages	D	E	Q/PA	MIK
11.47	Checks numbers of 'look in'	MO	GI	Q	TER
11.52	Checks/queries tonight's deliveries	D	GI	LS	PAC
11.55	Gives routes/delivery runs and quantities	D	SA	PA	BRI
12.00	Request for transport	TO	RH	PA	
			XCA	Q	
12.05	Availability of drivers' mates for twilight shift	TO	SI	Q	RON
			DA	PA	
12.07	Call for information (no one there)	TO	RH	Q	
12.09	Request to J. for transport and driver	TI	GDI	PA	ANON
	J. goes out to talk to driver	MO	SDI	Q	Driver

Figure 1.4 Activity log compiled for John Walton, Transport Manager
(Entries would in practice be handwritten)

Time	Activity				
12.13	Request for situation report	TI	GDI	PA	RAY
			DA	PA	
12.14	Checks up on transport availability	TO	SDI	Q	VIC
		D	SA	PA	TER
	Do we have a car? Do we have a driver?		SA	Q	
12.19	Spare driver?	D	SA	Q	MIK
12.19		TO	SA	Q	CLI
12.20	Situation report	D	E	PA	MIK
12.21	No driver	TO	GDI	PA	
12.22	Briefing caller	TI	BV	PA	RAY
			GDI	PA	WIL
12.23	Situation report	D	BV	PA	MIK
		TI	DA	PA	PAU
		D	SA	PA	WIL
		TO	GDI	PA	CLE
12.25					
12.28					
Lunch					
1.49	Planning procedures	D	GDI	PA	CLE
1.51	Making up loads for tomorrow	AW	DA	PA	CLE
2.06	Phone call	TI		PA	?
2.11	Clarifying schedule	D	PA	PA	MIK
2.12	Taking message	TI	A	PA	DIC
2.14	Phone (wrong number)	TI	A	PA	?
2.15	Call TER	TO		PA	out
2.17	TER calls back	TI	XCA	Q	TER
2.22	Goods (southern deliveries)	TI	SDI	Q	PAT
2.24	Meeting	MI	SDI	Q	NOR
			GI	PA	
2.28	Goods (midlands deliveries)	TO	SA	Q	PAT
2.30	Parcel arrives — goods components				PET
2.31	Makes out rail notes	MIO	DSI	PAQ	
2.32	Clarifying/explaining procedures	TI	E/BV	PA	CLI
	+ action: sorts out detail		O/DA	QPA	JON
2.42	Parking ticket from driver	M	XCA	QPA	Driver
2.42	Clock card	D	GI	PA	PAC
2.44		D	GI	PA	Driver
2.50	Calls for notes	D	SA	X	Driver
2.57	Writing	D	SA	PA	CLE
2.57	Sorts out midlands/north deliveries	D	E/	C	ART
			GDI		
3.09	Delivery of two reels of cable	D	SDI	Q	Driver
3.10	Electricians call	TI	BV	QPA	RAY
3.15	Ring for transport	TO	SA	PA	PAU
3.22	Needs information for PAT for goods (southern)	D	DA	PA	Visitor
3.24	Despatch priorities: goods (southern)	D	SA	PA	DER
3.28	Phone call	TI	SA	PA	DON
	Another call holding		SA	Q	ADR
	OBSERVER REJOINS PERSONNEL DEPT.				

Figure 1.4 *(Concluded)*

subordinates and push responsibility for solving problems back down to them?

- The very nature of a transport manager's role, especially when combined with that of chief despatcher, is fraught with fire-fighting problems. Being at the 'end of the line' inevitably means collecting everyone else's rubbish, to some extent.

  But, there is much that JW's immediate superior could do to reduce the pressure on John by:
  - sitting down with him and analysing the what, how, when and who of JW's work
  - assuming a higher profile and more assertive stance in managing the boundaries between finishing and transport/despatch.

  Ultimately, of course, many of the decisions to delegate or not delegate rest with John himself.

- Finally, there is the question of organisation. Is the structure of work done and current reporting relationships appropriate or is there a need to rethink and reorganise the whole question of ordering and using transport both at incoming and outgoing stages? This is obviously a far wider issue but inevitably the organisation structure is a major determinant of work loads, work patterns and comparative efficiency/inefficiency of managerial time.

ACHIEVEMENT OBJECTIVES AS A MEANS FOR SELF-DEVELOPMENT

Used either as a natural consequence of discussions at the end of a 'fly on the wall' exercise or as an alternative approach, specific achievement objectives can lend structure, direction and impetus to a manager's self-development. Based on a diagnosis of needs, set within the context of a manager's role and agreed with his boss, achievement objectives represent yardsticks of attainment against which the manager can measure his performance and development.

Obviously the practice of setting objectives takes various forms in business. These range from formalised management by objectives (MBO) schemes to informal (but specific) targets set between bosses and their subordinates or within a work group set up to resolve a particular problem. The very process of management is about moving from a current situation (X) to a requisite state of affairs (Y)

– usually within a set time limit. Typically managers work to the basic criteria as part of their day-to-day role, namely: quantity (how many and how much); quality (how well done or in what manner); cost (how much in financial terms); deadline (by when started/ completed).

At the most senior levels philosophy, policies and strategies are normally based upon certain corporate goals – even though they may be sometimes more implicit than explicit. Normally corporate objectives are then translated appropriately at different levels down the line so that, necessarily, there will be a mandatory aspect to managers' objectives as well as a discretionary one.

In setting and agreeing personal achievement objectives as a means of stimulating self-development and improving managers' effectiveness, Figure 1.5 illustrates the basic scope open to bosses and their subordinates. That scope can be refined by a structure which enables managers to select, define and sharpen objectives in a disciplined way that more closely relates the performance of individuals to the goals of others.

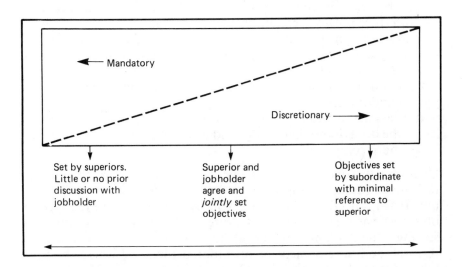

Figure 1.5   The extent to which objective setting between superiors and subordinates may be mandatory or discretionary
Some objectives will be mandatory themselves by their very nature (budget targets for instance) but *how* they are to be achieved may be largely discretionary within the boss – subordinate relationship.

First, it is helpful to determine what objectives are and what they are not. Management objectives:

are	*are not*
required results	activities
achievements	effort
accountabilities	duties
what is required	how it must be done
'musts'	'shoulds'

Second, there are different types of management objective. The principal categories are those which reflect the results to be achieved, under the following headings:

- targets: to meet a deadline, programme of activities or product launch;
- improvements: for example, to increase profitability levels, productivity rates or quality standards;
- resolution of specific problems: examples are the removal of obstacles or constraints in order to correct deviations and restore previous conditions;
- innovation and change: this would include introducing and implementing something new which represented a departure from previous practice;
- control: aimed at ensuring or maintaining a given set of conditions;
- personal or team development: principally aimed at acquiring the behavioural knowledge and levels of skill needed to operate more completely.

Undoubtedly some areas of activity are easier to measure than others in terms of results. It is usually possible to apply at least one specific, quantified objective. This is particularly the case where the type of objective has been determined ('target', 'improvement', 'problem solving', 'innovation' and so on). Even in areas of activity such as research and development or operational research, where the final outcomes might be very difficult to predict realistically, it is still possible to set quantified objectives. This can be done by making the objectives of the form 'submit and present an interim report at the progress review meeting on 13 May and show all findings to date' (for example).

Objectives need to be realistic, attainable, accurate and expressed in clear language if they are to appear credible and relevant as a self-development exercise. They must not be couched in vague terms. For example:

- 'Reduce the use of consumable materials on numbers 1 and 2 lines to budget level by the end of December, and by a further 10 per cent by the end of March' *not* 'Cut down drastically on consumables'.
- 'Submit proposals by the end of the month for reducing steel procurement costs by at least 12 per cent. Method: by the use of alternative transport arrangements from the mills' *not* 'Investigate methods for reducing steel procurement costs'.
- 'Revise your own and your subordinates' job descriptions by mid-January, clarifying the principal accountabilities for each person. Progressively ensure that only agreed principal accountabilities are retained and that all other work is delegated and reallocated to section heads by 31 January' *not* 'Delegate as much work as possible to subordinates'.

In some organisations people of high potential may be deliberately moved into the 'fast line' in terms of career progression by being appointed to specially designed 'development posts'. Although they usually carry out necessary functions the real purpose of their move is to groom them for a more senior, longer term position. In most organisations this probably does not happen and only selected tasks and objectives may be available for the jobholder's development. Where this is the case the opportunities for self-development could well lie outside the mainstream of the role in areas of:

- short-term tasks and objectives
- priority objectives
- innovation and change programmes
- trouble shooting and problem solving.

Figure 1.6 represents the typical structure of many managerial jobs where objectives are divided between mainstream and short-term goals.

SOME VEHICLES FOR SELF-DEVELOPMENT

Once the tasks and personal objectives have been agreed, there is the question of work opportunities through which to achieve those

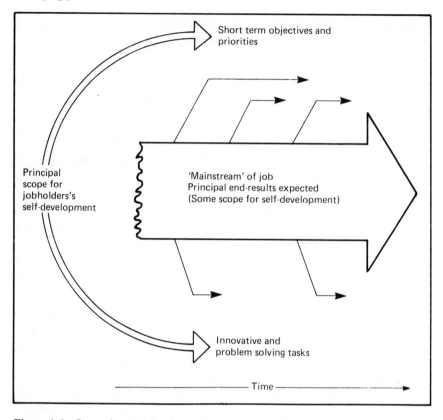

Figure 1.6   Scope for self-development within managerial jobs

objectives and ensure the process of development. A crucial factor in the process is the extent to which the manager's boss facilitates his subordinate's self-development by:

- providing the necessary 'trigger' and encouragement;
- sustaining and restimulating it;
- capitalising on it to the advantage of both the individual and the organisation;
- pressing on the appropriate 'nerves' when unnecessary obstacles get in the way.

Learning is fundamental to self-development and most people in managerial roles tend to learn as the result of *experience*. However, that experience needs to be analysed, discussed and worked through in order to draw the appropriate lessons from it.

Learning by experience, within a management job, is likely to involve the 'learner' in at least:

- *doing* – followed by analysis and review;
- experimenting with new or different experiences and activities;
- questioning and testing out existing knowledge, custom and practice, prejudices, values and beliefs;
- experiencing (and reviewing) both success and failure;
- examples and models (other managers) against which the learner can compare, assess and, if necessary, modify his own management style;
- study and reflection, in order to put experience into perspective and context.

Well-tried learning vehicles which provide opportunity for experiential learning and self-development include the following:

- Keeping a work diary which is reviewed daily, or at least weekly, by the learner with his boss and/or a management development specialist.
- Setting up projects which are *relevant* and *realistic* and which have *real pay-off* for the company, the department and/or the individual. Such projects often carry far more weight when there is major representation to be made by the trainee to the chief executive or a senior panel, so that a sense of occasion is attached to the experience and it is seen to be important.
- Cross-functional assignments involving multi-disciplinary teams of subordinates working together (for example marketing, product planning and engineering or production, industrial engineering and finance) where end results rely on cooperative, coordinated effort.
- Presentations on key issues – or contributions to key issues – to top management.
- Team development workshops in which members review:
  - 'our key objectives and priorities'
  - 'obstacles to achieving them'
  - 'my personal contribution to the team's goals'
  - 'our strengths and weaknesses as a team and as team members'
  - 'our action plan for the next 12 months'.
- 'Bespoke' tutorials for individuals or groups using external professionals who test thinking and action plans by inputs of expertise, rigorous questioning and a wider perception.

- 'Action learning', involving cooperation with managers from other companies and organisations, in the identification and resolution of each other's operational problems.
- Participation in junior 'boards', working parties, 'think tanks' or research teams, with or without senior executives involved, but where the outcomes are deemed to be important and relevant.
- Deputising for the boss:
  - by representing him at meetings, or on committees
  - visiting important external contacts, on his behalf
  - acting in his capacity for days/weeks/months at a time as appropriate.
- Setting up and running an entirely new product, department, function or small subsidiary company.
- Lecturing on personal accountability or a field of expertise to:
  - internal courses and seminars
  - professional courses run by universities, polytechnics or local colleges
  - educational programmes run by national, local or professional bodies.
- Planned reading, regularly reviewed and discussed with the trainee by one or more of the following acting in a mentor role:
  - his immediate superior
  - his superior's chief
  - appropriate in-company specialists, managers or supervisors
  - external professionals.

  Planned reading also involves keeping up to date by regularly choosing different areas of developing technology, important disciplines or relevant current events and systematically scanning the appropriate professional journals.

These, then, represent some of the learning opportunities that are available to enable a manager's self-development to take place at little or no cost to the company and with minimal interference with the day-to-day job that he is there to do.

The term 'self-development' means exactly what it says. The real drive to make it happen must come from within the individual himself, but his superiors can do much to ensure an encouraging supportive climate in which self-development can thrive and become regenerative.

SOURCES AND RESOURCES

Some organisations and bodies concerned with self-development

Organisation	Contacts
Anglian Regional Management Centre High Street, Stratford London E15 2JB 01-590 7722	I Cunningham
Association for Education and Development Polytechnic of Central London 35 Marylebone Road, London NW1 5LS 01-486 5811	M Greatorex
Centre for the Study of Management Learning University of Lancaster Gillow House, Lancaster LA1 4YX Lancaster 65201	J Burgoyne R Boot
Human Resource Associates 18th Floor St Alphage House Fore Street London EC2Y 5DA 01-638-4264	T Jaap
The Open University Walton Hill, Milton Keynes Milton Keynes 74066	B Lund
Polytechnic of Central London School of Management Studies 35 Marylebone Road London NW1 5LS 01-486 5811	J Bowden

Sheffield City Polytechnic   M Pedler
Pond Street, Sheffield S1 1WB   T Boydell
Sheffield 738621

Michael Williams & Partners   M Williams
Fairfield House
Quarry Park Road
Pedmore
Stourbridge
West Midlands DY8 2RE
Hagley 883485

FURTHER READING

Boydell, T and Pedler M (eds), *Management Self-Development*, Gower, 1981

Humble, J W, *Management by Objectives*, Gower, 1975

Jaap, T, *The Steps to Self-Development*, Human Resource Associates

Mumford, A, *Making Experience Pay*, McGraw-Hill, 1980

Pedler, M, Burgoyne, J and Boydell, T, *A Manager's Guide to Self-Development*, McGraw-Hill, 2nd edition 1986

Revans, R W, *Action Learning*, Blond & Briggs, 1981

Williams, M R, *Coaching and Counselling*, The Leadership Trust (Symonds Yat)

2

Manage your time

John Rogers

This chapter presents guidelines that will help you manage your time better. Six proven approaches are described – objectives and key task areas, diaries and planning, time logs, individual behaviour, managerial style and visual reminders. A discussion about the thinking behind each approach is accompanied by suggestions for self-assessment exercises. Your strategy in managing your time better may well involve a combination of several approaches.

INTRODUCTION

During this morning I have heard different people say:

- 'Yet more paperwork in the post, no wonder I can't get my proper job done.'
- 'I'm going to send the telephone on holiday, and lock myself away in a quiet room.'
- 'If I've told him once, I've told him a dozen times.'
- 'He wants me to re-write it yet again. Why can't he tell me what he wants in the first place; another evening spent working.'

No doubt you have heard similar comments today: what do they all have in common? And why do we feel so powerless to respond constructively? It occurs to me that all these basic statements relate to how we manage our time. It seems such common sense; after all, it's simply a matter of setting objectives, determining priorities and carrying out tasks. Or is it? If common sense was so common we wouldn't hear such statements so regularly.

Time as a resource

First, we need to recognise that time is a remarkable resource. Time is the limiting factor in achieving anything. You cannot hire it, buy it or rent it (although octogenarians may disagree), and you cannot obtain more than your allocation of 24 hours per day. In economic terms you cannot construct a marginal utility curve for time, and its supply is totally inelastic − no matter how high the demand, the supply will not and cannot be increased. Time is totally perishable; it cannot be stored in freezers, tins or deposit accounts, or slowed down like erosion. Time is totally irreplaceable, unlike plastics (for steels), bread for potatoes and automation for human labour.

Biologically we appear to be ill equipped to manage time. In an isolated darkened room, deprived of our main senses, we soon lose track of time. Similarly boredom apparently extends time, whilst excitement and deadlines compress it. Paradoxically, with unemployment levels high and an age of leisure approaching, managers work long hours suffering the consequences in a relentless battle 'to get things done'.

The changing world and time

The context of managerial work is changing rapidly. So in addition to managing our time well to carry out our existing roles, we need to adapt, learn and unlearn to cope successfully with our 'brave new world'. A branch manager of a bank, for example, is now responsible for selling up to 150 services to more sophisticated personal and commercial customers in an increasingly competitive market, whilst adapting to complex technological innovations. Such change is not unique − your context is likely to be changing just as dramatically. But in the last analysis, it is your responsibility to commit yourself to using time well to manage these changes.

Think of three managers you know well. Using the matrix shown in Figure 2.1 write down four areas of improvement for each manager that you believe would enable them to operate more effectively. It is very probable that you have included items basically related to time management − organising paperwork, running meetings, putting things off, consulting others etc.

A recent survey of over 1300 managers reported that poor priority setting is common. Despite the long hours worked, only 47 per cent of actual working time was taken up with managerial activities. Most of the remaining time was spent doing their subordinates' jobs; that is,

Areas for improvement	Manager 1	Manager 2	Manager 3
1			
2			
3			
4			

Figure 2.1   Areas of improvement for three managers you know well

doing the familiar and less threatening non-managerial activities they themselves *used* to do. When you consider that a salary of £15,000 per annum can be translated as £65.00 per day or £8.20 per hour (excluding employment costs) the cost of this time wasting can be rapidly computed into a fixed overhead, unless time use and behaviour change. And remember that there is *always* time to complete the most important matters.

This chapter looks at six approaches that will help you become aware of how you use your time, and then do something about it.

OBJECTIVES AND KEY TASK AREAS

Goals

What are your lifetime goals? Lakein claims that you should be clear about them. By writing them down you discover what you really want to do, generate motivation to do it and give meaning to your minute-by-minute use of time. Lifetime goals are linked to visions, purposes, missions and basic beliefs. Typical questions suggested by Lakein are:

- how would you *like* to spend the next three years?
- if you knew *now* you would be struck by lightning six months from today, how would you *live* until then?

Remember that goal setting is an ongoing activity which needs regular updating, recording, prioritising and reviewing for both long and short term goals.

When developing your goals, objectives or key task areas try to be aware of any inconsistencies or paradoxes: for example, becoming managing director is not usually compatible with having unlimited time with your family. Similarly to be liked by everyone is usually incompatible with having strong opinions which are voiced regularly. Look at your own lifetime goals for such incompatibilities.

Key task areas

So how do you establish your own key task areas? First you need some data about what you do and how you do it. This can come from a time log (see page 43); an alternative approach often favoured is to generate your own key task areas. The latter is more future orientated and likely to lead to more immediate results. Data to develop your key areas may come from considering the following checklist of business objectives:

- why is the company in business?
- what is it in business for?
- what do we need to do to remain in business?
- where do we need to be in two, five years' time?
- how can we get there?
- what parts do I have a direct influence upon?
- what are my department's objectives?
- what are my objectives?
- what must I contribute to achieve them?
- what powers do I have?

- who else must play a part?
- what do I expect of them?
- what do they expect of me?
- how can I improve my performance?

You may also have more personal sources, such as:

- job descriptions, but these may be out of date or static and in any case will not usually tell you much about priorities;
- appraisals and assessment interviews, which indicate potential strengths and weaknesses in attaining goals;
- colleagues, who will help you understand how you use your time, and how they think you *should* use your time;
- company goals, from notice boards, house journals etc.;
- professional journals and databases, which contain factual information about companies and managers in similar fields to yourself;
- your own life plans, what you really want to achieve with your life.

Examples of key task areas

As with your time log categories, key task areas should be of a manageable number, action orientated, cover *all* the tasks you do (or should do) and be vividly and concisely expressed. As an example consider a branch manager or assistant manager of a financial institution. Typical key areas in this job could be based upon the following:

- staff relations/effectiveness/training and development/motivation/delegation
- finance/administration (budgets, credit controls, statistics, routines)
- clients/customers/accounts (large – small, maintain – develop)
- new business (societies, directors, business clubs)
- local market information (competitors, potential clients)
- premises (building maintenance, equipment, security)
- internal coordination/communications (head office, boss, other branches)
- external relations (accountants, solicitors, schools, pensioners, estate agents)
- special projects/large one-off tasks
- professional updating
- personal development.

	Before course (%)	After course (proposed %)	After course (actual %)
Lending	20	35	20
Marketing	15	20	25
Planning	5	10	15
Improving profitability of existing services	5	10	15
Staff training	5	15	10
Administration	20	5	10
Achieving targets	30	5	5

Figure 2.2   Percentages of time spent in key task areas
The key figure shows the percentage of time spent by a manager in seven key areas before attending a time planning course, as proposed for the next six months and as actually achieved six months later.

Planning time allocation

One assistant manager in a large border county branch identified seven distinct areas of activity, estimating the percentage of time spent in each category

- before a time planning course;
- as proposed for the next six months whilst on the course;
- actual achievement as assessed six months later.

See Figure 2.2.

Exercise

Complete the past and proposed columns of the table shown in Figure 2.3. The differences between past and proposed percentages form the basis of an action plan that can be reviewed at a later date by completing the actual columns as in our example (Figure 2.2). Obviously your key task areas will be different.

DIARIES AND PLANNING

The need for information

You need some way of capturing and having ready access to important information. Apart from a sensible working environment with well labelled filing systems for static information, you will need some form of diary/notebook that is designed with good time management principles in mind. Most diaries bought at the start of a

Key task area	Past	Proposed (state time deadline)	Actual

Figure 2.3   Percentages of time spent in key task areas (your own)

new year from stationers are inadequate for anything but appointments.

Ask yourself, what kinds of information do I need to refer to on a regular and often unprepared basis? This might include:

- appointments and other dated deadlines
- tasks — to do, in progress and completed
- ideas and other notes
- key task areas — keep them 'in sight and in mind'

- birthdays, school terms and household/garden tasks
- maps and timetables
- books to read, films to see and places to visit
- expenses, budgets and other financial matters
- delegation, crisis and interruption logs.

Choosing a diary

When choosing a diary ask yourself:

- What size do I want? Sizes range from large wall charts and planners via desk diaries (about 20 × 25 cm) to pocket diaries about (10 × 15 cm) — but beware of running two or more diaries! Formats include one or seven days per page and one month per page. The increasing use of specially designed loose-leaf time management diaries helps you to create a system that works for you: some typical designs I find useful are shown in Figure 2.4.
- What information do I need a diary or time planner to contain? Traditional diaries usually contain standard information that may or may not be useful — a map of the London Underground system or the addresses of airports in Asia will be of little use to someone who never leaves Scotland. Diaries designed with time management principles in mind offer a wealth of information that you can choose from as it suits you — maybe even a road map of Glasgow and Edinburgh.

Suppliers of useful time planning systems are listed at the end of this chapter.

At this stage you should stop and consider what diary planning systems you use and whether they are adequate. If you find yourself hunting through scraps of paper, missing appointments, losing track of ideas and generally unaware of what you are really trying to achieve you should consider changing to something more suitable. But beware! If you are a perfectionist you may spend far too much time keeping the perfect neat time planner, without actually achieving anything other than administrivia.

Determining priorities

Whatever system you choose it is essential to list all activities that need doing. For many line managers this is best done daily, either immediately on arriving at work or just before leaving in the evening.

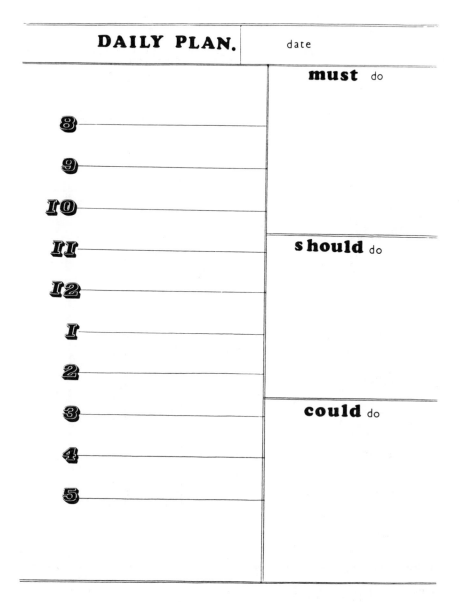

Figure 2.4 Typical planning forms for managing your time

	JOHN	GAIL	COLIN	HELEN	BARRY	DANIEL
MON						
TUE						
WED						
THU						
FRI						
SAT						
SUN						

Figure 2.4 *(continued)*

| weekly plan | WK NO: |
| | DATE: |

	MUST DO:
MON.	
TUES.	SHOULD DO:
WED.	
THUR.	
FRI.	COULD DO:
SAT.	
SUN.	

Figure 2.4 *(continued)*

| | wk no. |
| | period |

	1.
objectives	2.
of the	3.
week	4.

MON				
TUE				
WED				
THU				
FRI				

Figure 2.4 *(continued)*

month

OBJECTIVES OF THE MONTH

1.
2.
3.
4.
5.
6.
7.

1		17		
2		18		
3		19		
4		20		
5		1		
6		2		
7		3		
8		4		
9		5		
10		6		
11		7		
12		8		
13		9		
14		30		
15		1		
16				

Figure 2.4 *(concluded)*

If necessary you can find the mental space by arriving 10 minutes earlier, or leaving 10 minutes later. Where life is less hectic the list can be made weekly or monthly. But whatever your role do it when it suits you. What you will end up with is more activities than time available. Don't be overwhelmed at this stage: you need to prioritise. Go through your list and pick out priorities by the ABC method: 'A's are priority jobs, 'B's less so and 'C's not so important. 'A's are usually the hardest, most complex and difficult – and the most important! 'C's are often trivial, easy to do, look good when crossed off a list, but don't get you anywhere. So start with 'A's, not with 'C's or 'Z's.

Look at the 'A's. You may like to prioritise again (A1, A2, A3 ...) and then begin to see connections between tasks. By now you should be crossing off tasks and interlinking them: it may look a bit messy, but your left and right brains will be working away on speedy and effective methods of getting things done. If 'ABC's fail to appeal try prioritising using 'MSC's:

- tasks that *must* be completed;
- tasks that *should* be completed;
- tasks that *could* be completed (if only I had the time).

Avoid generating multiple lists, unmanageable numbers of priority jobs, items duplicated on several lists and constantly changing priorities.

Using a diary or planner

If you use a traditional diary make sure you transfer tasks and times into it in addition to the usual appointments. Do this by blocking out chunks of time. Be aware of the amount of time needed for project work, such as board reports and marketing programmes, and plan it into the diary. The alternative is a bulging briefcase to accompany the trek home and needlessly burning the midnight oil.

Similarly be aware of your continuing daily tasks and how long they take, and the average time that must be left unplanned to deal with crises, the unexpected and the unreasonable. An overall picture of your total work requirements can be built up which enables you to be clearer on where to say 'yes' and 'no' to the demands of others.

TIME LOGS

Why bother?

Many managers have at some stage in their working lives logged their time as it is actually being used, and analysed it later. But why bother? The answer is simply because you are probably unsure about how much time you spend on various activities. All right, you have some general ideas; but to effect *real* improvement a constructive survey and analysis is critical. Sometimes a manager will find that his time use is even more haphazard and fragmented than he previously believed. This realisation is a poignant lesson about the need to change. If a manager delegates more effectively, closes the door occasionally to plan and says 'no' as appropriate, he can complete a time log for two weeks at a later date to determine his relative success in changing.

The main advantages of the time log approach are:

- the self-development aspect, in that the results can be used by you personally and revealed only to those you wish to see it; thus you can be honest with yourself;
- it deals with real indisputable *facts* about how you spent your time;
- you learn from the actual process of doing it; for example, a salesman may be surprised at how much time he spends chasing low-yield prospects; a manager may learn just how much discretionary time is available to him.

However, it can be tedious to commit yourself to two–four weeks of logging, especially if your design is complex or you are too busy. If the latter is the case you would be strongly advised to find time to do a time log!

Designing and using time logs

In its most straightforward mode you will need to divide your working day into six–eight main categories of activities. These will normally be linked to your objectives or key task areas. You will need to note during the course of your day the amount of time spent in each category; activities outside these key task areas may be recorded in an extra catch-all category.

All time spent must be allocated. Ideally the noting should take place on changing activities or tasks; in practice, this may be impossible. In the turmoil of managing, a sensible compromise for the log to be useful and accurate without being laboriously detailed, is to complete your prepared sheets as convenient. But this should be a minimum of hourly — use the bleep on a digital watch, the memory being notoriously unreliable.

Other useful guidelines

In carrying out a time log analysis you should also bear in mind that:

- The log should be kept for a *typical* two to four-week period. You may find that there is no 'typical' period: indeed if you sense such a luxury on the horizon, you can guarantee some emergency or crisis will evolve. This will not invalidate your log. It will in effect enhance it with data about how you coped with unexpected events! Remember that the main purpose of the log is to excite you into wanting to improve your use of time, and not to define the mythical normal week.
- Your designed time log should be easy to understand and use so that revealing data will unfold. Do not make it so intricate that completing it every few minutes supersedes your role as a manager.
- Using symbols and abbreviations where you can is helpful, particularly in the notes column.
- You should acknowledge your log as soon as you get to work by getting it out and confirming your priority objectives or tasks for the day.
- Time spent travelling, working outside normal hours and meals should be included if relevant to you.

Sharing your time log with others

Whilst your time log is personal to you, it is useful if a group of managers performing similar roles get together to discuss their logs. A procedure that works is that each manager should take about 30 minutes of group time to give an informal chronological presentation of his time log data. The remainder of the group should act as devil's advocates and question the manager's explanation of his time use. The presenter's role is rotated until all managers in the group have experienced the 'hot seat'. Managers should identify and commit themselves to at least one specific aspect of improvement in their use of time at the end of their 30 minutes.

Some questions that may enable the group members to help in this process are:

- Where has time been used effectively? Why?
- What could/should have been delegated? Up, down, or sideways?
- Could some tasks (meetings, paperwork, interviews etc.) have been carried out more quickly? How?
- Should 'no' have been said politely but firmly to some jobs? Why wasn't it? How could it be in the future?
- Are there any tasks not done that should have been done? What has prevented them from being done? How may this be avoided in the future?
- What kinds of decisions are taken? Alone or with others? Who? How often?
- What are the main similarities/differences between the time logs in the group? Why?
- What do you like/dislike about what you have decided or been told about your own use of time?
- What might/are you going to do about it? How can we help you make those changes?

Examples of time logs

During a development programme a group of managers jotted down all the activities they spent time on over a period of several weeks. Over 50 activities were identified which were subsequently combined into 22 main activities and seven categories of activities, as shown in Figure 2.5.

A daily time log was used which included an assessment of achieving specified priority objectives. As can be seen in Figure 2.6 the categories of activities are listed horizontally, with vertical subdivisions representing time bands. The notes column was used for comments by the manager on levels of effectiveness, thoughts, feelings etc. For each daily sheet the columns were totalled and transferred to a summary sheet (see Figure 2.7).

Variations in time spent in key task areas

The minimum, maximum and percentage range of time spent in each key task area for each manager was summarised and is shown in Figure 2.8. The differences were explained in terms of unit size and

TIME LOG — CATEGORY SUMMARY

A   PLANNING, PREPARATION AND UPDATING
 	
    A1   Planning ahead
    A2   Preparation for interviews/visits etc.
    A3   Keeping your knowledge up to date

B   CUSTOMER INTERVIEWS (IN BRANCH)
 	
    B1   Lending interviews — personal and commercial
    B2   Other interviews with customers arranged to increase business etc.
    B3   Non-lending/non-business development interviews

C   CUSTOMER CONTACT — INFORMAL (IN BRANCH)
 	
    C1   Working at an enquiry desk
    C2   Meetint customers informally in the banking hall/casual meetings
    C3   Working at a till

D   STAFF CONTACT
 	
    D1   Checking/advising on the work of others
    D2   Briefing staff about changes in working routines/products etc.
    D3   Training staff/discussing progress/coaching others

E   OFFICE — ROUTINES AND PROCEDURES
 	
    E1   Dealing with correspondence/telephone calls etc.
    E2   Attending to faults, problems, priorities, administration etc.
    E3   Interpreting/issuing HO advices/procedures

F   ATTENDING MEETINGS
 	
    F1   Meetings with Area Manager or equivalent
    F2   Attending non-business professional meetings
    F3   Meetings with other departments (e.g. B.D., Personnel)

G   WORKING OUTSIDE THE BRANCH
 	
    G1   Seeing customers at their home
    G2   Visiting existing/prospective business clients
    G3   Meeting/lunching with professional contacts
    G4   Visits/talks/film shows outside the branch

H   OTHER CATEGORIES
 	
    H1
    H2
    H3

Figure 2.5   The 22 main activities and seven categories of activities for a managerial job in a bank

Time Log

Day No

Date

Priority Objectives

			Achieved?
1			
2			
3			

Time	Plan/ Prepare Update			Customer Interviews			Informal Customer Contact (in-branch)			Staff Contact			Office Routines & Procedures			Attend Meetings			Work outside the Office				Other -			Comments
	A			B			C			D			E			F			G				H			
	1	2	3	1	2	3	1	2	3	1	2	3	1	2	3	1	2	3	1	2	3	4	1	2	3	
9.00																										
10.00																										
11.00																										
12.00																										
1.00																										
2.00																										
3.00																										
4.00																										
5.00																										
6.00																										
Sub-total																										
Total																										

Figure 2.6   A daily time log for a managerial job in a bank

Time Log Summary

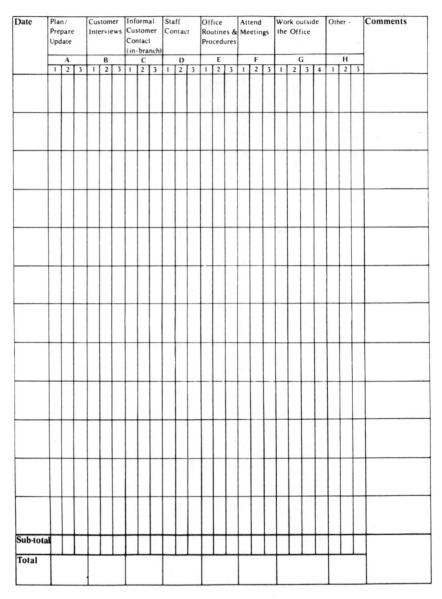

Figure 2.7   A summary sheet for collating daily time log data

geographical location, experience of staff, managerial styles, priorities and business mix – *and the manager's ability to use his time effectively!*

	Min (%)	Max (%)	Range (%)
Planning—preparing—keeping up to date	3	15	12
Customer interviews (in branch)	14	26	12
Informal customer contact/approaches (in branch)	0	20	20
Staff contact	4	14	10
Office routines and procedures	18	48	30
Working outside the branch	0	27	27
Attending meetings etc.	0	16	16

Figure 2.8 **Percentage minimum, maximum and range of time spent in each key task area for managers doing similar jobs**

In one unit the manager and assistant used four main areas of responsibility and the time log approach in developing their effectiveness in working together. There was a strong need to know what each other was doing over a period of time. In addition to achieving certain key objectives the percentage time spectrum shown in Figure 2.9 was seen as an appropriate goal.

	Manager (%)	Assistant Manager (%)
Business development (outside contacts)	30	5
Staff (training/development/motivation)	20	40
Administration	10	20
Customer interviews (lending/investment/tax)	40	35

Figure 2.9 **The overlap in key task areas and time spent in those areas by a manager and assistant**

These examples are described primarily to stimulate you to design a time log for yourself and to show you how it can be used, especially in contact with other managers.

INDIVIDUAL BEHAVIOUR – PROBLEMS AND SOLUTIONS

The need to have objectives, develop priorities and measure success in time management is well known and on occasions usefully practised. But what about all those behaviours we exhibit, often out of our awareness, that influence our ability to manage time? Some essential individual problems managers have are considered below.

Don't procrastinate

Do you have a house full of leaking taps, faulty electrical connections and doorhandles that you've often faithfully promised to put right? Do you *still* have that difficult customer who you must contact, or is that urgent sales report nagging away to be completed rather than gathering dust in your in tray, or that awkward appraisal interview that must be done before the end of the month, or that overdue apology? The gentle art of putting things off, procrastination, is an enormous time stealer.

Procrastination is a deep rooted habit that must be tackled while you are motivated to change. Take the first steps straight away using the following guidelines:

- Decide you are going to change as soon as you can – maybe *now*!
- List all those tasks you have been putting off. Make no exceptions; everything must be on your list.
- Remove one or two items on the list immediately by doing them.
- Plan how you will deal with the others, maybe relieving yourself of three each day. Try this first thing in the morning as it sets a positive tone for the rest of the day. You can tell yourself 'Great, the day's only 20 minutes old and I have already accomplished the most irritating tasks of the day.'
- If you stick to your plan reward yourself. If you don't, punish yourself in a way that makes it work in future.

Don't be a perfectionist

Do you have to retype letters because of a minor error, expect *no* customer complaints, or interruptions never to occur at work? Do you expect your pre-school children to have impeccable table manners, the garden to be perfect, or every day to be like Christmas?

Perfection is paralysing. There seems to be a fundamental difference between striving for excellence and striving for perfection. The former is achievable, realistic, healthy and personally satisfying; the latter leads to frustrations and neurotic behaviour. You will need to recognise in what areas of your life you really need to 'be perfect', and ensure such compulsions do not trap you into missing opportunities and achieving excellence elsewhere.

Set challenging objectives

Do you find yourself consistently failing to meet your objectives and being disappointed, annoyed or frustrated? Do you find yourself regularly underachieving, but meeting all objectives without too much physical or emotional effort?

Imagine spending an hour throwing tennis balls into a bucket, with success defined as a product of distance from which you choose to throw from and percentage of balls actually going into the bucket. If you set your objectives (i.e. distance) very low, say position 'A' in Figure 2.10, you will achieve some initial low level success. After a few minutes you will recognise a lack of a sense of achievement, an absence of risk, and experience increasing frustration and annoyance. Conversely if you set your objective (i.e. distance) very high, say position 'B', you may achieve some limited initial success in this high risk situation. Again motivation and achievement are likely to fall as frustration and lack of success become apparent. Position 'C' is a potentially healthy development position resulting in optimum success. With coaching, positive recognition, support and a few allowable mistakes C1 can be reached; with isolation, negative recognition and lack of support only C2 may be possible.

Have a look at your own objectives. How realistic are they? What happens to you personally if they are too difficult or too easy to achieve?

Learn how to learn

How children learn is well researched and understood; adult learning less so. Learning, un-learning and re-learning are key issues for good time management. You cannot rely on the occasional course or epistles from on high for your learning. In any case there is increasing evidence that mature adults have a strong need to be self-directing in their learning. However you must be aware of:

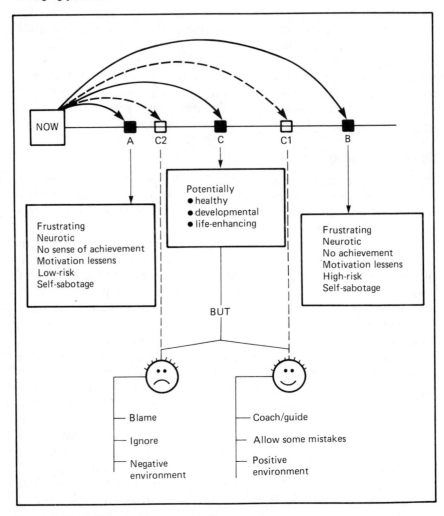

Figure 2.10   Setting challenging objectives
The figure shows the value of challenging but realistic objectives in achievement –
A is too low, B too high, with C about right in normal circumstances and C1 where
managerial support happens.

- the barriers you place in the way that hinder your learning;
- your preferred manner of learning for such situations;
- and what you did that enabled you to learn successfully in the past.

Modern learning methods such as distance learning, action learning and computer based training (CBT) help you learn at paces, styles and times of your choice; thus you can manage your learning time effectively.

Fight crises

There's nothing wrong with the occasional crisis; but if it is the same one that occurred last week, the week before and the week before that, you may not be learning from your crises. Good practices in a crisis are:

- to use your energies to find solutions (not for shouting or finding scapegoats);
- to focus upon the problem (not your performance or how it will look);
- to relax momentarily before considering options and then controlling that crisis;
- to turn the crisis into an opportunity for new ideas and methods. Contingency plans that help avoid future identical crises can be devised.

Other individual time problems

Five of the biggest personal time wasters have been described together with ways of resolving them. To manage your individual behaviour and time you also need:

- to plan (both short and long term);
- to concentrate and not be distracted by interruptions;
- to take breaks;
- to avoid clutter (physical and mental);
- to beware of becoming a workaholic;
- to learn to say 'no' firmly but graciously when appropriate;
- to access and use information well;
- to read and write accurately and quickly;
- to relax and reduce tensions.

MANAGERIAL STYLE

Think about the way people manage in your organisation. Who is more highly regarded:

- The manager who explains over and over in detail why a

problem cannot be solved or the manager who solves the problem and quickly moves on to other tasks?

- The supervisor who makes few decisions of any kind, even when decisions are urgently needed or the supervisor who makes the required decisions but occasionally makes a mistake?

- The boss who frantically dashes around solving his subordinates' problems again and again or the boss who develops his subordinates so that crises are avoided or that they can solve their own problems.

Managerial style and time

One model of management describes five styles of managing as follows.

Telling

An authoritarian style where the manager makes decisions himself, announces them and commands that they be carried out.

Selling

A style where the manager makes the decisions with some limited discussion and explains or convinces his subordinates.

Consulting

A style where the manager gets suggestions by inviting questions, makes suggestions himself, and consults subordinates before making decisions.

Sharing

A style where the manager presents the problem, defines the limits of any solution, and decision making is joint.

Delegating

A style where the manager allows subordinates to function within defined limits by defining constraints and by conforming with subordinates' requirements.

On going down the five styles the area of freedom for subordinates to make decisions increases, whilst the use of authority by the manager decreases.

Your own predominant style will influence the amount of time you spend with subordinates and others, and how you spend that time. The telling style will save time in the short term − it's easy to tell people what to do if they are willing to do anything you tell them. But it could mean extra time eventually being spent dealing with the dissatisfactions and mistakes that occur as the culture and individuals mature or give up. The consulting style will mean more time spent meeting subordinates, often at their request, to deal with the many ideas and options around; but good time management principles still apply.

Exercise

You should recognise your own predominant managerial styles and the advantages and limitations in time management terms using a grid shown in Figure 2.11. The actual and ideal percentages of time spent in each style should be completed, together with a statement about how you will make the changes occur.

| Style | Time management | | % of time spent | |
	Advantages	Disadvantages	Actual	Ideal
Telling				
Selling				
Consulting				
Sharing				
Delegating				

Figure 2.11 Managerial styles and managing time
The figure shows a matrix where you consider the advantages and disadvantages of several managerial styles in time management terms, before allocating your actual and ideal percentages of time spent in each style.

Key task areas and management style

Many models of management express success in terms of our ability to get things done and our relationships with people. Graphically a vertical axis represents task, the horizontal axis people. We can relate key task areas to this concept. Consider for example the seven key task areas (A to G) listed in Figure 2.5. Office – routines and procedures (E) and Working outside the branch (G) are primarily task functions, whilst Staff contact (D) and Customer contact – informal (in branch) (C) are primarily people functions. A spectrum of key task areas in terms of task and people orientations is shown in Figure 2.12.

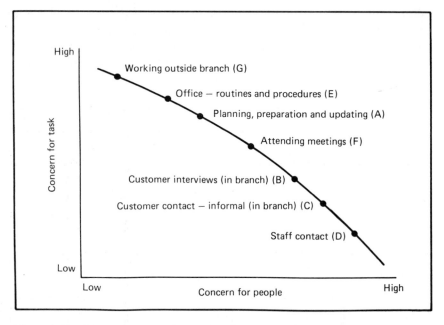

Figure 2.12   Key task areas and managerial concern for task and people
The figure shows how key task areas are related to the popular concept of a manager's concern for task and concern for people. Time spent in our key task areas reflects our managerial styles.

Exercise

You should now look at your own key task areas in a similar way by representing them on a task/people plot. Study the emergent picture carefully and identify what balance you need for success in your environment. You may need to develop some strategies to change the balance.

Functions of management

Other models of management look at the functions of management. One such function is delegation. 'Why should I be concerned with delegation?' I was recently asked. It is not easy to admit to doing too much yourself. It is usually simpler to do a task yourself than arrange to meet, explain, watch and critically assess a subordinate doing it, but the freedoms gained in delegation are enormous.

Delegation means giving responsibility, authority and sharing accountability rather than 'dishing out work'. Delegation can be difficult and it can go wrong, but it can be planned to work and be managed properly. Listing the advantages/disadvantages of delegation and the examination of how time is spent at work, often commit a colleague to the principles and practice of good delegation. One manager I met operates on the principle of 'never doing anything he can get someone else to do' – what's more, he is highly respected and extremely effective!

Other managerial time problems

In relation to our managerial style other common time wasters include meetings (as a leader or participant), dealing with crises, communicating through a hierarchy, control systems, using technology (including the telephone), decision making, working with a secretary and finding thinking time. You will find a number of these subjects dealt with in other chapters in this book.

VISUAL REMINDERS

Quotations and slogans

Despite all your good intentions and plans too much time still gets wasted. It seems as if there are mental blockages that allow you to default when the going gets tough and crises or the unexpected happen. To remind yourself of good time management principles on such occasions you really need an immediate stimulus.

Now, we have all heard quotations and slogans like 'time and tide wait for no man', 'master your time and you master your life', 'get a round tuit', 'to thine own self be true', and they make sense. One I particularly like is 'illegitimi non carborundum'. You will need to design or find slogans that work for you, and think about where to put them for maximum effect. A 'slogan of the week' is sometimes preferred.

Your own quotations

You can of course keep your 'slogans' in your head, repeating them like mantras until they reach an almost spiritual significance. Better locations could include your wall chart, inside your desk blotter, on a stand on your desk, in your time planner in bold letters where they will be seen, and on the telephone, especially if the telephone is your favourite time management problem. You may prefer initials DIBS ('Do it before sunset') or foreign phrases ('tempus fugit'); they are certainly more private and mysterious. Remember, if it works for you it works for you.

An organised office

More naturally recurring visual reminders will abound in your office anyway. Whatever the slogans you use, if your office looks a mess, your time management may be a mess. Bear the following general visual points in mind:

- Keep paperwork under control; where you can, handle paper only once. Decide whether to take action at the time (and pass it to the out tray), start some action (and place it in a pending tray), or read and store or GROAN ('get rid of it anyway – now!'). Chapter 3, Managing information in the office, will help you manage the paperwork.
- Choose and site your office furniture as appropriate for good time management. Filing cabinets should be well organised and work for you, especially if you have a secretary to help. Your files should not involve an exploration or paper safari every time you encounter them – nor should they challenge the exhibits in the local museum or company archives. Desks and chairs should be ergonomically matched and sited in a position to give you privacy when you need it – don't be your own worst interrupter and catch the eye of every passer-by.

SUMMARY

The main purpose and reward for managing your time well is the feeling of being in control that results. Having considered six successful approaches you should answer the following questions:

- Am I unclear and out of date with my lifetime goals, objectives and/or key task areas?
- Do my time planning systems (diaries, ABC priorities etc.) need revising?
- Would completing a time log help me understand where my time is being used, and for me to plan for improvement?
- Is there anything about my individual behaviour (procrastination, 'being perfect' etc.) that limits my effective use of time?
- Is there anything about my style of managing (concerns for task/people, delegation etc.) that limits my effective use of time?
- Does my work place look an administrative mess? Would revised systems and visual reminders help me?

If you answer an honest *no* to all questions, you can move on to the next chapter. Otherwise a final action plan exercise (Figure 2.13) should be completed. You will need to identify your strengths and weaknesses, before deciding on general improvement areas. Determine specific objectives and achievement dates, and write down the steps involved and possible problems that might occur on the way.

Will you complete the action plan? Or has that alternative and vital A1 loomed up from the nether reaches of your mind? Or are you procrastinating? As Lakein says – *what is the best use of your time right now?*

FURTHER READING

Lakein, A, *How to Get Control of Your Time and Your Life*, Gower, 1984. This classic book spawned several excellent training films and describes the author's system of time management, which includes simple but powerful techniques that succeed in life, work and in leisure. Unreservedly recommended.

Bliss, E C, *Doing it Now*, Macdonald, 1983. The author claims that successful people never procrastinate – they always do things now.

Improvement areas	Objectives	Stages toward objectives	Possible problems	Achievement date

Figure 2.13   Action plan for managing your time
The figure leads into developing an action plan that you can use to monitor your improvement in managing your time.

The book is in a very readable question-and-answer format, with good advice from the author's anti-procrastination seminars. A top 40 most commonly used reasons for putting things off are listed.

Mackenzie, R A, *The Time Trap*, McGraw-Hill, 1975. From studying people's work habits, the author presents practical, easy-to-apply tips and techniques for good time management. Particularly useful is a list of time wasters with their possible causes and solutions.

Pernet, R, *Effective use of Time* (Notes for Managers number 31), Industrial Society, 1978. A short neat booklet covering a broad band of time management items such as meetings, telephones and delegation plus some useful checklists.

Stewart, R, *Managers and Their Jobs*, Macmillan, 1967. A study of the similarities and differences in the ways managers spend their time, using a detailed research diary. The author presents the information and conclusions in a readily accessible way that has as much validity today as it did when published.

Reynolds, H and Tramel, M E, *Executive Time Management − Getting 12 hours work out of an 8 hour day*, Gower, 1979. The sections on writing clearly, conducting productive meetings and organising paperwork are particularly helpful.

Oncken, W Jr, *Managing Management Time − Who's Got the Monkey?*, Prentice-Hall, 1984. A book that deals in a unique way with using your time to achieve more visible, far-reaching results. Using 'organisational leverage' to concentrate efforts appropriately at the right time, capitalising upon intrusions and extending your influence are some of the more complex time management topics to write about and practise that are included.

Diaries and planning systems can be purchased from:

Norman and Hill Ltd
Filofax House
Forest Road
Ilford
Essex IG6 3HP
01-501 3911

Business Methods Ltd
Browells Lane
Feltham
Middlesex TW13 7EP
01-890 0085

Time Manager International
50 High Street
Henley-in-Arden
Solihull
West Midlands B95 5AN
05642 4100

Day-Timers (UK) Ltd
24A Bartholomew Villas
London NW5 2LL
01-267 5663

Sasco
27 Hastings Road
Bromley
Kent BR2 8NA
01-462 2241

3

Managing information in the office

Feona J Hamilton

When you walk into your office for the first time, have a good look round. Whether it is a new office, or one just vacated by someone else, the first impression will probably be the same. It will be empty and *tidy*. Maybe there are a few drawing pins left in the wall/notice board, or a scribble or two on the calendar, but that's all. The desk will be pristine – no overflowing trays (maybe no trays at all), lots of lovely space, pen tidy gaping open-mouthed back at you, perhaps a blotter with nothing in it but a clean piece of blotting paper. When all this neatness is imprinted on your memory, here's what you do: open your diary, and make a note to look again in a month's time.

You will probably see something very different. The trays will certainly be there, but they will be buried under piles of paper. There will be dog-eared and outdated memos on the notice board, and the phone will be ringing somewhere, under another pile of rubbish – sorry, information. Sounds familiar? I thought it might, but don't just nod despairing agreement, and turn the page.

This chapter is for you to read as a step in the direction of managing the information that comes into, and goes out of your office, and across the desk. It considers what you need to see and what doesn't matter, plus what you need to keep, and what you can discard. It will also indicate what you positively shouldn't see, and what you can have a look at outside the office, so that it need never come in and clutter up the place. Finally, there will be a quick glance at computers, since they certainly have their uses when it comes to controlling information.

WHAT IS INFORMATION?

Everything that comes into the office is information of some kind. It may come in many forms, such as:

- minutes of committee and other meetings
- scribbled memos from colleagues
- messages left by your staff
- reminders to yourself
- house magazine
- other published material — books, journals and so on
- correspondence
- reports written by you
- reports written to you
- telephone calls
- face to face conversations
- computer printout
- messages via the computer, if you have one.

YOUR DESKTOP

The top of your desk is the starting point from which you will control (or manage) the information which comes into your office. Any written or printed material is bound to land there, and spoken information you will either get through the telephone, or from someone speaking to you, when you will no doubt make notes as memory aids. If you don't do this, you should — it's a useful habit to get into.

One of the most basic things which you can do is to have two diaries — a large one for your desk, and a small one for your person. It is important to keep them both bang up to date. This means having to remember to put engagements in both of them, which is easy if you make an appointment over the phone, or face to face with someone in the office, but not so simple if you make it on the golf course, or during a working lunch. However, it really is not an onerous task, and both you and your secretary will be better informed about your movements as a result.

The diary and the telephone are not the only items which you should have on your desktop, useful though they are. Those filing trays which have already been mentioned do have their uses, if managed properly. A set of three — in, out, and pending — is usually sufficient, unless you're in charge of the post-room! Although it is possible, and very tempting, to spend an entire morning shuffling everything round from one tray to another, without actually achieving anything, you should try to resist. Nor, on the other hand, should you rely on the false premise that if you leave something in the in tray long enough, eventually you'll be able to throw it away. Some of the information sent to you will arrive because you are on a circulation list, and it is selfish, as well as inefficient, to delay sending it on its way to the next person, simply because you're too lazy − or too disorganised − to sort through the in tray regularly. Do it once a day, and you'll find that you can scan much of what should be passed on quickly in the time it takes to have a cuppa. You can then put it in the out tray and forget about it.

That 'out' tray can be one of the least used items in the office, if you're not careful. Some wits have been known to refer to the wastepaper bin as the out tray, and it *is* in a sense, but it cannot replace the real thing. An out tray, properly used, tells whoever else comes into the office to work with or for you precisely what they may remove without a qualm. Your secretary will be pleased to see an obvious pile of things to be removed, and any colleagues who wander in during your absence can succumb to the urge to see what other people are looking at without a twinge of conscience. After all, if it's in the out tray, and not in a sealed envelope, then you've finished with it and it's not confidential is it? Which brings me neatly to:

HAMILTON'S LAW 1: There is nothing outré about an out tray

The only tray not mentioned so far is the pending tray. Some people use the entire desktop as a pending tray, and leave little piles all over it, in some mysterious and unspecified order, which they understand at the time, but have completely forgotten by the next morning. This is another indication of lack of organisation, as well as being very difficult to cope with when searching for a specific, single sheet of paper with the information which you need for the meeting you should have been in twenty minutes ago. There is also the matter of having to find some space to make notes the next time the phone rings, as well as somewhere to put the next cuppa. It's better to have just one pile on the desk in front of you, work through that, place in appropriate trays, take the next handful from the in tray and so on. Remember:

HAMILTON'S LAW 2: Piles on the desk are also uncomfortable

EDITING YOUR INFORMATION NEEDS

However hard you try, you cannot possibly see everything of relevance – there is simply too much of it. The 'information explosion' is one of the more apposite phrases used today. Try stuffing too much into your brain, and it will have a pretty explosive effect on you, as well. If you suffer from the following symptoms: difficulty focusing on the page without the words jumping up and down; slight headache and dizziness; nausea; trembling hands, bursting feeling between the ears; you're either trying to absorb too much information, or you have just absorbed too much alcohol. If it's definitely the former – and be honest about this – there is a remedy: Divide the information you see into the following four categories:

1 What you must see. This will include minutes of any meetings which you have – or should have – attended recently; memos from the boss; relevant press cuttings; whatever the post has brought *that day* as far as possible (if you're on holiday, or out of the office on business, this cannot be strictly applied); telephone messages.

2 What you like to see. This means items for information which, while not vital to your work, are useful additions to those things which are included in 1 above. They will include minutes of meetings in related areas of work; general office memos; items of peripheral interest from journals or newspapers coming into the building; and items of interest which you are told about by a colleague, or friend, such as special supplements in newspapers – *The Times* often has some very useful inserts, on anything from Sussex University to Saudi Arabia. The relevance of such material depends, of course, on your job. Only you can make the decision.

3 What you want to impress others by seeing. This is usually a complete waste of time, as what you are looking at may well be of little or no relevance to what you are actually supposed to be doing. It can also be painfully obvious to whomever you're trying to impress that you don't actually understand much of what you're trying to read. Having said that, there can be times when something which you're reading for this reason turns out to be so fascinating that you decide to change careers, and go and find yourself a marvellous new job – but it is very rare.

4 What you don't need to see. You don't need to see all the bits and pieces connected with tasks that you've already delegated to somebody else. Delegation is an art which very few managers do really well. If they manage to pass on a task, they either check up so constantly that they might just as well do it themselves, or they take absolutely no further interest. The happy medium is to delegate, and ask for a progress report at properly spaced intervals. The information received thus is all you should want to see. Neither do you need to read every piece of advertising bumf that lands on your desk. Mail shots can be a good source of information on what the competition's up to, but you simply don't have time to scan it all. A quick look now and then is sufficient.

If you ignore the warnings, and try to read everything, you will find that you have no time to do any of the other tasks which make up your total job — i.e. you will be acting inefficiently. You will certainly find yourself becoming ever more muddled and confused, as you will be trying to stuff so much information into your mind that you will be unable to sort out the wheat from the chaff, and all you will have is a great lump of indigestible material, which you are unable to break down into its component parts. This means that, in turn, you will be unable to apply what you have read to the task in hand, and this will also lead to inefficiency.

HAMILTON'S LAW 3: Too much information gives you mental indigestion

KEEPING IT IN ORDER (SOMEWHERE)

As well as reading, or scanning, the material as it comes into your office, you will want to keep some of it. How you store it will depend on the reasons why you need to hold on to it, and the methods of storage available to you. Those most commonly used are:

- Typed, printed, or handwritten: cards, files, filing cabinets or folders.
- Tapes: cassettes or reels.
- Computerised: disks or magnetic tapes.

Some of these are interchangeable, e.g. you may have stored some information from a computer as printout, in which case it may be stored in a hanging file; or you may decide that something which is currently typed will be better stored on computer.

You will also wish to divide your material into that which is available to others, and that which you feel should be confidential. The most obvious candidates for the second category are personnel records, and business or development plans which you may be working on. If you are responsible for matters such as projects and contracts with other organisations, material relating to those will also be confidential. All these should be stored in a safe place – a locked filing cabinet or cupboard, to which only you and, perhaps, your secretary have keys, should give sufficient security. (Any members of the Civil Service or Armed Forces reading this will already know of the security arrangements connected with their positions.)

Once you've divided by format, and by confidentiality, it's up to you to decide on arrangement. This is one of those tasks which is often best delegated to the person likely to need access to the information most frequently. This is generally a secretary or an assistant rather than the manager in person. It is important for you to know how the system works, of course, so that you can get at the material yourself if necessary, but it's a waste of time and senior staff for you to do the setting up. Just remember, the simpler the system, the better, and alphabetically by subject is usually the best for the majority of filing systems. You should also have a very careful index to the files, so that you can trace material that is not where you thought, and find material on related subjects more easily. You do this by means of references and cross-references (see Figures 3.1 and 3.2).

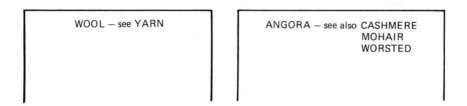

Figure 3.1   Reference   Figure 3.2   Cross-reference

Make sure that the person in charge understands what you're asking for, and then leave them to get on with it. Once the system is operational, all that's needed is to check that it's kept up to date.

Initially, your information bank will grow rapidly, and this is fine until you come to the perennial problem of lack of space. It's bound to happen before you anticipated, and the only way to solve it is to have rules for how long you hang on to material. It's impossible to draw up a rigid framework for this, as different types of information are important for different reasons, depending on the kind of manager you are.

There are some obvious rules you can set: the personnel records already mentioned will have to be kept for at least as long as the individual is employed by your organisation. In the same way, any notes or reports you may have concerning projects in which you are involved will also have to be retained at least for the duration of the contract. What about the rest — the memos and the press cuttings, the committee minutes and the journal articles?

If there is some kind of central archive held somewhere in the organisation, much of the decision making about what to keep and what to discard is solved for you. You will simply have the files weeded at regular intervals, and have whatever is older than a fixed length of time — a year, perhaps — sent for storage in the archive. If there is no central archive, then it becomes a bit more difficult, and you'll have to set your own rules. You can always suggest setting up an archive — it may be simply that no one thought of doing so before. Otherwise, you might decide to do this:

- Keep everything that you decide to retain for at least one year.
- Keep committee minutes and project reports for three years.
- Keep personnel records for one year after the employee has left the company.
- Keep all financial records for five years.
- Keep one copy of everything you write yourself forever.

HAMILTON'S LAW 4: Nobody needs two copies forever

It will probably be safe to discard the rest of the material — but this does not simply mean junking it. Someone else in the organisation may find it useful. If you have an information unit or library, offer the staff your press cuttings and back journals, at least. Check them carefully first; you may discover that 'your' copy of a journal was actually the library's originally, and that can be very embarrassing! When you've done all that, there should still be something to put in the wastebin, which is always satisfying. Sure as fate, there will be at least one thing which you will need tomorrow, but that's another law, already attributed to someone else.

INFORMATION SOURCES OUTSIDE YOUR OFFICE

As well as all the material that comes into your office, there will be other information available to you. This may be inside your organisation, or outside it. (I am excluding the results of industrial espionage and other illegal ways of getting hold of the stuff.) Apart from conversation with colleagues and others over lunch, there is another source, which may well be under-used by you. This is the library, or information unit, which may be housed right in the building with you. A few years ago many organisations closed down their information units, but most places have now realised the importance of such units, and either set one up, or reopened one.

If there is such a place in your organisation, when did you last visit it? Many middle and senior managers claim to have no time to do so, little realising what a useful place it can be. As well as its obvious function, a library/information unit can be a good place to retire to if you need somewhere quiet to sit and do a spot of writing, or thinking, without constant interruptions. This assumes that it is large enough to have room for a few desks and chairs, of course; some information units are so small that there is barely enough room for the stock and the staff, let alone people from other parts of the building!

It is a good idea to make yourself known to the librarian/ information officer, or whatever title is used. He or she can be a valuable friend. Well run units of this type keep profiles of all senior staff (at least), giving details of their interests and information needs. This helps them to feed you the right information, as it arrives, so that you are kept up to date with the latest developments. You will be a favourite if you pass on circulated journals as quickly as possible, and return borrowed material rapidly. The information staff will make an extra effort for you, and will do their best to get the information you require as soon as they can. Remember that it is often possible to order material which is not available in your own organisation via a national and international system of inter-library loans.

Computers play a large part in the information profession nowa-days, and most library and information staff are trained to use them. Tell them your needs, and leave them to it, but be reasonable, and don't always expect immediate results. Looking for a specific item can take some time, especially when you have not been able to give full details of your request. If you can give a title, author, and date, plus (in the case of a journal article) some idea of the name of the

Author *A EWING*					Office use
Title (Book/Journal) *CHEESE PLEASE : OR FETTA IS BETTER*					
Publisher	Date	Edition	Vol.	Part	
CHURN PRESS	*1986*	*1*	*-*	*-*	
Your name and department *ANN ONYMOUS — MICROBIOLOGY*					

Figure 3.3   Loan request form

journal, it will be found much more quickly than if you mutter vaguely about books with green covers that you saw last time you came in.

HAMILTON'S LAW 5: Even a librarian can't get it for you yesterday

A QUICK LOOK AT COMPUTERS

It would be impossible to write a chapter on information management without at least mentioning computers. Love 'em or hate 'em, they're here to stay, and they do help to speed up some of the functions we've already mentioned. There are some very simple filing systems — usually referred to as database management systems — which can be a real boon if you have the sort of job that means you have to keep large and detailed files. They can save space and time, provided you know exactly what you want to do with them. You may find at first that you quite like the idea of throwing yours through the window, but persevere, and you may find yourself wondering how you ever managed without it, within a relatively short time. You will also discover how important it is to be able to type — especially if, like me, you refused to learn for fear of being pigeonholed as a secretary.

As well as having useful filing systems, computers can also help with tasks like budget forecasts, development planning, and writing reports and other materials. (This chapter has been typed straight on to a computer, using a word-processing package. It has saved me a fortune in correcting fluid and paper.) Some people get so hooked on the computer, that they have a portable one, as well as the one in the office, which they use in the train travelling to and from the office. Working from home is also increasingly common, because of enhancements like electronic mail systems.

One word of warning, though: if you're inefficient and disorganised without a computer, you probably will be just the same with one. In fact:

HAMILTON'S LAW 6: Computers are not the automatic answer

CONCLUSION AND SUMMARY

Whatever kind of manager you are, and wherever you work, you will be an information user as well. If you try to see everything there is on your subject, and also try to keep it forever, you will rapidly become an inefficient manager, who is being pushed out into the corridor by the great mass of unsorted material lying around inside the office. You will also damage the efficiency of your colleagues and, eventually, the whole organisation.

If, on the other hand, you manage the information which comes into the office by the methods outlined above, you should be more efficient, because you will have it all under control, all of the time. So remember:

- Decide what you need to see, and what you would like to see.
- Forget about the rest.
- Pass on circulated material quickly.
- Make sure you understand your own filing system.
- Keep it up to date.
- Weed out the old stuff regularly.
- Use the library/information unit.
- Acknowledge copyright when quoting Hamilton's Laws.
- Read this chapter when you're stuck/depressed/bored.
- Enjoy your job.

FURTHER READING

Bakewell, K G B, *How to organise information*, Gower, 1984

Dare, G A and Bakewell K G B, *Manager's guide to getting the answers,* Library Association, 2nd edition 1983

Drucker, P F, *Changing world of the executive,* Heinemann, 1982

Torrington, D et al., *Management methods,* Institute of Personnel Management, Gower, 1986

Webb, S, *Creating an information service,* Aslib, 1985

4

Effective writing

Dorothy M Stewart

Management, it has been said, is the art of getting things done through and by other people. Much of the instruction (or persuasion) is done face to face, on the shop- or office-floor, day by day. But much also is done in writing – memos, telexes, letters, proposals, and reports.

Most people find business writing a chore, and many find it difficult. No wonder, as Figure 4.1 shows. When you meet face to face, you and your 'recipient' have three means of communicating – words, voice and body language. The figure shows the relative importance of each of these three as sources of information.

Words	10%
Voice	35%
Body language	55%
Total	100%

Figure 4.1 Relative importance of the three components of face to face communication as sources of information
Derived from J Townsend, 'Paralinguistics: how the non-verbal aspects of speech affect our ability to communicate', *Journal of European Industrial Training*, 1985, vol. 9:3, pp. 27–31.

Body language and voice are shown as the main sources of information. If you hesitate to accept this, try saying 'You will enjoy this' in different tones of voice, stressing different words each time, leaning back in a relaxed manner, leaning forward threateningly etc. The words contribute to meaning, but the other factors are clearly influential.

Writing consists of words alone. With writing, you must convey 100 per cent of the information through a medium which in everyday face to face interaction contributes only 10 per cent of the data. Body language and tone of voice are denied to you. In writing, you are communicating under a severe handicap. No wonder many people find writing difficult!

The handicap, however, can be overcome. This chapter sets out to provide you with guidelines on how to do just that in your business writing. You will find that the ideas will also apply to the other kinds of writing that you do, since the principles are the same.

WHY ARE YOU WRITING?

The first thing you need to know is your purpose in writing to someone. What do you want to happen as a result? If you are unclear about this, your writing will be unclear, and your recipient will be unclear about how he is meant to respond.

Consider the following extract from a letter:

> In case of any mistake on our part or your own, we felt that you would wish to be informed that at the close of business tonight your account appears in our books as £397.96 overdrawn.

The letter suggests that it is simply keeping you informed 'in case of any mistake on our part or your own'. The information being provided, however, is that you are overdrawn. This is being stated in a low-key, face-saving way which gives you the opportunity to put it right – if you wish. The bank are perfectly clear about their purpose, and so they have created an effective letter.

Not so, however, the writer of the next letter:

> Dear Sir,
>
> Many thanks for your application for a credit account at our store. As Credit Control Manager, it is my responsibility to check all applications and take credit decisions. I have found your application particularly interesting.
>
> You will remember we asked for information about other credit accounts you hold. You correctly mentioned those at Ace Sports Stores and Music Unlimited; your information on the amounts involved, however, was higher than supplied by these stores. Ace Sports Stores also informed me that you no longer work for Meltec Machinery Ltd. Meltec provided me with the

name and address of your current employer, Fraisons Plant Ltd, from whom I obtained necessary employment/salary details.

In the light of the above, I am happy to open a credit account for you with our store. I have carefully considered your circumstances and have decided that your credit should be £1000 per annum, not the £2000 you have requested. If you feel that there is sufficient change in your circumstances to warrant raising the limit, then I will be prepared to reconsider this in one year's time.

Many thanks for applying for a credit facility. If we can be of further assistance, please do not hesitate to contact us.

Yours faithfully,

Credit Control Manager

Here we have someone, perhaps new to their job or delighting in the power it gives them, forgetting that the purpose of their business writing is to improve their company's business. Instead, they use the opportunity as an ego trip and as a result alienate the customer, and lose the business on which their salary depends.

'Business writing' means that you are writing on behalf of the organisation that employs you. Your primary purpose in writing is therefore your company's purpose, and that is always a business purpose.

Part of the purpose is one of public relations. This includes not only making a good impression on your recipient, but making the *right* impression.

Consider your organisation. What kind of image do you think it has in the minds of people outside, e.g. bankers, customers, financiers etc? Try to pin this down by giving it a place on the organisational culture continuum in Figure 4.2. 1 is the most informal (found in advertising agencies, the pop record business), and 15 is the most formal (old-fashioned, traditional lawyers and accountants, for example).

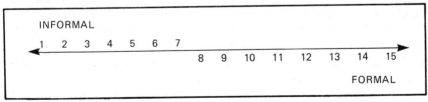

Figure 4.2 Organisational culture continuum

Now think about your own business writing style and the general style of written communication in your organisation. Are you on first name terms with colleagues and superiors and with outside correspondents? Or do you use the formality of Mr/Miss, or even the very formal 'J Brown Esq.'? Place the 'written culture' of your organisation on the continuum also.

You may find that the two scores match. This is a considerable measure of success in making the right impression. It may be, however, that old-fashioned writing styles are damaging your company's otherwise modern image.

This is very common nowadays especially in the traditional businesses, e.g. banks, insurance, shipping, where a strong lead from the top is transforming the business but at the lower levels the traditions hold firm, especially where writing is concerned. This presents a very confusing face to the outside world. Is the company really part of the twentieth century as top management insist – or is that merely a shallow façade behind which the business goes on unchanged from the Dickensian era of clerks scratching out their copperplate letters at high desks with quill pens!

These impressions are important to customers and financiers, who both need to have confidence in your organisation.

WHO ARE YOU WRITING TO?

The next step is to motivate your recipient to reply in such a way as to satisfy your purpose. This is not manipulation; it is more like good manners. There are ways of asking for another piece of cake!

First, you need to understand something of your recipient. Why should they read your letter or report, let alone agree with your request, send the information, promote you etc.?

Too many letters or memos begin, in effect, 'I have a problem . . . I want . . . I need . . . ' To persuade your reader to read, you must capture his attention. To do this, you need to capture his interest. And everyone is most interested in how things apply to *them*.

Think back over the people you have written to in the last week, and the nature of the correspondence. Think about the correspondence from *their* point of view. Can you identify the ways in which each was important to the recipient?

Now consider why your recipient should agree to your request, approve your report etc. Step inside his shoes and think about each from his viewpoint. How does it affect him? What benefits are there to him from agreeing/disagreeing?

Remembering what you actually wrote, you may find it revealing to ask yourself if you mentioned these things. Do you in fact know enough about your recipients to know how the contents were important to them, or what the benefits were to them?

There are a million claims on a manager's time. You need to give your readers good reasons for taking time to read your memos and reports, and good reasons for asking them to help you achieve your objectives. If you write with your *reader's* needs in mind rather than your own, you will find your success rate soars! See checklist in Figure 4.3.

- Catch and hold your reader's attention

- Show your reader why your message is important to *them*

- Show your reader the benefits to *them* from agreeing/replying etc.

- Aim for one page only for letters and memos

- Make it easy to read, understand and *act on* at one reading!

Figure 4.3   Checklist – writing for your reader's needs

HOW SHOULD YOU WRITE IT?

This is what most people would assume is the meat of this chapter. It is my contention that the most elegant style and structure will not compensate for lack of consideration of the earlier points. This understanding provides you with the basis for your strategy. Structure and style are your tactics.

Structure

Clear thinking leads to clear writing, and much of that clarity comes from good organisation. It is the poorly thought out letter or report which weaves uneasily through arguments and counter-arguments resulting in total confusion for the reader.

Whether you are writing a telex, a memo, a letter or a long report, time spent thinking and planning *before* you put pen to paper (or finger to key) is time well spent.

Structuring letters, memos and telexes

Begin by identifying your purpose. Are you providing information? You may like to think about the effect of the information on your reader along a continuum from good news to bad news. See Figure 4.4.

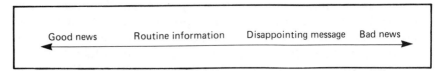

Figure 4.4   The information continuum

A successful good news letter (memo or telex) will require a different structure from that of a bad news letter. Good news or routine information, for example, has efficiency of communication as its goal. There is nothing to be gained from beating about the bush or wasting the reader's time with your warm-up sentence, so you can open directly with your main idea or central point, i.e. what it is about.

The bad or disappointing news letter needs to bring your reader in gently so that they are at least in a neutral frame of mind. This means starting with a buffer − neutral or positive information that the reader is not likely to disagree with. Then present your reasoning for the bad news. This should be in terms the reader will understand and agree with. Avoid the so-familiar over-complicated explanations and negative language. Aim for logic and clarity. Then, end on an optimistic note, offering a lesser alternative if that is appropriate and possible.

If your purpose is persuasion, you will need to get your reader's attention straight away. Do this by explaining your proposal in terms of the benefits to the reader. Do this crisply. Don't waste any words − you are already imposing on your reader's time! It is more courteous to state clearly the action you want rather than waste time with coyness. State the deadline and, if you can, suggest an incentive to act soon. It is useful to remind the reader at the end of the letter of the action you want and why they should agree.

Of all the three types, this is the most 'you-centred', focusing strongly on 'what's in it' for the reader. The pattern is probably very familiar from various mail shots you receive. These go on being sent out because of their proven effectiveness. Try the formula and see!

A general point about letters: do try to make letters look attractive. They are your letters; you sign them with your name, not your secretary's, therefore it is important that your letters convey the visual impression you want. This means that you must control layout. Many secretaries despair of vague bosses who provide no instructions on this and then complain about the results. If you do not have strong feelings or clear ideas on this, you may find it useful to look through your incoming mail and compare it with your usual layout style to see which you prefer.

Good news — routine information

- Be direct — main idea/central idea first
- Be complete — check you have put in all relevant details

Disappointing or bad news

- Buffer first — neutral or positive information
- Present reasoning — use logic and clarity; avoid jargon
- Optimistic close — offer lesser alternative if appropriate

Persuasive requests

- Get the reader's attention immediately
- Lead with your strongest motivator
- Explain your proposal in terms of the reader — what's in it for them
- Get their action — specify what action you want and when
- Offer an incentive if possible

Figure 4.5   Checklist — purpose and structure of writing

Structuring reports and proposals

As before, your first step is to consider your purpose since this has implications for the structure. If you are writing to provide information, the good news/bad news formula may help. See Figure 4.5. In any case, your readers will be expecting an emphasis on data, hopefully well organised, and possibly ending with a summary. If, however, you are offering a proposal, you will be expected to provide a description of the current situation, with a reasoned account of the steps leading to your conclusion, i.e. your proposal. If your report aims to solve a problem, your readers will want to see a clear analysis of the problem and recommendations for dealing with it.

Where a conclusion is required, there are three choices for the organisation of the report:

Choice 1	*Choice 2*	*Choice 3*
Introduction	Introduction	Conclusion
Body of the report	Conclusion	Introduction
Conclusion	Body of the report	Body of the report

Choice 1 is particularly useful where your recipient might tend to resist your conclusions, e.g. where the report contains bad news, or be contrary to your reader's opinions. It is also a good choice where your recipient may not be able to understand the conclusions until he/she has read the rest of the report. However, the main drawback of this choice is that busy people tend to flip to the end and read the conclusions first, thus defeating your strategy.

Choices 2 and 3 are the more modern ways of presenting reports. Introduced first in America, these patterns are preferred by most American companies and by senior managers who have worked for American companies or been educated at business school.

They are particularly appropriate when the report contains good news for the reader, or where the reader has enough background to understand the conclusions without further explanation. Readers may find the report easier to read since the conclusions provide a framework around which to interpret the detailed information.

The main benefit of these two structures is that they save the busy executive time. If you prefer (or your organisation insists that you use) the more traditional Choice 1, you may find that putting in a one-page 'Management/Executive summary' at the beginning will provide you with the best of both worlds. This should summarise your conclusions and recommendations, and how you got there, referenced to the main body of your report so that readers can follow up any points they wish.

This is a particularly useful style for reports presented to a committee. The management summary offers an overview and a ready-made agenda for discussion of the report, without the problems of getting bogged down in unnecessary detail.

See Figure 4.6 for a checklist before writing a report.

Organising the data

Once you have decided the general structure, you must marshal your data to best advantage within that structure. A prioritising system is a useful aid in this.

First list the main points on a piece of paper. Then think about each idea in turn and list the facts and ideas that go with each main point.

1 What is your purpose:

   ● provide information?
   ● write a proposal?
   ● solve a problem?

2 About your recipient:

   ● who is your recipient?
   ● what do you know about your recipient in relation to:

   expertise — how much do your recipients know about the topic?
             — will they understand the technical jargon you might use?

   interests — is there a preferred format you must use?
             — do they like tables, charts, pictures, statistics?
             — how much detail do your recipients want?

   opinions — will your recipients be for or against your recommendations?
             — do they think the topic is important?
             — what do they think of you, e.g. expert authority scribe,
               junior?

Figure 4.6 Checklist before writing a report

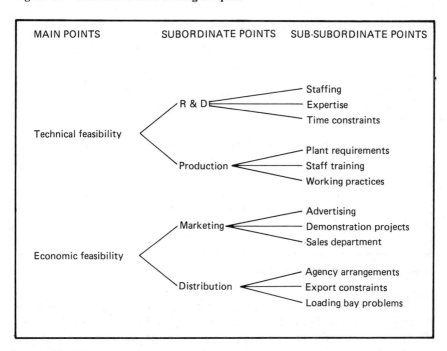

Figure 4.7 Example of a report outline

If the material is very detailed or complex, you may need a third stage where you add a further category of subordinate items. Figure 4.7 gives an example.

Now re-read your list to check that it is complete and you have missed nothing out. When you are confident that it is complete, take a few moments to consider your purpose and your recipient. What will motivate them best? What data will be most convincing or most interesting to them? Now look back over your main points and arrange them in the best sequence for your purpose, numbering them in order. Do the same for each set of subordinate points, using a decimal system as shown in Figure 4.8, until you have numbered each item. You may now want to rewrite your outline in order.

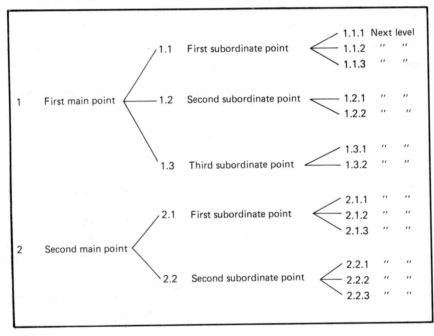

Figure 4.8   Numbered outline for a report

This provides you with a clear and well organised structure for your writing. You will find that it gets you started on your project and deals very effectively with any 'writer's blocks'. It cuts down substantially on writing time since all you need to do is follow the route map your outline provides. And for long reports, your first and second categories of points provide headings and sub-headings.

REPORTS GUIDELINES

- Plan carefully – think through the entire situation before you start to write.
- Gather all the facts and double-check them for accuracy and relevance.
- Choose an appropriate structure.
- Prepare a detailed outline.
- Anticipate objections and jot down ideas in response to work into your writing.
- Put yourself in the reader's place and try to imagine what materials would be most convincing.
- Beware of exaggerating, stating opinions as facts, or using biased statements.
- Edit every sentence and paragraph to make sure your meaning is clear.

Style

Style is a rather vague, literary term for the way you use words. To put it in more concrete terms, your chosen structure is your blueprint; words are the building blocks. Your vocabulary is your personal stock of bricks.

Some are everyday common-or-garden bricks; others are for special purposes. Many of the words you take for granted may be jargon to someone not in your industry or profession. Some of these words may be justifiable technical terms; others may be incomprehensible jargon to the outsider. The key to deciding which is which is your reader. What would he/she understand?

As well as jargon, there are a number of insidious 'weeds' which creep into our writing. These are the words and phrases we would never use in conversation; they are pompous, old-fashioned, and long-winded, e.g.

approximately	effected
assistance	terminate
commence	endeavour to ascertain
with all due despatch	concerning
in the event that	commendation
customary channels	

These are only a sample. I am sure you can think of many more. Can you find everyday, shorter ways of saying the same thing?

Clear English is the lifeblood of business communication. It can also make the difference between life and death as the following quotation shows:

> Of course, there were warnings about the fire risk at Bradford. I wish that they had been written in plain English, but they were written in the doughy, ponderous style that officials fall into, clearly under the impression that to use ordinary language is unworthy of their position. Anyone wanting to make the point would have written, 'people must be able to get away from the stand in two to three minutes. At present they cannot.' What the football club received was, 'Egress from the grandstand should be achievable in 2.5 minutes.' It was told that 'an appraisal of structural adequacy' was 'desirable'. Even the question of litter was put into terms that remove it a stage from reality '. . . there is a build-up of combustible materials in the voids beneath the seats. A carelessly discarded cigarette could give rise to a fire risk.'
>
> Was it beyond anyone to write, 'There are piles of rubbish under the seats. If someone drops a lighted cigarette into this lot, the whole stand could go up in flames in minutes'?

(This first appeared in *New Scientist*, a weekly review of science and technology.)

Grammar and spelling

A few words about two other bugbears: grammar and spelling. You need to be ruthlessly honest with yourself about these. Are you 'good at' grammar and spelling? If you are, no need to worry about them. If you are not, there is still no need to worry.

Grammar is something taught to children at school *after* the children have been communicating successfully for five or six years. Imagine learning Russian or Spanish, living in Russia or Spain for five or six years, speaking the language every day, and only then being taught the grammar. It's a crazy idea. Grammar is *part* of the language, not something complicated which is imposed on top of it. Grammar is something you know about; you use it every day speaking to people. The objective test for grammar is: do people understand you? If they do, and nobody complains about your use of English, then you are good enough at grammar. If, however, people complain about your use of English, help is required. Do *not* try to do this for yourself! Call in the experts, the people who complain, your secretary. State your problem: 'Never did get to grips with the finer points of grammar. I'd really appreciate it if you'd cast your eye over this and tidy it up for me.' The experts, especially those who complain, love to be asked to display their expertise. Don't get drawn into discussions (arguments), simply hand it over and let them get on with it. (If you do want to brush up grammar for yourself, you will find some ideas for this in the list of further reading at the end of this chapter.)

I believe that as far as spelling is concerned, there are only two types of people in the universe: those who can spell and those who cannot. It's rather like an ear for music. Either you have, or you haven't. If you have, rejoice. If you haven't, do not worry about it.

Have a good dictionary in your desk drawer and look things up. Don't be embarrassed about this. It's not a sign of failure. The secret of the perfect spellers is that they know their way round a dictionary. Not all dictionaries are the same in layout, presentation etc. Browse in a good bookshop and test out a few until you find one you really like. Then guard it with your life.

Again, do ask people for help, friends, colleagues, spouse, secretary — if they can spell. A simple request to 'check the spelling for me' will do the trick. It is very important for the manager who knows he/she is not good at grammar and spelling to ensure that their secretary is. Do include some test of these abilities in any selection process, then inform your secretary that she is responsible for the standard of grammar and spelling in anything she types for you. This should solve your problem, and end your worries on this.

CONCLUSION

Business writing is writing with a purpose. There is the PR purpose, representing your organisation and yourself in an appropriate way. And there is the result you wish to achieve from the communication, ranging from the swift return of required information to the final blessed silence of a long term complainer. Knowing your purpose is the first step to effective writing. This chapter has offered guidelines and ideas for achieving that purpose through the choice of structure, organisation of your ideas, and the use of language.

FURTHER READING

Austin, Mike, *The ISTC Handbook of Technical Writing and Publication Techniques*, Heinemann, 1985

Barrass, Robert, *Scientists Must Write: a guide to better writing for scientists, engineers and students*, Science Paperbacks (Chapman and Hall), 1978

Cooper, Bruce M, *Writing Technical Reports*, Penguin, 1964

Ewing, David W, *Writing for results in business, government, the sciences and the professions*, John Wiley, 2nd edition, 1974

Fowler's *Modern English Usage*, Oxford University Press, 2nd edition revised by Sir Ernest Gowers, 1968

Fowler, H W and F G, *The King's English*, Oxford University Press, 1975

Gowers, Sir Ernest, *The Complete Plain Words*, Penguin, 1962

Howard, Godfrey, *Getting Through! How to make words work for you*, David & Charles, 1980

Lesikar, Raymond V, *How to Write a Report Your Boss Will Read and Remember*, Dow Jones-Irwin, revised edition, 1984

Poe, Roy W, *The McGraw-Hill Guide to Effective Business Reports*, McGraw-Hill, 1982

Sussams, John E, *How to Write Effective Reports*, Wildwood House, 1983

Turabian, Kate L, *A Manual for Writers of Research Papers, Theses and Dissertations*, Heinemann, 1982

5

Effective speaking

Brian Sanders

We are all capable of speaking effectively to an audience large or small but many of us are woefully out of practice, some of us have never had any practice, and the vast majority have had no tuition in the skills involved.

This chapter provides a practical and basic introduction for the busy manager who has to talk to a group of people. The chapter is divided into four parts:

- The spoken word
- How to make the best use of oneself
- How to prepare the material
- Extending the vocal range

The word 'talk' has been used throughout and is intended to cover presentation, speech, address, lecture and synonymous expressions. The word 'audience' is used to include listeners, conference, meeting, assembly and similar expressions.

THE SPOKEN WORD

The art of speaking has been neglected in favour of writing. Few schools teach it. On a recent course a man of 45 said that the last time he spoke to an audience was at a primary school assembly!

Because of this neglect, confidence is lacking and the results may be disastrous. But with effort and practice much can be achieved. Preparation and practice are essential.

Effective speaking

The term 'effective speaking' has replaced the older 'public speaking'. The latter suggests a formal gathering with a platform and a large audience. Much work today is done in an informal situation and with an audience of only three or four.

But one must be effective. Do not underestimate the amount of effort required to talk to a small group. The world is full of mutterers. Do not be one of these. If you are to sound enthusiastic and convincing, vocal vitality is essential.

Whether you talk to 3, 30 or 300 the basic approach is the same. You need a conversational style. But both your physical self and your voice need enlarging and projecting to meet the needs of the larger audience.

Lord Curzon (1859–1925) was recognised as one of the finest orators of his time. He made a perceptive statement about talking to audiences. He said that the three most important things to remember, in their order of importance, are:

● who you are
● how you say it
● what you say.

At first sight the second and third statements may appear to be the wrong way round. But no matter how excellent your material, if you cannot present it in an interesting and entertaining way, if you cannot make it palatable, then you might as well not bother.

Who you are is your personality, relevant knowledge and experience. You must engage the whole of yourself – voice, eyes, face, hands, arms – the whole of your physical self to assist communication.

If you are extrovert then discipline yourself as necessary; don't completely overwhelm the audience. If you are a quiet and shy person, use these attributes to draw your audience towards you. Shyness does not prevent voice projection or vitality.

Don't be over-modest. Use relevant experience whenever you can. Anecdotes always stick in the mind.

How you say it demands the best use of your voice, the best possible presentation of your whole self and of the material.

Every effort should be made to increase and enlarge the vocal range and to keep the voice in trim with constant exercising. (Refer to the final section 'Extending the vocal range'.)

You must create the right atmosphere. Jargon and technical terms must be avoided if they will not be understood.

What you say requires careful selection and ordering. Everything must be relevant to the particular occasion.

Personality

You will be effective only if you are willing to disclose your personality. The actor hides behind the character he portrays. You must be yourself. You must be prepared to put yourself at risk.

But the element of risk causes nervous tension which will inhibit your performance. Relaxation will prevent this. Until you are relaxed you will never give of your best.

To learn relaxation takes some weeks of practice. But it can be done. Once relaxed you will enjoy the experience of talking to audiences.

HOW TO MAKE THE BEST USE OF ONESELF

Speakers sometimes fancy that if they take refuge behind an overhead projector or some sophisticated aid their lack of skills or nervous tension will go unnoticed. It is not so. In fact the more sophisticated the aids the more the weaknesses of a poor speaker are highlighted. A multiple projector presentation has often been followed by a disastrous question time because the speaker was tense, looked desperate and mumbled the answers. And this is what the audience remembered.

Relaxation will solve all the problems caused by tension. Practice will improve the speaker's performance.

Nerves and tension

It is important to distinguish between nerves and tension. Nerves are essential to set the adrenalin flowing into the blood stream. This has a stimulating effect on the system and gives the necessary 'edge' to our performance.

Some think, quite incorrectly, that eventually a person 'grows out' of nerves with the benefit of experience. This is not so. The time to worry is when you don't feel nervous!

Watch actors pacing, coughing and fidgeting backstage before a first entrance. See the effect of the red light in a BBC radio studio on the most experienced actors. But they have learned to control their nerves and so prevent the assault of tension.

Tension is a wrecker. It constricts the voice, prevents breath control, causes the speaker to look anywhere but at the audience. Clinging to a lectern or a piece of furniture, swaying, fidgeting and other distracting mannerisms are further manifestations.

Controlling nerves and eliminating tension

Useful exercises practised for a few minutes each day will eventually enable a person to relax at will. It is simply a question of mind over matter. Once relaxation is achieved speaking engagements become a positive pleasure. The speaker knows that self-control through relaxation will give an appearance of relaxed authority.

Some exercises for relaxation

1 On tiptoe, stretch arms upwards, fully extended; stretch fingers on hands. Stretch calves and thighs. Stretch the abdomen. Imagine yourself on a vertical rack with toes nailed to the floor and fingers pulled by unseen wires towards the ceiling.

Feel the discomfort of it. Hold the position for a few moments and then relax. Feel the pleasure of relaxation. Repeat this exercise three times.

2 Tense the arms from shoulders to fingertips. Feel the discomfort. Relax and feel the pleasure of relaxation. Repeat three times.

3 Keeping the soles of the feet on the floor, stretch the legs from thighs to tips of toes. (Keep the arms relaxed during this exercise.) Feel the discomfort. Relax and feel the pleasure of relaxation. When you relax keep both knees braced but not rigid. Repeat three times.

4 Stretch arms and legs together (as in 2 and 3). Feel the discomfort. Relax and feel the pleasure of relaxation. Repeat three times.

The shoulders and neck are most prone to tension. Breathing becomes difficult, the voice is stifled in the throat and the speaker is extraordinarily aware of hands and arms.

The following exercises are designed to help remove tension from these vital areas.

5 Shake the fingers loose on limp wrists and try to throw them on to the floor. Next shake the fingers and lower arms from the elbows.

Finally throw the arms from the shoulders. Feel all tension in the arms being flung out of the fingertips.

6   Roll the right shoulder forwards and then backwards several times in vigorous circles. Repeat with the left shoulder. Then exercise both shoulders together.

7   Relax the muscles in the neck and allow the head to fall forward. Roll the head round *slowly* three times, bending from the waist so that the weight of the head takes it round. Stop and rotate slowly in the opposite direction three times. Stop with the chin resting on the chest. Lift the head level.
Note: This exercise must be undertaken slowly.

CREATING A FEELING OF CONFIDENCE

Standing or sitting well creates a feeling of confidence in both speaker and audience.

For the speaker it aids relaxation, enables ease of movement, assists breath control and helps to free the voice.

The audience see someone authoritative, knowledgeable, confident and delighted to talk to them.

Standing well

The feet should be slightly apart. This gives a good grip on the floor. Never stand with your feet together. Brace both knees firmly but without tension. Bring the stomach wall under control so that it is firmly held but not pulled in.

Hold the chest freely without pushing it forward and settle the shoulders on the chest with two or three easy movements up and down. They should be very slightly braced.

Look comfortably straight ahead. The position should be 'head in the air' and not 'nose (or chin) in the air'.

Have the weight of the body on the front of the feet and not the heels. If you stand on your heels the blood flow is restricted and this will make you tense and tired. You should be able to stand on tiptoe without toppling forward. Raise and lower yourself on your toes several times.

Keep the feet anchored and swing the trunk left to the back and then right to the back. This will prevent any stiffness creeping in. See Figure 5.1 for examples of correct and bad posture.

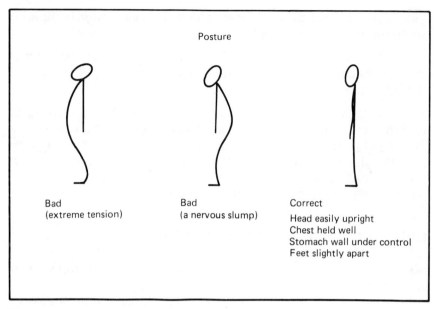

Figure 5.1 Posture: standing

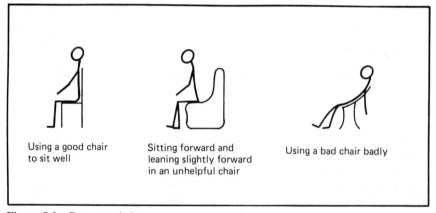

Figure 5.2 Posture: sitting

Sitting well

Choose a chair in which the seat and the back form a right angle. Place your bottom as far back as possible. When you sit up the back of the chair supports you. You can both sit comfortably and in a position which allows maximum freedom for movement from the waist upwards. It also allows freedom for breath control and voice projection.

If you are condemned to a badly designed chair sit forward on the seat and lean very slightly forward as well. See Figure 5.2 for examples.

Eye contact

Standing or sitting well enables an ease of eye contact with the audience. The top half of the body can move freely and, so long as the neck muscles are relaxed, the head will turn freely in every direction.

Eye contact with a large group is easier than with a small one.

When talking to an audience of less than 20 people the speaker's eye must light occasionally on each person. But don't 'searchlight' the group from side to side. This can be very wearisome all round!

With a large group the speaker should look for the most part about two-thirds of the way back. Occasional glances should be made to left and right of the front rows.

Gesture

Good gesture helps to underline what is said. All movement of the arm should be hinged at the shoulder and not the elbow.

The elbows give strength to gesture, the wrists enable precision and the hands contain power and control.

Bad gesture distracts. Twitches, fidgets and repetitious movements are fatal. The audience spots them and attention is diverted from what is said.

USING A MICROPHONE

There are times in a large hall or a room where acoustics are bad when a microphone becomes necessary. Neck microphones are preferable to stand microphones particularly if your talk requires movement. The neck instrument remains at a uniform distance from the larynx and allows you the necessary freedom to move about.

There are many types of stand microphone. Rehearse well before the event to discover what the instrument will and will not do. Take the advice of a technician if one is available. But remember that even technology cannot provide all the answers.

You must bring vitality to the microphone. There must be something irresistible about your performance. If you project both subtlety and vitality then the microphone will be most effective in transmitting them.

THE PREPARATION OF THE MATERIAL

Pre-preparation

Before attempting notes or jottings for the talk ask yourself the following five questions. Answer each as thoroughly as possible. This will help you to concentrate on material relevant to the specific occasion, will ensure that you pitch the talk at the correct level, will prevent last minute panics and will also save you time.

What is my aim? You may wish to inform, persuade, teach or stimulate. You will certainly always wish to entertain.

To entertain does not simply mean telling jokes. It is a combination of 'Who you are' and 'How you say it' together with the eventual selection and ordering of your material. It also includes relevant jokes and anecdotes. But if you are no good at telling jokes, don't.

Remember too that you cannot talk on technical matters or specialised knowledge for long without giving your audience a chance to relax a little.

Within your general aims consider your specific aim. What is it that you most wish your audience to remember, or action you wish them to take after the talk? This gives you a 'cutting edge'. It is worth noting now that your specific aim may change during the course of the preparation.

Who am I talking to? Find out all you can about the audience. Detailed research may be necessary but it is worth it in the long run. You must gear your talk as closely as possible to the listeners. Avoid jargon and technical terms if they will not be comprehensible. Find out what your audience wants to know, needs to know and doesn't need to know.

Where am I giving the talk? Know the size and shape of the room, the height of the ceiling, whether there are heavy curtains and a thick piled carpet. The room may resemble a concrete box. These things will affect the acoustics. A microphone may be necessary but don't use one unless you have to.

Decide where you will stand or sit. You must be seen easily by everyone. You should be in a dominating position though almost certainly not on a platform unless the audience is very big.

The natural light should always come from the side of the room unless the artificial lighting is excellent. If you are using electrical apparatus make sure that the sockets are conveniently placed.

Knowledge of these matters will help relaxation when the time comes.

What time of day am I talking? This may affect the arrangement of your material and will certainly shape your opening remarks.

After morning coffee is a good time to speak – probably the best. The audience are fully awake and ready for you.

After lunch – the siesta session – is a bad time. You will need to entertain to your utmost.

If it's an evening talk discover how your audience have been occupied during the day.

This information will enable you to gear the talk correctly from the start of your preparation.

How long are you expected to talk? 45 minutes is the longest time one person can cheerfully sustain. If you are given a couple of hours then you must organise the time carefully. After your opening remarks you might divide the audience into groups. Each group would appoint a secretary and go away to discuss some particular point. After a given time the groups would reassemble, each secretary would report back to the whole audience and then a general discussion might take place. It would then be your task to pull the threads together, summarise and point the way ahead.

Decide how you will organise question time and whether you may use visual aids.

Even when refurbishing an old talk it is still essential to answer these five questions.

Preparation time and the shape of the talk

The ideal time for preparing a talk is two or three weeks. Many have only two or three days, or even hours. The notes on assembling and selecting the material have therefore been divided into sections according to the time available.

All talks should have an introduction, a main part and a conclusion. Where should you begin? The principal facts or arguments go into the main section and this should be your starting point in the preparation. This section will comprise all but four to eight minutes of the total talking time.

Assembling and selecting material for the main part

Two weeks or more to prepare Write down on a large sheet of paper, notes and headings concerning the subject matter. Don't worry about the order at this stage. Check dates, figures, statistics; do necessary research.

Work at this in bursts of 15 or 20 minutes and then turn to something else. Return a while later and do some more. Your subconscious will work for you during the break and thoughts and ideas will flow more freely. Work again for only a short time and return again later or on the next day.

After five or six days, perhaps sooner, you will have a sheet or more of paper filled with a mass of material. There will be far more than you can possibly use in one talk.

Analysis on audience retention carried out some years ago produced most interesting figures. In a series of 40-minute talks it was found that an intelligent audience (an audience knowledgeable about and interested in the subject) could remember seven facts. An average audience could remember three facts. These figures are not sacrosanct but they are a positive guide.

Leave your jottings for a couple of days and allow your subconscious time to get to work again. Stored in your brain you have the answers to the five pre-preparation questions and all the rough headings and notes.

A burst of insight will tell you the theme you wish to pursue on this occasion because you are talking to that particular audience, in that place and at that time.

Now comes the vital moment of selection when you know what in your jottings is relevant and what is not. Strike out what is not relevant. Be ruthless. Take no matter you can dispense with. Better to say too little than too much.

Two days to prepare Notes and headings concerning the subject should be jotted down on a large sheet of paper. Don't worry about the order. Check facts and figures. This work should be completed in one day.

You will probably have too much material for one talk. Realise your specific aim for talking to this particular audience. Then remove any material not wholly relevant.

Two hours to prepare   Jot down all the headings which seem relevant. Leave the jottings for about half an hour. Return and delete irrelevant material. If you must add to the list then do so.

Two or three minutes to prepare   Should you wish to speak at a meeting and without prior preparation write down half a dozen key words on a sheet of paper. Then get them in a useful order. Speak for no more than three minutes and you may find yourself popular!

The main part of the talk

The skeleton of the main part is now to hand in what remains of your headings and jottings.

Get your headings in the correct order. If you are following a procedure or the way a piece of machinery works, then the order may be dictated by this. If there is no obvious order then arrange your points in order of importance.

Suppose you have six main headings. Arrange these in order of merit: 1 is your least important; 6 is your most important. Follow the Greeks who were masters of oratory. Begin your main section with point 5, your next-to-best; it will commend your whole case. Then proceed with 1, 2, 3, 4, and finish with 6.

You must work up towards a climax and not down. If you begin with your most important point ('They'll doze off after five or six minutes') then subconsciously you will know you have made the vital statement and you will 'run down' whether you like it or not. And they will doze off! Always work up to the point of greatest interest or intensity.

Next you must put the flesh on the skeleton of your talk. Write each heading on a separate large sheet of paper. Jot down your thoughts on how you may illuminate or develop that section. When you have completed the section in note form reshape your jottings to produce the right order. If you have stuck to notes and headings you will almost certainly find that the essential key words and phrases have emerged. Transfer these to the cards you will use for notes.

Pattern your notes in the way that suits you. Once you have found a satisfactory method of note making stick to it.

Having completed one section of your talk work on the others in a similar fashion.

The conclusion

This is a reiteration of the main points. Gather all the threads together and end on a conclusive or challenging note according to the purpose. Point the way ahead. Leave the audience with something to consider.

Introduction

This is the last section to be prepared and falls into two parts: the general introduction and the introduction of the subject matter.

The general introduction   It is essential for the audience and yourself to 'tune in' to each other. They may never have seen you before. If so they will size you up visually before they are fully prepared to listen to you. If you begin with some vital matter most of them will miss it.

If you are a stranger they need to be told who you are, your relevant experience and background. Your host may do this but it is often helpful to reserve some of this information for yourself.

If possible compliment your audience. Find out something about their organisation. Show you are interested in them outside the specific subject matter. Make them feel you are delighted to talk to them. If this is sincerely done the effect will be positive and helpful.

This general introduction can be done without reference to notes. This enables you to make eye contact with everyone and allows you to hear your voice projected to the back rows. If you can manage a smile as well − so much the better!

You may be addressing the firm's board of management or colleagues at a weekly meeting. Then much of the general intro-duction will be inappropriate. They may already know far too much about you! But an audience of colleagues still requires about a minute's 'settling time'. An appropriate observation or two will induce all eyes and ears in your direction.

Introduction of the subject matter   Your subject and objectives must be made abundantly clear. Avoid startling and striking openings. A clear, quietly stated opening is best. Tell them succinctly the ground you are about to cover and your aims.

NOTES

When these are completed number each card in the top right-hand corner. Then punch a hole in the top left-hand corner and tag the cards together. This makes it easy to turn them over and, should you drop them, they will remain in the right order!

Always carry your notes with you. There is no one to prompt you if your mind goes suddenly blank. And it is easy to miss something out. Discipline yourself to glance at the notes from time to time even if you are familiar with the subject matter.

A GENERAL OBSERVATION

Remember that the people being addressed are receiving the information for the first time. Facts and ideas must be presented simply and logically. Precise English is essential.

Always proceed from the known to the unknown. Build bridges from one point to the next. Do not elaborate the obvious.

Support statements with examples and anecdotes; tell jokes if you can and if they are relevant. Keep to the point.

USING VISUAL AIDS

Visual aids are used to assist communication and to present information so that it will be quickly grasped. They convey what words cannot get across.

Always let the subject matter speak for itself. Words are not visual aids. If using words keep them short and simple; make them forceful.

When showing a visual aid keep quiet for a little to allow the audience time to take it in. It is difficult, if not impossible, to read and listen at the same time. Remove the visual when you have finished with it.

Don't lose eye contact with the audience by talking to the flip chart or screen. Use a pointer or pencil and talk to the audience. But don't be afraid to write or draw on a flip chart or blackboard and talk a little at the same time, provided of course that you are talking about the matter on the board. Project your voice a little more at the same time.

The projector is better than other means for maps, charts, graphs and diagrams.

Visual aids should never be used merely as a concentration break or as a cue for the speaker.

Never display all headings at once. Use an overlay and limit strictly what is being looked at − that is what is being talked about.

Take care with colours. Blue and green together appear the same to the partially colour blind. Some colours are weak when projected.

Do not use too many visual aids. This confuses the audience and often confounds the speaker.

Prepare carefully and rehearse assiduously. Check equipment and always carry spare bulbs and extension leads.

Know beforehand what you will do if for any reason you are unable to use your visual aids.

ANSWERING QUESTIONS

In most cases a question session is essential unless you are satisfied you have given a complete performance. It is a matter of getting nearer to the whole truth and of meeting the needs of the audience.

Unless the talk is 'in house' it may be necessary to have a short interval when you have finished your talk. An audience cannot go into reverse at once. Tell them that questions will follow in two or three minutes. This will give them time to consider.

Answer as shortly as you can. Having answered the question don't go on answering it beyond the point of satisfaction.

If you do not know the answer say so. Call on somebody in the audience or offer to find out and write. Or suggest sources. Never invent an answer.

If you should know the answer but don't the fault is probably in your lack of preparation.

Rephrase a bad question before you answer it to avoid possible misunderstanding and embarrassment.

Repeat each question so that the back rows know what is being answered.

In the face of hostility remain courteous and keep your sense of humour. If a heckler persists and if there is no one in the chair to intervene offer to discuss the matter at the end as time is short and others wish to be answered.

When time is running out say, 'There's just time for three more questions', and hope to finish on a high note.

EXTENDING THE VOCAL RANGE

The human voice is a unique instrument. Unless physically impaired we each possess the necessary equipment and may do wonderful things with the voice. But we must learn to use it properly and to realise its full range. Relaxation and good posture help to free the voice.

Breathing

Correct breathing assists projection, helps avoid strain, gives the voice the necessary vitality and helps the speaker to sound enthusiastic.

For any form of public speaking we need to inhale quickly and deeply. In normal conversation we breathe through a slightly open mouth. This enables speedy and silent inhalation.

To breathe more deeply we must learn to expand the chest cavity. In normal breathing the rib cage moves upwards and outwards, and the diaphragm (a powerful muscle separating the chest from the abdomen) contracts and descends. These movements increase the volume of the chest cavity, a partial vacuum is created and air is sucked into the lungs (see Figure 5.3).

The more movement of the ribs and diaphragm the more air is drawn into the lungs. The more air in the lungs the better our voice control.

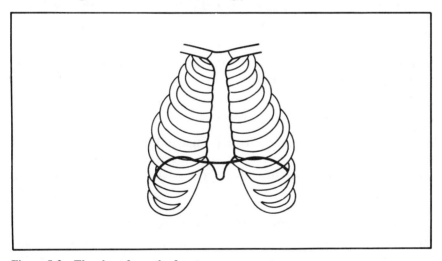

Figure 5.3   The chest from the front
The thick black line indicates the position of the diaphragm before inhalation.

Exercises for expansion and control

These exercises are best done near an open window or in a room with plenty of fresh air. (Outside is best of all − if you dare!)

Spend only two or three minutes at a time on breathing exercises. Should you feel dizzy then stop immediately. Overdoing things may result in hyperventilation.

1   Practise heavy sighs. This is a natural way of relieving tension. Sigh heavily and feel the rib cage collapse. Sigh several times. As you draw breath before the sigh feel the upward and outward expansion of the rib cage.
    Note that the shoulders play no part in breathing. They should be slightly braced (as for good stance), relaxed and still. On no account should they hunch at the time of inhalation.

2   Stand at one end of a large room. Inhale deeply and whisper 'One, two, three, four, five' using all the breath. Send the whisper on the stream of breath to the far end of the room.

3   Hum quietly. On the same note intone (or chant) 'One'.

4   Fill the lungs and intone 'One, two, three, four, five'. Repeat two or three times.

5   Once able to complete exercise 4 with ease and with 'five' fully projected repeat the exercise to 'ten'.

6   When you can complete exercise 5 with ease gradually extend the counting to 'fifteen'. The final number intoned should always sound as resonant as the first. When you run out of sufficient breath then stop.

7   When 'fifteen' is accomplished extend the counting to 'twenty'.

The exercises are to employ the rib cage and diaphragm so that they may work fully and easily: they are not voice exercises. Constant practice (a little at a time) will help to ensure an ease of deep breathing.

Resonance or the human amplification system

We should strive to make the best use of our vocal tone by ensuring that we are fully resonant.
    All hollow chambers above the voice box (larynx) act as resonators. These are the pharynx (the back of the throat), the nose and all the cavities and chambers connected to it, and the mouth (see Figure 5.4).
    The key exercise is humming.

1   Moisten the lips with the tongue and hum gently on an 'm' sound.

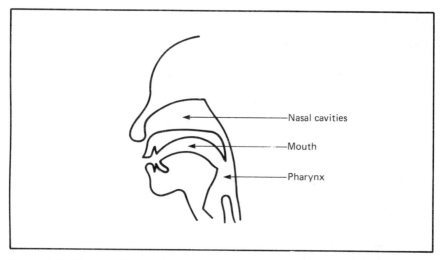

Figure 5.4 Cross-section of the head showing the resonating chambers
Note: The term 'nasal cavities' is intended to cover the nose and the various tubes and chambers associated with it.

The lips should be lightly together and the teeth slightly apart. When you hum a tingling sensation should be felt on the lips.

If no sensation is felt part the lips slightly and make a sound like a foghorn by blowing through them. Repeat this but after three seconds bring the lips together for the hum.

The tingling should resemble that when playing the comb and tissue paper. Quality of humming is more important than volume.

2   Hum, feel the tingle, open the mouth slowly and as wide as possible and sing 'ah'.

3   Intone 'Mary had a little lamb' feeling the tingle at the beginning and end of the line.

4   Speak this sentence with conviction, 'I must keep my voice in the front of my mouth'.

5   Do 3 and 4 together. Attempt to speak the words of 4 in the same place that you intoned 3.

6   Hum up and down the scale with a slow, smooth beat. Think and feel the sound on the mask of the face.

7   Hum any tune you know and keep the sound forward.

These exercises help to produce a forward voice and a well balanced resonant tone.

Clarity

Good articulation helps to make speech clear and distinct. The key instruments are the tongue, the teeth and the lips.

1 Say 'Articulation is a form of gymnastics between the tip of the tongue, the teeth and the lips'.

2 Say 'the tip of the tongue, the teeth and the lips' three times as nimbly as you can but without gabbling. The letter 't' is made by the explosion of teeth and lips parting.

3 Say ttt ttt ttt ttt (don't say tee tee tee).

4 Practise 't-say', 't-sow', 't-sigh' and then try 't-snake' 't-slave' 't-star'.

5 Practise precision of consonants:
   ppp ppp ppp ppp (lips)
   bbb bbb bbb bbb (lips)
   ttt ttt ttt ttt (teeth and tongue)
   ddd ddd ddd ddd (teeth and tongue)
   kkk kkk kkk kkk (body of tongue and soft palate)
   ggg ggg ggg ggg (body of tongue and soft palate)

6 Practise tongue twisters.

Modulation

To modulate means to vary or to change. Vocal modulation helps to highlight important words and phrases and makes it easier for the listener to comprehend the meaning.

The communication of technical information is particularly dependent on a well modulated voice.

Vocal modulation depends on inflexion (glides or kicks up or down on one word), changes of pitch (usually on a phrase), the use of pause, and pace (here defined as a slight speeding up or slowing down of the rate of speech in reaction to the matter). A voice that is not modulated is monotonous.

1 Use inflexion to change the meaning of the following words:
   hello; goodbye; yes; what.
(e.g. 'Hello' when you are delighted to meet someone has a different inflexion than when it is said with suspicion.)

2   Change the meaning of the following groups of words by changing pitch (steps up or down) and using inflexion:

what is that; if I must; why me; yes sir.

3   Using inflexion, pitch, pause and pace, how many ways can you say:

You are coming home with me tonight.

Phrasing

A phrase is a group of words which makes sense. Phrasing is the grouping of words in a way which is calculated to bring out the meaning. All words forming a phrase belong closely together and nothing should spoil or break this sequence. A phrase therefore should be spoken on one breath.

Exercise: Practise reading aloud from good prose. Stories for children provide excellent material.

The voice

The voice is our main and easiest means of communication. It can also be the most effective. But we must learn how best to use it, and to keep it in trim.

Athletes, singers, boxers, golfers, rugger and tennis players and people in many other professions practise daily. So should we if we have a professional approach.

FURTHER READING

Cole, Wilton, *Sound and Sense: a handbook on Elocution*, Allen & Unwin, 14th impression 1976

Kapp, R O, *The Presentation of Technical Information*, 2nd edn revised by Alan Isaacs, Constable, 1973

Burchfield, R, *The Spoken Word* – A BBC guide, BBC 1981

Gowers, Sir Ernest, *Complete Plain Words*, Penguin, revised by Sir Bruce Fraser, 1973

Partridge, Eric, *Usage and Abusage*, Penguin, 1963

6

Managing your health

Dr H Beric Wright, MB FRCS MFOM

HEALTH AND WELLBEING

To the extent that management is about taking decisions concerned
with the allocation of resources and the settlement of priorities, an
individual's health – your health – can increasingly be viewed
against a similar grid. Starting with genetic inheritance and the degree
to which one has learnt from experience, health is, in my view, very
much a reflection of general wellbeing and adjustment.

On the whole, well adjusted people, enjoying what they have set out
to do and not being continually stretched beyond their capabilities,
and involved in good relationships, are unlikely to be ill. Illness is
largely dis-ease, and wellness, as I have said, is a function of general
wellbeing. As the World Health Organisation said shortly after the
war, 'health is a state of physical, mental and social wellbeing'.

This somewhat pompous definition implies that to be well, one
must be reasonably in tune with the physical, mental (emotional) and
social parameters of one's life. In other words, the avoidance of too
much dis-ease in one's lifestyle is likely to influence mortality and
morbidity.

Lifestyle is very much a matter of choice and discipline. Diet, and
more particularly calorie intake, largely determines weight. Animal
fat consumption against a genetic background determining metabolism (the way in which the body deals with nutritional essentials) plays
a part in coronary risk rating. Smoking, drinking and exercise are well
within the control of a reasonably motivated and knowledgeable
person.

As will become apparent, in the present state of our understanding
of the common killer diseases, lifestyle, which is very much open to

choice, is a significant determinant of disease risk. And conditions like coronary thrombosis (CHD) which still kills at least a fifth of all men in the UK, can be usefully 'risk rated'.

Such an assessment of the odds, which can be made from the results of a detailed health check, will give you the probability of suffering a coronary. It does not necessarily mean that you will get one, or even avoid one entirely, but it does measure the likelihood and you can make your own choice as to what you do about it.

To make such a choice, it is necessary first to understand the various risk factors and the causes and incidence of common diseases; also to know about yourself, your aspirations, attributes and a few other basic facts. For instance, you cannot know what your blood pressure is, or the balance of lipids (blood fats) in your blood unless these are measured periodically.

We know that what becomes an overt disease, like CHD, is the end result of a process that in its early stages produces no symptoms and that the process can often be halted and reversed if caught early enough and dealt with vigorously.

To give another example, breast cancer kills about one in every 13 women. Breast and lung cancer are the commonest cancers in women; the former is increasingly treatable if detected early and the latter is very much smoking-related. Thus it is sensible for a woman to attend a breast screening clinic and practise regular self-examination to maximise the chances of early diagnosis and treatment by minimal surgery. Similarly anyone who chooses to smoke cigarettes must do so in the sure knowledge that they are reducing their life expectancy. This is then their free choice, based on the facts as they know them.

Management, as I have said, is about taking decisions in the light of the best information available, to obtain a desired objective: in this case optimum health and functional efficiency. As I hope to be able to explain, your life is largely in your hands because you *can* decide how you live and what your priorities in living are. Traditionally, doctors treat established disease. This doctor wants to keep you out of the hands of his colleagues!

Health is probably our most precious asset and good managers are a company's least replaceable one. Thus, as I see it, there is both a joint responsibility and mutual benefit in contriving a situation in which both flourish. Some companies, which in my view are badly run, have a propensity to consume people by driving them too hard. Managers, on the other hand, can be bribed or seduced into becoming full-time workaholics to the neglect of their other relationships and the needs of a compensatingly reasonable physical and emotional 'other life'.

These again are matters of conscious choice and not necessarily the inevitable rat race that they might seem. Living successfully is very much a matter of facing realities and making the right choices. Although it is difficult to prove statistically because there are always exceptions in all things biological, reasonably fit people are on the whole more lively and effective. As is often apparent, disciplined people are more effective because they know what they are trying to do and have the right priorities.

What I am trying to say is that health is very much a matter of choice and that the overall ground rules for making these choices do exist. As we tend to work in one group and live in a family unit, it is the 'climate' in these and the rules that are set up for them, that largely determine our wellbeing. Exercising the right options and understanding the odds are what is critical, plus a willingness to change if the equations don't balance.

WHAT YOU HAVE TO SURVIVE

If management is about understanding and choosing priorities and backing probability, management of your health should follow a similar path. Although you may inherit good, long lived genes or bad, short lived ones, because of genetically determined diseases or predispositions, it is useful to know something about the commoner hazards to your survival.

Two short examples will help to make this point. Coronary heart disease (CHD) still kills at least a fifth of all men in this country before retiring age, and this amongst other things creates a lot of widows. The incidence of CHD in developing countries increased rapidly after the war and has been rightly regarded as an epidemic. In America the incidence has fallen significantly over the last few years. In Scandinavia it is under control and falling as it is also at last beginning to here. Most of the predisposing or 'risk factors' for CHD are lifestyle related, i.e. they are well within an individual's or community's control and can thus be considered as a management problem.

Cigarette smoking, or the inhalation of tobacco smoke, increases the chances of a man getting a coronary by three or four times. It is the largest cause of lung cancer, the commonest cancer in men, and through chronic bronchitis, often euphemistically disguised as 'the smoker's cough', is responsible for a great deal of lost time and serious disability during the working life, as well as seriously clouding the retirement years through breathlessness and a weak chest.

Similarly, breast and lung cancer are the commonest killers in middle aged women. The latter can be avoided by not smoking and the former to an increasing degree mitigated by early diagnosis and early removal of small lesions by minimal surgery. This depends, as does the more acceptable cervical smear for cervical cancer (which has about one quarter the incidence of breast cancer), on the woman's willingness to attend a specialised Well Woman clinic.

These then are some high priority areas which are very much a matter for individual decisions, but decisions which significantly determine life expectancy.

Going back to probabilities, all this can be regarded as a relatively simple equation in which the overall odds are made up of the incidence and risk factors for various common diseases and the denominator provided by genetic inheritance and personality factors. Thus, if there is a family history of heart disease, it does not mean that all the sons of a coronary mother will be so afflicted but it does make it more likely that they will be. Thus, it is prudent for them and indeed for all of us, to know what the odds are and then to proceed more wisely through life, to minimise the overall risks.

Equally, someone with long lived parents can more safely risk being mildly overweight and perhaps eating more animal fats because they may well have a less vulnerable metabolic system. Obviously to make such decisions the facts must be known: hence the prudence of regular health checks so that you know what your blood pressure is and how your lipid and blood fat levels are behaving. If you like, this personal data is as important to health management as is regular information about your company's cash flow and sales ledger.

What this means is that having your staff, yourself and your family regularly serviced should be seen in the same light and with the same priority as servicing your car, plant and machinery. These are serviced to minimise breakdown and it is, I suggest, merely a matter of wise asset protection and a legitimate and tax deductible cost for a company, to encourage health servicing of staff.

Another and sadder denominator, about which space precludes detailed consideration, is the factor of social class or occupation. Although the incidence of the common diseases has been falling in the professional and managerial classes over recent years, the gap between them and the semi-skilled and unskilled workers has been widening. Thus the incidence of CHD, hypertension (high blood pressure), and lung disease is several times higher in these groups. This is partly for socio-economic reasons and partly because the 'lifestyle message' has not got through to these groups. Smoking, for instance, obesity, alcohol consumption and so on, have a higher incidence in social classes IV and V than in classes I and II. Sadly, this reflects a major failure of the NHS to really improve the health of the nation and does provide management with a chance to improve the health of its own work force.

Seven or eight years ago, the Electrical Contractors' Association and their division of the ETU put in a health screening scheme with BUPA. More recently, IBM in the UK have made a similar facility available to all their staff on a countrywide basis. In both cases the screening activity revealed a significant amount of untreated disease and provided an opportunity and the motivation for lifestyle counselling.

As this is so obviously important and valuable, employers are now under increasing pressure to provide 'on site' screening facilities for shop floor and office workers and this is becoming more widely available through organisations like the BUPA Medical Centre. Marks & Spencer in the UK pioneered the provision of cervical screening for all women employees and soon extended this to include breast screening. Many larger companies have in-house medical departments which will play a growing role in health promotion as well as the more traditional one of monitoring for toxic hazards and the provision of a 'works' surgery' for rapid treatment.

New regulations regarding toxic exposure to potentially harmful agents will make such monitoring obligatory and it should be easy to combine it with a simple health check at the work place.

Incidence of common diseases

Figure 6.1 shows the commonest causes of death in men and women at various ages in the UK. Although the numbers are small in the younger age groups, it is for instance significant that accidents and suicide do figure for those up to age 44 and must be regarded as to a degree preventable. But the most significant figure in this table is, of course, the incidence of heart disease and strokes. Cancer begins to figure from middle life onwards and the individual cancers are shown in Figures 6.2 and 6.3. This shows, as I have already said, that cancer

Age	Men			Women		
25–34	accidents (875)	cancer (507)	suicide (484)	cancer (619)	accidents (185)	suicide (128)
35–44	cancer (1,359)	heart disease (1,332)	accidents (690)	cancer (1,992)	stroke (229)	suicide (211)
45–64	heart disease (24,472)	cancer (20,098)	stroke (3,628)	cancer (17,806)	heart disease (7,074)	stroke (2,823)
65+	heart disease (62,898)	cancer (51,168)	stroke (23,108)	heart disease (61,265)	cancer (45,575)	stroke (41,136)

Figure 6.1 **Most common causes of death in the UK 1984 (totals in brackets)**
Source: HMSO Social Trends

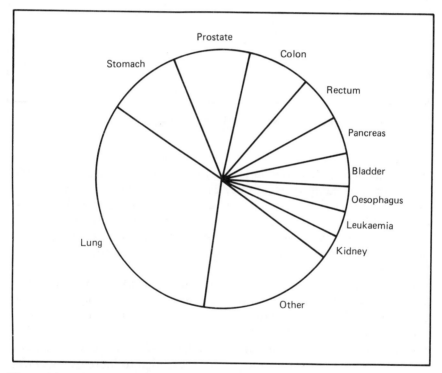

Figure 6.2 **Frequency of cancer deaths in the UK (men)**
Source: OPCS Monitor DH2

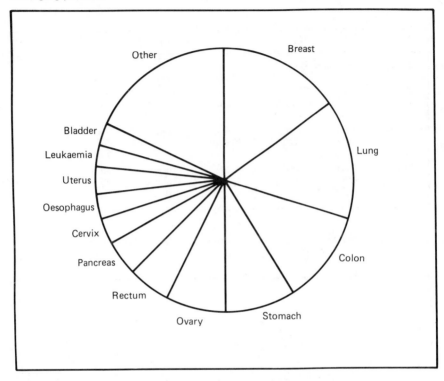

Figure 6.3   Frequency of cancer deaths in the UK (women)
   Source: OPCS Monitor DH2

of the lung and breast in women are top of the league and to a degree are either avoidable or treatable. There is also now a growing conviction that there is an environmental element in many cancers due to diet, pollution and so on. These again represent management and personal decisions about which more will be heard. Recent tragedies and near misses in the nuclear industry make such decisions more pressing.

One particular factor of survival, with considerable social consequences which cannot be discussed in detail, is the fact that at all ages women live longer than men. In spite of what I have said about the incidence of conditions like CHD, we are in the UK an ageing population and the biggest bulge will be, between now and the end of the century, in the over 80 age group, scheduled to increase by about 10 per cent. Most of these will be women living alone and perhaps on reduced means. The problem of the frail elderly is, in my view, the biggest social challenge of the next decades and requires individual consideration in the planning of one's later years. It will also require much more 'management' in terms of providing social, financial and medical support.

In summary, it is worth making the point that there is a virtue in managing your health sensibly but it is an advantage first to have good genes, second to be a woman and third to be in social classes I or II.

A much more detailed description of these critical underlying factors determining mortality, morbidity and their demographic implications, will be found in the author's *Ease and Dis-Ease*. (Longman Professional, 1986).

Coronary risk factors

As many of the keys to living sensibly, particularly for men, relate to avoiding CHD, it is worth describing briefly the factors which predispose to this still too prevalent killing disease.

Genetic factors

Reference has already been made to the fact that CHD can run in families. As will be apparent from the risk factors to be described, CHD is a multi-factorial disease, i.e. it has no single cause but results from an amalgam of factors which perm differently in different people. Similarly there is no gene responsible for, say, blood pressure, lipid metabolism or personality. But we do know that a serious condition called hypercholesterolaemia, in which blood fats are raised, is genetically determined. And there is reason to believe that some aspects of the way in which the body deals with fats, either well or badly, lies within the genes. Thus, it could be that in the years to come, genetic engineering will become a factor in coronary control. At the moment, however, this is highly speculative.

You will, I hope, remember that the genetic set-up, good or bad, is the main denominator of the coronary equation.

Blood fats – cholesterol

When I started being interested in the prevention of CHD in about 1960, it began to be apparent that men with high cholesterol levels in their blood were at greater coronary risk. This started the interest in low cholesterol diets by reduction of animal fats and established cholesterol as a risk factor.

But it did not explain why some thin men with low cholesterols got CHD and conversely why some fat men with high levels avoided it. We now know much more about the 'cholesterol package' and have refined ways of measuring its individual components. From this, it has been found that the two main factors are called High (HDL) and Low (LDL) Density Lipoproteins.

Very briefly HDL is metabolically good and the main way in which usable fats, for energy, are transported round the body. LDL on the other hand is more unfriendly and is the substance that gets deposited in the walls of blood vessels to narrow them and predispose to blockage. A coronary thrombosis is a blockage of the coronary arteries which supply the heart muscle, which if severe enough destroys the muscle itself and the heart's capacity to function as a co-ordinated pump.

What we now know is that it is the ratio, within the cholesterol package, between HDL and LDL which largely sets the coronary governor, high HDL levels being much less important than raised LDL.

Two things seem to govern the way in which an individual deals with his or her cholesterol. The first is, fairly obviously, the amount and nature of the fats eaten, and the other is the genetically determined governor that deals with these fats. The latter is more important than the former but a strict low cholesterol diet will reduce cholesterol levels and bring the ratio back into better and less harmful balance. It will also remove at least some of the LDL out of the vessel walls.

Diet

We are now, in developed countries, on the verge of a dietary revolution. There is a growing move away from a high protein, high animal fat diet, towards a more vegetarian − fruit, fibre, vegetable − one. Since the war the consumption of meat, dairy products and sugar has gone up significantly, and so has the incidence of CHD.

In America, Norway and Finland, careful long term studies have shown that by changing diet not only do cholesterol levels alter for the better but the coronary rate falls. Obesity is said to be the commonest 'disease' in developed countries, particularly America and Germany. That thin people live longer than fat people has been known for years by life insurance companies. This is largely but not entirely through the relationship between weight and blood pressure but there are other considerations as well.

Lack of exercise, as will be seen next, is also a risk factor and it is obviously more difficult for an overweight person to be physically active without putting undue and dangerous strain on his bones, joints and muscles.

Obesity again is genetically determined through body build but essentially if you eat more calories (energy) than you need for daily living, these will be banked within your body as fat. A calorie overdraft is in fact starvation. We do all mostly eat far more than we need and hence have a podgy credit account.

Sugar and fats account for most of this and their over-consumption has become a serious reflection of postwar life now being reversed by health re-education.

Eating is very much a culturally based habit pattern. We like what we are used to and have been brought up with. Being human, we resent change and are reluctant to experiment. This is very true of salt consumption. We eat salt in most prepared foods without knowing it is there but would miss it if the level was reduced. Some of us also add extra salt.

High blood pressure is again a complicated multi-factorial condition. It relates to arteriosclerosis which is part of the coronary picture. Hypertensive people are more coronary prone but also get strokes, heart failure and blood vessel disease. Salt is very much one of the factors relating at least to some forms of hypertension. There are thus good grounds for reducing direct and indirect salt consumption and at least demanding that food manufacturers state the salt content of their products.

Much more detailed information on diet and nutrition is given in the *BUPA Manual of Wellbeing* listed at the end of this chapter.

Exercise

The body is a machine designed for constant use. Joints need to be put through their range of movement and muscle strength, including that of the heart itself, can only be maintained by constant load carrying. Your heart muscle is as flabby and as fat as the rest of you.

In addition to living longer, because thin people have a lower coronary rate, physically active people largely feel better, sleep better and are more mentally and physically lively. Reasonable fitness puts up HDL and lowers LDL in the blood. Taking enough exercise is again a family and personal discipline which has an obvious reward, hence the current interest in jogging and other outdoor activity.

Smoking

Inhaling tobacco smoke is an addiction which has a higher mortality and morbidity rate (death and disability) than all the other 'drugs' like alcohol, heroin, etc. Until very recently it was socially acceptable and of course the government obtains a large slice of revenue from tobacco tax. Additionally money spent on advertising and sponsorship oils many of the wheels of our social life.

Tobacco smoke is chemically complicated but nicotine, a substance with a direct effect on the autonomic nervous system and a depressant or tranquillising effect on mood, is the addictive element.

The tars in the smoke are irritant and the lungs, being an efficient filter, absorb substances from it which are both locally irritant and chemically harmful. Efficient inhalers, that is those with relatively undamaged lungs, can raise the level of carbon monoxide in their blood significantly above that allowed under industrial legislation. This carbon monoxide damages the lining of blood vessels, which in turn facilitates the deposition of cholesterol and the narrowing of the vessels, reducing blood flow and increasing the chances of blockage by thrombosis.

Smoking is harmful because it raises the level of LDL and smokers are three or four times more likely to suffer a coronary thrombosis. As has been said, lung cancer is uncommon in non-smokers. Chronic bronchitis and emphysema cause a great deal of respiratory disability and ultimate death.

The incidence of smoking has been declining significantly over the last ten years, so that in social classes I and II smokers are in a growing minority. The problem now is to reduce smoking in social classes IV and V and to stop youngsters getting hooked at an early age.

It is never too late to stop and some of the benefits are immediate. Physically active smokers appear to be better off than their less athletic brethren but still a lot worse off than abstainers. Pipes and cigars which are not inhaled appear to be relatively safe and in spite of the publicity, the real risk of passive smoking is minimal.

Alcohol

Alcohol is not a direct coronary risk factor. Indeed, modest drinkers, particularly of wine, have a lower CHD rate. This may be because alcohol raises HDL. Nevertheless alcohol, which is socially acceptable and encouraged, i.e. a drink is offered at all social occasions, remains a dangerous addiction with social and directly medical ill effects.

We do not really know why a few people become uncontrolled or truly dependent drinkers but the probability is that there are both biochemical and personality related factors which predispose. Individuals have to be careful about how much they drink because unlike smoking there is a tendency, as tolerance develops, to drink more, rather than to stay at the same level. Individuals and organisations thus have, in my view, a responsibility to set modest personal and corporate standards and to set appropriate examples.

Alcohol is a useful social lubricant and enjoyed by many people. It is now vital that we try to control consumption to avoid penal taxation and legislation. This is, I suggest, a legitimate area for management intervention by both setting standards and providing counselling and discipline for their staff who drink too much and perform badly.

Alcohol has two quite different harmful effects. The first is to damage the liver, which is responsible for most of its metabolism. This damage is called cirrhosis and unless caught early will lead to death from liver failure. This effect can be measured by blood tests done as part of a health check. As a result it is possible to tell a patient that he is drinking more than his liver can deal with and that he ought to stop for three months and then proceed at a lower level.

The second effect is the behavioural decline of the alcohol dependent. This reduced performance disrupts families and will end either in Skid Row or with cirrhosis.

Experience has shown that what the Americans called 'job jeopardy' is the strongest weapon for dealing with an alcohol dependent employee, hence the value of a firm company policy. Everyone in the organisation knows who the drinkers are and they must be seen to be discouraged.

Stress and relationships

Stress is discussed in detail in the next chapter but as it is a variously interpreted phrase, I must make my position about it clear. All living things, including man, require challenge from the environment to keep them alert. Indeed it is by meeting challenge in a variety of ways and at various levels that we get most of our satisfactions in life. Conversely failure or inability to cope causes conflict and frustration.

Stress is a term borrowed from engineering where it implies an ability to withstand strain. If the strength of the substance is exceeded by the load, it will distort and collapse. Thus, in my definition, stress is *not* challenge but is what happens to an individual when he or she cannot cope with the challenge. It is a biological defence reaction to get them off a hook, or solve a conflict.

This may sound simple but in fact it is a very complicated and subconscious or 'automatic' reaction, without necessarily obvious relation to the cause of the stress. The reaction can be physical, in terms of pain, a skin eruption or a peptic ulcer, or purely behavioural in emotional or performance terms. Thus, anxiety, insomnia, irritability etc., are just as much diseases as are more traditional physical disorders.

Another complication is that stress thresholds vary for different types of challenge and relate to personality and past experience. Calm, extroverted people react differently to tense, anxious, introverted ones. It is also essential to realise that stress can arise from too much challenge or conflict in any aspect of life. It can be work or home based or to a degree due to lack of outside, relaxational satisfactions balancing out the other pressures.

This concept of stress and its relationship to wellbeing is obviously the basis of the whole man or holistic approach to dis-ease. Why someone is ill − or out of balance − is just as important as what is wrong with them. Symptoms may be treatable by drugs but it is better to deal with the cause. This involves understanding and insight or objective knowledge about oneself.

In my very general terms, even busy people who are succeeding are not necessarily stressed but managing to carry a heavy load of challenge. They may be tired but they are on top, particularly so if they have good relationships at home.

One of the skills of survival, then, is both to know your own aspirations and attributes and to pick, as far as possible, the right challenges for you. There are horses for courses and no one person has all the skills. Under-employment or being in a dead end is just as stressful as having too great a load.

Management must organise the enterprise so that unnecessary stress is minimised and energies directed in productive rather than frustrating directions. Jobs must have a discernible end point within the skills and experience of the individual.

Across the biological spectrum most of the challenge to living things comes from the physical environment: the need and competition for space, nutrition, warmth, water and so on. Species that live in social groups, like monkeys, elephants and many others, have evolved a series of harmless rituals to settle the problems of aggression and competition with minimal trauma to the participants. Very seldom does a species prey on its own members as we do.

In developed countries, however, a reasonable physical environment is largely available and the majority of challenge – and stress – comes from the psychosocial and interpersonal environment. Our successes and failures tend to relate to people rather than things. It is our ability to deal, in biological terms, with our own species at work, at home, in our social groups and then in the world as a whole, that provides the stress and the conflict. At personal, national and international levels, we do not seem to be very good at it.

A last point in this brief overview of the stress field, is that there is nothing new about stress or being stressed. Each generation tends to pride itself that its life is more complicated and difficult than it was for its parents, so that ergo, they/we are the most stressed. This is nonsense because, as I have said, challenge is essential and there have always been individuals and 'tribes' who cannot cope with it. All that alters is the nature of the stress and as we learn to cope in the here and now, society evolves to throw up new problems.

It worries me at the moment that because of lack of understanding about the difference between stress and challenge, being stressed has become a bit of a status symbol. Busy people tend to think that they cannot be flat out unless they are stressed but in fact if they are keeping on top they are largely winning and coping well. In very general terms stress is a manifestation of failure rather than success.

But essentially it is our ability to deal with interpersonal relationships and get ourselves into positions in which our aspirations and attributes largely match, that determines our stress.

It may, in these terms, be better to change a job, a marriage partner or a place of residence, than to be perpetually torn by conflict which cannot be resolved. At work, particularly, interpersonal relations tend to be hierarchical so that it is difficult for an individual to deal with incompatibility from above, unless the organisation is sensitively structured so that these things can be discussed openly and objectively. For most of us, however, it may be better to be brave enough to do our own thing in a smaller pond than to be continuously buffeted by an uncongenial system. But remember too that work is only one source of stress. It comes from all aspects of life and impinges on our whole personality and not just a bit of us. Work, home and play do interrelate with the 'whole of us' to determine who we are and how we react.

MANAGING HEALTH

Two points, I hope, are now clear about the management of health. The first is that it is manageable and that the odds are both worth playing for and reasonably understood. The second is that in the medium and longer term there are considerable benefits, in terms of both survival and effectiveness, to be obtained from successful management.

To this I would add two further points. First, that in spite of the hazards I have listed, living prudently is in no way living miserably. Good or sensible habits are just as enjoyable as over-indulgence. Prudence and survival are very much a matter of getting into a sensible habit pattern and sticking to it. The second is that in terms of at least the larger working groups, the management of health is also very much the joint responsibility of the individual and the organisation. Their interests should be mutually devoted to health and survival.

Thus, the individual should set himself the right priorities and have the requisite understanding of the pitfalls. As part of management, particularly at a senior level, he should insist on providing a 'healthy' environment; not so much in physical but in psychosocial or dynamic terms.

Companies should be organised so that the challenges of individual jobs are appropriate, communications are good, end products obvious and satisfying, with minimal frustrations. It is also sensible to create an atmosphere in which problems and frustrations can be brought into the open and discussed objectively. I think too that regular assessments of performance against defined targets are helpful, and so is the availability of counselling and career guidance, particularly on promotion. When an interpersonal problem or a failure becomes overt and may even lead to possible job loss, the individual may often complain that 'nobody ever told me about this weakness'.

It is assumed that because a person is deemed to be good enough to promote, he or she will be, *ipso facto*, capable of doing a more demanding job without training or indoctrination. I often used to see rapidly promoted youngsters stressed by having to run to stand still. This is particularly true when a technically trained person, good at doing things himself, is promoted into a role where he has to deal with people, ideas and hierarchies.

Neither individuals nor organisations themselves realise clearly enough that there are inevitably and necessarily management styles into which individuals have to fit. Within this framework there are senior people with whom subordinates have to be reasonably compatible if they are to flourish. Thus, in choosing a job or appointing a person, there must be a large degree of congruence between the individual and the overall climate, which means that individuals should be prepared to change their jobs, even to ones of lesser status and income, rather than be driven to a coronary by perpetual frustration or boredom. Doing one's own thing, even in a small way, may be more fulfilling than being a small cog in a vast but safe bureaucracy.

In these terms, then, management can control the environment in which their staff can be healthier. I think that regular health checks are part of this because they provide both a database, an early warning and a counselling service. But at a more mundane but nevertheless useful level, should management actively discourage smoking at work? Many now do. Should they employ non-smokers who are known to have a better health record, in preference to smokers? Should they take more interest in what their canteens serve? Do they have sensible standards about alcohol consumption both in house and in relation to expense accounts? Along these lines the list is endless but the issues are important. The standards they set must feed back into the individual's lifestyle.

In more positive terms, should management encourage staff to take exercise and even provide facilities for this? A number of companies are beginning to provide their own fitness centres. (Fitness for Industry, 116 Pall Mall, London SW1, will advise on this.) Similarly, it is sensible to see that people take their holidays, do not overwork for prolonged periods and look out for signs of stress, like a fall-off in performance, irritability, increased drinking and work taken home but not done effectively.

It is wise to monitor sickness records because it is certain that an individual who has previously had a good record and suddenly 'goes bad', has a lifestyle related problem which needs sorting out. If one group has a worse record than another, something could have gone wrong with the motivation and supervision within the group. The probability is that there are personality clashes or frustrations that need attention. Although it may be superficially expensive, attention to the welfare of staff and help with personal problems will raise morale and increase productivity.

What then for the individual? He or she needs to realise the ground rules for their own health maintenance and be prepared to adopt the disciplines. These are relatively simple and to a degree have their own reward. Smoking, drinking and weight must be controlled within reasonable limits. Diet should be sensible and 'modern', in terms of less animal and dairy products, and more fresh food and fibre. Regular exercise of any sort is a must and will promote a sense of fitness.

But most important is the matter of relationships, both at work and at home. In my view, couples still get married too young and without thinking through why they want to get married and what is in it for both of them. These targets change with age and status and need occasional renegotiation. The conflicts of career development and home life are considerable and unless faced and agreed lead to a lot of unhappiness, particularly for the isolated wife. The needs, for instance, of job mobility and business travel can cause considerable conflict and merit open discussion.

The vital thing about dealing with relationships is to be honest and open enough to discuss the problems and differences, rather than to bury them as a smouldering grievance which may surface as total incompatibility years later. There must at all times be enough in it for both partners. Children as they grow up must be established as independent adults and not expected to be obedient and grateful dependants.

Relationships are difficult, complicated and require constant attention but for most people they provide life's greatest single satisfaction. They need more work and attention than they mostly get both at home and in the work place.

I would suggest that periodically you do three things: first, ask yourself what you are like to work for, how you are perceived by your peers and whether you are giving them a square deal in terms of delegation, supervision and encouragement. Second, ask yourself what job satisfaction you think that your spouse gets out of being married to you. A useful extension of this would also be to try and assess yourself as an effective parent.

The third and more complicated point is to be brave enough, particularly in middle age, to review your self-image. Look, as it were, at yourself in the mirror and try to see yourself as others see you. Are you brisk, alert and reasonably well dressed? What do the whiskers all over your face convey to others? More important, are you reasonably happy and fulfilled or are you frustrated and miserable? If the latter, what are the real options and what are you going to do about them? Much of stress and frustration stems from the feeling of being caught helplessly in some interpersonal trap. It is useful to try to analyse the situation by listing the things that bug you and the various options. It may be that you are caught and cannot move, in which case live with it, find other outlets and stop worrying.

If you are a tense, nervous and rather stressed person, it is also worth remembering that relaxation can be learnt and that there are techniques and teachers about. In a similar way, there are coping skills that can be acquired for dealing with stress from work or home and by learning these you can reduce the heat in the kitchen. But if at a moment in time this does get too hot, be brave enough to hop out of the frying pan before you get burnt. Life is for living rather than mere endurance. A smaller house on a lower income, doing simple things, can be far more satisfying than endlessly commuting to a boring or uncongenial job.

What all this adds up to is that there are two keys to 'health'. The first is to know the main hazards to survival and how to avoid them. The second and more important is to understand that health is a reflection of general wellbeing which can be cultivated by understanding, insight and discipline. If you achieve this you should join the 80-year-old bulge, and this will present other problems! But it is important to maintain your wellbeing as long as you live. The more successful you are at this, the longer you *will* live.

FURTHER READING

The BUPA Manual of Fitness and Wellbeing, Macdonald, 1984
Wright, Dr H B, *Ease and Dis-Ease,* Longman Professional, 1986
Wright, Dr H B et al., *Allied Dunbar Retirement Planning Guide,* Longman Professional, 1985
Relaxation for Living — for advice on relaxation and coping, from 29 Burwood Park Road, Walton-on-Thames, Surrey KT12 5LH

7

Coping with stress

Andrew M Stewart

The subject of stress, and the way it affects people at work, has been receiving a great deal of attention recently. There have been radio and television programmes about it, and there is a wide range of published work available. This work tends to be at one of two extremes. It is either academic and rather heavily research based, or it is popular and inspirational but based only loosely on fact. This chapter aims for the middle ground, and poses the following questions:

- What is stress?
- What does it cost?
- What causes it?
- What are the signs?
- What can the individual do about it?
- What can organisations do about it?

After reading this chapter you should have some answers to those questions.

This chapter concentrates on stress at work, but people are not divided up into watertight compartments. What happens to you at work will affect you at home, and vice versa. Because the home or leisure environment can affect your performance at work, this chapter will also look briefly at a few of the main domestic considerations. This is not a medical chapter, so clinical problems are mostly avoided. People who find themselves in difficulty at work are usually normal, healthy, sane individuals who find themselves for the time being in an environment which is, for them, abnormal, unhealthy or insane.

People sometimes use stress as an excuse for not performing as well as they should, or for failing to do what they said they would. It is true that many people do experience levels of stress which are too high, but others might be helped by increasing their level of stress. The aim should be to help people find the best level of stress for them in their particular circumstances, and to help them to maintain it and adjust it to change. This will sometimes mean increasing it rather than necessarily reducing it. Stress management is about *managing* stress, not about making people so relaxed that they forget to *do* anything.

WHAT IS STRESS?

It looks as if it ought to be easy to define stress clearly and simply, but it is harder than it might seem. We might be talking about strain instead of stress. The word 'stress' is used to describe the cause of the problem, the problem itself, and the effect of that problem upon its victim. People vary enormously in the amount, intensity, type and duration of stress that they can cope with. Finally, it is useful to distinguish between the stress itself and what someone is doing to compensate for it. This often shows itself when someone produces a very strong reaction to something quite small that has annoyed or upset them. The event itself was of no great importance, but they are discharging a backlog of stress built up while they cope with the continuing, day-to-day grind of the major problem.

It is important to realise that stress is not something strange and separate, unrelated to normal things that happen to normal people, but that it sits firmly on a continuum. This continuum runs from having too little to do, through normal healthy levels of activity, to rushing around trying to do too much too fast. Either too much or too little to do will trigger changes in your physiology. People are quite good at detecting some of these changes, but it is often more difficult to do anything about them.

The motivation connection

To understand stress you need to understand a little about motivation. Some managers still appear to believe that motivation comes in little bottles, so that it is possible to inject 5 cc into an employee and that will fix the problem. This idea survives because of a basic misunderstanding of how motivation operates.

Motivation is not a single-shot event, but a cyclical process. One of the more stressful aspects of managers' lives is that the task of motivating their subordinates is truly never-ending.

The cycle is illustrated in Figure 7.1. It begins with a motive, drive, or need. You want to do something (motive). This could be in the form of a positive drive towards something, or a need created by the absence of something. Whichever it is, you do something as a result. If what you do takes you closer to your desired goal, then you will experience relief. If what you do is unsuccessful, then you will feel no relief, and there may be an increase in the drive or need. In either event, the cycle does not end, since you are now merely in a new motivational state, and ready to do the next thing on the way to attaining the next goal. Put briefly, people are never satisfied for long. This is an ample source of stress for managers, since it implies that they can never win.

It may be possible for managers to reduce the stress they put on themselves when thinking about how to motivate their staff. Perhaps

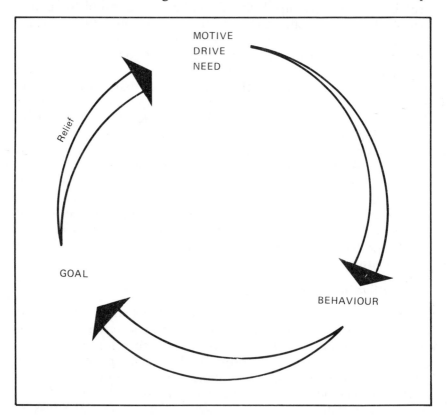

Figure 7.1   Motivation: a cyclic process

it is not possible to motivate other people at all, at least in the sense of doing something to them directly which will make them 'motivated'. It may be possible, however, to create the conditions under which people are more likely to motivate themselves. This is both an easier task for the manager, and more likely to bear fruit.

There is an old-fashioned view about motivation which can be expressed as: the more you push people, the more they will do for you. This theory of motivation is illustrated in Figure 7.2. It is wrong – or at least inadequate.

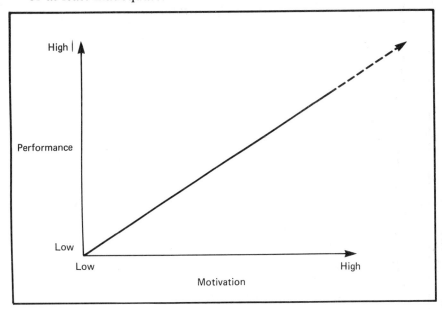

Figure 7.2 An over-simple view of motivation and performance

The truth is more complicated. Up to a point it is true that people will do more for you if you push them harder. After that point their performance will level off. If you try to start them on the upward path again after that, you are likely to achieve the opposite of what you want. You may actually impair their performance.

This curious state of affairs was first demonstrated by two psychologists called Yerkes and Dodson. In 1908 they found that motivation works in this way over a wide range of circumstances. They also found that it did not matter much whether the motivation was self-generated or created by someone else. Two factors will modify the picture, however. First, the simpler the task, the higher the level of motivation it can tolerate. Second, the shorter the task, the higher the level of motivation it can tolerate. Thus, if you are digging the garden and someone shouts that lunch is nearly ready, you can probably get that last row dug in double-quick time. It is a simple job and you know it will be over in three or four minutes. On the other hand, if you are sitting at your desk trying to work out next year's budget you are unlikely to respond well either to being shouted at or being hurried up. That is a complicated job and needs unhurried consideration to make it more likely that you will get it right.

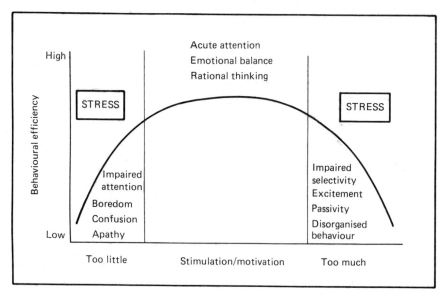

Figure 7.3   Motivation, performance and stress

The relationship between motivation, performance and stress is shown in Figure 7.3. In Figure 7.2 it becomes clear that either too much or too little motivation can lead to stress related behaviour. The most important point to note, however, is that for most people, stress is not something peculiar which means that they are losing control or actually ill. Stress is just what happens to motivation when there is a bad match between the person, what they are being asked to do, and the way they are being asked to do it. Stress is, if you like, motivation gone bad.

Fear and anxiety

Fear is a special kind of stress. Fear experienced during an event or, more usually, fear experienced before the event, will cause the same changes in your physiology as stress. Not many of us meet real fear very often, but most of us experience anxiety. Anxiety might be described as the fear of something which has not happened yet or which may never happen. You may experience fear half-way up a rock face, but your anxiety beforehand may prevent you from even starting the climb. Many outdoor development programmes have special techniques for helping people meet and cope with this sort of situation. The idea is that you are then better equipped to deal with less obvious sources of fear or anxiety at work.

Free-floating anxiety occurs when you have acquired the habit of being anxious, whether or not there is actually anything to be anxious about. If you cannot think of anything to worry about, you will worry about that! This kind of anxiety is quite difficult to deal with because there is no obvious or concrete source, so it can be hard to find anything to do to fix the problem. Because free-floating anxiety is often about things that may never happen, sufferers sometimes get rough treatment. 'Pull yourself together. It's all in your imagination.' If you could pull yourself together, you would. The fact that it is irrational does not make it any less real for the sufferer.

The physiology of stress

To understand and cope with stress, it is useful to know what is going on in your body when you experience fear, stress or anxiety. It all starts when you perceive some kind of threat. This could be a bump in the night, someone stepping out suddenly in front of your car, or a sharp comment from your boss. Whatever the source, as soon as the message reaches your brain and is perceived as actually or potentially threatening, a number of changes take place.

First, part of your pituitary gland is activated. This little organ sits under the centre of your brain, about an inch or so back from the bridge of your nose. It is at the junction of your body's chemical and electrical control systems. Nerve impulses from your brain, which are partly electrical in nature, reach the pituitary gland and trigger it into releasing minute quantities of a hormone into your blood. Blood goes everywhere in your body quite quickly, so putting a message into the blood stream is more efficient than the nervous system if you need to communicate with many different parts of your body fairly fast.

Nerve messages tend to go only to very specific parts of your body and are less good at general communications.

The hormone from the pituitary gland will reach your adrenal glands. These sit like small hats in the small of your back, one over each kidney. The adrenal glands release adrenalin and some allied substances, and these produce further physiological changes. You will now be able to notice some of these changes directly. Up until now you will not have been aware that anything is going on at all.

The main changes are listed below, together with the reasons for them. None of these changes is without one major purpose: to help you survive.

- The pupils of your eyes will get larger. More light will enter your eyes so that you can see any potential source of danger earlier and better.
- Your hearing may become more acute, again so that you can detect danger further away and give yourself more time to think of something to do about it.
- You will breathe faster. This increases the amount of oxygen in the blood, which is your fuel for action.
- Your heart will pump faster and harder, so that the flow of fuel is speeded up, and also so that any waste products caused by the burning of the fuel are quickly carried away.
- You may go pale. This is because blood has been taken away from the outside of your body, so you will bleed less if wounded. Another agent ensures that your blood will clot quicker, reducing blood loss if you are cut.
- You may feel sick or have upset bowels. This is because blood has been removed from your digestive system as well, and, in extremes, you will empty yourself either by vomiting or diarrhoea. This is to get rid of surplus weight if you have to run fast.
- The fuel-rich blood is sent instead to the muscles you may need to use in a hurry if the threat is real.
- You may sweat more. This is because physical effort generates heat. You only work efficiently over a quite small internal temperature range, so your cooling system is switched on. You lose heat by evaporating fluids from the surface of your skin — sweating.
- You may shake or tremble. This is partly because your muscles have tensed up generally. It may also be be to warm you up if the cooling system has come on but you have *not* done anything physical to actually generate any heat.

These changes are all normal, healthy, and aimed at ensuring your survival in an emergency. They were extremely useful when we lived in caves. They can be a real nuisance in the office or at home.

What has happened is that your body has been prepared for *fight or flight*. You may be in no position to do either. Many of the problems of coping with stress have to do with finding some way of discharging all this potential energy in a harmless or constructive way. If the energy is not discharged it will eventually cause damage. You will find that you have been pushed over the top of the curve in Figure 7.3, and your performance will suffer. At home or at work the problems may become worse. An anxiety spiral has been started.

THE COSTS OF STRESS

Managers usually prefer to spend money in ways which show some measurable return. There is no point, commercially speaking, spending money managing stress unless it is costing more money to ignore it.

In the days when you had to have a certificate for any spell of absence from work through sickness of more than three days, it was easier to estimate the commercial damage caused by stress related disease. Even then, the bulk of absences were not covered because they were for only half a day or a day, and therefore did not appear in the official figures. Even working on those reduced figures, the number of working days lost through psychosis, psycho-neurosis, nervousness, debility and headaches was well over double the days lost through industrial accidents. Other forms of sickness thought to have a psychological component, such as indigestion, skin complaints, muscular aches and pains, back problems, ulcers and heart disease, are *not* included in those figures. A fairly modest estimate of the working days lost through stress related problems each year is around 120 million. That is expensive.

Worrying though that figure undoubtedly is, it still does not address the whole of the problem. There is no estimate of the cost of mistakes made by people who remain at work while under stress. The figure relates largely to losses at shop floor level, where you can measure losses in production, orders not sent on time, poor quality products and paperwork errors fairly easily. But how do you assess the costs of lost management days? It is even more difficult to assess the costs of wrong decisions, wasted time, over-long lunch hours, together with too much alcohol and tobacco, and poor or inaccurate monitoring of performance. Evidence of the cost of poor decision making is all around us.

Industrial unrest may well have some of its roots in stress. The boredom (under-motivation) of routine production line work probably contributes to the readiness of some production workers to strike, even if only to generate some variety! The girl working on the supermarket till who would much rather talk to her friend than serve you is quite likely to be thoroughly bored. Even worse, the only feedback she may get on her performance is the occasional and unpredictable ticking-off from her supervisor when she happens to be spotted doing something wrong. How often is she rewarded specifically for good customer work? Can she predict which actions will get her into trouble and those which will lead to some form of reward? If not, why should she bother?

At management and shop floor levels, staff and line, stress in its various forms is squandering resources we can ill afford. The cost of cure is a very small fraction of the total bill. Prevention would be even better. The whole cost might even be recovered simply from reduced labour turnover costs.

THE CAUSES OF STRESS

Different people react in different ways to the same situation. What you find merely stimulating might be uncomfortably heavy pressure to someone else. With that reservation in mind, some of the common causes of stress at work are now reviewed.

Physical causes

Noise is a source of stress for many people, and its occurrence is the most usual source. This has now been recognised in legislation about maximum noise levels. Many workers have now been persuaded to wear ear protection who might have scorned to do so before: tractor drivers, road drill operators, boiler makers and chain saw users, for example. Attention is also being turned to domestic noise generators, such as vacuum cleaners, washing machines, food processors and the nuisance of other people's radios. The damage that is being inflicted by discos is also well understood.

It is less well known that things can also be too quiet! British Rail met this problem when building new modern coaches. The level of soundproofing was originally so high that the quiet interior made it too easy to hear other people's conversations. It was necessary to re-introduce some noise to mask the distraction from other passengers, and to allow relatively undisturbed reading, conversation or thinking. The level of quiet in a jumbo jet is very near to this disturbance level.

Tiredness causes stress as your ability to perform decreases. Worse, at the early stages of tiredness, you may not know that your performance is declining, and therefore you may assume that all is well and go on to make expensive errors or omissions. On top of that, because you are tired, you will be less willing to hear warnings about your performance from anyone else. The ability to assess your own performance accurately is one of the earliest things to go when you are tired, coupled with your emotional resilience.

Shift work patterns sometimes allow or encourage people to do other jobs during their off-periods. Split-shift patterns for bus crews often lead to this problem. As a result neither the official nor the side job is done well. In the case of drivers of any kind this has immediate and obvious dangers. Few managers in the UK work shifts, but some of them put in very long hours. Not all those hours are productive because of fatigue. Midnight oil burners can make bad mistakes. Frequent changes of shift pattern are also disruptive. It is better to have a long stint on nights, then a good break, followed by a long period on days, rather than changing every two weeks or so.

Jet lag is a special sort of tiredness, made worse by changing time zones and upset body rhythms. It is most unwise to make important decisions immediately after a long flight, especially if you have travelled from west to east. Few organisations seriously advise their people to rest for at least 24 hours before doing anything that matters, however.

Temperature and humidity also need to be controlled. Legislation lays down working limits, but greater extremes of temperature can be tolerated at lower levels of humidity. There are suggestions that increasing the level of negative ions in the air is beneficial, but this is quite hard to do on a large scale and the results are not yet certain.

Amount of work

Too much to do is a familiar idea, although it is often claimed before it is a fact. There are three different types of overload:

- the skill level demanded may be too high for the person;
- the speed may be too high for them;
- the volume may be too much;

or some combination of these.

Too little to do is also possible, but less often talked about. Again, there are three kinds of underload:

- the skill level may be too low (asking a graduate to do a school-leaver type of job);
- the speed may be too slow (when a meeting takes all day to decide something you could have done on your own in ten seconds);
- the volume can be too small (when a bright secretary is asked to do two letters and some filing in a whole day);

or some combination of these.

A sure sign of underloading at work is when the level of office politics starts to rise. People who have too little to do may fill the time with politics. The long term unemployed have met the underload problem. They often find it difficult to get out of bed and go out at all. The level of stimulus in their environment has dropped to the point where they actually need help to get going again. This is not deliberate idling at all, but a genuine psychological problem induced by boredom, loneliness and a sense of defeat.

Nature of work

New or unfamiliar situations, such as your first day in a new job or organisation, will be stressful because full of uncertainty.

Personal threat may be felt if your personal space is invaded by crowded conditions or by your boss standing too close when talking to you. If you feel that you are the victim of unreasonable control or arbitrary decisions about personal matters, such as going to the lavatory, your stress level will rise. Too little personal threat can also create problems. If nothing much happens when you fail to meet standards, then your standards of performance are likely to fall.

Pacing. The inability to pace your own work is highly stressful, as many production line workers will tell you. Likewise, if you happen to work in an office where your colleagues, your manager or your customers make frequent and unpredictable claims on your time, your performance will suffer.

Ambiguity. People vary a great deal in the amount of ambiguity or lack of clarity which they prefer. Some salesmen like very little uncertainty and prefer to work in the short term. They like to know at the end of each day how much they have sold and how much they have earned. On the other hand, a salesman dealing with large computing systems may have a long wait and a lot of work before he knows whether he has the order, and the nature of the installation may change during the course of implementation. It is much more difficult to establish a direct link between sale and reward; nor would that kind of salesman seek it. If you are a manager, the relationship between performance and reward can seem very indirect and uncertain indeed.

Feedback needs to be reliable and undistorted, frequent, and based on clear standards. Unclear standards and unreliable, distorted or non-existent feedback are the surest way to stress employees. They often lead to the use of some form of punishment as the only feedback offered, with no obvious connection to performance.

Fear of freedom

Most of us kick against rules and regulations. 'If only "they" would get off my back ...' is the frequent cry. When the restrictions are removed, the reaction often surprises. While it is a true liberation for some, for many it leads to great uncertainty, stress and even complete inability to act. We seem to need rules to react against. They provide a map which lets us know where we are and how to get somewhere else. If there are no rules and no map, many people simply feel lost and unable to move. Many managers, who have been excellent performers on their way up the organisation, disappoint when they finally reach the top seat because they suddenly find that there is no one to tell them what to do and no one to react against. They are fine as subordinates, and their impatience to succeed may have driven them on well, but now they have 'made it' they are no longer sure what their target should be. Their reaction can be to sit very still and to do the bare minimum necessary to keep out of trouble.

Domestic troubles

Stressors are also found at home. Domestic troubles, ranging from bereavement to marital discord, often coupled with financial problems, can severely affect performance in all spheres of your life.

Communication is a common problem amongst married couples. Imagine you have come home after a bad or boring day. The last thing you want to do is talk about it. You have just lived it. You do not want to go over it all again. Your partner, on the other hand, has just spent the day in the company of your three-year-old offspring of apparently manic and suicidal bent, is desperate for someone adult to talk to, and wants to know what you are doing so that some sharing of your life is possible. You are both right. Here lie real problems which can lead to marital breakdown. Worse still is the case where both partners work and may wish to discharge some of their day's problems. A perfectly reasonable response might be. 'Don't tell me. You want to try my job!'

Relocation is an increasingly frequent source of difficulty for families. When one partner is promoted, or finds a new and better job which involves moving house, who has priority? The male? The higher earner? The one who stayed put last time? The children's education? Will 'week ending' offer any solution, or will that simply lead gently to total and permanent separation? Pressure on the family will be heavy, and the solution may well affect the career prospects of one or both partners, quite aside from any personal damage that may occur.

THE SIGNS OF STRESS

The signs become easier to detect if you recall the fight or flight reaction mentioned earlier in the chapter. Under short term stress the fight or flight nature of the reactions is quite clear. Under long term stress it is not always so obvious.

Short term stress

The fight reaction when escape is possible is usually to have a short, sharp row on the spot with whomever is seen as causing the problem. The form of the row can vary from verbal abuse to a punch on the nose.

The fight reaction when escape is not possible, which is what most of us experience, is either to take it out on others or to punish yourself. If you take it out on others, then your staff may suffer because you have had a difficult meeting elsewhere. If you take it out on yourself then you may spend the rest of the day sunk in gloom.

The flight reaction when escape is possible is to go sick, take long lunch breaks, resign, or retire early. The main point is to remove yourself from the situation.

The flight reaction when escape is not possible may involve slowing down, withdrawing commitment to the business, delaying, acting with extreme caution, withdrawing from involvement with the business, or simply sleeping a lot more than before.

Long term stress

Psychosomatic illness may occur where there is no obvious physical cause for a physical ailment. It is arguable that ulcers, some heart attacks, strokes, indigestion, headaches, migraines, skin irritation, acne, over- and under-sleeping are all associated to some degree with stress.

Predisposition to illness can be caused by stress. You become vulnerable to illnesses that otherwise you would have brushed off, and your recovery is slower. The self-employed tend not to get colds!

Absenteeism may occur, ranging from lateness, through continuing small bouts of illness, to complete withdrawal by striking or leaving.

Indecision may increase to the point where it is difficult to get anything done at all without setting up a committee.

Capriciousness in decision making may appear. There is little hesitation, but there is equally little reason underlying the decisions. You may also see surprisingly light-hearted behaviour from the normally serious, or sexual promiscuity from the previously well behaved. You will find it increasingly hard to predict their behaviour.

Excessive consumption of food, drink and tobacco are fairly sure signs. No one should smoke anyway. Alcohol taken in more than moderation is damaging, and may be lethal if combined with driving. Too much food leads to obesity and all its associated health problems. It is also possible to consume material possessions to excess (cars, furs, jewels, and so forth). Excessive consumption of the opposite sex is often a sign of serious, unresolved stress.

Theft may increase under stress. When a factory is about to be closed, security should be tightened because anything not actually bolted to the floor may be considered fair game. On a smaller and more day-to-day scale, stationery, personal phone calls on company time, over-long lunch breaks, and a decision not to return to the office after an appointment that ended at three o'clock, are all forms of theft. Theft of goods is readily detectable. Theft of time, which may be more costly, is harder to see and control.

Workaholism. It is sometimes necessary to put in unusual hours to get a job done. If it becomes a habit, your job needs reorganising or you are running away from something.

Displacement activity. You find yourself doing all kinds of things except the really important one that is actually causing the problem.

Identification with the aggressor. Your boss is difficult with you. You cope by being unpleasant with your staff. They pass it on down the line. Soon everyone is having a terrible time.

Over-reaction to normal events. The phone rings and you leap out of your chair to answer it, rather than taking things in a more measured fashion. Your boss calls to say you are to meet at five o'clock. You assume that you are being fired, or promoted, instead of assuming that that is the only available time for a routine discussion of something.

Change is the key to detecting stress. Whatever your normal pattern of behaviour, any sudden change should be looked at briefly, in case it indicates some unsuitable level of stress. If someone you work with is always miserable, that may not be a sign of stress. That is just how they are. But if they suddenly become amazingly cheerful, something has obviously changed for them. It may well be perfectly pleasant and understandable. On the other hand, they may have decided to jump!

WHAT CAN THE INDIVIDUAL DO ABOUT STRESS?

Physiological and physical action

Control eating. Surplus is surplus. You do not need to consume it. You do not need to carry it around. It is a waste of time and energy.

Control alcohol intake. There is some medical evidence to suggest that a little wine may be positively beneficial, but treat alcohol with care. If you drink a bottle of brandy in one go it will probably kill you. Alcohol is high in calories and will allow your other food intake to go into store as fat.

Abolish smoking. Smoking kills about 100,000 people a year in the UK.

Take some exercise. Walk until you sweat slightly. Try swimming. Find something you can enjoy doing that makes your heart and lungs work a little harder than usual. Try to do it three times a week. *Warning:* if you have just spent 25 years getting unfit, do not leap on to the squash court and try to knock it all off in half an hour. You could damage yourself seriously. Taper into physical activity; do not slam into it.

Control posture. Sit up so that your lungs can breathe properly and your digestive system has room to function. Walk as if your pelvis were a bowl full of water which you must not spill. Keep the spine stretched and head erect. Make sure you get up and move about during the day.

Control breathing. Sit somewhere comfortable. Take a normal breath. Hold it for a slow count of three. Let it out with a slight huff. You may find it helpful to have your eyes shut while you are doing this. Do this twice a day for three weeks. See how you feel.

By controlling your breathing in this way you are breaking into the alarm reaction that you read about earlier. When your system picks up that your breathing rate has dropped, it will assume that the threat has gone or at least lessened, and will automatically run down the rest of the alarm system. Do not try to interfere with this process. You have a perfectly effective automatic system for doing all this, which you can trigger with the pause breath. Over a period of three weeks you are likely to find that you have become generally calmer and more alert, as well as being better able to cope with stress when it occurs.

Aim for contrast. Whatever you do during the day, try to find something different to do in the evening or at weekends. Try to find ways of varying what you do during the day. Vary the pace. Vary the intensity. Vary the importance. Do some things alone and some with other people. We thrive on variety, provided we feel that it is of our choosing and under our control to some degree.

Voice management. When you get upset your voice is likely to become higher, louder, and you will speak faster. You can control this. Deliberately speak a little slower, a little lower in pitch, and softer. Be careful not to overdo this. The adjustment is very slight. Men who go over the top can sound like a bad imitation of Louis Armstrong.

Females can find that they sound patronising, which will have the opposite effect to that intended. Not only will you find that this slight change in your voice calms you down, but it will be difficult for others to remain upset around you. Do not try this on your marriage partner. They know you too well, and it has been known to make a minor problem much worse!

Action against stress at work

Recognise that you can be a victim of stress. You are not invulnerable. If a problem does occur for you, you can waste a lot of time denying that it exists when you should be getting on and fixing it.

Analyse the probable causes. Keep this simple. They are not usually hard to find. They may be harder to admit.

Can you leave the situation? This is not a cop-out, but simply a quick check to establish whether you really do have to put up with the interview, training course, car journey, meeting, conversation or social gathering in which you find yourself. What is the price of leaving? What is the price of staying? Do your arithmetic. Act.

Decide when to cut your losses. Make a date with yourself. By then, you will have resolved the situation, or you will take more emphatic action (leave, go over your boss's head, fire your subordinate, dump the customer etc.). Once you have made this kind of deal with yourself, stick to it. If you break your word to yourself, you will never quite trust yourself again to do what you set out to do. This can be very destructive, so think over your bargain carefully before you commit yourself.

Control the pace. Good tennis players do not spend all their time up at the net. Sometimes they need to get to the back of the court so they can see what is going on in time to plan what to do next. Someone may be firing questions at you very fast and hard. You do not have to let them control the speed of your response. Play it your way. They have no control over your choice in this matter. If things seem to be slipping away from you, make sure that, whatever your answer, your final sentence is a question. This puts you in control of the conversation. You can even induce stress in others by delaying your replies just a fraction longer than they are comfortable with.

Discharge. Make sure you have something explosive to do to wash out any unresolved anger or frustration at the end of the day. If you play a high activity sport, that will help. If not, try digging a hole in the garden, thumping something inanimate, or just shouting loudly, once. Be careful who is around when you are doing any of these! Again, you are fooling your physiology into believing that the violent physical activity for which it has been preparing itself (fight or flight, again) has actually happened, and it can now relax.

Set your own objectives and life goals. Decide what you want to do, then go for it. This goes broader than merely work, and extends beyond retirement.

Medical aid. If you are in trouble, ask for help. This is not weak, but sensible self-management. Drugs will not solve your problem, but they can sometimes help you temporarily to a frame of mind in which you *can* solve your problem. Tell your doctor the moment you are not happy with what you feel the treatment is doing to you. There may be another way of dealing with the problem.

Review before relaxing after you have coped with the problem. Celebrate when you know *why* what you did worked. That way you know what to do if the problem ever occurs again.

Action against stress at home

Recognise it can happen to you and yours. No household is immune.

Analyse the probable causes.

Discuss the problems openly and early, before they become too difficult to talk about.

Recognition mechanisms exist for most people. Offer the signs that you are getting upset to your partner. Accept their signs in return. This way you can both spot when trouble is looming before it gets too developed.

Share some planned time and activities together. Do not spend all your home time in retreat.

Communicate with your partner and family. They need information from you and you need information from them so that difficulties can be dealt with early and opportunities for pleasure and reward can be developed.

Financial information needs to be shared. Many wives have been blamed by their husbands for spending the family into debt, when their husbands had never let them know what was happening and how much money was on hand. There are large cultural differences within the UK on this point, so check your family's expectations before acting on financial matters.

Consult on domestic arrangements. It is not a good idea to bring three colleagues home from work unannounced on a Friday night for a meal. Similarly, it is not helpful to announce as your partner comes in the door that Uncle Joe and Auntie Ethel have moved into the spare bedroom and are here for a week, especially if you have known that they were coming for some time.

Territory. Everyone needs somewhere that is their own. It need not be large. A desk; a dressing table; a small patch in the vegetable plot will often be enough. But that territory should be unique to the individual 'owning' it, and other people should only enter by invitation.

Solitude. Even in the most affectionate families, people sometimes need to be alone. This should be respected. It is not rejection. It may even be a statement of confidence that the relationships are so good that it never occurs to the person concerned that it would be seen as rejection. It can be difficult to find a moment of quiet in a busy family, but it is important to have the freedom to try.

WHAT CAN ORGANISATIONS DO ABOUT STRESS?

Organisations, as such, can do nothing. If you are a manager, you may be able to, however. What you and your colleagues choose to do can be understood as the organisation doing something.

Remedial action

A problem has occurred. You now have to try to cope.

Recognise that it has happened. Do not ignore it or hope it will go away by itself.

Removal. Does the person concerned have to stay in that situation? If not, move them. If so, plan with them how they can cope better.

Expert help. If the person has had a serious problem, and especially if they do not seem to be improving now that the apparent cause has been removed, get help. This is probably beyond you as a manager, and you possibly should not be spending that much time on it, even if you could do something about it. This is not your only subordinate. You could be adding significantly to the stress of others by over-concentration on this one problem.

Frequent feedback on performance will help restore confidence and ability. Give the person a lot of short term tasks which are well within their capability. Make sure they know they have done them well. Gradually increase the difficulty and length of the tasks, giving positive feedback all the way, until they are back to strength again. Do not make a big deal if they fail on some of the tasks. Just go back a step and try again. Do not expect or seek thanks for your help. They need to feel that they are standing on their own feet, and acknowledging any kind of dependency may make this difficult for them. This is part of your job as a manager.

Preventive action

It is far better to stop undue stress occurring in the first place than it is to cure it once it has arrived. You may never know if your efforts have worked. That is why prevention is not popular. Cure is much more obvious and dramatic. There are some measures which you can take as a manager which are highly likely to pay off by leading to a better managed organisation anyway.

Recognise that stress can occur.

Collect stress related data. This includes labour turnover, absentee-ism, lateness, pilferage, accidents, performance appraisal ratings, and employee attitude surveys. Be especially alert for sudden change.

Cut out deliberate stress. This includes lack of feedback and poor communications generally; sudden and unannounced moves of people and offices; and making people wait unnecessarily.

Working conditions may be at fault. Check lighting, heating, ventilation, humidity, noise, smoking, shift patterns, and the possibility of flexible hours at work.

Selection. There are few organisations that could not improve their initial selection methods. Having the wrong person in the wrong job is bound to cause problems.

Induction. Having got good people on board, make sure they know what they are supposed to do and help them form the connections and gather the information which will help them do it.

Training. We all need training and retraining to cope with the changing demands of work. The UK has a bad record of inadequate educational preparation for work, followed up by poor or non-existent training and development at work. You will become stressed if you are being blamed for poor performance but no one is helping you in any concrete way to do it better.

Potential assessment needs careful attention if you are to avoid appointing people to more senior posts who then fail to produce results. It is bad for them and bad for the organisation to promote people to positions which they cannot cope with.

Feedback. Give frequent, reliable feedback on performance.

Performance appraisal. Check that the formal annual appraisal is doing what it is supposed to do. Has it become an administrative chore? Is it too formal or too complex?

Job design. How well matched are people's capacities and what they are being asked to do? Do they have too much or too little to do? Is it too fast or too slow for them? How much control do they have or want over what they do?

Face up to bad news early, and then take action before the problem gets out of hand.

Avoid indecision. You will hardly ever have all the information you would like to help you make your decision. Do not take rash risks, but do not hesitate over-long either. Do not create indecision in others by your own unwillingness to make decisions or to let them do so.

Use stress positively. Remember stress and motivation are part of the same continuum. There is a large healthy area under the middle of the curve in Figure 7.3. People can take a surprising amount without burning out if they know what is going on. If there is too little going on they may rust. Find something for them to do – or face up to bad news early and get rid of them before more damage is caused to them, their colleagues and the rest of the organisation.

Counselling. Have a confidential counselling service available. People need someone to whom they can go to talk freely about their problems, of whatever scale. Companies which run such programmes claim that they make a major contribution to the health of the organisation and the people within it, but the confidentiality must be absolute.

Medical/psychological help should be available at short notice. When you hit a crisis, or one of your employees does, you cannot wait three weeks for an appointment. Something needs doing *now*. You might want to consider routine health checks for all employees as part of your action to prevent stress building up in the first place.

You can manage stress – both your own and others'. Your objective should be to achieve that level of stress which best matches the person, what they are being asked to do, and the circumstances under which they are working. Sometimes this may mean increasing their stress level to help them achieve more, but never to the point of asking them to risk damaging themselves.

It might be as well to conclude with a warning. Do not overdo your concern with stress. Not every problem is stress related, and attempts at do-it-yourself psychiatry for trivial upsets are likely to be a waste of time, and may do more harm than good. But managing yourself and others to avoid inappropriate stress is a highly profitable venture.

FURTHER READING

Popular

Booth, A L, *Stressmanship*, Severn House Publishers, 1985

British Medical Association, *The BMA Book of Executive Health*, Times Books Ltd, 1979

Cooper, C L and Marshall, J, *Understanding Executive Stress*, Macmillan, 1978

Rudinger, E, *Living with Stress*, Consumers Association, 1982

Selye, H, *The Stress of my Life*, Van Nostrand Reinhold, 1979

Wood, C, *Living in Overdrive*, Fontana Paperbacks, 1984

Technical

Cooper, C L and Payne, R, *Stress at Work,* John Wiley & Sons, 1978

Goldberger, L and Breznitz, S, *Handbook of Stress: theoretical and clinical aspects*, The Free Press, 1982

Kutash, I L, Schlesinger, L B and Associates, *Handbook on Stress and Anxiety*, Jossey Bass, 1980

Marshall, J and Cooper, C L, *Coping with Stress at Work*, Gower, 1981

Paine, W S, *Job Stress and Burnout*, Sage Publications, 1982

Price, V A, *Type A Behaviour Pattern*, Academic Press, 1982

8

Career planning

Michael Williams

At its simplest, career progression depends upon the interaction of two factors, or 'forces' – *personal ambition* and *organisation needs*. Figure 8.1 illustrates how these two forces act as the main determinants in the development of the individual's career path through his working life.

The more junior he is, the more will personal needs and ambition tend to be the predominant factor in the growth and direction of his career. By the time he has reached senior or top levels in the management hierarchy, the organisation's needs will usually be exerting the major influence over his career progression.

In up to 30 years in a managerial career the individual may have, typically, five or six different posts. It is unlikely that he will spend similar amounts of time in each. Generally, he may spend as little as one or two years in his earlier roles while in each of his final two posts he may spend seven, ten or more years, as Figure 8.2 shows.

The career 'plateau' apparent in this illustration may be due to many factors, both personal and organisational but it might also be due to the onset of 'middlescence' and mid-career stagnation from which the individual never really recovers. The problem of 'died at 40, retires at 65' is a common one and results in far too many career casualties, especially if there is an inadequate 'social support system' within the organisation to provide timely career counselling. Figure 8.3 shows the effects of the process on the career path of such a manager.

For many managers the mid-life period during the 40s and early 50s may be something of a crucial personal 'stocktake'. It is for many a time of re-decisions, as well as decisions about career development, personal life and how the two can more satisfactorily coexist.

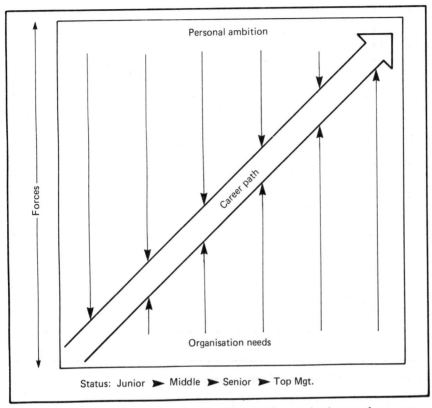

Figure 8.1 **The influence of personal ambition and organisation needs on career development**

Fundamental reorganisation or technical change is also likely to have a significant impact upon the individual's career progression and, presupposing that the manager is prepared to respond to the organisation's needs, the picture of his career path may look like that shown in Figure 8.4. Similarly the shift from a predominantly technical role to largely managerial responsibilities which often comes with career progression to more senior levels will create learning demands upon the individual, as Figures 8.5 and 8.6 show. Whether the manager's career is largely one of transition from technical to managerial roles or a linear progression through the management hierarchy, the shift in the *type* of skills he will need to develop is depicted in Figure 8.7.

147

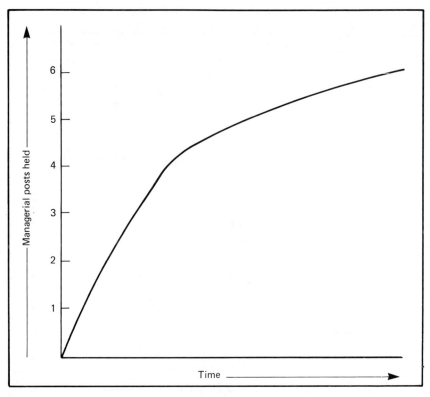

Figure 8.2   Typical managerial career progression

In the longer term, self-development needs to be related to the individual's career plans based upon where he or she wants to get to, within self-determined time scales.

The process begins when an individual starts by asking himself a whole series of personal questions such as:

- What do I want from my career?
- What don't I want from it?
- What do I do well and what do I enjoy doing?
- What do I want to be doing in two, five or ten years' time? Can I actually visualise the sort of job I want to be doing then?
- What do I need to do better, or differently, to be more effective in my present job?
- What do I need to do in order to prepare and develop myself for the jobs I believe I want to do in the future?

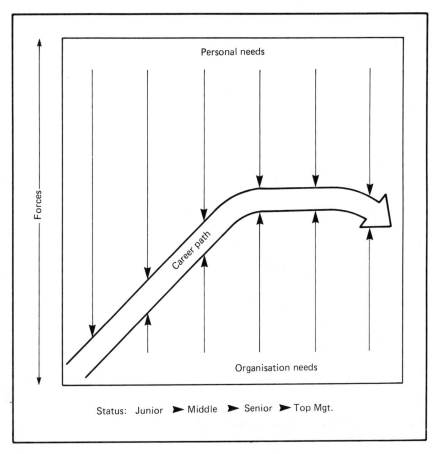

Figure 8.3   Impact of 'middlescence' on career path
This phenomenon appears to be complicated by a 'chicken and egg' argument about which comes first – the so-called 'mid-life crisis' or 'mid-career' crisis. The two are, however, often related.

● Where do I go to get the best possible help, guidance and advice about my career?

IDENTIFYING THE 'PLUS-ME' AND 'PLUS-JOB'

A first step to the process of deciding the right career path and self-development strategy might well take the form of a detailed personal 'stocktaking'. This involves identifying the 'plus-me' and 'plus-job'

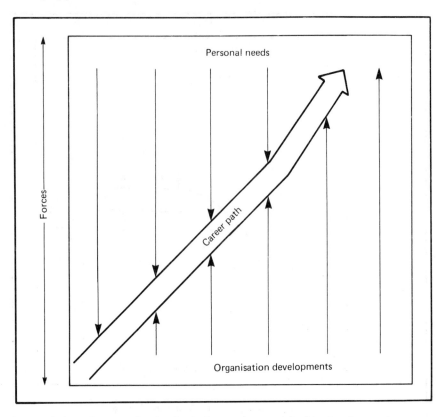

Figure 8.4 Influence of technological or major organisation developments on career path

referred to in Chapter 1. The 'plus-me' exercise in Figure 8.8 invites you to make an assessment of you as you currently see yourself, and then to rate yourself (along the same dimensions) against the demands of effective performance in your current job. Simply use 'G' for good, 'S' to denote 'satisfied' with your performance or 'I' to indicate that improvement is needed.

When you have completed the 'As I am now' column, cover up your scores before filling in the right-hand column. When both columns have been completed, examine the results.

● What are your priorities for development action?
● Is there any pattern in your improvement needs – for instance, a lack of confidence – which inhibits your effectiveness?

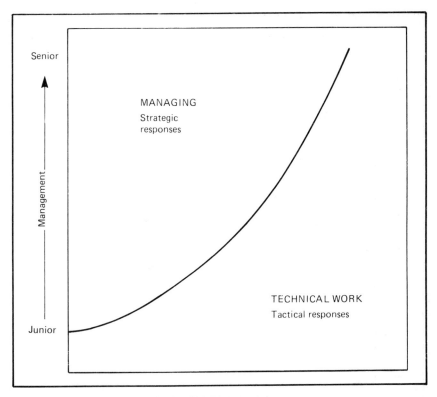

Figure 8.5   Shift in the nature of primary work
Generally the more junior levels of management (especially in technical functions) are characterised by a considerable technical work content. This diminishes significantly with promotion (although the manager may still cling to his original technical love).

- Are there any marked 'I' that you really cannot improve? How will you handle that?
- What about those marked 'G' — how will you build on those strengths and capitalise on them?
- What patterns emerge in your strengths? For instance are there any significant links between the 'G' scores? What clues do the patterns give you about your potential?
- What changes do you need to make to your job and work relationships to capitalise on the 'G' scores?
- What other key strengths do you have that make up your 'plus-me' and how do you intend to build on them?

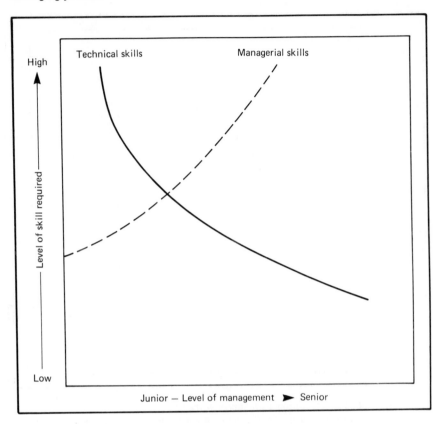

Figure 8.6   Changing patterns of skills required to match primary work shift

The next part of the process is to consider your present role and the *attainable* 'plus-job' which may exist within it.

The 'plus-job' may not be your whole job, but the parts of it which match your strengths and which offer scope both for personal growth and increased contribution to your work group and your organisation. The 'plus-job' *consists of those activities that fulfil you and motivate you personally and professionally.*

Typically, the process takes the form illustrated in Figure 8.9.

●   Begin by listing those aspects of your work which are attainable within the overall scope of your current work which you identify as 'plus' features.

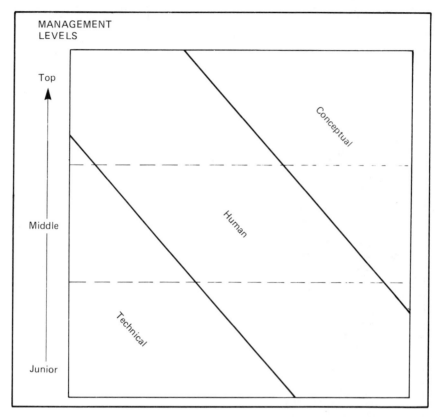

MANAGEMENT
LEVELS

Top

Middle

Junior

Conceptual

Human

Technical

Figure 8.7   Evolving needs for different skills in 'linear' career progression
This figure shows the changing skills needed as the individual moves vertically
through the hierarchy from supervisory or junior levels to the most senior executive
posts.

- Then against each of these features identify those strengths and
  positive attributes which you possess and which *strengthen* the
  plus aspects of your job. In other words, where do you excel, or
  have strengths, in the areas that motivate you?
- Next, identify 'plus' features which you consider to be attainable in your present job, but which are not yet present.
- Against each of these potential plus features write what *action*
  you should take to make it feasible.
- Now, write down any personal strengths you possess, related to
  what you see as your 'plus-job'. Especially consider those

My behaviour	As I am now	Demanded for success in my current job
1 Securing commitment from others		
2 Managing conflict		
3 Giving praise and appreciation to others		
4 Getting enough praise and appreciation from others		
5 Defining problems accurately and realistically		
6 Exercising judgement in technical decisions		
7 Exercising judgement in managerial decisions		
8 Being sufficiently tough when I need to be		
9 Saying what I do, or don't, want from others		
10 Being assertive (*not* aggressive) when feeling insecure or threatened		
11 Listening effectively		
12 Confronting others who violate my basic rights		
13 Owning my own problems — and their solutions		
14 Asking for help when I need it		
15 Allowing others to manipulate me against my will		
16 Capacity to put my role and contribution into proper organisational context		
17 Giving unpopular instructions face to face		
18 Expressing myself when I need to in front of a group or audience		
19 Thinking before I speak		
20 Remaining in control of myself when under real pressure, face to face		
21 Analysing situations thoroughly before acting		
22 Giving encouragement		
23 Giving others credit for their ideas		
24 Taking risks in my decisions and actions		
25 Collaborating with others		

Figure 8.8   The 'plus-me' exercise

'Plus' features of job	Personal strengths
1 Dealing with large groups face to face	1.1 Confidence to get up and talk to people in groups 1.2 Ability to 'sway a crowd' 1.3 Keep cool under pressure
2 Taking significant decisions	2.1 Job knowledge 2.2 Innovative thinker
etc.	etc.

Figure 8.9   The plus-job

which are not fully used at present and which you are therefore not developing as effectively as you could.

- Next, prepare an action plan for developing your attainable 'plus-job' and your strengths for discussion with your boss.
- Discuss it, implement what you can and follow through.

Particularly in the context of self-development and personal career planning, 'improvement' begins with 'I'. Other people are necessary to help the process, but only the individual himself has the ultimate responsibility for his development and growth.

CAREER TRANSITIONS

A considerable amount of research has gone into studies of the impact of major career changes upon executives and managers and most indicate that such transitions are usually accompanied by high stress and anxiety. Gaining the first real job, obtaining significant promotion, feeling trapped in a routine 'prison', depression following redundancy, or apprehension about impending retirement are typical transition stresses.

At best, they are periods of considerable vulnerability where the individual may be unsure of:

- what is expected of him in terms of skill, knowledge and performance;
- whether he can cope with and come through the transition successfully;

155

- what the ground rules, or guidelines (formal, or informal) are, which dictate how he should behave;
- which are the key relationships he needs to make and use – especially who to turn to as the real source of support, help and guidance.

By definition, a crucial career transition occurs, through promotion, job stagnation, or job loss where the individual needs to *change* his:

- beliefs, assumptions and perceptions about roles, jobs and possibly work itself;
- relationships with superiors, peers and/or subordinates.

Both changes usually involve breaking new ground where a cycle of stages normally follows, including:

exploration
↓
testing and probation
↓
building and consolidation
↓
recharging and maintenance

These four phases of career progression relate, to some extent, to the stages of development identified by Dalton, Thompson and Price in *Organisation Dynamics* (issue no. 19, 1977):

Apprentice → Colleague → Mentor → and Sponsor

Both concepts suggest a series of transitions which 'peak out' at some stage which, typically, is then followed by a significant change in role, influence and relationships.

However, *before* the peak is reached, there is usually – especially in managerial and technological career progression – a crucial move, often around the age of 35, which may have far-reaching consequences for the rate of climb to the peak, the level of the peak itself and possible subsequent stages (see Figure 8.10).

Evidence from both surveys and writings about career progression suggests that many managers did not prepare for the crucial move as they subsequently feel they should have done. Equally, many feel that they were not helped by their superiors, as much as they could have been, to understand and cope with the transition surrounding the crucial move in their careers. Role conflict and identity strains are two

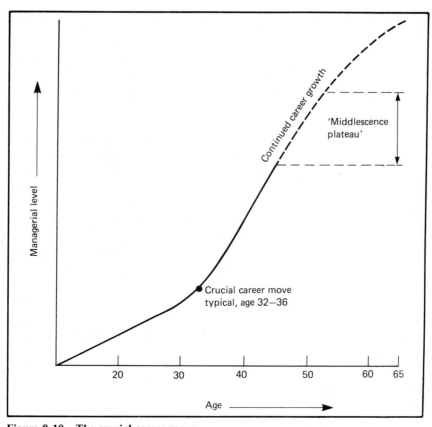

Figure 8.10   The crucial career move

frequently cited problems facing managers and executives at this stage. Role conflict emerges because of the pressures imposed by the promotion upon the manager's domestic life, wider interests or clash with his previous lifestyle at work. Identity strain often manifests itself in the form of confusion about:

- how to relate to key figures in the organisation;
- how to preserve 'territorial' rights and boundaries;
- what to do about in-company 'politics' and what roles or stances to adopt;
- what image to maintain and project and who to use as a model for management style.

Neither role conflict nor identity strain is confined to the most crucial

157

career change in the early or mid-30s. Such crises may occur at any stage in a manager's career, but particularly may re-emerge in a 'post-plateau' period, when the individual may find himself demoted, overtaken by far younger people, or made redundant. What is more, these two phenomena are likely to be aggravated, or considerably added to, by other stresses if they occur during post-plateau 'middlescence'.

For example, general anxiety and depression – the two 'common colds' of psychology – may well be at their most severe during the middle years or mid-career crisis and may, additionally, give rise to: over-protective (but counter-productive) behaviour; increased resistance to change; loss of incentive and motivation; low morale; loss of tendency to innovate and take risks; increased suspicion of others' motives, withdrawal, self-imposed constraints and 'self-pity' cliques; or loss of perspective and sense of reality.

Any, or all of these, are likely to lead to a reduction in personal effectiveness, at a time when the individual's impact and contribution are of prime importance.

WHAT CAN THE INDIVIDUAL MANAGER DO ABOUT CAREER PROGRESSION?

A fundamental need in career planning is *information* – whether the individual is:

- at a crucial stage in shaping his career
- about to lose his job
- conscious of being 'boxed-in', or on a plateau
- taking stock and considering the next stage
- close to retirement.

Another crucial need is likely to be for support, in the form of 'sounding boards' to test out perceptions, perspectives and options. The difficulty here is that of finding objective and valid views – or even other people's experiences which are closely related to one's own – and, therefore, an appropriate basis for comparison. Obviously vocational guidance specialists exist — both in private practice and in many city offices of the Department of Employment. Additionally several universities have conducted surveys into career planning, though much of the research is associated with mid-career crisis, redundancy and pre-retirement planning, rather than with the crucial

32-35 transitions. There are also books on the subject which are worth reading, *selectively*, in order to pick up ideas about career planning and the crucial importance of preparing oneself systematically for job and role changes. Some of these texts are listed at the end of this chapter but one worth mentioning at this stage as a practical guide for women in management is *The Managerial Woman* by Hennig and Jardim published by Pan. Men normally have a wide range of executive 'models' provided by other male managers, executives and directors whose styles they can imitate, refine or avoid, as the case may be. By contrast, women still have comparatively few female success stories in the management world to provide suitable models.

Whether there is a proliferation or scarcity of managerial models, the problem remains of what to avoid and in which fields to ensure timely action is taken.

Probably the fastest disappearing years in any executive's life are those that take place between 35 and 40. Too often, managers find themselves living out their working lives and planning − or, rather *reacting* − on a day-to-day basis with little long term thinking about their work, jobs, skill development, or managerial *style*. Specialists, particularly, are prone to career myopia and their preoccupation with their technological specialism, their pursuit of perfection or refinement of detail tends to inhibit long term planning *away* from technology and into general management. If these patterns are well established, the chances are that the elusive years between 35 and 40 come and go with no energy having been put into conscious long term career planning or development. The sudden awareness of one's own mortality — the true onset of 'middlescence' — usually coincides with the realisation that it is now too late to look forward to real advancement; and many managers drift into the mid-years plateau to escape into a niche, rut or sinecure and, eventually, retirement.

The effective counter is systematic long term career planning at the early stages of managerial life. This involves identifying the many cues that signal a manager's need to:

- acquire new knowledge and skills;
- develop understanding of the managerial and business world in breadth, as well as technical depth;
- experience leadership and managerial roles, where there is both accountability and the exercise of *authority*;

- become increasingly aware of his own behaviour and the impact other people have upon his operational effectiveness;
- recognise the supreme importance in management of self-confidence, which becomes more and more put to the test as the manager moves away from technology into line roles and general management.

Part of the process of career planning is to be aware of the personal 'horizons', referred to in Chapter 1, rather than to try to assess 'ultimate potential'. Horizons, based upon the time spans of two or three years, within a context of a five- or ten-year planning period, provide the manager with realistic time scales within which to work out the experience, learning, training and development necessary to make the planned moves a reality. Finally, it is vital to accept that, come the point of transition, there will inevitably be the moving out of the 'womb' of familiar roles, relationships and organisation into new fields where unfamiliar issues and problems must be confronted.

The tendency at such stages is to turn inwards, inhibited by anxiety and the wish to remain with the present, familiar world. It is, in fact, by turning *outwards*, to other people, that an objective view of the transition is to be had. By seeing how other people cope, by asking questions admitting to ignorance, the manager can acquire much of the necessary knowledge about his new role, *on the job*. The important thing is to get to know how the organisation *works*, who can provide what help, support and information and to recognise, as quickly as possible, the strengths and weaknesses of different executives' management styles in critical, but constructive and analytical, terms. In career planning – especially the development of realistic and flexible management styles – the manager's most powerful asset is an inquiring mind and a refusal to accept the present way of doing things is necessarily the best. Too often, management practices become organisational sanctities, hallowed by little more than the passage of time – and that is no guarantee of effectiveness, especially in today's rapidly changing world.

FURTHER READING

Dalton, G, Thompson, P H and Price, R. L, 'The Four Stages of Professional Careers – A New Look at Performance by Professionals', *Organizational Dynamics*, 19 (1977)

Robertson, John P, *You and Your Next Job*, British Institute of Management, 1982

Sofer, C, *Men in Mid-Career: A Study of British Managers and Technical Specialists,* Cambridge University Press, 1970

Weiss, R S, 'Transition States and Other Stressful Situations, Their Nature and Programs for Their Managment', in G Caplan and M Killilea, eds, *Support Systems and Mutual Help: Multidisciplinary Exploration,* Grune and Stratton, 1976, pp. 213–232

9

Skills for women managers

Valerie J Hammond

More women in the UK are becoming managers and they now hold 15 per cent of all management posts *(New Earnings Survey* 1986 Part E, Table 135). At the same time, values in society are changing. Traditional tough autocratic management is challenged by the need for a participative, cooperative style with the emphasis on teamwork and short-life projects. It is sometimes suggested that this style is associated with women and that women might influence organisational structures and practices to make them more appropriate for today's needs.

However, the experiences that women typically have as they grow up do not always fit them to take adequate stock of the organisation. They do not necessarily 'see' things in the same way as male colleagues and they have fewer opportunities to find a role model or mentor who understands their perspective and likely difficulties. Too often, it seems, women do not recognise the skills they need and do not use to best advantage the skills they have.

For these reasons it is worth looking at 'skills for women managers'. These are skills which women — and indeed men — may wish to look at afresh. They are not alternatives. All managers must acquire appropriate functional and general management skills but a review of five 'keys' will help unlock individual potential: understanding the organisation, building a personal management style, communicating effectively, managing oneself, taking account of personal development.

UNDERSTANDING THE ORGANISATION

Women tend to believe that doing the job well is what counts for success but that is not in fact enough. The number of people who know you and your work and the seniority of those people is an important determinant in career success. Being visible is crucial but the way to achieve visibility must be handled carefully. In some companies this is an acceptable activity; in others it is not. Understanding the organisational culture and its politics will help you decide what to do.

Understanding organisational culture

Culture has been defined as the glue that holds the organisation together; it derives from the values, beliefs and expectations that members come to share. But culture is elusive. It is often hard for us to be aware of it and how it influences what passes for acceptable behaviour, yet it is impossible to escape its effect. You can use it or even try to change it, but you cannot ignore it and succeed. An important step before joining an organisation is to find out as much as possible about its culture and value system, to see how this fits with your own personal values.

People who epitomise the business are important pointers to the culture. They might be founders or leaders, inventors of new products or systems. These people are visible demonstrations − even if only by reputation − of 'what you have to do to succeed'. In most organisations they are men. Exceptions occur in professions and organisations directly associated with women. Florence Nightingale and Helena Rubinstein both fulfilled this role in the organisations they created. A modern day counterpart is Steve Shirley who founded and heads F International, the organisation that marries computing expertise with the work patterns typical of women.

Values are at the heart of the organisation's culture because they define success in concrete terms. Values are about what and how things should be done and how people should be treated. Steve Shirley, for example, describes her mission as 'to develop through modern telecommunications the unutilised intellectual energy of people unable to work in a conventional environment'. She does not waste time checking up on people, believing that instead they are linked by trust as well as telecommunications. The result is that 'everyone of us saves company money carefully, as we would our own'.

Customs exist in all organisations and show 'how things are done'. They include meetings and ceremonies and informal events like always meeting in the bar or taking part in the company squash ladder.

Customs may serve to reinforce traditional sex-based roles so it is important that women understand their significance and act outside the stereotype when this is appropriate.

The cultural network is the primary and informal means of communicating organisational values. It carries the inside stories about how things really work. It is essential to be linked to this network and to be part of it.

You can learn a lot by just standing back and looking at your organisation. Try answering the questions in Figure 9.1.

Look back over your answers. Underline any aspects you had not

- What clues are there to your company's culture in its appearance? Think about buildings, general environment, furnishings, facilities.

- What clues are in the company literature — annual reports, recruitment literature, statements to financial analysts, press releases, announcements to staff etc.?

- Is the emphasis on business performance, on people, or both?

- Does what the company says apply in practice?

- How are visitors treated? Think about reception, furnishings, staff, telephone callers.

- How do staff refer to customers and members of the public?

- How do people refer to their employment with the company — with pride or something else?

- Write down one or two stories or anecdotes about your organisation.

- Note down any customs that exist in your organisation — think about awards, privileges, etc.

- List any outstanding company people — current or past — that you have heard mentioned. Think about who started the company, what kind of people do well etc.

- What do you have to do to get promoted? Is it based on job competence, results, loyalty, long service, being in the right department?

Figure 9.1 Diagnosing your organisational culture

considered before about the culture of your organisation. How does this fit with your own values and aspirations?

Organisation politics

Many women dislike organisation politics intensely but as Professor Andrew Kakabadse points out in *The Politics of Management* (see Chapter 21), it is impossible to avoid politics in organisations; even if you simply wish to be left alone to do your job you have to understand the politics of the place. This will help you to get things done, to identify and influence the actual decision makers, to get yourself promoted.

Sources of power

Women sometimes feel 'powerless' but everyone has some power. There are different types of power, for example:

- formal, delegated authority to make decisions (providing other people allow you to exercise it);
- expertise – specialist knowledge and skills;
- control over resources – physical, financial or information;
- interpersonal – the ability to influence and to build good relationships.

Sources of power exist in your personal qualities, skills and knowledge and in the position which you hold in the organisation. You may have personal or positional power but clearly it is an advantage to have both.

Take a look at your own potential for power (Figure 9.2). Put yourself in the centre of the power net (Figure 9.3). In the other circles put people who have an important effect on your work: they may be higher or lower in the organisation, they may be outside it, customers or suppliers, for example.

To exercise power you must influence another person to do what you want. Ask yourself why they will do it and you will see the type of power you have.

Power flows

Organisation politics is seldom a one-way process; usually both parties have some power. Look back at your power net. Have you indicated the two-way flow of power? Women tend to give away power. Check that you have not fallen into this trap and that you are using the power that you have.

- What type of power does each person in your net have in relation to you?

- Do they have the right to decide what you do?

- Do they have control over the information you need?

- What is their power based on?

- What sort of power do you have in relation to them?

- Who depends on you and for what?

- On whom do you depend and for what?

Figure 9.2 Personal power

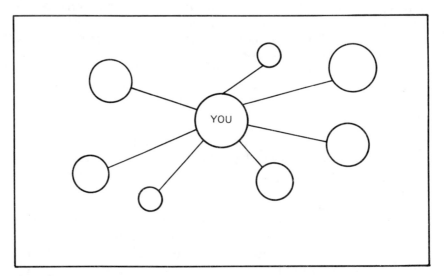

Figure 9.3 Personal power net
This exercise first appeared in Margaret Ryan and Rennie Fritchie, *Career Life Planning Workshops for Women Managers – a Tutor's Guide,* Manpower Services Commission, 1982.

One reason for being treated as 'powerless' is that you may not have clearly signalled your source of power. You will not be able to capitalise on 'expert power' if you are not perceived as an expert. If you have special knowledge and abilities, make sure that you are seen to exercise these. This might mean 'banging the drum'; it certainly means taking risks and using your skills rather than waiting to be consulted.

Even if you have relatively little acknowledged power, you can exert considerable influence by developing effective influencing skills and building good relationships. This will give you access to informal information channels which can be as important as formal ones. Use your skills to build links across departments, specialisms, hierarchies, inside and outside the organisation. Use these networks to gather early warning of developments that affect you so that you can take appropriate action.

Power: a moral issue? You may accept the need to understand organisation politics but still feel that you do not want to be part of the system. However, it is not really possible to opt out. If you disagree with the values but do not challenge them, then you are in fact supporting them. If you wish the values were different, then you can exercise some influence. In the short term, conforming to dominant values can enhance your own position; this might in turn allow you at a later stage to exercise power in line with your own values (if these are different). Obviously, this is a personal decision but none of us is powerless and it might be argued that women have a duty to bring values as well as skills and abilities to the business world.

BUILDING A PERSONAL STYLE

If you are the first woman in your post, recognise the extra challenges. You will not have a role model and those who have to react to you may not be sure what to expect. Take the opportunity to develop your own particular style.

Management style

Management style generally refers to the way a manager gets the job done. It concerns behaviour, what managers actually do. Style depends on personal qualities and the culture of the organisation, so incorporate your own experience and values to create a style with which you feel comfortable. There is no need to abandon so-called feminine qualities of care, concern, warmth and intuition. These can be combined with the qualities of rationality, decisiveness and objectivity. Organisations, and the men in them, are increasingly valuing the skills and different approaches which some women bring. In a London local authority women are perceived as being able to empathise more easily with the needs of the community. Women in that organisation are also seen as more effective in creating teams and in drawing support from subordinates and colleagues.

Long-established management styles – authoritarian, consultative, participative – are being joined by different approaches. These include Marlow's 'ferryman', who navigates the route for the team, and Bradford's and Cohen's 'manager as developer'. These newer styles meet the needs of the changing business environment and they build on the skills and qualities which women bring to management.

An effective manager will be able to use several styles, selecting the most appropriate for a given situation. It is important to keep the right balance on getting the job done, being concerned about individuals and taking care of the group. Check that anxiety about the task does not blind you to the needs of your staff.

Rosabeth Moss Kanter in her book *Men and Women of the Corporation* links a focus on the task with authoritarian behaviour and argues that women behave in this way because of uncertainty about power. So, clarify power issues, stop being defensive, start delegating and let yourself explore the participative, team building approaches that are appropriate to the modern organisation. Teams are more likely to be the norm for the future and women are seen to be good team members and managers of teams when they feel secure enough. Trust your instincts and intuition and work with and through your team. This is an area where women's natural tendencies appear to be suppressed to match the style of colleagues when in fact men are looking to women to bring different viewpoints and approaches.

Decision making style

Research into the way the human brain operates, particularly activity in the right and left hemispheres of the brain, has led to the suggestion that women may reach decisions in a different way from men – not better or worse, but different. Women tend to use a conceptual and intuitive (right-brained) approach whereas men are more likely to use an analytical and logical (left-brained) style. This may contribute to problems in meetings when people tackle issues in quite different ways. On the other hand, the interaction of these two styles could release creativity into the organisation.

The Japanese are also high scorers on right-brain activity and this is stimulating interest in the West about ways to develop intuition, particularly amongst business leaders. It is thought that such leaders will be better able to steer their organisations through unpredictable times ahead. If you are aware that you use intuition to good effect, this information should encourage you to have confidence in your own decision making style.

Leadership style

It is increasingly recognised that organisations need better leadership not only at the top but at all levels of management. At the same time, it is evident that conditions for the future call for a different kind of leader — one who helps to create change by helping people to find more of themselves to contribute than they thought possible. It is also suggested that women are particularly well suited to this leadership style. See Chapter 10 for a discussion of leadership.

Although there are relatively few women in national leadership positions, a perusal of newspapers and journals shows that there are more women leaders than one might think. Some adopt a traditional or conventional leadership style: Margaret Thatcher is an obvious example, a modern Boadicea. But others are increasingly trying to blend feminine and masculine behaviours to achieve a style that has become known as androgynous. Such women draw out the very best that their people have within them and use their energies to harmonise the needs of the organisation, individuals and society. Have confidence in your own leadership style and take every chance to develop it.

BUILDING RELATIONSHIPS

The organisation has already demonstrated its support by appointing you. There are after all usually more men than women from whom to choose. A statement has been made; be aware of the strength this gives you.

Boss and colleague relationships take time to build effectively. You may be their new experience and they may look to you for a guide about how best to develop a two-way relationship. Make time for informal conversations. Get to know people outside your immediate work area. Use every opportunity to become part of the informal communication net.

Staff. Use the skills of everyone, including your secretary, in the department. Provide the right circumstances for them to do their best. Work with them to gain a reputation as a good people-developer. This is a good way to ensure they will want to work with and for you.

The world outside should not be neglected. Be active in your professional associations. Make sure you are in the main stream and not side-tracked into groups which are 'marginalised'. Your value and standing in the wider community can help you to value yourself – something which women are generally poor at doing.

Women's networks, in or outside the company, can also give you the support and information you need.

COMMUNICATING EFFECTIVELY

Communicating effectively involves speaking out clearly and within the framework of the other person's experience. When face to face, women and men are sometimes divided by use of the same language and behaviour to which are attributed different meanings.

Gestures, posture and even dress must support the message you wish to convey so that you avoid sending out conflicting messages. For example, if you are unable to get the promotion or opportunities that you seek even though you have the experience and ability to handle the job, check whether you are acting in a way that suggests the opposite, and speaking in tone and manner that belies your expertise and authority.

There is less emphasis in the UK on the 'dress for success' image building that exists in the USA. However, successful women pay attention to this aspect of personal communication and dress with flair and style but in a way that complements rather than competes with the message.

Assertiveness

Assertiveness is an essential behaviour for effective communication but women are generally dicouraged by social conditioning from being assertive. It is a skill that every woman should acquire.

An assertive woman is open and flexible, genuinely concerned with the rights of others, yet able to establish easily her own rights. Assertiveness means taking charge of yourself, setting goals, making choices. It does not mean winning at the expense of others. It has to do with valuing the other person and their needs as well as valuing yourself. If you often:

- feel disregarded;
- feel obliged to come to agreements you find unsatisfactory;
- go away without the information you want;
- cannot attract attention when you need to;
- say 'yes' when you mean 'no';

then you almost certainly need to work on your assertiveness skills.

Assertiveness has to be practised. You can read about techniques but you will probably find it more helpful and you will certainly make faster progress if you join short courses.

If you fear that becoming more assertive will make you 'aggressive' it is worth taking a few minutes to distinguish the behaviours. Most courses and books identify three: aggressive, passive, assertive.

An aggressive person wants to win, even if this means disregarding the rights and feelings of others. She overvalues self and attacks or accuses others. Her behaviour makes them feel defensive, resentful, hurt and upset. She uses threatening questions, makes assumptions and tells people what to do. She looks and feels angry.

A passive person lets others use her. They have rights, she does not. She lets others take responsibility. She shows no reaction but resents being put upon. Her behaviour frustrates others, or makes them feel guilty. In speech she hesitates and apologises, uses qualifying statements to create an escape route if things go wrong. She seldom asks for what she wants or needs. She looks and feels nervous.

An assertive person stands up for herself but recognises the rights of others. She communicates clearly and honestly, sharing her opinions and intentions. She makes others feel good, lets them know she values their opinions even if she has to disagree. She takes responsibility for herself and explains her beliefs and ideas. She looks and feels comfortable.

Check your own level of assertiveness. Think about your behaviour in each of the situations in Figure 9.4. How would you rate your typical reaction? Be honest with yourself!

Look back at your evaluation. Ask friends or colleagues if they assess your behaviour in the same way. Try working with them to practise role playing assertive behaviour in any situation where you know you typically adopt an aggressive or passive stance.

	Aggressive	Passive	Assertive
Wine not chilled in a restaurant			
Reminding friend that she/he owes you for goods bought			
Upset by sexist comment at work			
Asking for a rise			
Discussing an appraisal which you think is unjust			
Dealing with a staff member who has BO			
Confronting a senior colleague who put forward your idea at a meeting without giving you credit			
Asking people not to smoke in your office			
Making your point at a meeting when the chair seems to avoid you			
Dealing with your home help who you know is taking advantage of the fact that you are not at home			

Figure 9.4   Level of assertiveness

When you are acting assertively you will:

- state your needs, wants, opinions and feelings in a clear direct way;
- make statements that show you empathise with the other person's point of view even when it differs from your own;
- point out the difference between what has been agreed and what is actually happening;
- make clear to the other person the effect their behaviour is having on you;
- make sure that the other person understands the consequences of not changing their behaviour;
- find out what are the needs, wants, opinions and feelings of the other person.

Assertiveness techniques

Broken record – especially useful when you have to make a refusal in difficult circumstances. Keep repeating your original statement. Avoid being side-tracked into discussion about other issues or justifying yourself. Stay calm. You will eventually convince the other person you mean what you say.

Empathy – helps you to say no in a 'softer' way. Your response includes a statement that shows you have heard what the other person wants, that you understand, but you cannot do or agree with what is requested.

Workable compromise – helps to get out of win – lose situations. Offer a compromise solution that enables both parties to maintain self-respect.

Fogging – helps you to cope with unfair criticism instead of responding emotionally with feelings of guilt or anger. Fogging allows you to take the steam out of the situation by showing that you have heard, even accepted, the words and by making sure you respond only to what is said – not what is implied.

Negative assertion – best summed up by Robert Townsend's advice to 'admit mistakes'. Doing this openly and honestly avoids loss of face.

Negative enquiry – used to get feedback. Invite criticism, respond to the words, not to the implications. Do not counter-criticise and do not become defensive.

Improving communications in one-to-one situations

Although you may be dealing with people in the same way as other managers, their impressions will be coloured by past experience. Some people will not have worked with a woman manager before. Others find it difficult to disentangle attitudes to women in work and personal situations.

In one British health authority informal communication took place in pubs and other convenient stopping-off points as the managers moved between the different hospitals. When women joined the senior management team, they did not foresee difficulties but the men felt very uncomfortable about frequent meetings as a duo in such surroundings. Informal communication between men and women managers stopped. Soon the men started to complain about the 'female mafia' which communicated quickly and easily amongst its members. The women saw this as the men's problem but it was wider than this for it inhibited essential communications. The situation was only resolved when the managers, men and women, recognised the problem and worked out a way of meeting everyone's needs – in this case it was by arranging to meet regularly for lunch in the staff restaurant where there would be good opportunity for building informal relationships with less risk of gossip.

Be open to feedback. Many male managers find it extremely difficult to give clear critical comment to women so when you get it, don't be resentful but value it. Jean Denton, Director of Burson Marsteller, says if you are told 'that was bloody stupid', listen, learn and then get on with the next job.

Improving communication skills for meetings

In meetings you are highly visible and have a chance to display your ability to senior managers. It is vital to participate. Do not throw away the opportunity to display your verbal skills. Be aware of the politics; a lot of informal assessment takes place as you interact with colleagues.

Meetings demand preparation, so do your homework. If you are in the chair, work out carefully what you want to achieve at the meeting, what contribution you need from each person and make sure you ask for it. Involve all the members, even those who do not volunteer information whether these are women or men. Beware the trap of seeming to favour women but, equally, encourage them to speak.

When you are a meeting member, take time to prepare. Identify your contribution or view on the subject in hand. Arrive early. Choose a seat where you can easily catch the eye of the chairperson. When the meeting starts, try to say something in the first ten minutes. Women who do not do this tend to be overlooked. Natasha Josefowitz, author of *Paths to Power*, describes how in meetings at the University of San Diego where she is Professor of Management, if she hasn't anything to say at this stage, she nevertheless grunts 'just so they'll know I have a voice and they won't be surprised when I speak later'. To check your performance at meetings, see Figure 9.5.

If there are aspects about your involvement in the meeting that you would like to change, try some of the techniques mentioned here, not forgetting assertiveness at your next meeting. You will find more about meetings in Chapter 20.

Think of a meeting you attended in the last week or so.

What was your role?

What unique knowledge/experience could you bring to the meeting?

Who were the other participants?

What were their roles/specialisms?

Draw a plan of the meeting — show the seating of the participants including yourself

What contributions did you make?

When did you make these?

What were the outcomes?

Was it easy to catch the eye of the chairperson?

Did you get a fair amount of 'air space' in comparison with others?

Did other people talk over you?

What did you do about this?

Did other people present your ideas without reference to you?

What did you do about this?

Figure 9.5   Check your performance at meetings

PERSONAL EFFECTIVENESS

Personal effectiveness often depends on being able to take control of things which seem uncontrollable such as time and stress.

Time management

If you are always late, work with a backlog, feel guilty about not having enough time for family and home, then take a look at your time management. These aspects are particularly relevant for women but it is also worth completing a full personal time audit.

Spending time at home

It is not possible to work effectively if you are worrying about what is happening at home so take time to organise it properly. Involve everyone in the household in running it, husbands and partners, sons as well as daughters, parents and other dependants. Recognise that you will almost certainly have to invest some of the household income, whether it means hiring child care and domestic help, buying labour-saving equipment or sending everything possible to laundry and other contractors. You can create employment whilst making yourself a more effective manager – and you will be able to enjoy the time you spend at home!

Stopping others spending your time

Check whether you are creating problems for yourself by being too accessible. Natasha Josefowitz reports from research that women managers were twice as accessible to their staff as men. Almost all the women admitted that they found it difficult to say 'no' to interruptions.

Having an open door policy can be beneficial. It helps build staff loyalty, strengthens employee morale and ensures that there is a steady flow of information between you and your staff. However, it also incurs costs. You will have less time to handle other tasks, to plan for the future or to be creative. And fewer communications with your superiors and colleagues means reduced chances for upward progression.

To maximise the benefits and reduce the costs:

- set priorities;
- start each day with a 'must do' list;
- organise the day so that staff know when you are available to them;
- ask your secretary to screen calls and visitors;
- use door signs saying 'please come in' and 'please do not disturb';
- set time deadlines for meetings and conversations; keep to them – agree to continue later if necessary.

Saving time at work

Most of us have tasks and activities that we enjoy but they are not always the most effective way of spending time. Senior managers often comment on women's capacity for the detailed work that is appropriate for specialists. It is sometimes quoted as a reason for not promoting women because this type of work is less relevant in general management. If you have been promoted, check that you are not hanging on to work that can be done by more junior people, including your secretary. It can be a development experience for them and release you for tasks that demand your skill and expertise.

Check that you are not falling into the 'superwoman' trap. Do not be seduced into having a reputation for agreeing to achieve the impossible. Even though you might want to emulate the paint advertisement which says 'we stretch when others crack', it puts extra stress on you and your team. A busy person can achieve a great deal but to do this you must be well organised, keep your eye on the main goal, be able to mobilise resources and above all make the right choices. Take time to:

- identify key objectives and write them down;
- keep a diary of how you use your time;
- check whether the way you spend time now helps you to meet these objectives.

If you are not meeting your objectives, set about making changes — now.

Remember time is a currency to be saved and spent just like any other resource. Make sure you are making your investment where it will give you the best return.

Stress

Stress comes from feeling or working under pressure. Tolerance of, and need for, stress varies from person to person and from situation to situation but research by Marilyn Davidson and Cary Cooper shows that women managers typically experience high degrees of stress. This is in part because women who succeed in management today typically have personality type 'A' (based on research by Friedman and Rosenman) which is characterised by the need to compete, to achieve, to do everything at the double. At the same time, our society is not organised to expect women to be high achievers at work. Socialisation still places most emphasis on a home and family role for women. A frequent reaction is to try to meet all expectations – to fall into the trap of the 'superwoman syndrome', to work harder and faster, to pile on the stress.

Stress is not intrinsically bad. Stress can help us to perform well by mobilising the energy and adrenalin we need to meet the challenge. Problems arise when pressure is maintained, or we maintain the pressure on ourselves, so that the stress level remains high over a long period and we move from stress to strain.

Reducing stress

Recognising the symptoms and the circumstances which cause them are the first steps to reducing stress. Marjorie Hansen Shaevitz, author of *The Superwoman Syndrome*, says 'decide what's important in your life'. Learn to recognise situations that cause you stress and take time to prepare for them.

Try consciously to do things differently, to slow down. When the pressure is really on a change of scene or pace for a short while can help. Have your hair done, go shopping, stop and have a chat, take some exercise.

Check your diet and eating patterns. We all have to skip meals occasionally. When this happens, aim for balance – fruit, cheese, nuts, mineral water rather than a quick, stodgy sandwich and coffee, and take time to savour it. When the business lunch is the problem, again look for lightness, fish, eggs and salads rather than meat and spicy food. Experiment to find a drink to suit you. For example, tonic and angostura bitter is refreshing. It looks like (but doesn't have the same effect as) gin or vodka. Coffee and tea are often consumed in large quantities in stress situations – try instead herb teas which can be refreshing and yet soothing.

When you are really stressed, share your feelings: don't bottle them up. Make sure that family and colleagues know what is causing your stress and that it is not something they have done (if it is, of course you should tell them). If it's hard to talk when you're feeling really pressured, agree some signals of your feeling.

Let go of things you cannot control. Colleagues described the relief they felt when, after trying to avoid a traffic hold-up, they finally decided they were not going to arrive at the meeting on time. They telephoned the meeting partners, went off for a cup of tea, allowed the hold-up to disperse and then travelled smoothly on their way, arriving unruffled even though they were later than originally anticipated. (For more on stress and how to manage it, see Chapter 7.)

PERSONAL DEVELOPMENT

Career planning

A top flight career can exact a high price in terms of the impact on private life. This is obviously an area of personal choice. However, almost all senior women who are also married emphasise the importance of a partner who is supportive. There are after all likely to be negotiations about career moves, precedence at different times as well as all the usual domestic issues. If you have or plan a family then you need to pace your career in line with your personal plans. It is good stress-removing practice to make sure you give adequate time and space to meeting all your objectives, those at home as well as at work.

Getting trained and qualified

Identify the appropriate qualification or development experience for your specialism or work area — and get it. Women are still in the minority at business school and on management training courses. These often serve as 'rites of passage' essential for career progression as well as providing basic knowledge and skill. If this is so in your organisation or specialism, then it is doubly important that you attend.

The question of women only or mixed courses is a personal issue. Some women feel reluctant to join women only courses feeling that this is artificial, but there are advantages in single-sex training especially early in career. Men, after all, have always had such training. The key is to choose the situation where you will be prepared to risk most for it is only by reaching high and risking failure that you learn.

There is an increasing trend for individuals to take time to study for qualifications like an MBA and women should form a larger part of this trend. It is now possible to study for an MBA at many universities and other centres in the UK and this can be organised on full-time, part-time and modular bases. The Business Graduates Association will provide information.

Role models and mentors

Role models and mentors are invaluable in helping women to move up in management but they can be hard to find. This is because we tend to look for people most like ourselves, i.e. other women. However, as relatively few are in senior positions, it can be difficult to find a woman who has experience and is accessible. We can overcome this. First, let's clarify what we mean by role models and mentors.

Role models are people we admire and wish to be like. We may admire them for many different reasons, for their skill, the way they 'ride out' problems, how they manage staff, the balance they maintain between work and home, the way they dress, their social poise, confidence and so on. They are usually senior but they may not work for the same organisation or even do the same type of work. We may know them quite well or we may admire them from afar.

Mentors have some of the same characteristics. They are senior people, often, but not always, working in our own organisation. They are successful and have a lot of experience to share about the informal aspects of the organisation as well as straightforward factual information. We may not necessarily like them, but we certainly respect their opinion.

There are some important differences. An individual can be a role model without being aware of it but a mentor has a personal relationship with the person they sponsor. It is possible to have many role models, to value people for different qualities and to be quite selective about the aspects we wish to copy. It isn't even necessary to know the model personally. Mentors, on the other hand, offer a closer relationship and, therefore, whilst some people have more than one mentor (perhaps one in work and one outside) it is rare to have several at the same time.

The importance of the mentor relationship is increasingly being recognised. It gives the younger person access to help and advice, to knowledge and experience. This is not confined to learning how to do the job but how to cope with the political processes that operate in organisations and in personal relationships. The mentor may give feedback on performance and, because s/he is usually outside the direct reporting line, such feedback can be very direct and constructive but without the evaluative overtones that exist in similar discussions with one's boss.

In many cases the mentor will be a man and this can present some problems for women. The mentor–protégé relationship is usually a close one. In mixed sex pairs, this can be open to misinterpretation. It can result in office gossip or, in bad cases, in jealous misunderstandings with spouses. Also men are not socialised to criticise women and may find it difficult to give the frank feedback that is essential. It is also obvious that the experience of men differs from that of women and that they might not therefore be able to empathise sufficiently with the situation of the protégée. Take these factors into account when thinking about possible mentors.

Identify your own mentors

Your immediate boss may not be your best choice for a mentor – you may eventually be wanting his or her job!

Look for people who

- have a reputation for developing others;
- have a wide range of skills to pass on to you;
- know a lot about the organisation, how it works, where it's going;
- are patient, have time for you and whom you respect;
- can link you into a wider network of contacts.

Agree meeting places and times where you both feel comfortable. Be aware that it is unfortunately true that if your mentor is a man, or if you in your turn mentor a man, your meetings may give rise to gossip. Think how you will handle this. Allow sufficient time to build a good relationship.

Drop mentors if they are not effective and, in any case, recognise that mentoring relationships eventually come to an end. In your turn, mentor a younger woman. Be accessible. Don't be directive but be open with information, contacts, how and what to do.

Networks

Networking can help enormously by giving you access to information and contacts, encouragement and support. There are now many networks of different degrees of formality and membership so you should find one to suit your need. Most networks provide a membership list and the opportunity to meet as often as you need. They may produce news-sheets, run events and carry out studies. A network, however, will only be as useful as you make it. Use the contacts it gives and be ready to help in return.

SUMMARY – A WOMAN'S WAY

You will inevitably be visible. It's a strength – use it.

Be proud of your aspirations and announce them. People can't read what is in your mind.

Be demonstrably on top of your specialism.

Have a repertoire of management styles and move between them – don't get stuck in an authoritarian mode.

Use feminine qualities of compassion and understanding. Show concern for the individual and the team as well as for completing the task.

Treat everyone with respect – have high expectations and people will rise to meet them.

Don't be too proud to do mundane jobs – taking minutes, pouring tea – but make sure such jobs are shared with male colleagues.

Overcome traditional feminine submissive behaviour; don't apologise for asking for things to be done; don't be overly accessible.

Take care always to be well groomed and appropriately dressed. Present an image of a successful woman who cares about herself. Travel light – one bag.

Develop your own network. Help every woman who asks, whether you know her or not. Don't forget to use the network yourself.

FURTHER READING

Deal, Terrence E and Kennedy, Allen A, *Corporate Culture, The Rites and Rituals of Corporate Life*, Addison-Wesley, 1982

Kakabadse, Andrew, *The Politics of Management*, Gower, 1983

Josefowitz, Natasha, *Paths to Power*, Addison-Wesley, 1985

Kanter, Rosabeth Moss, *Men and Women of the Corporation*, Basic Books, 1977

Marlow, Hugh, *Success Individual, Corporate and National*, Institute of Personnel Management, 1984

Bradford, D L and Cohen, A R, *Managing for Excellence*, Wiley, 1984

Sargent, Alice G, *The Androgynous Manager, Blending male and female management styles for today's organisation*, American Management Association, 1983, 1981

Dickson, Anne, *A woman in your own right – Assertiveness and you*, Quartet, 1982

Garratt, Sally, *Manage your time*, Fontana, 1985

Shaevitz, Marjorie Hansen, *The Superwoman Syndrome*, Warner Books, 1984

Cooper, Cary and Davidson, Marilyn, *High Pressure Working Lives of women managers*, Fontana, 1982

Clutterbuck, David, *Everyone needs a mentor. How to foster talent within the organisation*, Institute of Personnel Management, 1985

Part II
MANAGING OTHER PEOPLE

Introduction: Understanding other people

Management involves getting things done through or by other people. Here is where most managers make their first mistake. 'It's quicker to do it myself', they say. 'The only way to make sure something is done correctly is to do it yourself.' And so on. This is not what management is about.

If you insist on doing things yourself, instead of getting them done by or through other people, a number of things happen:

- You fill your days doing things that should be done by other people.
- You waste your organisation's money: calculate the rate per hour your organisation is paying you and the rate per hour for those subordinate to you who should be doing what you're insisting on doing yourself. Subtract the difference. That is what your organisation is losing.
- You have less time available to do the things you are actually paid to do. This may be deliberate — you're too unsure of your ability to operate at the level you've been promoted to so you spend your time doing things you know you *can* do.
- Your subordinates do not have enough work to do and have to find other things to do, e.g. office politics, rumour mongering, industrial relations.
- Your subordinates do not have the opportunity to learn new skills.
- Morale and motivation drop.
- Your stress levels rise.

The answer, of course, is management through people: achieving *your* targets through *their* contribution, *their* work.

First, you need to be clear about what your targets are: what are you meant to achieve? Next, who are 'your' people? What are their skills, their strengths and weaknesses? A brief review of these points will provide a valuable basis for assessing current performance and planning for the future.

But it does not touch upon the heart of the matter. How do you marry 'your' people and their skills with the tasks and targets you need to achieve? In this section, we cover a range of skills you may need to help you: the people skills you may find useful; leadership and motivation; developing your people and using your support staff to best advantage; team building; performance appraisal and counselling; selection and interviewing; the skills of communication with staff, and making meetings work. And finally the skills of managerial politics, ever-present in organisations.

FURTHER READING

Handy, Charles B, *Understanding Organizations*, 3rd edition, Penguin, 1987. Detailed yet very readable introduction to organisations and the people who 'are' those organisations. An illuminating and useful overview of organisational theory, designed to be of practical use for the intelligent manager who wants to understand as well as manage.

10

Leadership and motivation

John Adair

Ideas about leadership have changed considerably in recent times. People today are better educated and more articulate. They can no longer be commanded in the same way as before. In industry trade unions are certainly more vigilant and often more militant. There needs to be much more involvement and participation at work — everyone recognises that fact. But to achieve these ends industry has to see its managers more as leaders. Indeed, every kind of working enterprise has acknowledged that it needs more and better leadership at all levels. How can it be developed?

The aim of this chapter is to help you to improve your own abilities as a leader. I am assuming that you have a direct personal interest in leadership. You may be in a position which you suspect — or have been told — requires leadership. You may already be an experienced leader, or you may be on the threshold of a career in management which will expect you to become a leader. In each case leadership matters to you. So how can you improve your leadership ability?

- You need to stimulate your own *awareness* of leadership in all its aspects. That means being aware when it is required in a given situation and aware when it is lacking. It also entails an awareness of the changing values of society (and industry which reflects those values) which will deepen your awareness of the importance of good leadership if free men and women are to cooperate effectively.
- You need to establish your *understanding* of the principles, requirements or functions of leadership. The poor leadership of many managers can be attributed, in part, to ignorance. No one ever told them the functions of leadership. So they miss out

some vital factor. A good leader understands the whole spectrum of leadership behaviour, and knows when a given function is required.

● You need to develop your *skills* in providing the necessary functions, not only *when* to do a particular action, and *why* it should be done, but also *how* it should be done.

WHAT YOU HAVE TO BE

'It is a fact that some men possess an inbred superiority which gives them a dominating influence over their contemporaries, and marks them out unmistakably for leadership.' So declared an eminent lecturer on leadership before the University of St Andrews in 1934. Since time immemorial people have sought to understand this natural phenomenon of leadership. What is it that gives a person this influence over his fellows?

The traditional or *qualities approach* to leadership suggests that the person who emerges as a leader in a group does so because he possesses certain traits. This view has been rejected by academics. They emphasise the lack of agreement among researchers on what constitutes these distinctive leadership qualities. Such a notion of leadership also seems to run counter to their assumptions about democracy.

Some researchers concede that leaders do possess the qualities expected or required in their working groups — the coxswain of the lifeboat, for example, clearly needs to exemplify the qualities of a good lifeboatman. But are there more general or universal qualities of leadership? Most people accept that leadership implies *personality*. Enthusiasm and warmth are often deemed to be especially important. There is also an impressive testimony in history that *character*, incorporating moral courage and integrity, matters enormously.

The following is a ranking of attributes rated most valuable at top level of management by a cross-section of successful chief executives.

1	Ability to take decisions	8	Understanding of others
2	Leadership	9	Ability to spot opportunities
3	Integrity	10	Ability to meet unpleasant situations
4	Enthusiasm		
5	Imagination	11	Ability to adapt quickly to change
6	Willingness to work hard		
7	Analytical ability	12	Willingness to take risks

13	Enterprise	20	Ambition
14	Capacity to speak lucidly	21	Single-mindedness
15	Astuteness	22	Capacity for lucid writing
16	Ability to administer efficiently	23	Curiosity
17	Open-mindedness	24	Skill with numbers
18	Ability to 'stick to it'	25	Capacity for abstract thought
19	Willingness to work long hours		

You may find it useful to complete the checklist in Figure 10.1 and consider what it reveals about your leadership qualities.

An understanding of leadership in terms of the qualities of personality and character which one person has to a greater degree than his fellows *is* relevant, but it is far from being the whole story.

WHAT YOU HAVE TO KNOW

The second major approach to understanding leadership focuses upon the situation. Taken to extremes this school declares there is no such thing as a born leader: it all depends upon the situation. Some situations will evoke leadership from one person − other situations from another. Therefore it is useless discussing leadership any longer in general terms. This *situational approach*, as it is called, holds that it is always the situation which determines who emerges as the leader and what 'style of leadership' he has to adopt.

This 'horses-for-courses' approach has some obvious advantages. It emphasises the importance of *knowledge* relevant to a specific problem − 'Authority flows to the man who knows', as one writer put it. There are broadly three kinds of authority at work:

- the authority of *position* − job title, badges of rank, appointment;
- the authority of *personality* − the natural qualities of influence;
- the authority of *knowledge* − technical, professional.

Whereas leaders in the past tended to rely upon the first kind of authority − that is, they exercised mastery as the appointed boss − today leaders have to draw much more upon the second and third kinds of authority.

List the five key characteristics or personal qualities which are expected or required in workers in your field:

	Good	Average	Weak
_____			
_____			
_____			

Now rate yourself in terms of each of them — Good, Average or Weak
Circle the number where you would place yourself on the following continuum:

Very introvert   Very extrovert
        5   4 3 2 1 2 3 4   5

(Leaders tend to be slightly more extrovert than introvert on this scale, i.e. they are ambiverts — mixtures of both)

	Yes	No
Have you shown yourself to be a responsible person?	☐	☐
Do you like the responsibility as well as the rewards of leadership?	☐	☐
Are you self-sufficient enough to withstand criticism, indifference or unpopularity from others and to work effectively with others without constant supervision?	☐	☐
Are you an active and socially participative person?	☐	☐
Can you control your emotions and moods — or do they control you?	☐	☐
Have you any evidence to suppose that other people think of you as essentially a warm person?	☐	☐
Can you give instances over the past three months where you have been deliberately dishonest or less than straight with the people that work for you?	☐	☐
Are you noted for your enthusiasm at work?	☐	☐
Has anyone ever used the word 'integrity' in relation to you?	☐	☐

Figure 10.1 Checklist — do you have some basic leadership qualities?

Technical competence or professional knowledge is a key strand in your authority. Yet expertise in a particular job is not enough; other more general skills are also required. These focus upon leadership, decision making and communication. These can be *transferred* as you

192

	Yes	No
Do you feel that your interests, aptitudes (e.g. mechanical, verbal) and temperament are suited to the field you are in?	☐	☐
Can you identify a field where you would be more likely to emerge as a leader?	☐	☐
How have you developed the 'the authority of knowledge'? Have you done all you can at this stage in your career to acquire the necessary professional or specialist training available?	☐	☐
Have you experience in more than one field or more than one industry or more than one function?	☐	☐

Do you take an interest in fields adjacent
to your own and potentially relevant?

sometimes	☐
never	☐
always	☐

How flexible are you within your field? Are you:

Good	You have responded to situational changes with marked flexibility of approach; you read situations well, think about them and respond with the appropriate kind of leadership	☐
Adequate	You have proved yourself in two situations, but you fear some situations; you are happiest only when the situation is normal and predictable	☐
Weak	You are highly adapted to one particular work environment and cannot stand change. You are often called rigid or inflexible	☐

Figure 10.2   Checklist – are you right for the situation?

move into a different situation in your field or change to a new sphere of work. Within your field you should aim to widen your knowledge of the work and develop the general abilities of leading others. That will increase your *flexibility*.

Even within the broad continuities of a particular industry or business the situation will change. Social, technical or economic developments will see to that. Are you ready?

The checklist in Figure 10.2 reviews the situational approach, and offers an opportunity for assessing your flexibility.

WHAT YOU HAVE TO DO

A third line of research and thinking about leadership has focused on the group. This *group approach*, as it may be called, has tended to see leadership in terms of functions which meet group needs: what has to be *done*. In fact, if you look closely at matters involving leadership, there are always three elements or variables:

- The leader − qualities of personality and character.
- The situation − partly constant; partly varying.
- The group − the followers: their needs and values.

The most useful theory about groups for the practical leader is that they are rather like individuals − all unique and yet all having things in common. What they share, according to this theory, is *needs*, just as every individual does. These needs are related to the *task*, *group* maintenance and the *individual*.

Task

One of the reasons why a group comes together is that there is a task which one person cannot do on his own. But does the group as a whole experience the need to complete the task within the natural time limits for it? Now a man is not very aware of his need for food if he is well fed, and so one would expect a group to be relatively oblivious of any sense of need if its task is being successfully performed. In this case the only sign of a need having been met is the satisfaction or elation which overtakes the group in its moments of triumph, a happiness which social man may count among his deepest joys.

Before such a fulfilment, however, many groups pass through a 'black night of despair' when it may appear that the group will be compelled to disperse without achieving what it set out to do. If the members are not committed to the common goal this will be a comparatively painless event; but if they are, the group will exhibit various degrees of anxiety and frustration. Scapegoats for the corporate failure may be chosen and punished; reorganisations might take place and new leaders emerge. Thus, adversity reveals the nature of group life more clearly than prosperity. In it we may see signs or symptoms of the need to get on effectively with whatever the group has come together to do.

Team maintenance

This is not so easy to perceive as the task need; as with an iceberg, much of the life of any group lies below the surface. The distinction that the task need concerns things and the second need involves people does not help overmuch. Again, it is best to think of groups which are threatened from without by forces aimed at their disintegration or from within by disruptive people or ideas. We can then see how they give priority to maintaining themselves against these external or internal pressures, sometimes showing great ingenuity in the the process. Many of the written or unwritten rules of the group are designed to promote this unity and to maintain cohesiveness at all costs. Those who rock the boat, or infringe group standards and corporate balance, may expect reactions varying from friendly indulgence to downright anger. Instinctively a common feeling exists that 'united we stand, divided we fall', that good relationships, desirable in themselves, are also essential means toward the shared end. This need to create and promote group cohesiveness I have called maintenance need.

Individual needs

Third, individuals bring into the group their own needs; not just the physical ones for food and shelter, which are largely catered for by the payment of wages these days, but also their psychological needs: recognition; a sense of doing something worthwhile; status; the deeper needs to give to and receive from other people in a working situation. These personal needs are perhaps more profound than we sometimes realise.

These needs spring from the depths of our common life as human beings. They may attract us to, or repel us from, any given group. Underlying them all is the fact that people need each other, not just to survive but to achieve and develop personality. This growth occurs in a whole range of social activities — friendship, marriage, neighbourhood — but inevitably work groups are extremely important because so many people spend so much of their waking time in them.

The work of A H Maslow forms a useful springboard into the deep water of understanding 'what makes people tick'. He suggested that individual needs are arranged in order of prepotence — the stronger at the bottom and the weaker (but more distinctively human) at the top (see Figure 10.3).

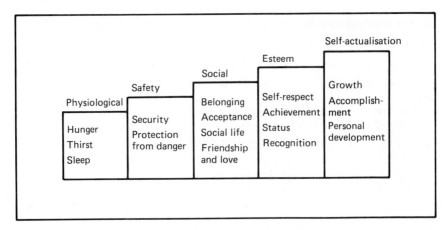

Figure 10.3   The hierarchy of needs

Physiological. These are man's physical needs for food, shelter, warmth, sexual gratification and other bodily functions.

Safety. These include the need to feel safe from physical danger and the need for physical, mental and emotional security.

Social. This covers the need for belonging and love, the need to feel part of a group or organisation, to belong to or be with someone else. Implicit in it is the need to give and receive love, to share and to be part of a family.

Esteem. These needs fall into two closely related categories – self-esteem and the esteem of others. The first includes our need to respect ourselves, to feel personal worth, adequacy and competence. The second combines our need for respect, praise, recognition and status in the eyes of others.

Self-actualisation. The need to achieve as much as possible, to develop one's gifts or potential to the full.

Maslow makes two interesting points about these needs. First, if one of our stronger needs is threatened we jump down the steps to defend it. You do not worry about status, for example, if you are starving. Therefore if you appear to threaten people's security by your proposed changes as a leader you should expect a stoutly defended response.

Second, a satisfied need ceases to motivate. When one area of need is met, the person concerned becomes aware of another set of needs within him. These in turn now begin to motivate him.

THE INTERACTION OF NEEDS

The three-circles diagram (Figure 10.4) suggests that the task, group and individual needs are always interacting with each other. The circles overlap but they do not sit on top of each other. In other words, there is always some degree of tension between them. Many of an individual's needs – such as the need to achieve and the social need for human companionship – are met in part by participating in working groups. But he can also run the danger of being exploited in the interests of the task and dominated by the group in ways that trespass upon his personal freedom and integrity.

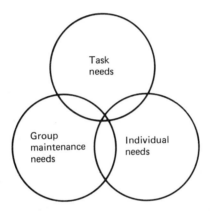

Figure 10.4   The three-circles model

It is fundamental that each of the circles must always be seen in relation to the other two. As a leader you need to be constantly aware of what is happening in your group in terms of the three circles. You can imagine one circle as a balloon getting bigger and another shrinking, or you can visualise the situation as if one circle is completely blacked out. Cut out a disc or use a cup to cover one circle now. At once segments of the other two circles are covered also. Using the disc and doing the following exercise you can begin to develop this awareness yourself.

Contrary to assumptions in the group dynamics movement, the

roles of leader and members should not be entirely confused. Leaders in real situations, as opposed to artificial 'laboratory' ones, are appointed or elected or they emerge – usually a combination of two of these methods. All group members share responsibility for the three areas but the appointed or elected leader is *accountable* for all three. By performing the functions of leadership he guides the group to:

- achieve the common task;
- work as a team;
- respect and develop its individual members.

See Figure 10.5 which shows these applied to the three circles.

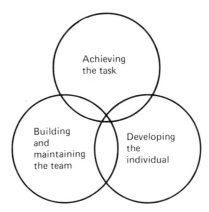

Figure 10.5   What a leader has to do

Understanding your position as the leader in relation to the three circles is vitally important. You should see yourself as half-in and half-out. There should be some social distance between you and the group, but not too much. The reason for maintaining this element of distance is not to enhance your mystique; it is because you may have to take decisions or act toughly in the task area which will cause reactions to be directed at you from the group and the individuals who face, in consequence, some unwelcome change. You have weakened yourself if you are on too friendly terms, or rather you have exposed yourself to pressures – 'we didn't expect that from *you*' – which you may not be able to handle.

There is an especial problem for leaders who are elected or appointed from among their workmates and remain with the same group. To exchange the close friendly relationship of colleagues for that of a leader and subordinates is not easy.

You can begin to see why a degree of self-sufficiency is important for a leader. Leadership is not about popularity, though it would be inhuman not to enjoy being liked. Because leaders tend to have social, even gregarious, natures they can find the inevitable brickbats that come their way hard to endure. But what matters in the long run is not how many rounds of applause a leader receives but how much *respect* he gains, and that is never achieved by being 'soft' or 'weak' in the task, team or individual circles. See Figure 10.6 for some relationships between leader and group.

BEHAVIOUR	USEFUL	NOT USEFUL
Leader emphasises distance	Where group knows him well before he became a leader. When group seems to want over-familiarity. When unpopular decisions are in the offing. When taking charge initially of a new group.	Where group already has a strong traditional sense of distance from its leaders. When people can be fully trusted not to become too familiar anyway.
Leader minimises distance	When there is lack of communication and trust between management and employees. Where all are roughly equal in knowledge and experience	Where the distance is already fairly minimal owing to the predecessor's style. Where it can be misinterpreted as familiarity
Leader strikes balance between closeness and distance	Most working situations.	Where the group needs corrective treatment after either too remote or too friendly leadership.

Figure 10.6   Position of leader in relation to group

The leader's social needs can be met partly by relations with his team, but it is always lonely at the top. He can never fully share the burden with those who work for him, or open his heart about his own doubts, fears and anxieties: that is best done with other leaders on his own level. If the leader's superior is doing his job he will help to make such meetings possible (they are often called management training courses!). Even more important, the leader's superior will himself be a resource; a pillar of strength and – at times – a shoulder to weep upon, should the leader require it.

	Yes	No
Have you been able to give specific examples from your own experience on how the three circles or areas of need — task, group and individual — interact upon each other?	☐	☐
Can you identify your natural bias:		
You tend to put the *task* first, and are low on group and individual	☐	☐
For you the *group* seems most important; you value happy relationships more than productivity or individual job satisfaction	☐	☐
Individuals are supremely important to you; you always put the *individual* before the task or the group for that matter. You tend to over-identify with the individual	☐	☐
You can honestly say you maintain a balance, and have feedback from superiors, colleagues, and subordinates to prove it	☐	☐
Do you vary your social distance from the group according to a realistic appreciation of the factors in the situation?	☐	☐
Can you illustrate that from experience?	☐	☐

Figure 10.7 Checklist — the three circles

Until you can do the essential work illustrated in Figure 10.5 your appointment as a leader will not be ratified in the hearts and minds of the group. Try out the checklist (Figure 10.7) to help you assess your performance.

MOTIVATION

Individual needs are especially important in relation to motivation, which is closely connected with leadership. One of the things that leaders are supposed to do is to motivate people by a combination of rewards and threats — the carrot and stick approach. More recent thought and some research suggests that you and I motivate ourselves to a large extent by responding to inner needs. As a leader you must understand these needs in individuals and how they operate, so that you can work with the grain of human nature and not against it.

Douglas McGregor has pointed out that managers often operated mainly under one of two sets of contrasting explicit or implicit

Theory X	Theory Y
People dislike work and will avoid it if they can	Work is necessary to human psychological growth. People want to be interested in their work and, under the right conditions, they can enjoy it
People must be forced or bribed to put out the right effort	People will direct themselves towards an accepted target
People would rather be directed than accept responsibility, which they avoid	People will seek, and accept responsibility under the right conditions. The discipline people impose on themselves is more effective, and can be more severe, than any imposed on them
People are motivated mainly by money People are motivated by anxiety about their security	Under the right conditions people are motivated by the desire to realise their own potential
Most people have little creativity — except when it comes to getting round management rules!	Creativity and ingenuity are widely distributed and grossly underused

Figure 10.8   Assumptions about people

assumptions about people, which he labelled theory X and theory Y (see Figure 10.8).

McGregor made the point that what we believe about a person can help that person to behave in that way (*the self-fulfilling prophecy*). If you tell someone you believe that they are bone idle, for example, they will tend to live up to your prediction. If you have a high regard for them, although that is not strictly justified by the facts, they may well rise to meet your expectations.

Another approach was taken by Frederick Herzberg. In the mid-1950s Herzberg and his associates interviewed 203 engineers and accountants in Pittsburg to find out why they found some events in their working lives highly satisfying and others highly dissatisfying. Herzberg divided the factors involved into two factors, which he called 'motivators' and 'hygiene factors' (see Figure 10.9). The motivators provided longer lasting satisfaction to individuals. The hygiene factors cause us dissatisfaction if they are wrong. But if you give a person more of a hygiene factor you will only either reduce their dissatisfaction or else give them a short lived sense of satisfaction.

Herzberg's 'two-factor' theory has been the cause of much controversial debate. Like most black and white, 'either–or' pieces of analysis, binary interpretation achieves the appearance of simplicity but only at the cost of sacrificing elements of the more complex truth. Money, for example, cannot be regarded only as a hygiene factor: it can serve as a tangible and necessary expression of recognition in some spheres. Nonetheless, Herzberg has had a powerful influence on the movement to increase job satisfaction in industry, a practical application of the wider understanding of individual needs.

Although Herzberg includes 'supervision' in his set of hygiene factors – those which cause great dissatisfaction when they are not met or are 'wrong' – he is clearly mistaken on this point. Leadership, a word he did not use, is more than just part of someone's job context; in many instances it is integral to the job itself. You only have to look at the list in Figure 10.9 to see that leaders can play a large part in the 'motivators'. Here are some of the ways.

Achievement

The function of evaluating means that the leader will give both the group and the individual feedback when the task is achieved. Sometimes there is direct feedback to the group or individual not involving the leader, as when a football team scores the winning goal in a cup final or a construction crew contemplates a finished suspension bridge. In other situations the feedback may come via the leader, who then needs to communicate success to the group.

Recognition

Managers are sometimes tempted to claim the credit for themselves after a success. If so, they are thinking of their own advancement. As a leader, however, you should seize every opportunity to motivate people by recognising their worth, services or contribution. Credit has to be shared, while you take the blame for yourself. At the first level of leadership, good leaders naturally meet recognition needs by acknowledging the contributions of individuals or of their team as a whole. If they receive some symbolic reward, such as a medal or citation, they interpret it as a recognition of the group's achievements as a whole. Equally, at a higher level, the leader may show recognition of the contributions of groups, departments or units to the success or prospects of success of the whole organisation.

HYGIENE FACTORS	DEFINITION/EXAMPLE
Company policy and administration	Availability of clearly defined policies; degree of 'red tape', adequacy of communication; efficiency of organisation
Supervision	Accessibility, competence and personality of the boss
Interpersonal relations	The relations with supervisors, subordinates and colleagues; the quality of social life at work
Salary	The total rewards package, such as salary, pension, company car and other 'perks'
Status	A person's position or rank in relation to others, symbolised by title, parking space, car, size of office, furnishings etc.
Job security	Freedom from insecurity, such as loss of position or loss of employment altogether
Personal life	The effect of a person's work on family life e.g. stress, unsocial hours or moving house
Working conditions	The physical environment in which work is done; the degree of discomfort it causes

MOTIVATORS	DEFINITION
Achievement	Sense of bringing something to a successful conclusion, completing a job, solving a problem, making a successful sale. The sense of achievement is in proportion to the size of the challenge
Recognition	Acknowledgement of a person's contribution; appreciation of work by company or colleagues; rewards for merit
Job interest	Intrinsic appeal of job; variety rather than repetition; holds interest and is not monotonous or boring
Responsibility	Being allowed to use discretion at work, shown trust by company, having authority to make decisions; accountable for the work of others
Advancement	Promotion in status or job, or the prospect of it

Figure 10.9   Herzberg's two-factor theory

The individuals or groups with high prestige or obviously vital functions tend to get all the recognition. A wise and able leader, however, will make sure that the apparently weak and insignificant individuals or groups also get their fair share of recognition. This equalising work both promotes or builds up a sense of being a team and also meets the needs of some individuals (or groups) who would otherwise receive no recognition in the world's market place, where such rewards go naturally to the most powerful, best looking, most active or simply the most apt at edging themselves into the limelight.

Job interest

If work is to be restructured in order to allow more job satisfaction someone has to have the vision to undertake it and the consultative skills to bring about the change. That means leadership. In particular it calls upon the leader's organising ability.

Responsibility

The leader is accountable for the results of his group. Marshal Pétain, when asked after the First World War, 'Marshal, did you personally win the Battle of Verdun?' replied, 'I've no idea, but I know very well who would have lost it'. But as a leader you should share the sense of responsibility as widely as possible.

The clue to developing responsibility is to extend the boundaries of trust. There can be an element of risk in this process, but there is no other practical alternative. Delegation, the entrusting of authority to someone to act as your deputy, is a major expression of trust and a means of creating responsibility. But delegation has some inherent risks that make otherwise excellent leaders reluctant to do it.

Advancement

Leaders play a vital part in promoting people. That gives them a certain power to motivate ambitious and able subordinates. They may not have the necessary jobs in their gift directly, but their word is often influential if not decisive. You can often motivate such an individual by reminding him that the prospects for advancement in position or status do exist.

Of course promotion is not a motivating force if it is not related to merit and performance. No one is going to work harder if advancement is reserved for the company's 'blue-eyed boys'. By stressing that ability and results are the necessary condition for promotion, you can create the right bracing atmosphere to motivate people to give their best.

Therefore, if you examine closely all the factors which positively motivate people at work, you can see that good leadership plays an important part in all of them. Consider your reactions to Herzberg's hygiene factors (see Figure 10.9), those elements that have the power to dissatisfy you if they are inadequate, but do not provide more than modest or short term satisfactions.

Leadership enters into all these factors whether we wish it to or not. If poor organisation and an apparently unfair rewards system leaves people dissatisfied, someone has to organise things properly, and that 'someone' is usually a leader. Good leadership resolves most of the dissatisfying factors implicit in being supervised and working with others: much of this chapter has been concerned with just those interpersonal relations. Your leadership should also contribute to reducing insecurity.

Status as one's position or rank in relation to others is an inescapable fact of life in working groups and organisations. Roughly speaking, higher status goes to those individuals who contribute more or hold the more responsible jobs. Most dissatisfaction over status is caused by apparently petty grievances over status symbols, such as parking space, offices or job titles. These often are symptoms of a deeper disease. For example, a very competitive person may make an issue of not having an office of his own because he sees that a potential rival has one, and he fears that he is being left behind in the race for promotion. Here the cause − insecurity − must be treated, not the symptom.

Personal problems may be caused by the effect of work on family life or the reverse process − some unhappiness at home which is causing difficulties at work. A good leader is sensitive to the individual: he can detect changes in norms of behaviour. As a leader it is important for you to demonstrate in some way or other that you are aware and that you do care. Even if you can do little or nothing, as in the case of a bereavement, the very fact of showing your sympathy does matter. In many instances, however, you can do something yourself to remove the obstacle which is damming and diverting natural motivation.

To assess your skills and attitudes, consider the checklist in Figure 10.10.

Managing other people

	Yes	No
Have you agreed with each of your subordinates his main targets and continuing responsibilities, together with standards of performance, so that you can both recognise achievement?	☐	☐
Do you recognise the contribution of each member of the group and encourage other team members to do the same?	☐	☐
In the event of success, do you acknowledge it and build on it? In the event of setbacks, do you identify what went well and give constructive guidance for improving future performance?	☐	☐
Can you delegate more? Can you give more discretion over decisions and more accountability to a sub-group or individual?	☐	☐
Do you show to those that work with you that you trust them, or do you hedge them around with unnecessary controls?	☐	☐
Are there adequate opportunities for training and (where necessary) retraining?	☐	☐
Do you encourage each individual to develop his capacities to the full?	☐	☐
Is the overall performance of each individual regularly reviewed in face to face discussion?	☐	☐
Does financial reward match contribution?	☐	☐
Do you make sufficient time to talk and listen, so that you understand the unique (and changing) profile of needs and wants in each person, so that you can work with the grain of nature rather than against it?	☐	☐
Do you encourage able people with the prospect of promotion within the organisation, or – if that is impossible – counsel them to look elsewhere for the next position fitting their merit?	☐	☐

Can you think of a manager by name who (a) delegates more effectively (b) less effectively than you do? What are the results in each case?

(a)

(b)

Figure 10.10   Checklist – motivating

A FUNCTIONAL APPROACH TO LEADERSHIP

The three approaches − qualities, situational and group − in the foregoing sections can be visualised as paths leading up to the summit of a mountain. If you go up one path you will be led nearer to the other two. In other words, rather than seeing them as *alternative* theories you should look upon them as *complementary* to each other. You may be content to hold all three approaches as distinct entities or 'paths' in your mind, or you may want some closer integration of them, a 'general theory' that will reconcile their differences.

In some respects I believe that the general approach that I have evolved over the last 20 years does serve to integrate or pull together those three threads. The functional leadership approach sees the functions as touching upon *all three circles,* either directly or indirectly. Moreover, it adds other functions to supplement the traditional list, especially in the team maintenance area. Functional leadership draws upon a number of traditions but subtly changes their offerings. The well established lists of management functions, for example, are applied to all three circles. Qualities can be interpreted in functional terms as well. Do they help you to achieve the task? Do they contribute to unity or are they disruptive? See Figure 10.11 for some examples.

Some qualities are especially important because they apply to all three circles − *enthusiasm* is an excellent example. Some enthusiasts are not leaders, but if you have the gift of enthusiasm you almost always will spark it off in other people. It produces greater commitment to the task, creates team spirit and enthuses the individual.

Other qualities are more latent. They can be called out and express themselves in behaviour in any of the three areas.

THE DIFFERENT LEVELS OF LEADERSHIP

Leadership happens on different levels. Originally work on leadership focused upon the small group. Recently my own work has extended the functional leadership concept to leaders at all levels within the sphere of work, including the chairmen and chief executives of organisations employing more than 100,000 people.

According to the well known 'Peter Principle', people tend to be promoted to the level of their incompetence. Some people are perfectly good leaders at one level, but they are less able to cope at the

Leadership characteristics	
Quality	Functional value
Task *Initiative*	A quality which appears in many research lists. It means the aptitude for initiating or beginning action; the ability to get the group moving
Perseverance	The ability to endure; tenacity. Obviously functional in many situations where the group is inclined to give up or is prey to frustration
Team *Integrity*	The capacity to integrate; to see the wood for the trees; to bind up parts into a working whole; the attribute that creates a group climate of trust
Humour	Invaluable for relieving tension in group or individual, or, for that matter, in the leader himself. Closely related to a sense of proportion, a useful asset in anything involving people!
Individual *Tact*	It expresses itself in action by showing sensitive perception of what is fit or considerate in dealing with others
Compassion	Individuals may develop personal problems both at home and work. The leader can show sympathetic awareness of this distress together with a desire to alleviate it

Figure 10.11 The functional approach to leadership qualities

next level up. What can help you to determine your own level is your ability to appreciate the subtle changes which take place in the task, the team and the individual as you go higher up the mountain.

The three circles still apply. In the task area the top leader is concerned more with longer term and broader aims. In the team area he has the double job of building and maintaining his immediate team of senior executives, and promoting a sense of unity among the diverse parts of the organisation. These two jobs are clearly inter-related. Again, the individual for him is both a senior leader – a known person in the senior team – and also each individual in the organisation. The latter will not be known personally or even by name in organisations of more than 500 people, but the top leader still needs to think constantly about that individual – and talk to him whenever possible.

At whatever level of leadership you are fitted for, by nature, training and experience, you should encourage thought about the task in terms of values as well as needs. Then the common purpose will overlap with the values of the groups and individuals in the organisation — including your own.

FURTHER READING

Adair, John, *Effective Leadership: a self-development manual,* Gower, 1983

Cribben, James J, *Effective Managerial Leadership,* American Management Association, 1977. A readable, research-based guide to the subject.

Hunt, John W, *Managing People at Work,* McGraw-Hill, 1979. A readable introductory guide to the fields of organisational behaviour — motivations, perception, communication, groups, roles, power, organisations, structures, managers, leaders, participation. Besides distilling some of the more enduring concepts and theories, the author does offer some interesting ideas of his own.

Garnett, John, *The Work Challenge,* The Industrial Society, 1973. Gives the Industrial Society's practical and down-to-earth approach to 'the human side of enterprise' with plenty of examples of good practice.

Prior, Peter J, *Leadership is not a Bowler Hat,* David and Charles, 1977. A rare example of a chief executive in industry giving his personal philosophy of leadership.

Gibb, C A (ed.), *Leadership: Selected Readings,* Penguin, 1969. An introduction to academic research on the subject. Some classic articles — and some opaque ones.

Stogdill, R M, *Handbook of Leadership,* Free Press, 1974. This weighty book sets out to be a systematic analysis and review of the literature on leadership, and is undeniably a useful collation of the published evidence on this subject, but practical leaders are likely to find it of limited value. The 'Summary and discussion' in Chapter 40 may, however, be found useful.

Herzberg, F, et al., *The Motivation to Work,* Wiley, 1959, and *Work and the Nature of Man,* World Publishing Co., 1966

McGregor, Douglas, *The Human Side of Enterprise,* McGraw-Hill, 1961

Maslow, A H, *Motivation and Personality,* Harper, 1954

11

People skills

Dr Peter Honey

People come in all sorts of shapes and sizes, which is another way of saying that people are complex and infinitely variable. Remarkably, however, there are some fundamental skills for handling people that are not dauntingly complex. This chapter will introduce you to those fundamentals and give sufficient practical advice to help you become even more skilful with people.

The chapter is written on the assumption that you have already acquired some people skills through an ad hoc process of learning from experience. There will undoubtedly be things you already do well, that no longer require any conscious effort on your part. The problem is that, quite understandably, we all tend to stick to the tried and tested and therefore repeat over and over again the same skills. In effect, therefore, we stop acquiring any new skills and this may mean we risk having too narrow a repertoire of skills to equip us adequately for the variety of people situations we are likely to encounter. This chapter will encourage you to experiment and broaden your repertoire of people skills.

WHAT ARE PEOPLE SKILLS?

People skills are behaviours, used face to face, that succeed in helping progress towards a useful outcome. Let's separate these ingredients and examine them more carefully. *Behaviours* are everything you say and do. As we shall see they are important because they are so immediately apparent to everyone you come face to face with and therefore have a direct effect on other people. *Face to face* covers a whole multitude of different interactions between people. It might be an informal chat with someone or it might be a formal meeting with a group of people. The point is that it is only during face to face en-counters that your behaviour is totally evident. During phone calls, by contrast, only what you *say* counts. Written communications are different because whilst what you write represents your behaviour even though you are not present, it isn't happening 'in flight' as is the case with face to face behaviours. A *useful outcome* is the third ingredient, for what would be the point of skills that led you to a useless outcome? The proof of the pudding is in the eating and the proof of people skills is that they make it as likely as possible that we achieve our objectives with people.

The trick is to get all three ingredients to come together in a smooth and easy symmetry. Face to face situations provide the context, objectives spell out the desirable end and behaviours are the means (see Figure 11.1).

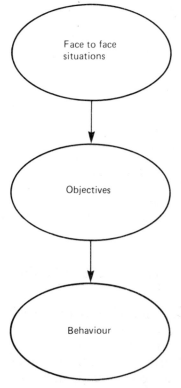

Figure 11.1 **Behaviour is the means to achieving your objectives in face to face situations**

WHY THE EMPHASIS ON BEHAVIOUR?

Quite simply because your behaviour is the only part of you that other people can observe. So far as other people are concerned, you are your behaviour for they cannot observe your underlying thoughts, motives, attitudes or feelings (see Figure 11.2). It follows, therefore, that your behaviour influences:

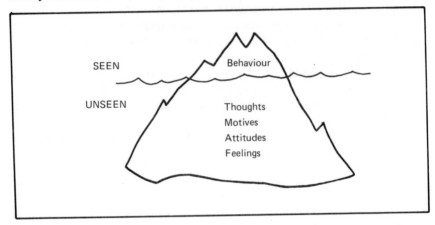

SEEN

Behaviour

UNSEEN

Thoughts
Motives
Attitudes
Feelings

Figure 11.2   Your behaviour is the only part of you that other people can observe

- other people's perceptions of you (i.e. whether they like or dislike you, trust or mistrust you and so on);
- other people's reactions to you (i.e. whether they behave helpfully or unhelpfully towards you).

The only people skills that matter, therefore, are encapsulated in the things you say and do when face to face with other people: in a word your *behaviour*.

WHAT ARE THE ADVANTAGES OF IMPROVED PEOPLE SKILLS?

There is no doubt that improving your people skills by extending your repertoire of behaviours is not easy. As with the acquisition of any skill it requires conscious effort as each skill is practised to the point where it becomes effortless. Since an investment of time and effort is required it is important to be sure that it will all be worthwhile. Some of the advantages of improved people skills are that you will be better at:

- Assessing and understanding face to face situations. You will thus benefit from fewer misunderstandings.
- Setting specific and realistic objectives for face to face encounters with people. You will thus benefit from being clear about what you are aiming at and successfully achieving it more often than not.
- Choosing and using behaviours that complement the circumstances and are appropriate to the objective. You will thus benefit by having an easier, and pleasanter, interaction en route to achieving your objective.
- Being aware of other people's behaviour and influencing it. You will thus benefit from being able to use your own behaviour as a powerful influence.

These are just some of the potential benefits of enhanced people skills. There are others which will emerge as the chapter pinpoints the skills more precisely.

CAN PEOPLE SKILLS BE IMPROVED?

The straight answer is yes, or course they can. You learned to behave the way you do now and there is nothing to stop you learning new behaviours. The secret of success is to learn from experience by:

- experimenting with new and different ways of behaving;
- reviewing what happened;
- concluding from the experience;
- planning what to do next (i.e. continue with the experiment, modify it to make it more successful, or try something quite different).

Unfortunately, people are often reluctant to embark on this learning process. There are all sorts of excuses to stay exactly the way you are now. 'You can't teach an old dog new tricks', 'Leave well alone', 'A leopard cannot change its spots'. Pessimism abounds. There is, however, nothing to prevent you from improving your people skills except yourself. If you don't want to enhance your skills, then no one or anything can force you to do so. The door to development is locked with the key on the inside. Other people can hammer on the door imploring you to open it; they can even entice you with attractive learning opportunities, but you and you alone hold the key. The choice is yours.

WHAT ARE THE FUNDAMENTAL PEOPLE SKILLS?

The fundamental skills are those which give us a process that is equally applicable in all situations. This is preferable to having a 'shopping list' of skills where the items on the list will inevitably vary in importance depending upon the situation. If, for example, you were in a foreign country where the water is suspect, then bottled water would be high on your shopping list. It would not, however, feature as a necessity on a shopping list in the UK. It is the same with people skills. If you are discussing how to solve a problem with a person who has more experience than you, then listening would be high on your list. If, on the other hand, you knew much more about what had to be done to solve the problem than the other person, then communicating clearly and testing the other person's understanding would be higher priorities.

We avoid this 'it all depends' qualification if we have a few fundamental skills on our list that apply in *all* situations. Just six are sufficient:

1 Analysing the situation
2 Establishing a realistic objective
3 Selecting appropriate ways of behaving
4 Controlling our behaviour
5 Shaping other people's behaviour
6 Monitoring our own and others' behaviour

The first three skills are essentially about thinking; the last three are about doing. It is the combination of both that is vital for there is no point in thinking without doing, nor in doing without thinking.

Notice also how these skills provide us with a timeless wisdom, applicable to all 'people situations' anywhere. Analysing the situation helps us to detect the circumstances that need to be heeded when setting a realistic objective. The objective, in turn, provides a backcloth against which to make choices about how best to behave. Each thinking skill cascades into the next and the three combined help us to be aware of the situation and to have worked out what to do about it. By consciously controlling our behaviour we are more likely to do the things that need to be done to achieve the objective. In so doing we influence other people's behaviour in the only way possible, via our own behaviour. And all the while we monitor, to keep tabs on what is happening and to get the feedback we need to make in-flight adjustments.

Let us look more carefully at each of these skills.

How to analyse situations

Remember that in the context of people skills we are concerned only with face to face situations. There are six key questions to ask of any situation you encounter:

1   Is the task/problem/subject matter to be discussed complex or routine?
2   On balance, who has the most know-how, you or the other people involved in the face to face discussion?
3   Is time very tight (as in a crisis) or is there sufficient time to discuss all aspects thoroughly before reaching a decision?
4   Is commitment from everyone essential or merely desirable?
5   Are the risks of making a mistake unacceptably high (financially and/or physically and/or from a credibility point of view) or are the risks within acceptable limits?
6   How many people will be present at the face to face discussion: just one other person, or a small group of say 6 – 8, or a medium sized group of 9 – 15, or a large group of 15 plus?

The answers to these key questions render enough data to move you on to the next skill.

How to set objectives for face to face interactions

An objective (for any activity, not just for face to face interactions) is a forecast of what you want to achieve at some point in the future. It might be a long term, medium term, or short term objective.

An immediate objective forecasts what you want to achieve by the end of the interaction.

Here is a recommended procedure for setting an immediate objective: First set yourself an *end result*. Do this by answering the question 'What do I want to achieve by the end of the interaction?' Second, work out some *indicators of success*. Do this by answering the question 'How shall I know that I have successfully achieved my end result?'

Here is an example of an objective set this way. Imagine you are going to meet someone (let's call him Bill) for the first time and you want to get off to a good start with him.

End result
By the end of the meeting I will have established rapport with Bill.

Indicators of success
Bill has asked at least six questions about me/my work.
Bill has 'opened up' to me about a significant current problem.
Bill has relaxed sufficiently to volunteer at least a couple of personal details (about outside interests, family, etc.).
We have booked a date, time and place for our next meeting.
Bill has specifically asked me to provide some additional data for our next meeting.
All achieved within 1½ hours (longer than Bill originally scheduled, i.e. he was 'happy' to overrun).

How to select appropriate behaviour

The secret is to limit the choices so that the vast spectrum of different behaviours is reduced to something manageable. It is best to think of your behaviour as a mixture of verbal (i.e. the things you say) and visual (i.e. the non-verbal things you do such as facial expressions, gestures with hands and arms and so on). Both verbal and visual aspects need attention. Let us look at verbal behaviour first.

Verbal behaviour

Limit yourself, at least initially until you become practised at using this method, to nine alternative behaviours:

1 *Seeking ideas.* Asking other people for their ideas.
2 *Proposing.* Putting forward ideas (possible courses of action) as statements.
3 *Suggesting.* Putting forward ideas as questions (i.e. 'How about doing so and so?').
4 *Building.* Developing someone else's idea.
5 *Disagreeing.* Explicitly disagreeing with something someone else has said.
6 *Supporting.* Agreeing with something someone else has said.
7 *Difficulty stating.* Pointing out the snags or difficulties with something someone else has said.
8 *Seeking clarification/information.* Asking other people for further clarification or information.
9 *Clarifying/explaining/informing.* Giving information, opinions and explanations.

These nine behaviours are not an exhaustive list but you will find they give you adequate scope. When it comes to selecting the most appropriate behavioural recipe, think of the behaviours as offering you a series of alternatives in the following way.

In a face to face interaction you could either:

seek ideas	or	give ideas (proposing or suggesting)
build	or	disagree
support	or	stating difficulty
seek clarification/ information	or	give clarification/ explanation or information

You will quickly see that the left hand side is a recipe for being participative and supportive towards other people. By contrast the right hand side is a recipe for being more directive and challenging towards other people. In the case of meeting Bill for the first time (see page 215) with the objective of establishing rapport with him, clearly the left hand behaviours are going to be more appropriate than the right hand ones. This will not always be so. With a different objective, an alternative mix of behaviours would be necessary. This illustrates the importance of first being clear about the objective, and second, thinking about which behaviours are appropriate to achieve it. As the objective alters so will the recipe of appropriate behaviours.

Visual behaviour

Visual or non-verbal behaviour covers a wide range of different aspects including:

- facial expressions
- eyes
- hand movements
- gestures with hands and arms
- leg movements
- body posture
- spatial distance and orientation.

In addition, there are some fringe areas such as clothes, physique and general appearance.

There is overwhelming evidence that visual behaviours play a larger part in communications between people than is usually supposed.

It seems that, without necessarily being able to describe how they do it, people make judgements and form impressions based on the visual behaviours they see other people using. Perhaps the most dramatic example of this is when people meet for the first time. Within seconds visual behaviours are sending signals which create a favourable or an unfavourable impression. Initial judgements are formed about whether the other person is friendly or unfriendly, confident or timid, trustworthy or untrustworthy, nice or nasty. Sometimes these first impressions are so strong that they linger stubbornly and defy revision even when different signals are being transmitted by subsequent visual behaviours.

Clearly the great advantage of thinking about your visual as well as your verbal behaviour is that you can choose visual behaviours that help rather than hinder progress towards your objective. You may be in the habit of using some visual behaviours that run the risk of giving the other person a poor impression of you. The secret of success is to concentrate on some simple combinations. If you do just one thing in isolation it probably will not have the desired effect because people gain a general, overall impression from a combination of:

- your facial expression and head movements
- gestures with your hands and arms
- the rest of your body including your legs.

All three aspects need to be practised so that they all come together to give the right impression.

Here are some combinations of visual behaviours. Practise doing less of the left hand ones and more of the right hand ones.

People will tend to see you as **defensive** if you:

Face and head
Don't look at the other person. Avoid eye contact or immediately look away when it happens.

Hands and arms
Clench your hands.
Cross your arms.
Constantly rub an eye, nose or ear.

If you want to come across as **friendly and cooperative** adopt the following combinations:

Face and head
Look at the other person's face. Smile.
Nod your head as the other person is talking.

Hands and arms
Have open hands.
Hand to face occasionally.
Uncross arms.

Body
Lean away from the other person.
Cross your legs.
Swivel your feet towards the door.

People will tend to see you as **anxious** if you:

Face and head
Blink your eyes frequently.
Lick your lips.
Keep clearing your throat.

Hands and arms
Open and close your hands frequently.
Put your hand over your mouth while speaking.
Tug at an ear.

Body
Fidget in your chair.
Jig your feet up and down.

People will tend to see you as **overbearing** and **aggressive** if you:

Face and head
Stare at the other person.
Have a wry 'I've heard it all before' type smile.
Raise your eyebrows in exaggerated amazement or disbelief.
Look over the top of spectacles.

Hands and arms
Point your finger at the other person.
Thump your fist on the table.
Rub the back of your neck.

Body
Uncross legs.
Lean forward slightly.
Move closer to the other person.

If you want to appear **confident** adopt the following combinations:

Face and head
Look into the other person's eyes.
Don't blink your eyes.
Thrust your chin forward.

Hands and arms
Keep hands away from your face.
'Steeple' your finger tips together.
If standing, have hands together behind you in an 'at ease' position.

Body
If seated, lean back with legs out in front of you.
If standing, keep straight.
Stay still, no sudden movements, no wriggling.

If you want to appear **thoughtful** try the following combinations:

Face and head
When listening, look at the other person for about three quarters of the time.
Tilt your head to one side slightly.

Body
Stand while the other person
remains seated.
Stride around.
If seated, lean right back with
both hands behind your head
and legs splayed.

Hands and arms
Hand to cheek.
Slowly stroke your chin or
pinch the bridge of your nose.
If you wear spectacles, take
them off and put an earframe in
your mouth.

Body
Lean forward to speak.
Lean back to listen.
Keep your legs still (no jiggling).

How to control your behaviour

Obviously there is little point in using the first three skills (analysing
the situation, setting objectives and selecting appropriate behaviours)
if, come the important face to face interaction, you fail to keep your
behaviour under control. The whole point of controlling your
behaviour is to avoid doing things that will be detrimental to achieving your objective and to force yourself to do sufficiently the things
that will aid and abet its achievement. The word 'force' is used
deliberately since you will undoubtedly find that, initially at any rate,
you will need to stick consciously to a behaviour plan. You are more
likely to be able to do this if your plan is:

- specific in spelling out precisely which verbal and visual
  behaviours to use;
- realistic in pinpointing a few key behaviours to use or avoid,
  rather than being over-ambitious by listing too much.

The other important aid to good control is to be selective about when
you will consciously practise using your people skills. Initially, it may
be sensible to choose face to face interactions where the risks of
making mistakes or being more hesitant than usual are not too great.
It also helps to practise on people who are likely to be supportive of
your efforts rather than apathetic or hostile.

How to shape other people's behaviour

This is the key to the whole business. Clearly if your behaviour made
no difference to the reactions of the people you dealt with then people
skills would be of no consequence and this chapter would never have

been included in this Handbook. The plain fact is, however, that the way you behave has a considerable influence on the way other people behave in face to face situations. The precise effects of the verbal behaviours have been more thoroughly investigated than those of the visual behaviours. Let us look at each behaviour in turn and see their shaping abilities.

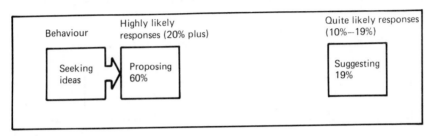

Figure 11.3   Responses to seeking ideas

Seeking ideas is a powerful behaviour. Nine times out of ten it is successful in provoking some ideas from the other person (Figure 11.3). It is a helpful behaviour to use whenever you need to pick someone else's brains.

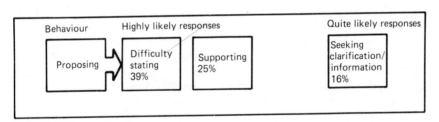

Figure 11.4   Responses to proposing

Proposing ideas unfortunately provokes difficulties or objections more often than it wins support (Figure 11.4). If you want to 'flush out' people's reservations then proposing is a good behaviour to use. If, on the other hand, you want to make it more likely that there will be agreement to your idea then the next behaviour is a safer bet.

Suggesting ideas is a more effective way of gaining agreement than proposing ideas (Figure 11.5). There are, of course, no guarantees that it will succeed because your idea may be such a rotten one that even though it is suggested it runs into difficulties. The actual

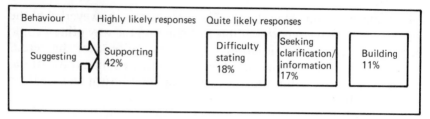

Figure 11.5   Respones to suggesting

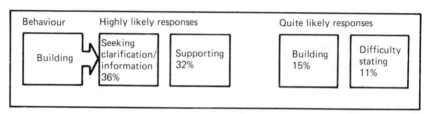

Figure 11.6   Responses to building

statistics reveal that four times out of ten a suggestion is followed by an agreement and that isn't a bad rate.

Building on someone else's idea is a powerful way to get their wholehearted support. Despite this, building is a fairly rare behaviour. It seems that people find it easier to find fault with ideas than to build them up into something better (Figure 11.6). This is a good example of having a choice. People who think about their behaviour are more likely to try building than people who are in the habit of immediately criticising ideas. The fact that seeking clarification is so prevalent reminds us what a potentially confusing behaviour building can be. The lesson is to 'flag' building so that people are in no doubt, and then supporting and more building are the most likely reactions.

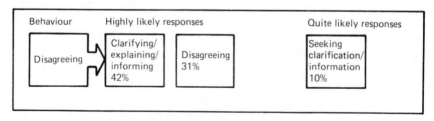

Figure 11.7   Responses to disagreeing

Disagreeing on seven out of ten occasions triggers a defensive reaction or even further disagreements (Figure 11.7). It is interesting how often people get locked into a disagreeing 'spiral' where one disagreement breeds another which, in turn, breeds another and so on. Disagreeing is very much a last resort. It is best to try some of the more constructive options first.

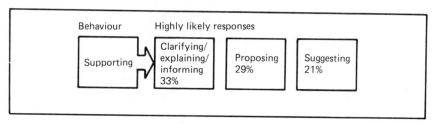

Figure 11.8   Responses to supporting behaviour

Agreeing with something someone else has said is a powerful way to encourage them to go on and say more. Eight times out of ten this will be the effect (Figure 11.8). Agreeing is therefore a useful behaviour if you want to gain more information from the other person. It isn't an appropriate behaviour if you want them to shut up.

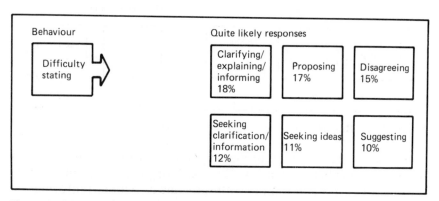

Figure 11.9   Responses to difficulty stating

Pointing out difficulties is a very common behaviour but it is one of the riskier ones because research shows that it is far from certain how people will take it (Figure 11.9). Marginally, the most likely reaction is to offer some clarification or explanation. However, people often take umbrage and start disagreeing or, if you persist with difficulties, they may give up and go and find someone more positive to talk to. You need to watch carefully to see whether pointing out difficulties is hindering or helping the proceedings.

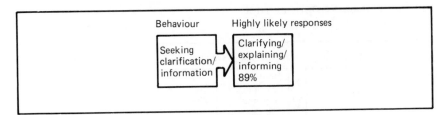

Figure 11.10   Responses to seeking clarification/information

No surprises with the next category (Figure 11.10). If you ask for clarification then nine times out of ten you will get it. Seeking clarification is a frequent behaviour that exerts a powerful influence over the behaviour of the other person. This is very useful behaviour when trying to get to the bottom of things and when you need to tease information out of the other person.

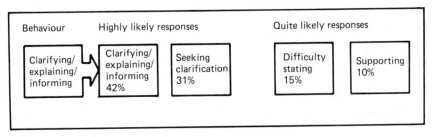

Figure 11.11   Responses to clarifying/explaining/informing

Informing is the behaviour that happens more often than any other in conversation between people. This isn't surprising, of course, since the overall purpose of talking with someone is to impart information of some kind. The most interesting aspect is how informing breeds informing, which breeds informing and so on in what can be a time-consuming loop (Figure 11.11). Sometimes this is appropriate and necessary. At other times the loop amounts to going round in circles and not getting anywhere fast enough.

The reason why people often prolong the informing loop is because it is a relatively 'safe' way to pass the time. When you offer a piece of information, you don't commit yourself in quite the same way that you do when you propose or suggest an idea.

The lesson from all this? Simply that the behaviours you use have known shaping effects on the behaviours you get back from other people. The data underline the fact that you are more likely to succeed with people if you think about your behaviour and select and use behaviours that help rather than hinder progress towards your objective. This process is enhanced still further if you adopt visual behaviours that reinforce what you are saying. It is the combination of verbal and visual that has the desired effect.

How to monitor your own and others' behaviour

This is purely a matter of practice. Since all behaviour, whether verbal or visual, is observable in a straightforward way there is no reason why you shouldn't develop your powers of observation. When you next attend a 'boring' meeting where some of the agenda items do not directly involve you, try monitoring the behaviour of the participants. See if you can spot the differences between proposing and suggesting, disagreeing and difficulty stating. Count how many times clarification is sought and given. Study people's attempts to build on one another's ideas. Scrutinise each person in turn to see what non-verbal characteristics they display when they are speaking as opposed to when they are listening. Watch to see when people lean forward in their chairs and when they lean back. Monitor who speaks to whom. Are any patterns that emerge associated with where people are seated round the table? There is no end to it, and certainly there is no excuse for being bored at a meeting ever again! Another obvious source of practice is when watching television, especially debating programmes such as *Question Time*. To study visual behaviour, just turn the sound down.

The whole idea of gaining practice in these ways is so that monitoring behaviour becomes second nature. When you yourself are a busy participant in an interaction it is best to monitor behaviour on an exception basis rather than try to cope with everything. So, for example, concentrate on the unexpected behaviours. If you were hoping that someone would be positive and develop your ideas, be especially alert to their disagreeing and difficulty stating and think hard about how best to respond to nudge their behaviour towards building and supporting. (Do this by being careful to suggest rather than propose and by seeking ideas from them and proceeding to build on them yourself. There are always hopeful things you can do *if* you use your people skills).

ARE THERE ALTERNATIVE PEOPLE SKILLS?

That concludes our examination of the six fundamental people skills. Acquiring them is not easy but the advantages of doing so are considerable and the skills are both sensible and pragmatic.

There are, of course, many different ways of describing people skills. We have focused purely on verbal and visual behaviours. Once you have mastered the fundamentals, what other skills could you practise? For the sake of brevity we will finish the chapter by looking at three interesting possibilities.

Management styles

You might find it useful to think about your characteristic style of management, when it is appropriate and when it isn't, and when to adopt consciously a different style from your usual one. One of the simplest ways to classify alternative management styles is shown in Figure 11.12.

Since most managers seem to find it easier to be directive than to use the other styles it is good advice to:

● Think delegative first.
● If delegative is inappropriate in the circumstances then next think collaborative.
● If collaborative is inappropriate in the circumstances then next think consultative.
● If consultative is inappropriate then go ahead and be directive.

This plan ensures that you consider all the alternatives. All four styles are appropriate at some time. The skills we looked at earlier of analysing situations and establishing objectives are the key to deciding when to use which management style.

Ego states

You might have come across an approach to people skills called transactional analysis. It originated from the bestseller *Games People*

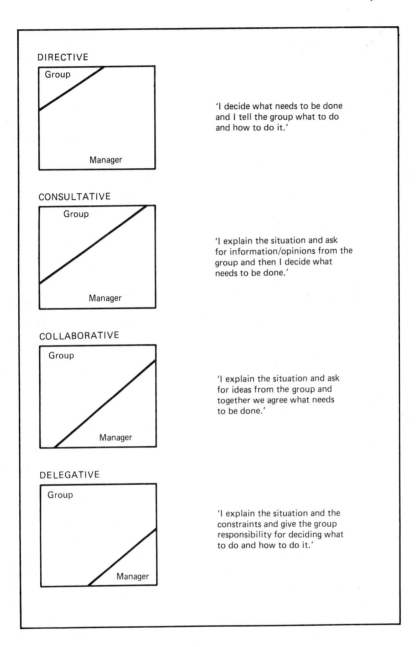

DIRECTIVE

Group

Manager

'I decide what needs to be done and I tell the group what to do and how to do it.'

CONSULTATIVE

Group

Manager

'I explain the situation and ask for information/opinions from the group and then I decide what needs to be done.'

COLLABORATIVE

Group

Manager

'I explain the situation and ask for ideas from the group and together we agree what needs to be done.'

DELEGATIVE

Group

Manager

'I explain the situation and the constraints and give the group responsibility for deciding what to do and how to do it.'

Figure 11.12   Alternative management styles

Play by Dr Eric Berne. A core concept in transactional analysis is a framework for describing three different ways of behaving.

The three behaviour categories, or ego states, are called Parent, Adult and Child. In TA they are distinguished from *real* parents, adults and children by the use of capital letters.

Parent behaviour stems from feelings about what is proper, right and wrong. This provides discipline and protection. The Parent speaks in dogmatic, autocratic terms with a heavy emphasis on controlling. Parent behaviour is subdivided into:

- Critical Parent behaviour: critical, prejudicial, moralising or punitive. Typical non-verbal clues are the pointed finger, shaking head, handwringing, arms folded, foot tapping, wrinkled brow, sighing, impatient snorts and grunts. Typical verbal clues are 'always, never, remember, you ought to know better, you should do better, don't do that, you should never do that, that's wrong, stupid, ridiculous, absurd, how dare you'.

- Nurturing Parent behaviour: nurturing, protective, sympathetic and comforting. Non-verbal examples are: a comforting touch, patting a person on the shoulder, consoling sounds. Verbal examples are: 'there, there, you poor thing, try again, don't worry'.

Adult behaviour involves gathering information, evaluating it and using it to make, and implement decisions. The Adult has the capacity to monitor and, if necessary, update Parent and Child tapes. Adult behaviour stems from thinking rather than feeling. Non-verbal examples are; postures indicating interest, listening, thinking and generally being 'with it'. Verbal examples are: 'why, what, where, when, who, how, alternatives, possible, probably, relatively, practical, feasible'.

Child behaviour stems from feelings, either of joy or of sorrow, and, therefore, tends to be spontaneous. Child behaviour is subdivided into:

- Natural Child behaviour is entirely dictated by feelings; it includes being impulsive, inquisitive, curious, affectionate and playful. NC is also fearful, self-indulgent, self-centred, rebellious and aggressive. Non-verbal examples are: tears, temper tantrums, no answer, biting lower lip, downcast eyes, shoulder shrugging. Verbal examples are: 'look at me!, Nobody loves me. That's mine, can't, won't, that's fun, I love you, whoopee!'

- Adapted Child behaviour is a toned down version of Natural Child: it is literally an adaptation of completely natural impulses so that they are more acceptable to other people. Non-verbal examples are: giggling, teasing, flirting, pouting and whining. Verbal examples are: 'please, thank you, I wish, I'll try, please help me, I don't care, I don't know'.

The whole idea of this classification system is to have a practical method of monitoring different modes of behaviour in ourselves and in others we encounter. A main tenet in transactional analysis is to practise using our Adult ego states to weigh up situations and decide whether Parent, Child or Adult behaviour would best suit. In other words, the Adult is encouraged to use the six basic skills that we examined earlier in this chapter. Many people have found the ego states a helpful way of looking at behaviour and bringing it under conscious control.

Assertiveness

Finally, you might find the assertiveness approach a useful way to enhance your people skills. This approach tends to specialise on behaviour in tricky situations where your needs are in conflict with the needs of other people. Such situations are made worse or better depending on how you handle them. Broadly you have three choices. You can be assertive, submissive, or aggressive.

Assertive behaviour involves standing up for your own rights in such a way that you do not violate another person's rights and expressing thoughts, feelings and beliefs in direct, honest and appropriate ways.

For example, someone keeps disagreeing with your ideas. An assertive response would be:

> I appreciate that you want to see improvements as much as I do, and yet you keep finding fault with my ideas. What can I suggest that would be more acceptable to you?

So assertiveness is based on the beliefs that we have needs to be met, others have needs to be met; we have something to contribute, others have something to contribute. It is characterised by statements that value ourselves and also value others.

Submissive behaviour – you are being submissive when you:

- fail to stand up for your rights or do so in such a way that others can easily disregard them;

- express your thoughts, feelings and beliefs in apologetic diffident or self-effacing ways;
- fail to express honest thoughts, feelings or beliefs.

For example, someone keeps disagreeing with your ideas. A submissive response would be:

> Well, I suppose you've got a point. My ideas probably wouldn't have worked out in practice.

So submission is based on the belief that our own needs and wants are less important than those of other people. It is characterised by long, justifying explanations, often putting ourselves down whilst accommodating others.

Aggressive behaviour. You are being aggressive when you:

- stand up for your own rights in such a way that you violate the rights of another person;
- express thoughts, feelings and beliefs which may be honest or dishonest, but in inappropriate ways.

For example, someone keeps disagreeing with your ideas. An aggressive response would be:

> To hell with all your objections. Just listen to me and I'll spell out what I want to happen.

So aggression enhances ourselves at other people's expense; it puts the other person down. It is based on a belief that our opinions are more important than other people's. It is characterised by blaming other people, blaming outside factors, by showing contempt and by being hostile/attacking or by being patronising.

The assertiveness approach urges us, when faced with a conflict situation, to hang on to assertive behaviour rather than succumbing to our emotions and either being submissive or aggressive. Once again this is only possible if we think about our behaviour *vis-à-vis* the situation we are in and the objectives we wish to achieve.

CONCLUSION

Here, finally, is a checklist (Figure 11.13) of behaviours that hinder and behaviours that help. It is not an exhaustive list but you will find more than enough to start you off. To succeed, practise doing less of the hindering behaviours and more of the helpful behaviours.

HINDERING BEHAVIOURS	HELPING BEHAVIOURS
Lean away with hands clenched, arms crossed and legs crossed	Lean forward with hands open, arms uncrossed and legs uncrossed
Look at the other person for less than 50% of the time	Look at the other person for approximately 60% of the time
Listen silently with no continuity noises and/or interrupt before the other person has had their say	When listening nod and make 'I'm listening' noises such as 'um' 'yes' 'really'
Have a blank expression	Smile
Sit opposite the other person	Sit beside the other person or if this isn't possible, at a 90° angle to them
Don't use the other person's name or use it artificially so that it jars	Use the other person's name early on in the transaction
Don't ask questions or ask closed questions	Ask the other person open questions
Offer no summaries and don't check your understanding	Summarise back to the other person what you think they have said
Stick rigidly to saying things that are routine and standard	Say things that refer back to what the other person has said
Don't acknowledge the other person's expressed feelings or point of view	Show empathy by saying you understand how the other person feels and can see things from their point of view
Acquiesce or never explicitly agree with the other person	When in agreement with the other person, openly say so and say why
Pick holes in the other person's ideas	Build on the other person's ideas
Criticise the other person	Be non-judgemental towards the other person
Disagree first then say why	If you have to disagree with the other person, give the reason first then say you disagree
Be defensive and never admit to any inadequacy	Admit it when you don't know the answer or have made a mistake
Be secretive and withhold information from the other person even though it affects them	Openly explain what you are doing, or intending to do, for the other person
Have visual and verbal behaviours out of step with each other	Be genuine, with visual and verbal behaviours telling the same story
Remain aloof and don't touch the other person	Whenever possible, touch the other person
Don't give the other person anything	Give the other person something even if it is only a name card, or piece of paper with notes on it

Figure 11.13 Checklist — hindering and helping behaviours

Remember the choice is yours and, so far as other people are concerned, *you are your behaviour*.

FURTHER READING

If Looks could Kill: The Power of Behaviour, Video Arts, 1986

Honey, Peter, *Face to Face: A Practical guide to Interactive Skills*, Gower, 1987

Back, Ken and Back, Kate, *Assertiveness at Work: A practical guide*, McGraw-Hill, 1982

Morrison, James H and Hearne, J J, *Practical Transactional Analysis in Management*, Addison-Wesley, 1977

12

Recruitment and selection

P T Humphrey

No matter what has been written or said about recruitment and selection, everyone believes that he is an expert in this field. It is probably the one area of personnel management where 'the professional' is inevitably challenged by 'the layman', whatever the circumstances. Nevertheless, it is one of those situations where often a manager or supervisor has to face up to the problem of becoming totally involved in the recruitment and selection process without quite knowing how to tackle what is in reality a complicated task, in spite of the apparent simplicity of the ultimate decision to be taken — 'to hire or not to hire'.

However, before going into detail a few basic points must be established and emphasised. Almost everyone in any organisation has at some stage the responsibility for requesting materials or finance in order to carry out their work effectively. These requests which can lead to heated discussions between superior and subordinate, or between peers, are essentially concerned with inanimate objects — 'vegetable, mineral or abstract'. But the request for a replacement as someone is leaving the organisation, or for more staff to carry out the work, will inevitably lead to consideration of the 'animal' category. The true relevance of this is the ability, apart from the right, of this 'animal' category to hold and undoubtedly voice opinion and comment, constructive or destructive, about the way in which the recruitment and selection process is handled. This 'answering back' facility is acknowledged by all professional recruiters, who ignore it at their peril. It is probably the one point which many managers do not appreciate, for when they are dealing with the accustomed human problems within their own job functions they are dealing with known people, in a specific and generally accepted framework. But job applicants are not subject to, nor do they hold, the corporate values (real or imaginary) that form part of the everyday working lives of those already employed.

The second point, which follows on naturally from the first, is that the principle of 'do unto others as you would be done by' underpins the total recruitment and selection procedure. The job applicant, whatever the level expects to receive the normal human courtesies not only in the face to face situation but also at all other points of contact during the decision making process. In spite of the obvious economic nature of employment, a great deal of attention must be placed on the underlying social processes.

Third, it is important not only to acknowledge but also to understand that the situation is not one sided as far as the decision taking process is concerned. The conclusion of a recruitment task does not occur with the decision 'we'll offer you the job', this is merely a unilateral decision. The conclusion in reality only comes when the applicant says 'thanks, I accept your offer'.

In any organisation there is at the same time both a buyer's market and a seller's market as far as jobs are concerned. It is important to distinguish between them, for while the same basic administrative approach is both necessary and applicable, the tactics to be adopted can differ widely. This is equally true of shop floor and boardroom situations. The recruitment process has its part to play in the public relations policy of the organisation. The projection of the corporate image is reinforced through the job advertisement and even more in the handling of candidate response by the recruiters who themselves have a unique opportunity for reinforcing as well as maintaining the image. Many recruitment 'failures' can be attributed to the lack of consistency between the organisation's perceptions of itself and those it projects through the media and its current staff. Bearing these points in mind the objective now is to provide managers at all levels no matter whether they are experienced or inexperienced, with positive guidelines to tackle the job effectively, and to gain, by the end of the day, a sense of personal satisfaction from a task well done.

BASIC PLANNING AND PROCEDURE

Everyone will realise and readily acknowledge that all organisations including one's own family must have financial resources in order to function at all, and in order to utilise these financial resources correctly some systematic methods must be devised and implemented to account for income and expenditure. But not everyone is prepared to acknowledge that the same principle has to be adopted in relation to recruiting and terminating staff, in spite of the fact that no organisation can function without staff! The total cost of recruiting an employee of average skill can be assessed at approximately three to four times the weekly wage, and very much more for senior grades. So any organisation that does not set up an effective system for handling recruitment is likely to put at risk sums of money in the immediate short term which under normal circumstances would be referred to board level for approval.

Statistical information on the numbers already employed in the organisation categorised by status, department, works or site, and subdivided in relation to occupational skills required, levels of work involved or merely by job titles, must be available in order to provide a reference point from which the whole procedure begins.

The subsequent steps are as follows:

Stage 1   Run-up

1   Preparation, authorisation and issue of a requisition for replacements or additional staff
2   Gathering information about the job
3   Checking against obvious internal sources
4   Advertising the vacancy – internally and externally
5   Processing of applications

Stage 2   Face to face – the employment interview

6   Setting up the interview
7   Conducting the interview
8   Administering appropriate tests
9   Making the appointment

Stage 3   Follow-through

10   Introducing the new employee to the organisation
11   Following up the progress of the new employee
12   Reviewing and evaluating the recruitment and selection process.

On examination, even the most ad hoc example of recruitment reveals that the above procedure has been followed and that often the tactics/approach/mechanics vary in relation to the nature of the job to be filled. In many instances it is the level of the vacancy which is the determining factor. Therefore, where applicable, attention will be drawn to the different requirements in recruiting staff at the following levels:

- managerial, including supervisory
- clerical and technical
- operational.

STAGE ONE: THE RUN-UP

Requisitions

The need for a sound method of producing the right statistical information, such as number employed, labour turnover and absenteeism, has already been stressed. However, even in cases where this information exists, many organisations are quite indifferent to the way in which requests for replacement or additional staff are made. In many respects the underlying attitudes which permitted this have been altered by economic circumstances. Closer scrutiny of labour costs is taking place and the requisition for staff at all levels has almost the same cachet now as the capital requisition.

A staff requisition form should include:

- Name and location of originating department
- Job title
- Main job function
- Salary or grade
- Reason for requisition
  (a) replacement
  (b) new appointment
  (c) additional appointment
- Required by: (date)
- Signatures .... Department Head: Authorised date

While it is appreciated that it does take a certain (minimal) amount of managerial time to complete such a requisition, nevertheless its value to the person responsible for recruitment is incalculable. The main advantage is that it leaves no room for doubt. No one has to rely on the recollection of what was said about the job during a lunchtime conversation which ranged from detailed shop talk through gossip to personal letting hair down. Far too much valuable managerial time can be wasted in reference back by telephone or by personal visit to verify the position. Certainly the time of the recruiter can be spent to better effect in the next step of the process.

Job information

A great deal of confusion exists over the different terms used in this area. The term 'job description' means different things to different people, and indeed the context in which the term is used can alter its apparent meaning. Nevertheless an attempt has been made by the Department of Employment in its publication *Glossary of Training Terms* to standardise usage of such terms:

> A *job description* is a broad statement of the purpose, scope, duties and responsibilities of a particular job.
> A *job specification* is a detailed statement of the physical and mental activities in a job.

However, jobs must be viewed as part of a dynamic organisation, with the result (as so many management writers have said) that the job description presents at best only a point-in-time interpretation. Consequently many managers who inevitably feel 'pushed' in the everyday situation will question the necessity of having a job description at all. But there are simple operational reasons which can help in the argument to overcome such resistance. These are:

- The job description acts as a basic means of communication between the manager and the recruiter as far as the position to be filled is concerned.
- It is an invaluable mechanism for discussing and finalising the tactical approach to the selection process.
- It can yield vital information for the candidates who have come to have a high level of expectation in terms of job information. This certainly has a useful 'plus effect' in promoting confidence about the organisation amongst the candidates.
- It ensures that there is an accepted factual basis from which information can be selected for advertising purposes.
- Finally it provides the reference point against which all decisions taken and judgements made can be evaluated.

Time sensibly spent on this important preparatory work can yield significant dividends in preventing over-interviewing and indeed in ensuring that advertising and other expense is used to maximum effect.

The job description

What information, therefore, needs to be included in the job description? The following items are essential no matter what level of appointment is being considered:

- Job title: this must be self explanatory wherever possible and certainly where either unusual technical terms or terms specific to the organisation are used, adequate explanation must be given.
- Name of department: as above.
- Accountability: the job title of the person to whom the job holder is responsible.
- Main job function: a brief but lucid statement of the purpose of the job.
- Responsibilities for people and/or equipment. No need to detail every nut and bolt, but include categories and numbers of people to be supervised together with major items of equipment.

Additional items are required when considering managerial, supervisory or technical positions. These include:

- Limits of authority – particularly in relation to spending money.
- Levels of contact – this is of special importance in a multi-divisional organisation and with working relationships outside the organisation.

Useful questions to keep in mind during this process of gathering information and writing the job description include:

- Is the informant's statement accurate?
- What degree of bias is contained in the statement?
- Who can provide a second opinion?
- Does the written description contain all the relevant facts?
- Is it accurate?
- Can the layman understand it? (In other words is it too simple or too complicated?)

The job specification

The job description now has to be extended and interpreted specifically in relation to the physical and mental activities of the job, and the consequent demands to be made on the job holder.

While it might appear that there is considerable difference in requirements at the various levels of appointment, nevertheless, five basic categories of the job specification can be defined as follows:

- qualifications, knowledge appropriate to the job
- specific skills, abilities and aptitudes required
- experience required
- personal attributes
- physical attributes.

These categories can be qualified as appropriate for each selection by a scale of relevance – vital/desirable/of no consequence.

Qualifications. This category is the bane of every recruiter's life, for more heat can be generated over this than almost any other topic to do with recruitment. The standpoint to take must be 'is it relevant?'. Is a PhD really vital to do the job of sales manager in an electronics firm? It might be. On the other hand it is certainly not a vital qualification for the sales manager with a confectionery firm. A sense of reality must be maintained, for it is just as easy to be swayed by degrees and professional qualifications as it is by medals and decorations. Indeed the relevance of City and Guilds qualifications to the craftsman and technician is probably more deserving of the recruiter's attention than has been the case in the past.

Instead of qualifications it is often more advisable to list areas of knowledge which are required, e.g. plastic injection moulding for a production manager, standard costing for a senior cost clerk, export procedures for a shipping clerk.

Specific skills, abilities and aptitudes. This category is not to be regarded as a rag-bag for glossy management 'in' phrases, which result merely in directing attention away from the main purpose. Rather the intention is to define accurately (and quantify if at all possible) those factors which are regarded as necessary to achieving success in the job. For instance the skills required in negotiating with trade union officials, or the different skills required in the negotiation of commercial contracts with suppliers, must be stated in the appropriate specifications. Abilities to be considered can include the ability to sell 'an idea' or a product, or even the ability to see 'the wood for the trees'. Aptitudes that readily spring to mind are verbal, numerical and mechanical, where great strides have been made in assessing and quantifying them among the population at large. All this must be geared to reality, and fanciful ideas of what might be required should be discounted. Simplicity really is the keynote in this section.

Experience required. This is most important, and every attempt should be made to build up an accurate picture of the previous experience required. Accuracy in this respect can often lead to better advertisements, easier pre-selection and more searching interviews. What kind of detail then is necessary? Early 'formative years' experience – apprenticeships, studentships, exposure to more than one commercial or industrial situation, or maybe service in the Armed Forces or Merchant Navy.

First post of responsibility – chargehand, section leader – technical responsibility, e.g. in chemistry laboratory, secretary to a departmental manager, territory salesman. Subsequent responsibility requirements can then be added depending on the nature and level of the post being specified.

Indeed a relationship must be established between the foregoing and the environments in which the experience was gained. For instance with the post of foundry manager, experience of working with specified materials or in making a certain size of castings is very relevant. So also is information concerning the general standing of the companies or organisations in which the experience was gained.

The other most important aspect of the experience required is in relation to the major tasks of the job. This is just as important at operational as well as the other levels where, for example, garage fitters in general are not experienced in maintaining high-speed packing lines at peak performance. Another example can be taken from a supervisory situation which calls for experience in handling a large department of 600 employees. However, unless it is specified whether the employees are all males or all females, there is considerable scope for some fascinating misconceptions!

Personal attributes. More attention is being paid now to this category. The impact of the new individual on an existing work group and vice versa can be vital, particularly where incentives are based on group performance. Some attempt must be made to analyse the 'chemistry' of the situation – acceptability is probably the key word in this context.

However, on occasions it may well be absolutely necessary to specify what might appear to be unwelcome attributes. Abrasiveness is one such attribute which nevertheless can be vital in stimulating complacent teams at all levels. Preparedness to accept a challenge, to work under trying circumstances, or to subordinate one's own convictions in certain situations are other examples.

Physical attributes. A great deal of emphasis has been placed, through legislation, on the employment of the disabled. This is more obvious in relation to physical disabilities, but it is often found that only lip service is being paid to the mental health aspects of the working situation. The question of stress and the individual's capacity to absorb stress is very important, especially at certain decision making levels; also where working hours (such as 12-hour shifts in noisy, dusty conditions, or train or aeroplane crews having to 'stop over') can have a serious effect on an individual's necessary domestic or social relationships.

These attributes must be specified accordingly and whenever possible professional advice must be obtained. The amateur doctor or psychologist can do untold harm, and such an occurrence must be avoided.

Having gone through all these steps in describing the job and obtaining the specification, a firm basis has been established. The recruiter can now proceed with great confidence to find 'Mr or Ms Right' for the post in question.

Internal sources

Many companies still have the tendency to overlook the bank of talent contained in their existing work forces despite publicity aimed at management succession plans, or schemes for 'growing your own'. It is therefore very important to look inwards to try to identify potential internal candidates from all parts of the enterprise. In doing this the political pressures of the organisation will come into full play, and therefore it is essential to maintain a very independent stance throughout the exercise. This independence is sustained by the very nature of the factual information contained in the job description and the subsequent specification. Nevertheless if potential internal candidates are found, it is vital that they are subjected to the full selection process. This must not be regarded as an act of 'bloody mindedness' or 'bureaucracy', for its very purpose is to safeguard, for the organisation, the integrity of the process itself as well as of all those who play a part in it, especially the candidates.

Advertising

The job advertising market is now a multi-million pound business, and inevitably it produces fads and fashions from time to time. Special job advertising agencies have been set up, and selection consultants, office staff bureaux and appointment registers have followed the trend by extending the range of services available. A great deal of material has been published on the subject and indeed many professional recruiters, depending on their own personal inclinations, are either disappointed or delighted if their daily postbag does not include at least one printed circular on job advertising.

The main purpose in advertising a job is to attract sufficient candidates of the right calibre, thereby securing a reasonable field from which to choose the most appropriate person for that job. How does one tackle this attraction process?

- Define the audience (i.e. the type of people to be reached).
- Decide on the means and establish the cost of making the contact.
- Write the message.
- Monitor the results.

The audience

The level and nature of the position to be filled will largely define the audience both in terms of volume and geographical spread. At the operational level there is on most occasions a local audience which can be tapped, but from time to time instances occur when special skills are sought, which are not available from the local audience. When this happens, some preliminary investigation is called for, in order to establish the location of the required audience as well as the potential available. This also applies in the clerical and technical level, though there is a tendency for technical people to restrict their own availability by becoming too clearly identified with particular processes, even within the one organisation. However this does not seem to be the case with computer staff whose skills and knowledge have almost universal application and whose mobility transcends national boundaries.

It is at managerial level that the audience becomes national in character. It is also pertinent to define the audience at this level in broad functional terms e.g. accountants, engineers, buyers. In addition, consideration must be given to defining current salary levels from which potential candidates can be drawn.

242

The means

A great deal of detailed information from many sources is available to the recruiter on such matters as circulation of papers or publications of professional bodies, types of people who can be reached and the costs involved.

Decisions therefore have to be made on the worth of national coverage against local coverage, the amount of space needed, and whether any apparent extraneous points, i.e. company image, or wider public relations exercise, need to be taken into account. While it seems natural to turn to press advertising, consideration must also be given to other methods. These can include:

- television or cinema advertisements
- posters in places where the appropriate audience is likely to congregate – newsagents, public halls, schools and colleges
- leaflet distributions, especially on housing estates
- word of mouth – with the inevitable discount for mis-statements
- notice boards outside the place of work
- notice boards inside the place of work
- Job Centres
- 'recruitment circus' i.e. using a caravan as a travelling recruitment centre, e.g. for the armed forces
- use of a pre-recorded message on tape or video which can be distributed.

Most of the above means are more appropriate when considerable numbers of people are required at the same time, especially when a new site is being manned or expansion is taking place. The 'milk round' for graduate recruitment has become firmly established as part of our national recruitment scene. Most organisations involved use a number of the above methods in a variety of combinations, depending on their own requirements. Eventually and inevitably cost must play its part in the final decision.

The message

Above all simplicity is the keynote, together with the need to use technical terms on a restricted but meaningful basis. There is certainly an art in constructing the message, for a basic emotional appeal to the audience is necessary. However, not only must one present this appeal, but also sufficient hard information. These two together must make the appropriate candidates reach for their writing pads, cause them to telephone, or make them sufficiently curious to make a personal visit. However, the message must be tailored to suit the means chosen. Consideration must also be given to technical detail, especially size of print, headlining, number of words that can be used, for the message includes everything within the defined physical boundaries of the medium, whether it be words, white or black space, line drawings, or company symbols. Indeed from time to time it is necessary to consider whether or not it is important to write in English or another language. But advice on many of these details is readily available from advertising agencies and public relations consultants. Most organisations have working relationships with services of this kind, either on a local or national basis. A great deal of help can be obtained from such sources, particularly on technical matters.

The results

It is extremely useful to keep a record of the response to advertisements whatever the means used. This enables the user to evaluate in financial terms the relevance of certain media in reaching the required audience. The main statistic is 'cost per reply' which can be refined in relation to numbers interviewed, candidates shortlisted and appointed from that particular source. A relatively simple form can be designed and maintained at negligible cost by a clerk or a secretary. The type of information required includes:

- appointment title
- media used
- size of advertisement
- cost
- number of replies
- cost per reply
- numbers interviewed
- numbers shortlisted
- numbers appointed.

It is quite surprising how useful this information can be, not only in relation to developing realistic advertising budgets but also in settling arguments and destroying preconceived ideas.

Equally at this stage use can be made of the advertising agency in obtaining comparative data on a confidential basis from other agency clients, in order to place one's own data in a wider and perhaps more meaningful context.

Processing of applications

The greatest sin in recruitment is not so much to lose an application (which is bad enough) but to ignore it, to leave it unacknowledged. Most applicants are prepared for the occasional 'mislaying' of letters, but not one will tolerate being ignored. This again is in the realm of extending natural courtesies to the people who have been sufficiently interested to respond to the message.

Keeping track of applications over the selection period which can extend on occasions to several months demands a good administrative system, preferably one which dovetails with the sorting process. A suggested outline appears in Figure 12.1.

Most organisations revise their application forms from time to time, but it is important to remember that the form itself can be so designed to promote effective administration by allocating space for action signals at appropriate points.

With the advent of word processing there is an even stronger argument for having individually addressed standard letters. The amount of time that can be saved is considerable, apart from the important question of maintaining cordial relations with the candidates. Admittedly a certain amount of time is taken up initially in constructing standard letters, but it then avoids the necessity for dictating individual replies. This is doubly relevant when 50 to 60 replies are received and demand equal attention. The major standard letters should cover:

- acknowledgements of receipt of application;
- invitation to interview;
- request for further information;
- rejection.

A well thought out and well tried system will not only keep candidates and recruiter happy, but will also avoid the unwelcome letter to the chairman from an aggrieved candidate, which will inevitably lead to an embarrassing post mortem!

STAGE TWO: FACE TO FACE: THE EMPLOYMENT INTERVIEW

Up to now all work on which the recruiter has been engaged has been directed inwardly on the job to be filled and outwardly only in terms of the audience to be contacted. However, the next stage — 'face to

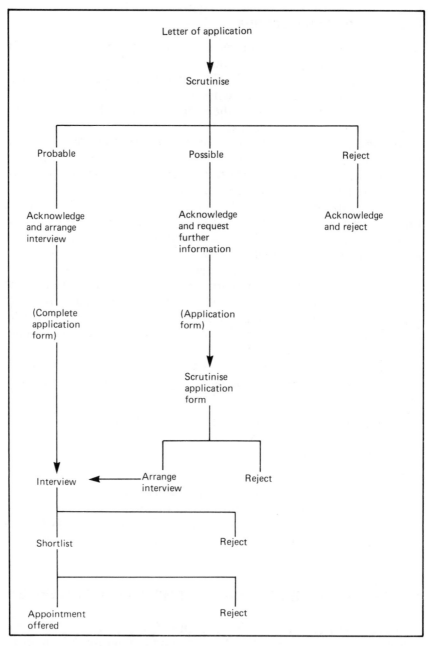

Figure 12.1 Processing of applications

face' — is the one where many managers feel quite exposed. Chapter 13 deals with this in detail. We shall touch on just a few important points for the recruitment and selection process.

Recording

Often a great deal of information about the candidate will have been recorded already — either in correspondence or on an application form. However, interviewers can never hope to remember the answers to all the questions put to the candidate; therefore it is necessary to have some policy and method for making notes during the interview. Most candidates will expect this, but it must be done in the least obtrusive way possible. A common document for all interviews is useful, particularly one which allows the interviewer to complete a preliminary assessment after the candidate has left. One such example is shown in Figure 12.2. Quite often it is suggested that a person cannot really do more than one thing at a time, but the proficient interviewer should be capable of asking questions, listening closely to the answers and taking notes at the same time. However there are times when something is missed, and then the interviewer must be strong enough to ask the candidate to repeat his answer.

Administering appropriate tests

A great deal of space in management literature has been devoted to arguing the case for and against using tests of various kinds in the selection process. Although it does not generally appear under this sort of heading, the most common test applied is the medical one, whether it be a screening by a trained nurse before engaging operators for a food factory, or a full blown medical conducted at the medical centre of the Institute of Directors. The case for even this test can be argued both ways, although enacted legislation does tend to set some basic parameters. Nevertheless most companies or organisations have a reasonable defined policy and practice to follow, and therefore guidance is probably already available to the recruiter.

However, in non-medical areas questions inevitably arise over the value of using tests in the selection process. In many instances a case can be made for using appropriate tests, especially where there is already sufficient information available to establish the validity of the tests in that particular context. But a word of warning is necessary, for certain safeguards have been introduced by the National Foundation for Education Research in England and Wales, in

Date:	Time:	Ref. Number:
Name:	Age:	Job:

Education, training and qualifications	Impact
	Appearance
Relevant experience	Personal

Figure 12.2 Interview notes

conjunction with the British Psychological Society, into the administration of many tests in the UK. Where there are any possible problems over the use of tests in a selection or management development situation, reference to the above bodies, to a qualified person, to the test constructors or to a commercial organisation such as the Independent Assessment and Research Centre is a must.

What can tests test? Skills like manual dexterity, intelligence, aptitudes, abilities, interests, colour blindness and various aspects of the personality are some of the areas where additional and important information can be gained about candidates in order to make a full and final assessment about their suitability for the job in question.

Managerial level

This is an area where the impact of an individual personality can make a great deal of difference – both positive and negative. In terms of tests, therefore, thought must be given to the main personality characteristics which can contribute to successful performance, and to those which could be contra-indicators, i.e. would detract from successful performance. Abilities, interests and aptitudes are important especially in making decisions about people who are starting out on a managerial career for the first time, and especially at this time when many people are likely to find themselves switching career paths once, twice, or even three times in their working life. Therefore in constructing a test package for a particular selection procedure leading to a managerial post, professional advice must be sought, and due weight given to professional opinions in the final assessment.

Clerical and technical

Here keyboard skills are obviously crucial, but in many routine clerical jobs tasks such as checking information against source documents are important. Tests of accuracy are available, and indeed, with the growth of computerised accounting systems, quite a number of tests of proven validity have been constructed and developed. Sometimes it is important to administer even simple arithmetic and verbal comprehension tests which can be constructed to suit local needs, provided of course that the recruiter knows what he is trying to achieve.

Operational

Tests for would-be apprentices, dilutee craftsmen, plant operators and assemblers are available to those qualified to use them correctly and interpret the results properly. The test of their acceptability is one which can only be resolved in each individual case. But since a great deal of time is required in training those selected to do the job properly, the use of tests must often be justified on financial grounds.

While most tests give detailed instructions on procedure, test administration is nevertheless important, and the recruiter should make certain that he achieves as near to optimum conditions as possible for all test sessions. The correct physical conditions and the right psychological tone are essential to good test performance by the candidates, and if these conditions are not available then the test session can become a futile exercise in apparent sophistication. A guarantee as to the confidentiality of the result is highly important to candidates, and the approach to be encouraged is that of the medical profession in dealing with personal information of this nature.

Making the appointment

The moment of decision has arrived! Again it must be stressed that the decision to offer the position to one of the candidates is one-sided, and until the offer has been accepted, the recruitment task has not been completed.

At this stage the 'evidence' on all the candidates should be available for review and final assessment. In all probability, at least two people will be concerned in the final decision, and in most cases they should meet together to discuss the matter as fully as necessary. Sometimes one candidate stands out among all others, and consequently the decision comes easily. But on many occasions a 'debate' occurs with an informal cataloguing of the pros and cons, and inevitably some sort of compromise has to be made in relation to the 'ideal' job description and candidate specification prepared at the beginning of the recruitment and selection process. Indeed in filling some positions the selection decision is made, not by comparing candidate against candidate, but by assessing the candidate in relation to the specification.

The important point here is to approach the decision making session in a systematic way, so that the reasons for the choice of one candidate and the rejection of the others become quite clear. No one should be afraid of stating and if necessary restating that a liking for a candidate has tipped the scales in his favour. As Robert Townsend says in *Up the Organization,* 'The important thing about hiring is the chemistry of the vibrations between boss and candidate; good, bad, or not there at all'. Any manager who denies this truism has already reached his level of incompetence.

Having made the decision, this must be conveyed in written form to the successful candidate. The formal offer of employment should always be qualified with the phrase 'subject to obtaining satisfactory references', unless of course references have already been obtained. No self-respecting potential employee will accept and act upon a mere verbal offer, and until an acceptance letter has been received the process has not been completed. It is also useful at this stage to clear with the appointee any remaining matters relating to the conditions under which he will be employed.

STAGE THREE: THE FOLLOW-THROUGH

Introducing the new employee to the organisation

Any new employee will require a period of familiarisation before he can begin to perform his job properly. In many cases it is possible to set up a formal introductory course through which new employees learn about the policies and practices of the organisation. Sometimes it is possible to put a number of employees through the same course, while for others the introduction will have to be tailor-made. The main aim of induction, whether conducted on a formal basis or informally by the new employee's boss, is to integrate the newcomer as soon as possible. This is not an altruistic concept, but is based on sound economics, for the sooner a person is settled the sooner performance reaches standard.

Perhaps the best basis from which to start the induction process is the question: what does the newcomer want or need to know? A programme of induction must cover such matters as conditions of employment, departmental information, general health and safety. Remember also that new employees will find it difficult to assimilate a mass of information at one sitting, and a suitable timescale should therefore be devised.

For induction programmes at technical, supervisory or managerial level, a useful guide is to be found in the pamphlet *Induction – Acclimatizing People to Work* by W R Marks, published by the Institute of Personnel Management. However, the important principle to bear in mind is that the programme must be constructed around the requirements of the job to be done, and the timescale must also be realistic, for most newcomers just want to settle down and prove their worth.

Following up the progress of the new employee

This is of specific importance where a probationary period of employment (not more than 12 weeks) has to be served successfully before confirmation of the appointment takes place. In these cases a formal procedure has to be adopted in order to maintain adequate records and background information for the decision which has to be taken. If the review takes place on a weekly or monthly basis then the employee should be given some idea of what progress he or she is making. This need not be on a formal basis, for given good supervisors, the effect of an 'informal chat' can result in either a mending of the ways or a spurring to even better performance.

In general terms, though, contact needs to be maintained with new employees until it becomes quite apparent that they have settled down and become part of the team. This contact between the recruiter, the new employee and his boss can be of considerable benefit in developing an awareness, in the recruiter, especially of the sorts of people who successfully survive the hesitation of the first week or month and become settled members of the company or organisation. In looking at labour turnover figures it is not surprising to note that in many instances most of the leavers quit within the first three months of being employed. There is therefore a real economic meaning and purpose to follow-up after induction.

Reviewing and evaluating the recruitment and selection process

In basic terms most organisations check their recruitment and selection methods on the exception principle – the new recruit who doesn't fit in becomes the stick with which the recruiter is beaten about the head, no matter how many 'successes' can be listed! However, it is possible to examine the actual methods by which the final decision is reached in a more objective way. Such questions must be asked: Are we advertising the vacancy properly? Are we attracting the right sort of candidates? Are we treating the candidates in the right way? Have we got the right system for obtaining the preliminary information about the job? Generally are the candidate specifications lucid enough? Are we getting the right sort of information about candidates from the tests we use? How long do new employees of various categories stay with us? Is this a result of over- or under-recruitment?

The answers to some of these questions will give an indication of what is going on in the selection process, and provide a reasonably sound base for further improvements.

In respect of the competence of the recruiter himself, it is to the advantage of the organisation to ensure that its 'gate-keepers' can discriminate (in the nicest possible sense) between those who should or should not be admitted. Apart from professional competence as an employment interviewer and a test administrator, the recruiter must be able to maintain the confidence of his peers and colleagues within the company, as well as enjoy the confidence of the candidates who come in front of him. Integrity is a vital word in this context both from a professional and personal point of view as far as the recruiter is concerned. Indeed all managers eventually build up a 'track record' on their effectiveness in taking on the right people for the tasks in hand.

Finally it must be stated that most companies and organisations are now beginning to realise that the recruitment of the necessary human resources requires the same attention, effort, and concentration as purchasing essential raw materials, plant and supplies. In the last analysis it is people who, collectively or individually, make or break the company as a viable concern. The cost effectiveness of the recruitment and selection process must be of prime concern for top management, especially as the annual company report now contains the average numbers of people employed over the year and the amount of wages and salaries paid to them. In the last analysis, value for money is the unspoken question in the selection decision.

THE IPM RECRUITMENT CODE

The Institute of Personnel Management first launched its recruitment code in 1978, after much debate and heart-searching amongst interested parties, recruiters and applicants alike. Its declared aims include the promotion of 'high standards of professional recruitment practice by encouraging recruiters and applicants to adhere to common guidelines', and the provision of 'guidance on those matters that most commonly cause difficulty to recruiters and applicants'.

Among topics covered by the code are such matters as dealing with unsolicited applications, failure of applicants to honour interview appointments, payment of interview expenses, the taking up of references, and discrimination against applicants on the grounds of sex, race, disability, or past convictions for criminal offences.

The code sets out the obligations of recruiters and applicants, and the following extracts are taken from the fourth edition.*

* Extract from The IPM Recruitment Code used with permission of the Institute of Personnel Management, IPM House, Camp Road, Wimbledon, London SW19 4UW.

Recruiters' obligations

1 Job advertisements should state clearly the form of reply desired, in particular, whether this should be a formal application form or by curriculum vitae. Preferences should also be stated if handwritten replies are required.
2 An acknowledgement or reply should be made promptly to each applicant by the employing organisation or its agent. If it is likely to take some time before acknowledgements are made, this should be made clear in the advertisement.
3 Applicants should be informed of the progress of selection procedures, what these will be (e.g. group selection, aptitude tests etc.), the steps and time involved and the policy regarding expenses.
4 Detailed personal information (for example religion, medical history, place of birth, family background etc.) should not be called for unless it is relevant to the selection process.
5 Before applying for references, potential employers must secure the permission of the applicant.
6 Applications must be treated as confidential.

Applicants' obligations

1 Advertisements should be answered in the way requested (for example telephone for application form, provide brief details, send curriculum vitae etc.).
2 Appointments and other arrangements must be kept, or the recruiter be informed promptly if the candidate discovers an agreed meeting cannot take place.
3 The recruiter should be informed as soon as a candidate decides not to proceed with the application.
4 Only accurate information should be given in applications and in reply to recruiters' questions.
5 Information given by a prospective employer must be treated as confidential, if so requested.

FURTHER READING

Higham, M, *The ABC of Interviewing,* Institute of Personnel Management, 1979
Plumbley, P, *Recruitment and Selection,* 2nd edition, Institute of Personnel Management, 1976
Ungerson, B (ed.), *Recruitment Handbook,* 3rd edition, Gower, 1983

13

Interviewing

John Courtis

For most managers, interviewing implies recruitment and selection interviewing but the same rules apply in other applications, such as appraisal, counselling and fact finding. The subject is massive and so is treated here on an exception basis with pointers to additional sources of specialist texts and advice. We start from the premise that most interviews are unsatisfactory in some way, a premise supported by independent research over many years. Many interviews are abortive or unnecessary.

OBJECTIVES

It may seem trite to mention that you should be certain about your objectives before starting or even planning an interview but the point is often forgotten or taken for granted. For example, in hiring, few people stop to consider whether they are involved in a selection interview or just a recruitment ratification. Selection involves a qualitative filtering process in which you choose the best, or none, from a number of people interviewed. Recruitment, on the other hand, implies that you choose the first person who matches up to the minimum criteria, or perhaps all those who meet them.

There are secondary objectives which, although peripheral in many cases, are none the less important. For instance:

- your time management objectives
- the public relations aspect of each meeting
- house advertising, as an investment for the future
- product and service advertising

- research
- counselling (during internal selection processes).

If you do not identify your objectives clearly, you cannot plan to achieve them. You may also emerge from the interview without enough data to enable you to meet the objectives when you later realise what they are.

ABORT THE ABORTIVE

Several of the objectives outlined above demand that you do not run interviews which, in retrospect, prove to have been abortive. If you know they are abortive your interviewee probably does too so that not only have you wasted your time and the victim's; you have also damaged your own and your organisation's reputation.

Better communication is the key. If there is an adequate exchange of information beforehand, some interviews will prove to be unnecessary. Others can be modified in content or objective to make them worthwhile. The simplest example is the person who is being interviewed for an inappropriate job, because details of the individual or the job have not reached employer and candidate respectively in a form which permits qualitative judgements by either or both. The defence which both sides usually offer for partial or non-disclosure is that they are afraid of 'putting off' the other side. This is at best shortsighted. It does not impress busy employers or busy candidates (usually the best ones) to find that time has been wasted for this reason. Worse, the chance to have a correctly planned interview which related more accurately to the individual and his or her potential within the organisation has almost certainly been missed.

Even at 'recruitment' interviews it is still discourteous to interview people who do not fit the candidate specification or know that they could not or would not do the job as finally described to them. There is a tendency to dismiss this sort of error with the thought that 'It's only half an hour', conveniently ignoring the candidate's travel time, inconvenience, disappointment, and loss of earnings at a level where pride, money and time may all be in short supply. So, sometimes, is self-confidence. Your moral obligation to do the right thing is actually greater the wider the gap in seniority between interviewer and candidate.

TIME FLIES

Given the preceding fairly discouraging introduction, you may be wondering how it is possible to perform a good or worthwhile interview in the time normally allotted. The quick answer is that you cannot! Even in the sort of interview which is planned to take several hours (rather than dragging out to that length by the incompetence of the interviewer or the loquacity of the 'victim') it is entirely possible that the results will be incomplete, misleading, or just plain bad.

The secret is discipline: discipline about the conduct of the meeting and discipline about preparation. I have a theory that much of management consists of the avoidance of error, rather than dramatic flights of flair, fancy or invention. Nowhere is this more true than in interviewing. Proper research and preparation before the interview will make all the difference. Part of the selection process, for example, can be conducted on the telephone. Five minutes per candidate is more than enough to form a preliminary opinion about the candidate's merits, without the need to meet or proceed further (except for a gracious written rejection later).

PREPARATION

The environment may be the most important ingredient in the interview preparation. Certainly the difference between good and bad can change an interviewee's chance of communicating well quite considerably. A stress-free room, free of interruptions, threatening layout (large desk, uncomfortable guest chair), sun in eyes, draughts, excessive heat and noise nuisance, is firmly indicated.

Getting them there

We should not need to labour this point. However, you will have colleagues who are not prepared to be flexible about interview timing, either in respect of the time of day or the day of the week. They may also be thoughtless about the lead time necessary for someone in a worthwhile and demanding job to plan absences. (Where selection and recruitment is concerned, the following is worth considering: other things being equal, the best people are those who are still trying to honour their contracts with their present employers. Excluding the idiots who play hard to get on principle, the elusive are likely to be better than the all-too-available.)

Final preparation
Read their paperwork again.
Read again what you have sent them.
Smile.
Go out and greet them.
Tell them who you are.
Make sure they are who you think they are.

Tell them what you want to achieve during the meeting. (Call it a meeting, not an interview.) Make sure they are there for the purpose you think they are. Tell them the structure of the meeting. Now go ahead.

THE INTERVIEW PROPER

Reasonable readers might assume that this heading highlights a distinction between the main body of the interview and the peripheral matters previously covered. Not so. The alternative in the author's mind is the interview improper, which is unfortunately the norm in many organisations!

The caring interviewer — especially the recruiter — when approaching an interview, must remember that the interviewee has almost certainly been conditioned badly for the interview, in one of three ways:

- lack of experience;
- guidance from friend or counsellor who considers the candidate's objectives without regard to those of the recruiter/interviewer;
- lots of experience with bad interviewers (the interview improper).

According to the *Oxford English Dictionary,* the primary meanings of 'improper' are 'Inaccurate, wrong, not properly so called'. 'Wrong' will do for our purposes. The ways in which other interviews are wrong and yours can be right are varied but they all come back to the questions of objectives and control. The interviewer must run the meeting and concentrate on matters relevant to the objectives outlined earlier.

The alternative is anarchy and a wasted hour or more. For example, the sort of interview where the candidate takes charge and launches into a biography which duplicates the written material already exchanged (or is necessary because adequate written material has not been exchanged in advance) is wholly unproductive except to demonstrate the candidate's poor grasp of the objective. Given that he or she has been badly conditioned, it may be unfair to make an adverse judgement on this basis. The effective interviewer, by controlling and setting guidelines for the conduct of the meeting, does both sides a service.

This is less stressful for the candidate who desperately wants to recite a biography if the objectives are clearly specified. Something like this may be appropriate:

> I want to achieve three things during this meeting. First, to clear up any queries arising out of the paperwork we sent you, so that you can clearly understand the job and the company environment. Second, a brief review of your track record so that I can make sure that I have understood its relevance to the job. Third, I want to give you a chance to mention any experience or evidence of excellence that is not brought out in your CV.

It is useful at this stage to enquire whether the candidate has any timing constraints and to mention your own, if any. There are few things more damaging to an interview than one of the parties being under pressure on time, while the other is relaxed and could go on all day. Communication can be even worse when both have time problems and neither has disclosed them.

However, all interviews suffer from time pressures because no two people have the same idea of the right time to allocate. The solution is for the interviewer to make it very clear that the exchanges are on an exception reporting basis. If this is done, the candidate is forced to discipline the use of time and also is reminded that this is not going to be the sloppy norm experienced in other places. If he or she does not react to the message you have learned something about them.

This economy of effort creates one trap. The quality and brevity of the information exchanges may improve, but the staccato rhythm is seductive and may tempt you, as interviewer, not to probe too deeply when an answer is superficially acceptable. This is exceptionally dangerous because the most important things in an interview, apart perhaps from body language, are the answers to supplementary questions.

Information volunteered by candidates may well be useful but is of their choice. Answers to your questions are more important because, if you are doing your work correctly, they are more relevant to your objectives. Supplementary questions are crucial because they refine or highlight key matters arising out of the other two.

For instance, there are many questions to which a candidate can give a stock answer which is largely under his or her control and is no more informative than the carefully polished words on a CV. Getting behind that stock answer to the unplanned spontaneous reaction can be much more informative.

'Why did you leave the So and so Co.?' is a classic and deeply boring question which usually attracts a well polished reply like 'There was a promotion bottleneck. My boss was only two years older and unlikely to move.'

You can tackle this in one of two ways. Either change the primary question, so that you are asking questions which previous interviewers have not asked and which therefore demand thought and unique answers, or use the probing supplementary.

In the case quoted, the alternative question might be 'Why did you leave the So and so Co. so quickly, when you appear to have been well paid and getting new experience?' This is quite sneaky, because there are at least two and possibly three implied criticisms which the interviewee must consider and rebut. Listen extremely carefully at this point because most people will omit to answer you on one or two of these. Note them. Come back to them, either by way of supplementary questions or a later approach from another angle. Anyone who actually covers all three points without getting tied in knots is probably quite bright!

You may want to try several possible supplementaries, arising from the earlier conduct of the interview. The obvious one is 'Why didn't you consider this when you joined them?' Because it is obvious it may be less informative than something more open-ended like 'Does that mean your priorities have changed since you joined them?' This gives you a chance to ask later what the priorities are now; quite important if you are trying to weed out job-hoppers.

Open-ended questions are almost invariably better than those requiring yes/no answers, except when you are trying to pin down a candidate of suspect credibility.

Questions of all kinds, as implied above, are more important than statements from either side. Even the nature of the candidates' questions can be more informative than their answers to bad questions. A pattern should emerge which will tell you whether the candidate is obsessed with detail or is a 'broad-brush' operator. Again, it is very important to listen and analyse these.

Apart from the heavy set piece question there are some very useful interjections which can be as useful as the formal question, e.g.:

For instance?
For example?
How?
Why was that?
What, exactly?
Can you be more specific?
Tell me more.
Can you explain that?
I don't quite follow.

You probably have your own favourites. All are designed to provoke clarification or a fuller picture without interrupting the flow too much. Even 'Yes?' is both encouragement and reinforcement of this kind.

This is not the place for a detailed listing of all the possible 'good' questions. Instead, the general principle needs to be stressed. Questions are more important than statements, in both directions. The answers are even more important. If you think back over horrible interviews you have attended, it is almost certain that you have experienced the improper interviewer who has devoted massive effort to the construction and issue of a very good question and sinks back exhausted and deaf the moment he asks it. Do not be like the improper interviewer. Listen. Listen to the answers. Listen to their questions. Both are informative. Also, if you do not listen to their questions carefully you may respond with your slightly irrelevant stock answer. The second-rate candidates will not notice or, if they notice, may not mind. The good ones will notice and mind. Even if you decide they are worth offering the job to, they will not accept because they have formed an unfavourable impression. This is so even if they will not be reporting to you in the job, but doubly true if you are the potential boss.

If you are surrounded by improper interviewers who are very obviously unaware of these problems, there are three or four aids which may effect or influence a cure. Tape recording the meeting, overtly to permit later assessment, may aid self-awareness. Video recording and playback does the same thing more forcefully. A proprietary video training package by Melrose Films called *Listen* is very helpful on this point. So is the old Video Arts film *Manhunt* about the inverview process as a whole. Finally, D Mackenzie Davey wrote an excellent booklet for the British Institute of Management called *How to Interview.*

Tape recording your own sessions can also help. You will probably be unpleasantly surprised at first, both by your performance and by the number of non-sequiturs and other communication failures evident in the first few tapes, but this is the only way to learn discreetly, from self-example.

Replaying taped interviews will show you that abortive interviews are signalled very early in most cases. The candidate who comes to a meeting uncertain whether he or she is right for the job and vice versa is usually giving out warning signs, either in the nature of loaded questions, the absence of any questions, or a desire to hurry bits which should normally be taken seriously and slowly. For this reason the author nowadays goes immediately to the question of the candidate's interest in the job, without spending time on the candidate's relevance.

Other things being equal, unless you have a wide variety of jobs to fill, there is no point in interviewing in depth a candidate who is going to reject the job as soon as the nature of it is made clear. If this rejection can be identified early, both sides can save time and self-respect. The time saved can then, if appropriate, be devoted to exploring what the candidate can do which might be relevant to the organisation's short term management development plans. Or you can both go home earlier.

BODY LANGUAGE

Reading a good book on body language is doubly important. There are several. Two are called: *Body Language,* (Fast, J, 1972, Pan Books, London; Pease, A, 1984, Sheldon Press, London) and Desmond Morris's books *The Naked Ape* and *Manwatching* both have relevant content.

You need this background for two reasons. First, it can help you interpret what the interviewee is thinking, if what they are saying or not saying is not the whole truth. Second, you can use the positions and signals described in the books to demonstrate sympathetic interest, or anything else you feel like, at times when you feel far from sympathetic or interested, but the good conduct of the interview demands that you be supportive. Conversely, if you want to get rid of a verbose candidate, body signals can help to reinforce other messages, without overt rudeness.

THE CLOSE

Getting rid of people on time is a tempting objective in some circumstances, but it must not be allowed to interfere with the correct disciplines for shutting down the meeting.

You must both know what you have agreed and what comes next. Your next action must be mentioned, with a time forecast. If the interviewee has to send you something – remind him/her and agree how soon it is needed. If you are not sure where they stand about the job, for heaven's sake ask them!

If you are uncertain about a job candidate's relevance, tell them why, so they have a chance to agree or clear the air. Even if it is disappointing, this is better than having them feel hard done by when an unexplained rejection arrives later. You may also find that some candidates drag themselves back into the running, on merit, at this point. Finally, ask them if they would accept the job if offered (and if there is anything else coming to the boil elsewhere). This gives a clearer picture than general interest queries. It also clarifies your lead time, if any.

INTERVIEWS AND THE LAW

This section is about some of the legal pitfalls which can occur in the badly run interview. The first, of course, is the possibility that someone inadvertently makes a verbal job offer at interview, which is then accepted. This is extremely rare and, unless the candidate is litigious and armed with a tape recorder, this is not a financial problem, just a goodwill and time waster.

The second, much more common, is that the interviewer asks questions or makes statements which are or could be misunderstood to be discriminatory. Given the nature of current equal opportunities legislation it is important, as pointed out earlier, that interviewers are briefed on what not to ask, or say, and that for every interview they make adequate notes which indicate clearly the reasons why the candidates meet or fall short of the organisation's criteria. It is just as important that you record the reasons why Fred got the job as the reasons why Fiona did not. Tape recordings may help here in the training process. Even the most well intentioned manager can use words or phrases which in the mouth of someone with a desire to see the worst in everything can suggest a pattern of prejudice. If, for example, the use of photographs on application forms became discriminatory here as it is in at least one other country, interviewers who care about remembering which candidate was which would have to revert to a pen portrait of the candidate. When you have a spare hour, try writing such a description of a few strangers in a way that will permit instant recall without any potentially sexist or racist connotations. It is not easy.

THE SECONDARY OBJECTIVES

Interviews as PR

This is not as blatant as it may sound. Public relations in the better sense refers to your corporate communication with various audiences in and around the organisation. (Much more about this in Chapter 29.) Potential employees are an important part of several audiences. They may be, or may become, employees, shareholders, suppliers, customers, enemies or even advisers. The quality of your treatment of candidates, whether or not you know they are more than just members of the general public, can be very important to the organisation's future, even in small ways. To take an extreme example, a candidate who has first-hand experience of being properly treated and well briefed about the organisation is likely to be a powerful ally in any distant discussion arising from press misquotation. If the distant discussion includes a thoughtful MP who is going to vote about you the next day he or she is very likely to prefer a first-hand opinion to that of the press. All MPs know how the media misquote!

Interviews as advertising

Interviews often result from recruitment advertising. They can also replace future recruitment advertising, or product advertising. The warm interview with a good candidate who is of the right calibre for the organisation but not quite right for the current vacancy should leave the door open for either side to renew contact in the future. If the briefing has conveyed a sense of excitement about the products and services of the organisation, the candidates, their households and their present employers may be influenced as potential customers. Most sales staff would give a lot to have the attention of a prospect for an hour, half of which was to be spent discussing the excellence of the product. Good interviewing can be very effective marketing.

Interviews as sources

This does not refer to industrial espionage or illicit head hunting although, tactlessly handled, either might be suspected. In brief, if an interview goes well but both sides decide that there is not a match, there is a special professional bond between candidate and interviewer for a short while which sometimes makes it natural for the recruiter to ask if the candidate has ever worked with anyone who could and should do the job. It has to be left to the candidate to decide if there are any ethical constraints about such a contact but in most cases the new nominee is a past colleague rather than a current one or if current is known to be disaffected.

This also raises the question of the tow rope. It is not generally realised how many people move in groups rather than solo from company to company. Much publicised migrations, as in stockbrokers' specialist departments, are not worth mentioning by comparison with the key functional managers who pull one or more of their team along to the next outfit. Sometimes the initiative comes from above, sometimes from below, because the old place isn't fun any more without Fiona or Fred. Quite often, senior functional managers, perceiving other weaknesses in the new organisation, will also recommend members of their peer group or even their ex-bosses. Much more of this happens than is evident from the appointments column. The tow rope is very powerful. Do not ignore the potential of this when team building.

Finally, when exploring referees other than the conventional ones, do ask about their personal merits and their relationship with the candidate. This is not for head hunting purposes − you need this to evaluate the later reference properly − but there may occasionally be a by-product which can be used without any twinge of conscience. The other bonus is that you find out how candidates talk about people close to them and can differentiate between the constructive and the negative attitudes. It is a useful part of your qualitative filter. (All appraisals tell you more about the author than the subject of the appraisal.)

OTHER KINDS OF INTERVIEW

Although we have concentrated on recruitment interviewing for examples so far, the other types are very important.

These include appraisal, counselling, fact finding, termination and warning (in the statutory context). Some are easier for the interviewing manager, some more difficult, but the basic disciplines remain the same. (Chapters 15 and 16 deal with appraisal and counselling in detail.) It is up to the individual manager to identify the extent to which each example differs from the norm and the need for special techniques or preparation.

The general rules which remain the same include:

- Remembering that the 'victim' always feels nervous, sometimes even threatened, although he may outrank you.
- Allowing for the difference in context between the different types of interview. This does not just refer to the objectives of each participant, but includes timing, the extent to which the meeting is voluntary, the desire for communication, the threat, as above, ignorance about the reasons for the meeting (very prevalent, even when the alleged agenda has been declared in advance), suspicion about the motives of the interviewer or the organisation (not quite the same as the threat problem), and the extent to which the interviewer is dreading the meeting as much as or more than the victim!
- The need for preparation and for putting certain things in writing if they are to be remembered afterwards. This does not mean in typescript. It can be very effective to do a spontaneous handwritten note during the meeting to which the interviewee feels he or she has contributed. Indeed the content may well evolve naturally during the meeting. A photocopy for the interviewer and the original for the 'victim' (always this way — more courteous and more natural) suffices as an official but informal way of recording key points, whether one is explaining redundancy pay or listing points for personal improvement. In the latter case the use of the 'victim's' own words is appreciably more comforting.
- The need for communication, remembering always that communication is supposed to be a two-way process. Any alleged communication which is structured to flow only in one direction deprives the originator of a discriminating response. The feedback can amend or eliminate the need for the rest of the meeting. Always keep listening. Watch for non-verbal signals.

Appraisal

Here the key problem is to decide in advance the extent to which the objective of the meeting is compatible with the total disclosure sometimes mistakenly assumed to be implicit in an appraisal. There are some highly dangerous appraisal processes in which the corporate system requires that a document containing virtually all the victim's weaknesses is discussed with each subject. This is inimical to the achievement of the objective, in that it destroys or demotivates. The preferred position for appraisal disclosure (unless appraisal has to be combined with a statutory dismissal warning) is to concentrate on the curable and ignore the incurable. This raises a secondary problem – that of deciding what is and is not curable – which must be addressed. The knack here is to find a way of discussing the marginal points which you may suspect are incurable as if they were open to improvement, but without making it sound like the end of the world if they are not cured. The precise technique can only be decided in relation to specific faults in a specific context but, for example, suggesting that they are important for future career opportunities rather than crucial to current survival may get the message across without damage and with some chance that even an apparently insensitive employee may be interested in self-improvement.

A final thought on appraisal – people don't get worse at their jobs suddenly without good reason. If someone who was competent last year is substandard this year a change has taken place at work or at home which is creating problems. The appraisal meeting which ignores this is wholly wasted.

Counselling

This is often but not always a by-product of an appraisal system. It is less widespread than appraisal and rather more difficult. Ideally it should only be undertaken by someone with formal training. If this is not possible, someone relevant and sympathetic should be chosen. Allowing an untrained and even antagonistic boss to do it is not best practice. As with the pre-departure meeting, the choice of interviewer is the most important aspect of the preparation. The second aspect of the choice is that the interviewer must be given enough authority to help as a result of the counselling, which is seldom wholly one-sided. A good counselling interview will uncover faults in the organisation, not just review the employee's past failings.

This point applies of course to all appraisal meetings and should be tattooed on all interviewers. Listen, record, react, keep promises.

Compulsory interviews

There is one outstanding respect in which most non-recruitment interviews differ from recruitment interviews. Most are compulsory for one side or other. This makes the climate quite sensitive. By comparison a recruitment interview is easier because, although one or both participants may be nervous (actually, in a sample of all interviews everywhere, *most* participants are probably nervous − and if they are not, they ought to be) in the recruitment interview one party actively wants a job and the other actively wants to hire someone. This predicates a better climate than one could forecast for many other meetings.

The compulsory interviews do of course include appraisal, but there are different degrees of compulsion about the fact finding meeting which may be research, fact gathering from a departing employee or just formalised data collection in normal operations. All require discipline but they are relatively non-threatening, and goodwill plus a willing and sensitive ear makes them effective. Only the pre-departure meeting is tricky, because there may be an immense amount to be learned and the employee doesn't necessarily see any valid reason for total disclosure. Equally, the interviewer, if too close to the problems, may not want to hear too much. Choice of a neutral and sypathetic interviewer is more important than trying to add technique to an unreceptive boss, who may well be the cause of the trouble anyway

Firing people comes into the compulsory category, but need not always do so if the rule about listening is observed. If the organisation has been communicating properly with its people, the meeting itself may be compulsory but the firing may not. In a substantial minority of cases the meeting may evolve into a resignation, request for redundancy, philosophical debate about how things are not working out or even an announcement of an impending event whose imminence (undisclosed) has been a factor in the performance failures which were causing the rift. The lovelorn can be transformed both by engagements *and* by the departure of an unsatisfactory partner. Better still, they sometimes want to change employers as part of the therapy.

When all else fails, listen − and keep quiet.

WHAT WE HAVE LEARNED

This has not been an encyclopaedic dissertation on every facet of every possible interview situation. Instead, you have a series of concepts, principles, thought-starters and horrid examples which should enable you to formulate your own policy and practice in the light of your unique knowledge of your own organisation and indeed your own personal style.

There is no one right method of handling interviews or their preparation. What feels right for you is better than something which feels so alien that it impairs your performance, provided that you satisfy the basic guidelines given. You must satisfy them. Interview rules, especially in recruitment, are not made to be broken. If you want to break a rule, you must create an alternative discipline which satisfies the original objective. The best test has not yet been mentioned. It is very simple. If you were the candidate, would you be satisfied with what you and your colleagues are doing and not doing with each recruitment exercise? Even if you have not been a candidate for some time, it should be possible to answer this.

FURTHER READING

Melrose Films, *Listen*, video training package.
Video Arts, *Manhunt*
Davey, D Mackenzie, *How to Interview*, Professional Publishing, 1986
Morris, Desmond, *The Naked Ape*, Pan, 1981 and *Manwatching*, Pan, 1978

14

Developing your people

Cathy Stoddart

There is no chapter or section in this Handbook called 'Education and training' or 'How to choose the best courses for your staff'. This chapter is, however, entitled 'Developing your people' and although sending employees away from their place of work to attend courses is one way of developing parts of their competence, it is only one way.

The emphasis here is on the individual manager's responsibility for developing the people who report to him/her and less on what the personnel or training department can or should provide for those people. Considerable space is devoted to the 'small p' political issues and lobbying activities involved in gaining senior management support for training and development plans. The suggested route towards this support is by demonstrating how the implementation of such policies throughout an organisation will contribute to the effective achievement of that organisation's aims and objectives. This is as true for traditional manufacturing companies pursuing increased turnover, profitability or market share, as for service companies, non-profit making organisations, local authorities, community service bodies, charities or any other type of organisation which is concerned to produce a quality product or service.

Obviously, it is much easier for a manager who has the support of senior management to implement effective policies and programmes for developing his/her own people. However, this chapter does set out to demonstrate that even without the resources of a training department or the wholehearted support of senior management, it is still possible to reap many benefits for the department and the organisation from assessing training and development needs and taking action to meet them within one's own department.

THE POLITICAL ISSUES

An organisation which sees its education and training programmes as its sole contribution to employee development would not see development as a political issue at all. It would be likely to view expenditure on apprenticeship schemes, induction courses or external refresher courses on technical matters in the same way that it views expenditure on the maintenance of its buildings, that is, as a recurring item which could be cut in the face of financial pressure.

However, an organisation which sees education and training as one part of the organisation's strategy for achieving its objectives will have another view. This organisation may consciously group together training activities and the much wider development activities (described in a later part of this chapter headed 'Nuts and bolts') and describe them as Human Resource Development (HRD). Whether it explicitly labels its activities HRD or not, the organisation which views training and development as an essential activity harnessing potential to achieve goals will not be so ready to cut its budget in times of financial difficulty. Seen in these terms, the HRD budget competes directly with that of other functions for scarce resources (even though it is distributed across many departments to be spent). Some companies are so committed to the importance of their HRD strategies as vital contributors to business success, that their reaction to financial 'hard times' is to *increase* the amount they spend on it.

Decisions about how much to spend and what types of HRD will be supported therefore become inextricably tied up with organisational politics and cannot be considered in isolation from the culture and traditions of the organisation, its philosophy, and its aims.

Why bother to develop employees?

Many senior executives in business, commerce and public administration will put their hands on their hearts and agree that 'people are the most important asset in the organisation'. They may even, in their business plans and strategy documents, make some reference to manpower and management resources. However, it is highly unlikely that there will be any links between business objectives and people development which are articulated in terms of performance. This is quite different from financial, production, sales and marketing, pricing, capital investment and other objectives which will probably have quite clear performance outcomes as targets. So, if HRD were to have specific outcomes or targets, what might they be?

Competence, Commitment and the Capacity for change (the 3Cs) can best be demonstrated by looking at specific goals linked to business objectives. One of these might perhaps be the introduction of information technology.

For example, one well known British manufacturing company recently decided to invest in an extremely expensive American system of computerised stock control. The board realised that not only would the hourly paid workforce need considerable training in the mechanics of using the new system, but also that a fundamental shift in attitudes was required throughout the production function if implementation of the system were to be successful. Supervisors, foremen, and managers were going to have to liaise more effectively within their own function, and communicate closely with other functions. So, along with specific training to give employees the knowledge and skills to use the new system, they also instituted 'inter-departmental problem groups' of foremen and middle managers. These groups examined both 'old chestnut' problems and anticipated new ones arising from the new system. They worked out for themselves the need for better communications and changes in attitude and had prior board commitment that their problem group solutions would be implemented. Thus those managers took on 'ownership' of the problems and generated a commitment to their solutions.

This example is a good illustration of how HRD can contribute to the fostering of the 3Cs – Competence, Commitment and the Capacity for change (see Figure 14.1). Competition from other organisations is often a reason for bothering to develop employees. This may be in the form of intensified competition for the available recruits at any level – the brightest school leavers, the best qualified graduates, or the senior people with the most relevant experience. Increasingly, applicants are interested not only in salary and associated benefits, but also in what a prospective employer has to offer in terms of personal and career development, appraisal systems, and criteria for promotion. An organisation might suddenly realise that, in spite of competitive benefits packages, it was not managing to attract and retain high calibre employees. This could be because there is no evidence of succession planning, the appraisal system is a mechanical procedure used principally for the airing of grievances, and criteria for promotion take little or no account of an employee's overall performance in a job. They rely solely on easily quantifiable achievements.

In this sort of case, the competition could be coming from an

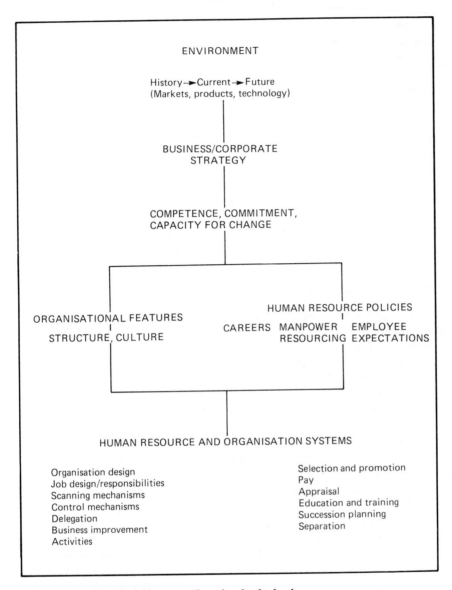

ENVIRONMENT

History→Current→Future
(Markets, products, technology)

BUSINESS/CORPORATE
STRATEGY

COMPETENCE, COMMITMENT,
CAPACITY FOR CHANGE

ORGANISATIONAL FEATURES

STRUCTURE, CULTURE

HUMAN RESOURCE POLICIES

CAREERS MANPOWER   EMPLOYEE
RESOURCING EXPECTATIONS

HUMAN RESOURCE AND ORGANISATION SYSTEMS

Organisation design
Job design/responsibilities
Scanning mechanisms
Control mechanisms
Delegation
Business improvement
Activities

Selection and promotion
Pay
Appraisal
Education and training
Succession planning
Separation

Figure 14.1   The human resource function in the business
This illustrates the central importance and essential interdependence of the HRD
function within a business.

enormously wide range of organisations; the only similarity need be that they are seeking to recruit a comparable type of staff.

However, competition can also provide the motivation to undertake some systematic HRD if it is seen that a competitor is gaining some advantages through its HRD policies. For example, your company may begin losing market share to a competitor whose in-house seminars on how to get close to the customer are beginning to bear fruit. Or, the competitor's well established quality circles may have given way to 'zero-defect groups' which are now achieving their objectives. Of course, if your company has no mechanisms, either formal or informal, for finding out what competitors are doing on any front, then it is unlikely that it would know of such developments. A company which attached importance to 'scanning its environment' would, on the other hand, pick up these things quickly and be motivated into doing something itself.

Whose responsibility is it anyway?

Reality often falls far short of the ideal — in organisations as in all else. However, it is helpful to look at an ideal situation in order to assess what is, or what should be, the right answer to this question in any particular organisation.

In an ideal world, the short answer to the responsibility question is that everyone in an organisation is responsible to some degree for identifying and then articulating his/her own development needs and to a varying degree for identifying the development needs of others.

Stimulus for HRD activity will come from at least three directions (see Figure 14.2). It will come from the bottom where those closest to the manufacture of the product or the delivery of the service are best placed to have innovative ideas for improvement, and to notice problems associated with existing procedures and practices.

Stimulus will also come from the top and cascade down through a management structure in which managers know that they have support in developing employee competence, commitment, and capacity for change. In this ideal world, the top stratum of management will have articulated clearly the organisation's aims and philosophy so that no employee has any doubt about where the organisation is heading and what values it holds most highly. In American and Japanese companies these intentions are often encapsulated in a very concise paper known as 'The Mission Statement'. This almost invariably includes statements summarising the

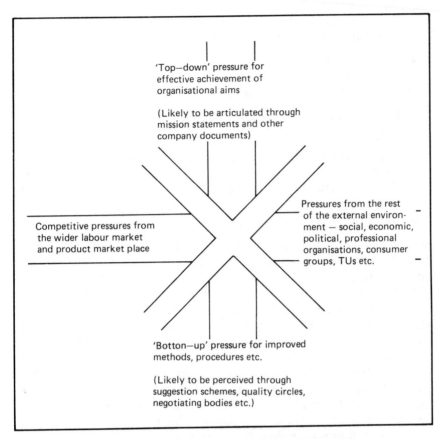

Figure 14.2   Pressures on an organisation for effective HRD policies

company's HRD aims and relating them to its strategic aims. As an example, one Japanese car maker describes its approach as follows:

BASIC EDUCATION PHILOSOPHY: to assist the company in its efforts to:

Offer the public superior products, thereby contributing to society through:

- research and development and creativity (good thinking, good products)
- marketing and after sales service (customer first policy).

Strengthen labour – management trust and promote a spirit of corporate involvement through:

- communications
- teamwork
- creativity, challenge, courage.

HUMAN RESOURCE DEVELOPMENT: employee education goals:

- development of personnel who can respond flexibly to their work
- development of personnel who understand the company situation
- development of creative personnel.

Statements such as these can leave no doubt in an individual manager's mind about the strength of commitment from above to positive policies for the development of human resources.

The third direction from which an organisation can experience pressure for effective HRD policies is the external environment. The activities of competitors have already been mentioned, but in addition to these there are many other forces at work of which an organisation sensitively tuned to its wider social, economic and political environment will be aware. For example, government exhortations to improve efficiency may be linked to grants from government agencies for training. Or customer tastes and preferences may be shifting towards those companies which provide 'the personal touch' as well as a reliable product or service.

So, in the ideal world, a departmental manager knows and accepts that the effective development of people at work is an important part of his/her job. This is fully recognised by senior managers, fellow line managers and functional specialists, as well as by subordinates. The role of the personnel, training or HRD department in this sort of company is likely to be that of a facilitator, enabler and specialist resource to be drawn on by departmental managers. Figure 14.3 breaks down the roles involved in an 'up and running' staff development programme to show the crucial role of line managers and also the enormity of the task facing them if they are lacking the clear support of the top management team.

In reality the situation may not look remotely like this. A manager who is already convinced of the benefits to his/her department and to the organisation as a whole may well wonder how and where to start.

Roles/actions	Top mgt team *	Managers	Staff	Specialist department **
Define policies	✓			Assist
Work within defined policies		✓	✓	✓
Allocate responsibilities	✓	✓		
Allocate resources	✓	✓		
Be committed	✓	✓	✓	✓
Encourage commitment amongst others	✓	✓	✓	✓
Clarify current and future priorities	✓	✓		
Analyse company needs	✓			Assist
Analyse departmental needs		✓	✓	Assist
Invest in staff development	✓			
Prepare training plans		✓		✓
Approve training plans	✓			
Prepare training programmes		✓		✓
Make and approve practical arrangements		✓		✓
Implement programmes		✓		✓
Coach others		✓	✓	✓
Participate in programmes	✓	✓	✓	✓
Check the results		✓		✓
Report on programmes		✓	✓	✓
Evaluate the total effort	✓	Assist		Assist
Brief and de-brief trainees	✓	✓		Assist

*   The 'top team' is deemed here to include the chief executive

**   The 'specialist department' here may be the personnel, training or HRD department. In any event, it will be the one coordinating activities

Figure 14.3   Breakdown of roles and actions required in a staff development programme

If s/he detects little or no support, enthusiasm or resources from above, receives few positive signals from subordinates, and is unused to considering external factors in relation to his/her job, an indirect strategy is probably most likely to succeed:

- The first step might be to identify an operational problem within the department. Ideally, this should be one which is not totally specific to one department, but might be mirrored elsewhere in the organisation.
- Propose a solution to this problem utilising one or more of the elements suggested in the section called 'Nuts and bolts' below.
- The benefits of employee development are likely to be indirect as well as direct and these can then be demonstrated to appropriate senior managers as but small examples of what could be achieved with organisation-wide programmes.

ASSESSING TRAINING AND DEVELOPMENT NEEDS

It is almost impossible to imagine an organisation that has no reasons for continuing training and retraining. The only way in which it would be theoretically possible never to have a constant training need would be in an organisation that could be cut off from change. This would mean that people in the organisation never changed, never changed their jobs, never got promoted, never died. It would mean the organisation produced the same product, subject to the same legislation, in the same market without ever making any technical adjustments or innovations.

However, back in the real world, there are many situations, both internally and externally generated, which give rise to training or development needs. For example, an organisation or department might be suffering from high staff turnover and low morale. One reason could be low pay. However, the problem might be more complex, stemming from lack of employee involvement and consequently lack of motivation to contribute more than their contracts require to the organisation. If the first diagnosis is correct, a pay review should solve the problem. If the second is closer to the truth, a comprehensive training and development needs assessment is indicated.

It is clear from this small illustration that training and development needs are generated both from organisations themselves and also, via the jobs that they do, from individuals in their departments.

What training and development needs are generated by organisations?

Different environments, products, markets and customers mean that organisations have different expectations of their employees. Therefore, different training and development needs arise and different strategies or ways of dealing with them are appropriate.

The Prospect Centre has developed four models which illustrate the range of environments and appropriate HRD strategies. Companies of even moderate size may harbour more than one type in different parts of the organisation. As change and uncertainty increase, companies need to increase the range of their response by adopting several strategies. Companies which adopt inappropriate stances can find their business strategies inadequately supported or even undermined.

As a first step, and to ascertain in which 'ball park' you are playing, it will help to decide which of these models is closest to your particular situation.

Ad hoc or unplanned maintenance

This strategy is, on its own, adequate for companies operating in essentially stable and predictable markets. The product/service is usually low-tech and is not subject to rapid change. The levels of knowledge, skill and competence required are relatively low. Any HRD needs which arise from time to time are easily identified because they spring from out-of-the-ordinary events or situations. They can be met on an ad hoc basis using whatever internal or external resources are available.

Planned maintenance

This model is best suited to a company operating in relatively stable markets. It can be assumed that it will operate successfully without too much change and that its competitive behaviour, its products/services, and its labour force will be much the same in three years' time as they are now. The company is responsive to some changes in consumer preferences without experiencing great competitive pressures. The product/service is essentially low-tech but may be complex and requiring considerable capital investment.

Companies which perform well according to this model have established programmes of new entrants' training, e.g. craft apprenticeships, graduate trainee schemes, induction courses etc. They

279

commonly run upgrading course (shop floor to supervision; supervision to management) and general management courses. They often have systems for manpower planning, career planning and management development. The purpose of these activities and systems is to keep the company in good shape. Ad hoc measures can also be taken in special circumstances.

A good system of planned maintenance HRD is not cheap. Money needs to be spent to ensure long term fitness but it is not seen as making a central contribution to survival or to vital changes in business strategies and objectives. It can therefore be, and usually is, cut in difficult times.

Business planning

This HRD model is needed by companies intending to change their business plans, or the strategies they use to achieve these plans, in order to achieve their goals. Such companies may be acting in response to important and foreseeable discontinuities in the market, in technologies, in products, in the political or social environment, or because management (often new management) have taken the decision to pursue a new range of business aims and objectives. This model is particularly appropriate when lead times are sufficiently long to be able to plan and implement the development of people as well as products and processes.

Formal off-the-job learning and a variety of job responsibilities have an important role to play in this model, as in 'planned maintenance'. The significant difference is that training and development activities are targeted towards change and innovation which will support identified business objectives. Typical activities include 'environmental scanning' and project teams, quality circles, innovation workshops − within and between functions.

Strategic capability

This model is particularly apt when environmental turbulence and uncertainty have become so pervasive that business success depends on the organisation's ability to cope continuously with and manage effectively new, unfamiliar and surprising situations. For example, it is appropriate in high-tech companies which operate in fast moving, highly competitive markets with short new product development cycles.

Such companies must rely on the exploitation of the knowledge and creativity of a great diversity of talent within their whole workforce.

Training and development activities need to go beyond those required for 'planned maintenance' by reinforcing the entrepreneurial, innovative culture in which learning and experimenting are part of everyday life. Typical activities help employees to accumulate a track record of positive achievement in novel and unpredictable circumstances. Activities may include secondments, sabbaticals, spinning off of products into little businesses and frequent changes of responsibility, as well as a vast array of other learning activities which are also associated with other models.

HRD in companies of this type is consciously embedded in day-to-day operational activities. Its costs are high but subject to considerable fluctuation. The non-budget element is likely to be much greater than in the previous model.

What training and development needs are generated within departments or functions?

The four models described above examine types of organisations in a 'macro' sense, in their wider environment. However, the manager who wants to undertake some staff development but is in an unsupported position needs to know where to make a start on the immediate, 'micro' level.

There is a variety of ways of approaching the analysis of training and development needs. Many of these, such as job analysis, task analysis and performance appraisal are well described elsewhere. They can also be very detailed, precise and consequently time-consuming in their application. Also, they tend to concentrate on the knowledge and skills components of jobs and tasks. However, if the subsequent training is then directed solely towards the acquisition of identified knowledge and skills, it does not help those being trained to develop their ability to manage or handle real work situations. A needs analysis which looks at the wider concept of 'job competence' (as in the 3Cs) is more likely to lead to a development plan which helps employees to manage situations in their jobs as opposed to simply carrying out instructions. 'Competence' therefore implies a capacity to use knowledge and skills for effective performance at work.

Five steps towards an analysis of training and development needs are shown in Figure 14.4 and might look like this:

Step 1 involves the usual methods of collecting information. Specifically:

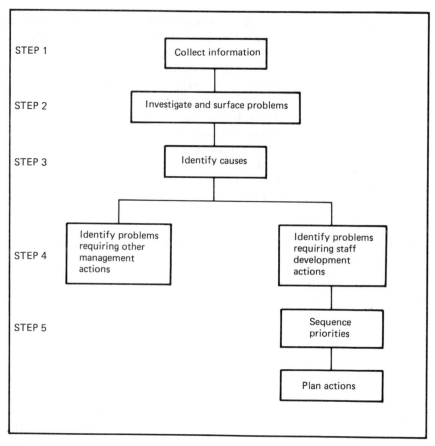

Figure 14.4 Five basic steps
The systematic process is presented graphically here. It involves five basic steps.

- interviewing and discussing with key personnel both inside and outside the department or function;
- observing the work place, working conditions, processes and outcomes;
- examining records and other relevant written information, both internal and external.

At least two of these methods should be used to cross-check the accuracy of the information collected.

Step 2 involves comparing the function or department's performance with its objectives, targets and standards as specified (formally or informally) by the organisation as a whole. Questions such as 'what is the key purpose of the department and in what respects is it not fulfilling that purpose effectively?' will help bring to the surface all sorts of problems.

Step 3 is crucial because the point in collecting information is really to identify the causes of problems faced by the company. Only then will management be able to direct or channel resources to solving such problems. Otherwise, the danger is that only the symptoms of problems are treated, not the actual problems themselves.

Causes may arise from some item or items that may be found to be inadequate or ineffective. They may also arise from a total absence of one or two items.

Inadequacy/ineffectiveness/absence of	Requiring staff development actions	Requiring other management actions
● Systems (e.g. production, distribution systems)	–	✓
● Resources (e.g. time, money, space, equipment, materials)	–	✓
● External environment (e.g. changes in working hours, employment laws, geographical location, economic/ market conditions)	–	✓
● Communication	Possible	✓
● Procedures	Possible	✓
● Control	Possible	✓
● Planning	Possible	✓
● Knowledge and understanding	✓	–
● Skills	✓	–
● Attitudes (e.g. motivation, cooperation, discipline)	✓	–

Figure 14.5   The major causes of problems
Check those parameters which are not meeting the department's objectives, targets and/or standards against the following major causes.

Step 4 takes account of the fact that although HRD is a highly significant factor, it is only one way to improve an organisation's performance or effectiveness. The illustrative checklist in Figure 14.5 may help to demonstrate this. Those problems and causes which produce a 'possible' indication in this checklist require further analysis and investigation. For example, communication may be seen by a manager as a cause of some of his department's problems. If he sees this as his supervisor's inability to present and convey policies adequately to their subordinates, then some development activities might indeed be required. If, however, poor communication is the result of a lack of proper information channels, such as the availability of newspapers or staff circulars, then the problem should clearly be addressed by other management actions.

Having identified the problems and causes requiring training and development activities, a manager can then sequence them into groups under different areas (see Figure 14.6). These groupings assist the manager in identifying what types of activities to embark on, for whom, and towards what purpose.

Entry training	which involves new recruits and staff required to take on new jobs
Problem resolution	training to meet a shortfall or deficiency in job performance
Training for change	to prepare staff for jobs identified for the near future
Development	to equip staff for organisational changes in the future

Figure 14.6 Grouping the actions

Step 5 requires actions to be listed in order of priority according to where the need is most urgent. However, it should be borne in mind that there are often unexpected and indirect benefits from staff development measures, which can continue to accrue over a long time. Therefore a problem may be a long way down the list of priorities, but some of the benefits from instituting the solution may relate clearly to a problem much higher up the list.

Step 6 is a further step which will be compiled with the help of the next section of this chapter, 'Nuts and bolts', and also, where appropriate, with the help of the personnel, training or HRD department.

If the manager following this systematic process is not entirely without support and resources from within the organisation, s/he must obviously at this stage consult with others to ensure that specific departmental plans fit in with any existing broad plan for the whole organisation.

THE NUTS AND BOLTS OF TRAINING AND DEVELOPMENT

This section is intended to help the manager find the most appropriate and effective methods to implement his/her action plan. Ideally, such a departmental plan will be a reflection of the organisation's overall staff development policy and so established methods will provide a good indicator as to the kinds of activities which best suit the organisation's culture. In the absence of such a plan, the manager should begin by selecting the sorts of activities which are compatible with the prevailing culture and support any more adventurous moves later on with full consultation and discussion.

Training and development activities can be classified loosely according to whether they take place on or off the job and within or outside the organisation. British managements traditionally favour off-the-job training methods, perhaps because these can be more readily quantified. That is not to say considerable on-the-job development does not go on in British organisations. Often activities listed here as falling within that category are simply not considered as such. They are often among the less expensive and less resource-intensive activities and yet can yield impressive and quantifiable benefits. For these reasons, more consideration is given to them here than to those off-the-job activities about which much has been written elsewhere.

Off-the-job training and development outside the organisation

The course-providing industry is one which seems constantly to be expanding. The problem therefore is one of choice. Training is offered by a wide variety of institutions such as training organisations; consultancies; trade, industry and employer associations; plant and machinery suppliers; and publicly funded bodies such as government departments or the Manpower Services Commission (MSC).

These external resources must be used with care. Many of them can do a very good job, but others may not satisfy the organisation's particular needs. At the very least when choosing a programme, it is important to see if what is being offered and expressed in terms of objectives and outcomes as well as methods actually fits the analysed training and development needs. It should also be remembered that however high the quality and/or the price tag of the external course or workshop, it cannot possibly do the total development job for any organisation. There is always a need to reinforce a trainee's learning through thorough preparation and then debriefing, and also to supplement that learning with further training by applying it in the work place. That way, the knowledge and skills gained can be translated into job competence.

There are other, less obvious forms of off-the-job training and development outside the organisation. These include periods of sabbatical study leave and secondments to other organisations. Secondments have been used in the UK to improve understanding of component manufacturing in assembly companies (and vice versa) and also for manufacturing companies to appreciate better the problems of the end user.

A large UK retailer also uses secondment as part of its personal development programme for senior managers. It seconds them for a year or more into charities or community enterprises which benefit from professional management expertise which they could not otherwise afford. The managers themselves benefit from the challenge of applying their competence in a very different environment.

Off-the-job training and development within the organisation

Examples quoted here are in no particular order of priority. Whether or not they are selected for any particular department or organisation will depend on the identified objectives for the training and development.

Subject workshops on specific issues

These can bring together all the personnel concerned with a particular issue or problem and focus their talents and energies on that issue. For example, a company in a highly competitive market might be concerned about keeping in touch with developments in its markets. The company could establish periodic 'competition workshops' whose purpose would be to provide information about competitors, create understanding about their people, plant systems and methods. This information could then be compared with the company's own, and ideas could be developed for beating the competition.

Senior management might be expected to participate in the first instance, but subsequently a wide range of employees (including supervisors and shop stewards) could be involved.

'By staff for staff' workshops/courses

These are used extensively by one well known American company in the highly competitive high-tech consumer goods market. This company's external environment and approach to staff development correspond closely to the 'strategic capability' model described earlier. They encourage staff members to prepare and give lectures, demonstrations or workshops on virtually any subject. These are advertised by the training department throughout the company. They begin in company time, but run over into personal time and are well attended. They accord with the company's general development policy of encouraging 'the habit of learning, the skills of learning and the desire to learn' amongst employees at all levels.

Quality circles and zero-defect groups

These can be used effectively to improve quality, to foster innovation and to increase employee involvement and commitment. However, they cannot simply be transplanted from the Japanese culture where they were born and grew up, to a completely alien one. Considerable preparation is needed through consultation and explanation. Also, specific training will be needed for circle participants and leaders in such skills as group work, statistical techniques, and presentation of recommendations. With considerable sensitivity to the prevailing culture, these circles and groups can make significant contributions.

Cross-functional project or problem groups

These can help in gaining the commitment of employees to, for example, the introduction of new technology affecting more than one functional area of the organisation. To be effective, members of the groups need undertakings from more senior people that their proposals will receive full consideration.

Training departments in larger organisations

These may have the facilities and resources to provide tailor-made courses and workshops or even training programmes using high-tech facilities such as interactive video.

There is obviously more scope to ensure that the design of programmes closely mirrors the 'client' department's requirements when they are to be run in-house. However it is still important, as with external courses, to ensure that objectives are expressed in terms of job competence, and not simply knowledge and skills. That is not to denigrate 'pure' knowledge and skills programmes which may sometimes be needed when operational requirements mean that someone who is already competent in their job needs additional skills, for example, a foreign language or an ability to operate a new piece of equipment.

Open and distance learning

This does not fall squarely into any of the categories of activities since it may occur on or off the job and either inside the organisation or in the employee's own time. In recent years open and distance learning materials have been produced which offer greater flexibility at lower unit costs than many traditional approaches. A survey of such materials, when considering the choice of development activities, might reveal that some of them support existing or proposed activities within the organisation. Although the initial investment is large, there is at least one large British car manufacturer who speaks very enthusiastically about the benefits accruing from its open learning centre.

On-the-job development

Learning to do a job while actually carrying out the tasks involved used to be universally denigrated by trainers as 'sitting Mary next to Nelly'. If that were all that was involved, it might be an apt description. However, an approach to staff development which incorporates structured experience gained in handling different aspects of a job with planned inputs of knowledge and skills training, and aims at competence in job performance is a long way from the Mary and Nelly syndrome.

Work experience

This has been used for many years in traditional apprenticeship schemes although it could be argued that they have historically been too narrowly skill-based and have paid too little attention to competent job performance as an outcome. Graduate entry schemes also often follow an off-the-job induction course with planned work experience in various departments.

The modern Youth Training Scheme is trying to alter the emphasis of post-school vocational education from education-led with some work experience, towards work-based learning with some education inputs.

Mentoring and coaching

These are ways of giving both organisational and individual support to someone's learning whilst they are in post. It can be as informal as a senior manager 'keeping a parental eye' on a recently appointed one who is not a direct subordinate. Alternatively, it can be used as a method of ensuring that someone in a technical or professional specialism gains and benefits from the right sort of work experience to progress to the next appropriate stage in their professional examinations.

Another form of 'assisted' learning is the 'Meister' training used in Germany for supervisor and foreman training. These programmes are designed for people with similar background and although they include advanced technical knowledge, they also go beyond that. The programmes cover supervisory competence, commercial understanding and the ability to plan and carry out training of, and coaching for, those for whom the supervisor is responsible.

Planned job development

This can be seen as a staff development activity or as something that any good manager does anyway. The choice might depend on how receptive the senior manager being 'sold' these ideas was likely to be and whether they challenged the prevailing culture or not.

An example might be job rotation. People should not be left in the same job for too long, but given opportunities for acquiring wider experience. This is not merely a matter of sensible preparation for promotion, but also a useful way of bringing fresh minds to bear on old problems. Equally, a planned system of deputising for absent colleagues (either on a similar or somewhat more senior level) could serve a dual purpose. The work of the person on holiday/overseas assignment/sabbatical would not just be left to pile up and the person 'standing in' would be adding to his/her personal development in a planned and anticipated way.

Finally personnel decisions about, for example, overseas postings or domestic relocations can be influenced as much by development criteria as say, promotion decisions are. It is all part of effective succession planning to ensure that personal development is a continuous process between promotional steps. A detailed and comprehensive database is of course an essential tool for a manager looking at these issues for his/her department.

Effective implementation of on-the-job development activities has been made much easier for managers in the field in the American 'strategic capability' company quoted earlier. That is because that company's training department has placed great emphasis on 'being close to the action'. Very few training officers are to be found anywhere near the training department. Instead, they are loosely attached to the various major functional departments of the company and are trained specifically to help departmental managers identify their training needs and plan suitable programmes within departments.

This is perhaps an extreme example of close cooperation between training and operating departments, but it serves to illustrate that appropriate expertise should be available to managers in companies big enough to have their own training departments. It is also clear from observing many other companies involved in this type of programme that any type of off- or on-the-job development programme needs meticulous planning and thorough training of any staff who will be used as trainers, mentors or coaches if it is to succeed.

FURTHER READING

Rae, Leslie, *The Skills of Training*, Gower, 1983

15

Performance appraisal

Andrew M Stewart

A large part of your job as a manager involves getting other people to do things that you cannot do, either because you do not have time or you do not have the necessary knowledge or skills yourself. Performance appraisal is intended to help you plan and control the process of managing your people so that they do what you want well.

Although a great deal has been written and said about performance appraisal few people report that they are satisfied with the way it is done in their organisation. This is perhaps because people have made a basically straightforward process too complicated.

The essence of performance appraisal is achieved when two people, the manager and the managed, sit down together about once a year to agree answers to the following questions:

- What did we set out to do during the last year?
- Did we do it?
- What are we going to do next?
- How will we know if we have done it?

This chapter offers some of the ways in which people have tried to answer those four questions.

THE PURPOSES OF PERFORMANCE APPRAISAL

People cannot learn unless you tell them how they are doing. Even this will not help much unless the feedback is both regular and frequent. Both successes and failures should be discussed. You should give feedback as soon as possible after the event. In the daily rush of getting things done you may well feel that you do not have time to do this. A formal performance appraisal scheme is supposed to make sure that even the most busy people get at least one chance a year to sit down with their manager to learn how they are doing, to correct their mistakes and to add new skills. Formal performance appraisal once a year is no substitute for daily contact and discussion with your staff about their work in the short term.

You will be reviewing past performance and planning to meet the needs of the future, so you are constantly preparing to manage change. You should be considering longer range targets, thus making positive and controlled growth for the organisation more likely through the planned efforts of individuals. You will find that you and your subordinate have an opportunity to move back from daily fire fighting to considering courses of action which may reduce the need for constant short term action. Finally, you and your people are expensive. It makes sense to try to encourage everyone's best efforts.

A performance appraisal interview can be one of the most motivating events in an employee's year. If you handle it badly, it can be a disaster. There are usually four parties to an appraisal: the appraisee, the manager, the central planning and personnel departments and external bodies. The external bodies may include training boards, trade unions, and various groups set up to monitor or enforce equal opportunities legislation. The interests of the appraisee and the appraiser are the most important. Performance appraisal done mainly for planning or defence purposes is unlikely to encourage people to perform well.

Appraisal systems are used for three main purposes: remedial, maintenance, and development. You need a mix of all three in about equal proportions. The remedial part of the discussion is concerned with putting right things that are going wrong. If you do too much of this, then the appraisal interview can become a disciplinary interview, and the record form becomes a charge sheet.

The maintenance part of the discussion is concerned with encouraging the appraisee to continue to do those things he does well. If you over-emphasise this purpose, then the interview can become little more than a nod and a steady-as-you-go message, without any depth or chance for your appraisee to raise new issues.

The development part of the discussion is concerned with what the appraisee needs to be aiming for next as a person. If there is too much emphasis on development, then you will find that you are spending too much time talking about the next job rather than the one currently in hand. You may even be seen as offering promises of future progress.

Above all, the appraisal interview is a time for you to listen. Your subordinate probably has a fairly accurate idea of how he is doing, and this is unlikely to disagree much with your view. In fact, your subordinate may well be tougher on himself than you would want to be.

VARIETIES OF SYSTEM

Many variations in appraisal systems have been tried. There is no single best method, but it is possible to list the main options so that you can select the ones that best fit your circumstances:

- Eligibility. Are all staff covered, or managers and salaried staff only?
- Appraiser. Is this the immediate line manager, the manager's manager, a technical specialist, a personnel specialist, or an outsider?
- Employee access. Do employees see all of their form, some of their form, or none of it?
- Self-appraisal. Is this done at all, formally, or informally?
- Preparation for counselling. Is this offered at all, formally or informally?
- Is past performance only appraised, or is there a separate opportunity to discuss present performance?
- Measurement. Is this against performance targets or objectives, rating scales of performance, rating scales of personality, or are no measurement criteria specified?
- Rating scales. Are they used? How many divisions are offered on the scale?
- Target setting. Is there an opportunity to set specific and measurable targets for future performance?
- Training and development needs. Are these discussed for the present job, the next job, or for the longer term?
- Potential. Is this assessed at all? If so, is it on a one-dimensional scale, multi-dimensional, or by some form of narrative?
- Salary. Is discussion of this forbidden, compulsory, or optional?
- Frequency and regularity. How often do appraisals take place? Is there a set time of year which is the same for all, or are the interviews conducted on the anniversary of arrival in that post?

- Disputes. Are these resolved by appeal to manager's manager, personnel, union, or by no set procedure?
- Access. Who else may see the forms apart from the main people involved? What for?
- Storage. How are the forms kept and for how long? Do you need to comply with the provisions of the Data Protection Act?
- Use. Are the forms used for central planning, day-to-day management, coaching, internal selection, or any other reason?

The design of your system should reflect the answers you give to those questions. If your system is not working well, it may be that it is being used for purposes for which it was not originally designed.

Linking salary with performance appraisal

Should you link salary with performance appraisal at the interview? If salary is seen simply as compensation for work done, then the link with performance is weak. If salary is used as an incentive, to reward outstanding work and to encourage rising standards, then a link with performance seems clear.

The best way to manage this link is probably to have both performance and salary rated on the same scale, but separated by six months. In this way, everyone understands the system, but you have some freedom to vary the salary rating if your subordinate's work standard has changed significantly since the performance review. If salary review and performance appraisal occur at the same time you may feel tempted to drift the rating upwards in order to be able to give a satisfactory salary. This introduces distortions which have to be corrected later, usually upsetting everyone in the process.

PERFORMANCE CRITERIA

The criteria against which people are judged should be genuinely related to success or failure in the job. As far as possible, you should avoid subjectivity. It is also helpful if the criteria are easy to understand and administer, and they appear fair and relevant to employees.

There are two main measures in use in performance appraisal: personality and performance.

Personality measures are not much favoured nowadays. They are difficult to apply reliably. They depend heavily on the quality of the relationship between you and your subordinate. There is little that anyone can do easily if they are told their personality is deficient in some way. This can be highly demotivating and helps no one.

Performance measures have largely replaced personality measures. They have two main forms: rating scales and objectives.

Rating scales are generally printed on the form and are held to apply to all employees. They allow you to measure change in an employee over time. They also allow you to make comparisons between employees. This is useful if you want to use appraisal records for central planning of salaries, careers or succession. The main disadvantage of rating scales is that managers may not be using the same standards when they rate people on the scales, so the comparisons are not as fair as they might seem.

Objectives provide an individual performance measure, agreed between you and your employee. This gives you and your subordinate much more freedom to decide how you want to measure performance. This can also help motivate you and your people because you will have to discuss and understand the standards that you are using, whereas rating scales can be centrally imposed without a real discussion of standards. The main disadvantage of objectives is that no common yardstick may exist between different appraisers and appraisees, making cross-comparison very difficult.

It may be possible and desirable to combine rating scales and objectives in one system, thereby getting the best of both worlds. If you take this option, however, be sure to keep both sections brief, otherwise no one will want to fill the thing in!

Precision in measurement is important and desirable, but not at the expense of having a system which people are prepared to try to operate. If quantitative measure is possible and appropriate, then use it. On the other hand, a qualitative measure, the meaning of which is clear to you and your subordinate, is usually preferable to a quantitative measure which assesses with great accuracy something that does not matter much.

Examples of the various types of measure, in increasing order of precision, are:

- Personality: drive, loyalty, integrity.
- Performance: accuracy, clarity, analytical ability.
- Objectives: 'sell x items by y date to z customers'.

Each organisation should seek out its own performance measures. An off-the-shelf prescription for the universal employee seems unlikely to be available for some time yet. You are much safer finding your own measures locally. Once you have found them, be prepared to change them as the needs of your people and the organisation change. If you do not do this, you can find yourself appraising people against criteria which are no longer relevant to what you are trying to do.

SYSTEM DESIGN

Each of the four main groups of people involved in appraisal has different but overlapping purposes. These purposes all have implications for the way the system is designed.

The appraisee will want to make a contribution to the appraisal. This implies a face to face interview. They may need to sign the form to show that they agree with its contents − or have at least seen them. If they want long term guidance the system will need to provide the chance to discuss ambitions, training needs, and abilities which may not be evident in the present work. If they want to undertake some form of self-development, then you should provide copies of written objectives to which both of you can refer whenever you need to. There should also be further mini-appraisals during the year to check that self-development is actually happening. Many employees also find that a formal preparation for counselling form helps them to conduct their own self-appraisal before you meet, leading to a faster, better focused, and more constructive discussion.

The appraiser will want the employee to work to agreed goals and standards. This means that the system must make it possible to set and record a number of objectives and personal goals, with standards. These goals may need coordinating with those of other employees, so it must be possible to record the information in such a way that it can be shared. The preparation for counselling form should provide the appraiser with clues about the aspirations, unused skills, and constraints on performance perceived by the subordinate. There should also be a record of training needs and the extent to which they are being met. If money is being used as compensation, then you can communicate a salary increase at the interview, since pay and performance are not directly linked. If money is being used as an incentive, then you should conduct the salary review as a separate but related exercise.

Central planning and control may wish to conduct a manpower skills audit. If so, then there must be some common performance criteria across all employees. For manpower planning purposes the form may need to record additionally information about age, job history, mobility, and family circumstances. Succession planning will require the assessment of employee potential, as objectively as possible, together with judged suitability, aspirations and current performance. Salary planning may require an overall performance rating across all characteristics for the productions of norms. The training function will need to know the overall picture of training needs to decide training priorities. Equity between employees can be checked by central monitoring of both quality and promptness of appraisals, and by a formal system for handling those who perform below standard.

Outside parties may have requirements which affect the design of your system. Training boards may lay down requirements for schemes. Local, industry or national codes of good practice may emphasise the need for job-relevant criteria, equity of treatment, and the handling of poor performers. Legislation concerning privacy and rights of access may require that employees be able to see the whole form, and that there be adequate safeguards against misleading interpretation, such as employee sign-off and a comment space. There will need to be a formal grievance procedure and a clear policy about who has access to appraisal information and for what purposes, together with location and duration of storage of records. There are particular requirements under the *Data Protection Act 1984* which may apply if you store any part of the information electronically.

DESIGNING THE FORMS

Because it is more complicated to approach appraisal system design in terms of the purposes of the various users, people often spend a great deal of time and effort designing the forms instead. The ideal appraisal form is sometimes said to be a blank piece of paper, so it may not be wise to spend too much time on elaborate forms. To keep the whole exercise as simple as possible, however, some suggestions may be helpful.

If individual objectives are to form the core of the process, then you need a blank piece of paper divided down the middle, with objectives on the left hand side and standards of performance on the right. You should be careful not to set too many objectives; nor should you try to cover the whole job. About half a dozen main objectives is enough. Anything more detailed than that is more suitable for day-to-day management rather than the overview of the year that performance appraisal is concerned with. Qualitative objectives, provided both parties understand them, can be just as useful as quantitative ones.

If narrative summaries are to be used, then the form will contain a list of key words, such as accuracy, speed, cash control, or timing. You will be asked to write a two-line summary of the employee's performance against each of these characteristics. This method has the advantage that it does apply common yardsticks across large groups of people, but does not ask for undue precision.

Rating scales will require that you rate the employee on each criterion, using a scale with a number of divisions. There is no point in offering more than five divisions. Scales with seven, nine or even thirteen points have been seen. Managers treat them as slightly vague five-point scales.

There are likely to be endless arguments about whether there should be an odd or an even number of points on the scale. Some people like a middle point. Others regard a middle point as enabling a manager to avoid making up his mind. You can avoid the whole issue in this way: label the points on the scale, avoiding the word 'average', so that the first four are concerned with above the line performance, and only the fifth records work that is below standard. For example:

- Exceeds standards in all respects
- Exceeds standards in most respects
- Exceeds standards in some respects
- Meets standards
- Fails to meet standards

In this case ratings are being made against the requirements of the job, not against colleagues. In addition, the scale can be described as a five-point scale, or as a four-point scale with an extra box for the unsatisfactory performer. You might also offer a 'not applicable' box for those cases where a particular measure is irrelevant to the job. Any overall rating should follow the separate rating scales. You could find it useful to consider a separate column to record immediate past performance. This emphasises the fact that appraisal is supposed to be a review of the entire previous year, and allows any recent, marked changes in performance to be noted without distorting the way you judge the rest of the year's work.

Finally, keep reviewing your forms and system to make sure they are still relevant and helpful. Use the system: do not be used by it. If it does not help you to manage better, change it.

TRAINING

Appraisal training falls into three parts. First, obtain the managers' commitment. Second, train them in the formal systems and procedures. Third, train them in the necessary interview and interpersonal skills.

Commitment is best obtained by holding a series of meetings at which all those who will be affected by the system have a chance to hear what is being proposed and to argue about it. The purposes of the appraisal system must be very clear. You can negotiate about system design, but try to avoid getting bogged down in form design. The form should be the simplest possible that will support the purposes. This will win you quite a lot of friends.

Systems and procedures training should not take place until commitment has been obtained, otherwise much time will be spent trying to answer the question 'why' when the training is designed to answer the question 'what'. The training should tell managers why there is to be an appraisal system, what organisational improvements it is intended to produce, what actually happens in the interview, how the form is filled in, when, by whom, who receives the form, what happens to the information, and whose job it is to see that the actions agreed on the form are actually carried out. Special attention needs to be given to the grievance and poor performer procedures.

Skills training is only useful after successful completion of the first two stages; otherwise disruption is highly likely. Three approaches to training may be worth considering.

Role play is used automatically by many trainers. The main dangers are that people can always opt out by saying, correctly, that it is not real life. It can be useful, however, where attitude change is important. Trainees can be asked to play the part of someone whose attitude they need to understand, such as someone passed over for promotion. Role play can also help to unfreeze people by asking them to experiment with a new appraisal personality.

Real life counselling involves one participant counselling another about a genuine work or personal problem, under guidance, while the rest of the participants observe. This certainly lacks the artificiality of role play, but can get out of hand. Perhaps because of this risk it can be a better vehicle for learning counselling skills than the normal role play, where there are no real consequences.

Live appraisal of real tasks uses the following sequence:

- one person performs an appraisable activity while the rest of the small group observe;
- all prepare to appraise the volunteer, who prepares to be appraised;
- one person appraises while the rest observe;
- all prepare to appraise the appraisal, while the appraiser prepares to be appraised;
- one person then appraises the appraisal while the rest observe.

Repeat the module as often as necessary, and conclude with a general review. The exact nature of the starting task does not matter, so long as there is enough to appraise. Subsequent appraisals quickly become surprisingly real, and issues to do with objectives, standards and the basis of measurement will soon emerge. Rich feedback is essential, and a videotape can help a good deal as people will sometimes not believe that they have done or said what the observers say they did. Keep the focus on objective matters, such as who was talking most at various points of the interview, the amount of tir e devoted to extremes of performance versus the amount of time used to talk about the regular performance, the use of open and closed questions, and the amount of positive versus negative feedback offered.

If managers are reluctant to appraise or to be trained to do so, try offering training to their subordinates in being appraised. As soon as managers get to hear that their subordinates are likely to know more than they do about appraisal, there will be a queue outside the training manager's door.

Common issues needing attention in the skills training stage include: knowing your own biases, being prepared to discuss both good and poor performance in a straightforward manner, using open, closed or reflective questions, handling conflict, listening skills, and summarising skills.

Common pitfalls met in appraisal, which therefore should be covered by the training, include: the halo effect, avoiding extremes of rating, talking too much, failing to support opinions with evidence, inadequate briefing of the appraisee, prejudging performance, not allowing enough time for the interview, not finding the right place for the interview, appraising on feelings rather than facts, overstating weaknesses or strengths, failing to take account of special circumstances, making false assumptions, and basing judgements on too short a time span. Training in these skills can have benefits well beyond the appraisal interview.

MONITORING AND CONTROL

All appraisal systems need monitoring. Particularly in the early stages of a new system you should be on the alert for two main kinds of problem: misunderstanding of terms, and misunderstanding the system.

Misunderstanding of terms may occur, particularly common ones such as objective, job description, man specification, training needs, development needs, counselling, personality, performance and behaviour. Trainers and management developers will be familiar with them but managers may not be, or may have developed their own peculiar definitions.

Misunderstanding the system will show up by forms going to the wrong place or being filled in late, inadequate coverage of certain employees or groups, peculiar use of rating scales, or partial completion of the forms.

Actions recommended on the appraisal forms should be followed up to see if anything is actually happening. The types of objectives being agreed can also be checked as part of this exercise. Predictions, particularly of potential, can be checked to see if they turned out to be correct in practice. Employee attitudes can be checked by means of a survey.

The following items have been found to be significant indicators of good interviews:

- I had a clear idea of his/her career path.
- He/she and I had the same idea about the direction of his/her career.
- My manager agreed with my rating.
- My rating came as no surprise to him/her.
- She/he accepted my rating of her/him.
- She/he fitted in with the rest of the work group.

- We wanted the same outcome from the interview.
- I could see him/her as my manager some day.

It made no difference to the effectiveness of the interview whether the manager had selected the employee for the job initially or not, nor whether the interview was conducted in the office or outside.

Any survey of employee opinions will raise their expectations. If you are not prepared to do anything differently as a result of what you find, do not start. There should be a policy about feedback of results, a method of feeding back locally useful results fast, and a commitment by top management to visible action if the results show a need for change.

IDENTIFYING POTENTIAL

Performance appraisal is designed to look backwards in order to look forwards. The best predictions of potential, using performance appraisal as the basis, are made when the next job is not very different from the previous one. The more different the new job is, the less likely is it that track record will be enough on its own. It would seem that performance appraisal is essential but insufficient as a predictor of future performance in a significantly different job.

There are many alternatives or supplements to performance appraisal as a means of identifying potential. These include assessment centres, psychological tests, assignments, secondments, peer and self-assessment, action learning programmes, career path appreciation, and so on. Ideally, any rating of potential will rest on more than one criterion or trait, more than one assessor, and more than one technique. In this way more reliable judgements may be reached in a difficult area.

If performance appraisal is to play a useful part in predicting potential, you should ensure that appraisal is on the basis of performance, not personality. The performance criteria should relate to success in the future job, not the present one. The appraising manager should know enough about the possible future job that he or she can actually make informed judgements. If you do not know much about the job, it is unlikely that you will be able to assess someone's suitability to do it.

Unsupported by other techniques, performance appraisal information can be seriously misleading as a predictor of potential. It can lead directly to appointing people to jobs just one level beyond their competence, since there is no information thus far in their careers that they are reaching their limit. You only find out by pushing them over it. This is neither kind nor efficient. However, the information yielded by a well designed and run performance appraisal system is a vital element in decisions about people's career potential.

PROBLEM PERFORMERS

People perform poorly for many reasons. Your first task is to discover which particular combination of reasons applies in the case in front of you. The problem may lie in a number of factors:

- Intelligence. Too little, too much, specific defects of judgement or memory.
- Emotional stability. Over-excitable, anxious, depressed, jealous, sexual problems, neurosis, psychosis, alcoholism, drug addiction.
- Motivation to work. Low motivation, low work standards, lack of organisation, frustration, conflict.
- Family situation. Domestic crises, separation from family, social isolation from peer group, money worries.
- Physical characteristics. Illness, handicap, strength, age, endurance, build.
- Work group. Fragmented, over-cohesive, inappropriate leadership, wrong mix of personalities.
- The organisation. Inappropriate standards, too little investment and management support, poor communication, span of control too large, responsibility without authority.
- External influences. Employment legislation, consumer pressure, health and safety legislation, changing social values, economic forces, change of location, trade union pressure.

Once you have found out what the causes of the problem may be, then you can use the appraisal system as part of the process of dismissal for unsatisfactory performance. Alternatively, and preferably, the system can be used to manage those people so that their performance improves and the problem no longer exists. Some of the options for action are:

- Counselling. Self-appraisal, preparation for counselling, some form of job climate questionnaire, vocational guidance, mid-career guidance, medical or psychological help, financial counselling.

● Training and development. As a reward and encouragement, not punishment; set up with precise, measurable objectives, careful monitoring and close follow-up.

● Changing the job. Physical layout, timing, induction, responsibility without authority, no feedback, late or distorted feedback, too many figurehead duties, little or no control over the job content, insufficient warning of changes, shared management of subordinates.

● Termination. This does not have to be rushed or without compassion; it can take account of financial arrangements, time off to look for a new job, vocational guidance, training in being interviewed, and an exit interview to try to ensure that all administrative loose ends are tied up and no residual resentments are unexpressed.

There is also an option to change jobs within the organisation. Some appraisal schemes specifically exclude this possibility. In those systems your options are to help your subordinate improve his performance to a satisfactory standard, or to dismiss him. This runs the risk of sending away someone who could do a perfectly good job if he were in the right post. The idea is to avoid managers shuffling poor performers around the system instead of coping with the problem, but it seems likely to be wasteful to make a rigid rule that stops you trying someone out in a different role.

There are particular groups who perform badly simply because they are unhappy or confused. You might have this kind of problem with new graduates who feeling that their abilities and expectations are not being met by what you are asking them to do. If people do not get a proper induction into the organisation they will almost certainly be uncertain and unhappy for a while, and their work may suffer permanently as a result of wrong conclusions drawn and poor attitudes developed through lack of early guidance.

Older employees might feel that they have reached their ceiling, or they might be experiencing difficulty with the increasing pace of change and the slower learning patterns that can occur with older people. People without clear career paths would appreciate information and options. People with a poor history in the

If you do the following things in the order listed you can be fairly sure that nothing major will have been overlooked.

1   Agree a time, date and place for the appraisal well in advance.

2   Make sure the place is private and free from interruptions.

3   Set aside ample time — at least two hours.

4   Bring all relevant results and information about the appraisee's performance.

5   Ask the appraisee to review his/her performance point by point.

6   Ask the appraisee about any problems which might affect performance.

7   Ask the appraisee about the implications of any problems or events, and their effect on the individual, the team and the work.

8   Ask the appraisee what needs to be done by either of you to help improve performance.

9   The appraisee should ask about anything which she/he feels is affecting her/his performance.

10   Agree the key result areas.

11   The appraisee should suggest and agree standards of performance for the next review period.

12   You should suggest and agree standards of performance for the next review period.

13   Agree future action.

14   Make sure the record is complete and agreed or signed off.

15   Close with a firm date for the next interim review.

Figure 15.1 Checklist – performance appraisal sequence

organisation need help to discover whether the problem is real and not merely a reputation which is following them around without any real backing.

The performance appraisal system should assist you to produce information, objectives and controls to assist with most of these situations, making the need to dismiss someone for poor performance rarer. The system should also help you to be more sure-footed when you do need to dismiss someone.

CONCLUSION

Your performance appraisal system should help you to be a better manager, and should save you and your subordinates time. If it does not do this, sit down and analyse where the shortcomings are, and work on changing them. Remember the four questions:

- What did we set out to do last year?
- Did we do it?
- What are we going to do next?
- How will we know if we have done it?

Make sure that you can answer these questions. If you find that you are required to do much more than this, ask what is done with the results of the questions. If the answer is nothing, do not ask them. If the answer is of no benefit to you or your subordinates, question whether the performance appraisal interview is the right place to be asking them. Keep the system simple and direct. In this way you will make it more likely that managers will actually do their appraisals, and you stand a better chance of understanding the results. For a checklist on performance appraisal sequence, see Figure 15.1.

FURTHER READING

Boyatzis, R E, *The Competent Manager*, Wiley, 1982

Gill, D, Ungerson, B and Thakur, M, *Performance Appraisal in Perspective*, Institute of Personnel Management, 1973

Handy, C B, *Understanding Organizations*, 3rd edition, Penguin, 1987

Margerison, C, Turning the annual appraisal system upside down, *Industrial Training International*, February 1976

Stewart, V and Stewart, A, *Practical Performance Appraisal*, Gower, 1977

Stewart, V and Stewart, A, *Managing the Poor Performer*, Gower, 1982

Williams, M R, *Performance Appraisal in Management*, Heinemann, 1971

16

Counselling in the work place

Mike Megranahan

The use of counselling and counselling skills in an employment context is growing as companies become increasingly aware of the benefits that can be gained, to both employee and employer, from these interactions. A trained employee represents a valuable asset which needs to be protected in the same way as plant and machinery. Counselling is one way of providing the company, as a whole, with the means of alleviating different problems which if not identified, discussed and resolved could erode the effectiveness of the person, not only as an asset in the organisation, but as an individual.

Every person at one time or another is likely to experience a domestic or job-related problem. Most people are unable to package problems neatly and confine them to specific areas and thereby avoid the effect that one may have on the other, e.g. home on work. If the employee perceives his manager or supervisor as potentially sympathetic and approachable, the opportunity to discuss the problem may be sufficient to help him see how it can be resolved. Any manager would be expected in the course of his job to undertake a number of formal and informal (or ad hoc) interactions with employees. The use of appropriate interactive skills in these situations should enable these contacts to be constructive, improve communication, and encourage trust.

This chapter attempts to demonstrate the differences between counselling and the use of counselling skills. It should also increase awareness of the respective uses of counselling and counselling skills, i.e. which should be used, when, how and by whom.

WHAT IS COUNSELLING?

Counselling may simply be described as a form of communication between two people. The person in the role of counsellor should be trained in counselling techniques; the person seeking counselling may need assistance with a particular area of concern. These elements set counselling apart as a form of communication. In addition, a number of important themes arising from different counselling strategies make counselling distinct from other forms of helping. For instance, counselling essentially adopts the premise that the person is the expert on their problem and the process of counselling is therefore used to:

- help the person talk about, explore and understand his/her thought and feelings, and work out what s/he might do before taking action; and further
- the person is helped to decide on his/her own solutions.

Other forms of helping

The need for counselling depends on the circumstances at the time; alternative strategies may be more appropriate and these may be enhanced through the application of counselling skills. The other forms of help which may be available to a person are summarised in Figure 16.1. Most can be readily identified with. We have all been in a position of giving or receiving most of these forms of interaction. In all these forms of assistance, the source needs to be perceived by the person to possess sufficient relevant expertise to justify contact. Where a person simply needs some information, for instance, counselling would be inappropriate, although counselling skills may help to establish and clarify the need for the information.

COUNSELLING SKILLS

Counselling skills may be applied in a variety of situations, forming an integral part of the manager's one-to-one interaction with employees. In addition to the use of the actual techniques of counselling skills, the manager needs to consider other important aspects. For instance, the manager needs to be consistent in the use of counselling skills across a range of formal and informal interactions with employees. He also needs to assess which situations merit the use of these skills: some situations may require more directive action.

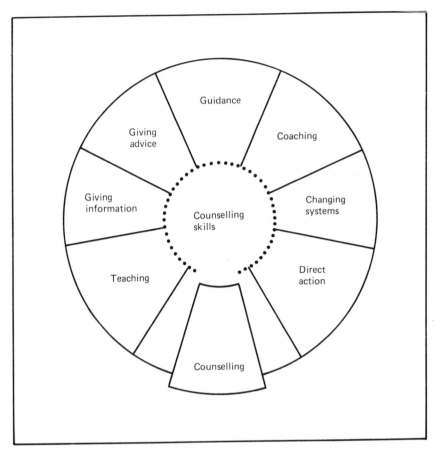

Figure 16.1 Helping interventions
Taken from Megranahan, M S, 'Counselling at work', *Journal of General Management*, Vol. 11, no. 1, Autumn 1985.

Areas where counselling skills would be applicable

The manager, through knowledge of his employees, should be able to determine when counselling skills may be usefully employed and would therefore form a useful addition to his 'kit bag' of skills. Further, the organisation provides the manager with the 'inbuilt' opportunity for him to demonstrate his approach to employees on a one-to-one basis through formal contacts. For instance:

● disciplinary interviews

- appraisal interviews
- coaching an employee
- redundancy
- pre-retirement
- career development interviews

Once employees become aware of a manager's style of interaction, e.g. enabling employees to communicate fully and in confidence, with a tangible end result, informal interactions may develop. These could include work- or home-related aspects which if confronted jointly by the manager and the employee at an early stage may avoid later deterioration of relationships and work performance. This mutual objective could help to identify ways in which the particular concern could be alleviated and may involve referral to a counselling resource. Examples of informal contacts are:

- ill health at home
- mounting debt
- feelings of isolation from work colleagues

The employee may or may not be keen to volunteer thoughts, feelings or other information which he may perceive as potentially damaging to his situation if revealed to the manager. Therefore, if suspicion exists between a manager and an employee, communication is likely to be limited and interaction poor. Directive action in this case may lead the employee to further suppress and withhold information. This cycle could also develop between the manager and other employees resulting in poor working relationships and repercussions on aspects such as morale, attendance etc. Counselling skills, if used appropriately, could avoid this downward spiral.

What are counselling skills?

For counselling skills to be effective, the manager needs to have an awareness of his existing style of interaction and its subsequent impact on employees. Once this awareness has been developed, the manager may consciously make use of counselling skills to improve or refine interactions and therefore communication with others.

Appropriate verbal responses associated with counselling skills are insufficient if used in isolation. Consequently the following guidelines need to be drawn upon to identify and utilise those facets necessary to a positive outcome. The guidelines are applicable to many formal and informal contacts and are as important as the person's ability to use spoken techniques effectively.

PRELIMINARY PHASE

The physical setting for the interaction needs to be comfortable for both parties. Consider seating arrangements, e.g. do not have the employee facing direct sunlight, the room should be sound-proof, there should be no interruptions and the employee should have the sole attention of the manager. If background information is available or applicable then this should have been read and digested well in advance of the meeting.

INTRODUCTORY PHASE

The manager should attempt to establish an open atmosphere for the meeting. The initial contact with the employee is important – rapport needs to be established quickly since this can set the tone for the whole interaction. It may take longer to establish this aspect with some employees but it remains an essential element of future progress.

If defensive attitudes are detected in the employee then attempts should be made to overcome these, for example, by explaining the purpose, structure and objectives of the meeting.

WORKING PHASE

The discussion with the employee should be conducted without the use of unfamiliar jargon or technical terms. Confidence and trust need to be developed as a result of the interaction.

Effective listening is very important and the employee needs to be able to recognise that this is taking place. This requires 'reading' beyond the actual words that are spoken, attending to what is *not* said.

There should be empathic understanding of the employee's difficulty; this requires an understanding from the employee's point of view, to see and appreciate the feelings he has in his situation as he experiences it. Non-critical acceptance of the employee's difficulty is important.

Interruptions to the employee's flow of dialogue should be avoided. Be prepared for periods of silence and therefore avoid feelings of awkwardness. Opportunity should be given to the employee to express feelings and emotions; and as far as possible these should be reflected.

PLANNING PHASE

At the conclusion of the interaction, what was said and decided should be summarised and agreed upon:

- define the action he wants/needs to take;
- express this in concrete attainable goals;
- identify the strengths and resources he possesses;
- what resources and skills he may need to acquire;
- provision to provide support and encouragement.

Appropriate interview techniques and question style

The introductory, working and planning phases of the meeting need to be supported by an awareness of the use of both verbal and non-verbal responses by the manager. The employee needs to be encouraged to consider and express his concern fully. He will also be very conscious of the way in which the manager is responding to him, an aspect which needs to be remembered. Various techniques may be usefully applied during the interview to assist both the manager and employee to ensure that important aspects are covered. Some of the main techniques and associated question styles are shown in Figures 16.2 and 16.3. The latter needs careful forethought, since the types of questions asked will either block or elicit responses from the employee. In addition, the nature and form of the questions needs to be supported by the non-verbal actions of the manager (discussed later).

Non-verbal communication — an area for caution

If what every person said could be relied upon to be a true expression of their thoughts and feelings then the above would suffice. However, this is rarely the case and the person conducting the interview needs to be aware of other indicators during the interaction which may be contrary to the verbal communication.

Equally the person conducting the interview will be projecting a range of non-verbal communications to the employee and it is essential that these support the type of questions asked. Very little

TECHNIQUE	PURPOSE	QUESTION STYLE
Paraphrasing	This involves rephrasing what the person is saying in order to interpret and clarify factual information for both parties	As I understand it So what you're saying is ...
Reflecting feelings	This requires careful listening to detect feelings, accurate interpretation to put them into words and suitable responses. It is very useful for exploring attitudes and opinions in detail. Empathy is important for this technique to be used effectively	You feel that ...? It seems to you that ...?
Confrontation	This enables the person to identify inconsistencies, logical sequences etc.	What would happen if ...?
Silence	This indicates to the person that more is expected and it should be accompanied by various non-verbal signals	e.g. Hmm? Ah? Oh? Uhh?
Supportive statements	Used to encourage the person to continue talking. Non-directive in form	I see ... That's interesting
Mirror questions	An effective technique if used carefully. Simple rephrasing of the question tells the person that you would like to know more	'I don't like the job' 'You don't like the job?' 'No, it is too boring' 'It's boring?'
Identification questions	These can be used effectively to isolate specific facts and information	When did you first notice the pains?
Extension questions	If further clarification or explanation of a subject is needed then a fuller answer should be encouraged	How do you mean? How can you be sure? How do you know?

Figure 16.2   Examples of positive measures during a face to face interaction

could be achieved by inviting an employee to talk about their problem in a loud demanding voice and an aggressive posture.

Figure 16.4 illustrates the range of non-verbal communications which may encourage (or not) an employee to speak openly and freely.

Review

It would be beneficial to consider the use and outcome of the positive

TECHNIQUE	PURPOSE OR OUTCOME	QUESTION STYLE
Multiple questions	This tends to lead to a confused response from the person. He is still trying to take in the questions, order the answers and recall the next question asked	Does your wife work? Can't you budget? Do you drive? Is it true that you're on holiday soon?
Trick questions	These may be used on the wrongful assumption that they may reveal some underlying aspects which have not yet emerged	Do you drink? When did you last see your doctor?
Leading questions	This type of question is suggestive in that it puts forward the right answer that the questioner expects from the person. Leading questions can take many forms.	You don't believe that ...? Isn't it true that ...?
Ambiguous questions	These tend to leave the person confused and the answer therefore of little value plus they interrupt the flow of interaction and make the person suspicious	What are you like with people? What about working with men?
'Why' questions	These should be avoided as far as possible since they may be perceived as threatening. They may also invoke justifications which prevent the actual causes being obtained	Why did you do that? Why have you asked to see me?

Figure 16.3   Examples of negative measures during a face to face interaction

and negative aspects which may occur in a manager – employee interaction. Two approaches are described below: the first is directive in form and tends to disregard the principles of counselling skills. The second approach is non-directive and utilises counselling skills. The position adopted by the person conducting the discussion determines which approach is adopted. The outcome for the individual is markedly different.

A directive approach to the person's problem

In this approach the pattern of interaction between the manager in the helping role and the person seeking help begins after a statement of the problem by either the directive manager or the person. The former controls the discussion. The manager may be seen to encourage the person, to offer solutions to his problem by directing a series of leading questions. An example of this would be an employee whose

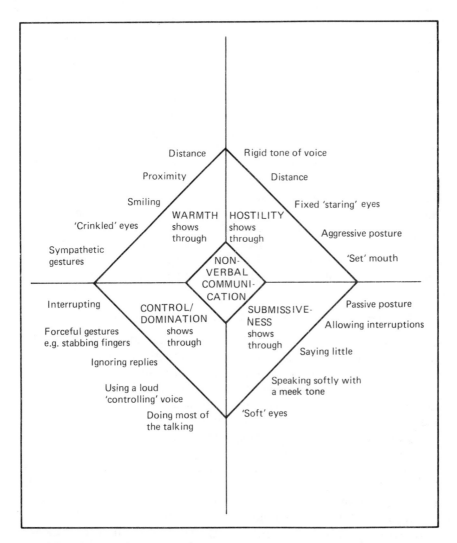

Figure 16.4 Non-verbal communication
Non-verbal communication can, during the course of face to face interaction,
provide valuable or detrimental projections which will be perceived by the employee:
adapted from Mackay, I, *A guide to asking questions.*

difficulty is one of poor time keeping. The directive manager, after condemning the behaviour, may ask why the employee has this problem. This will often result in a non-committal reply. The next stage may be for the manager to use a number of leading questions, e.g. Do you oversleep? Have you been ill? Is your car not starting? Is it the children? and so on.

Not only does this process seldom lead to the discovery of the real problem; it suggests to the employee possible excuses which the supervisor – subordinate may find acceptable.

The main forms of remedy offered to the person in this directive situation, once a problem has been determined, are advice, warning, praise, and reassurance. All these actions emphasise the superior position of the person in the helping role and the dependent one of the employee. The manager assumes full understanding of the basic nature of the problem and both determines and attempts to introduce changes in attitude or behaviour which will remedy the conflict. An alternative action from the directive manager will be to make use of praise and reassurance in order to encourage the employee to overcome problems, or to realise that no problem really exists.

A non-directive approach to the person's problem

This approach is based on the belief in the person's ability to solve personal problems with the aid of a sympathetic listener. The role of the manager is one of understanding rather than passing judgement. There is no attempt to create a superior – subordinate relationship, positions are more or less equal. The non-directive manager assumes that the person is in the best position to know and understand the problem. An appropriate atmosphere needs to be created through a permissive and friendly presentation by the person in the counselling role, with actions and statements which exhibit continuing interest but not judgement. Silence may be used as an invitation for the employee to speak further. Attention is given both to the words spoken and the feelings behind the words. The intention is that, as the employee talks about the problem, the situation will become clearer and a truer picture will emerge of what lies behind the difficulty.

Once the employee has gained greater awareness, new plans, actions or attitudes may be developed. At this stage the counsellor may assist the employee to check that as many alternatives as possible (and their consequences) have been considered. At no time must an exploration of this kind expose any bias towards any of the alternatives. A review of the actions taken at a later time may be useful for some people but that choice remains with the employee.

Summary

These approaches to interaction with an employee give different outcomes. The non-directive approach can take longer and create more demands on the manager. However, the end result is that of an employee determining his or her own plan of action through a realisation that they have the resources to confront and resolve the problem facing them. Since the plan is self-determined it is more likely to be carried out. The manager should never attempt to take over the employee's problem.

Directive action may discourage an open, honest and frank discussion of an employee's problem, and advice offered (with the best of intentions) may not be adopted and acted upon. This aspect alone may eventually give rise to further conflict and anxiety between the employee and manager if the problem recurs.

There may be occasions when the two approaches merge, and not every problem requires the depth that the non-directive approach offers. It is important to consider which features either prevent or assist the employee to express his/her thoughts and feelings about different areas of concern and to ascertain as complete a picture as possible before deciding a future course of action.

IDENTIFYING PROBLEMS

The early identification of an employee's area of concern may save both the person and the company loss of considerable time, effort and resources. There are usually a number of indicators of underlying problems and it is the early detection of these which, if explored with caution and sensitivity, may provide an insight to more serious problem areas. Indicators of any kind will always need to be checked with the person concerned; a judgement on the basis of subjective assessment may be totally inaccurate and would not lead to the resolution of any problem that did exist.

How then can a manager begin to identify an employee with potential problems? A number of factors arising from the employee's behaviour manifested in inconsistent or poor work performance, irregular time keeping, scruffy dress, constant daydreaming etc. may have been observed by the manager, prompting him to initiate contact with the employee to investigate. Alternatively the employee may not display any overt activity which may alert the manager to underlying problems. One example would be of an employee who regularly seeks information, perhaps not unusual in itself, but in practice it may be an attempt to initiate and sustain conversation. This type of behaviour is less likely to alert a manager to the potential difficulties being experienced by the employee, which in this instance take the form of firstly establishing contact, and secondly direct expression of the problem.

There may be a range of actions taken by an employee in order to 'sound you out' or to build up the courage to broach the area of concern. Personal experience and awareness of different employees should enable this form of activity to be recognised as potentially underpinning a problem area. Registering these flagging signals and thereby keeping communication open is not easy. However, to actively seek out flagging signals or potential indicators may lead to the misinterpretation of employee behaviour.

Examples of the range of indicators which may be observed by a manager and the types of underlying problems which may be their cause can be a useful guide. If any of the categories listed below are noted by a manager or supervisor over a period of time then these should be recorded and the employee invited to discuss these aspects in the context of employment-related issues, i.e. informally (as a work colleague) or formally (e.g. in a disciplinary interview). Where specific problem areas emerge concerning out-of-work issues or other serious aspects, e.g. alcoholism or where it is reasonable for the manager to suspect that other problems underpin the employee's behaviour, although the employee declines to reveal information supporting such concern, it may be beneficial for the manager and/or employee to have access to professional counselling resources. For the manager this would allow professional guidance on how to proceed with the employee, and for the employee recourse to an external help agency. Whether or not an employee takes up contact with these resources remains the employee's decision.

Potential indicators and their causes

CAUSE	INDICATOR
Marital – separation	Lack of concentration
– threatened separation	Irritability
Enforced change of residence	Indecisiveness

CAUSE	INDICATOR
Loss, e.g. bereavement, material	Poor memory
Financial difficulties	Verbal attacks
Reduced social contact	Panic attacks
Role ambiguity at work	Slow in thinking/speech
Work overload/underload	Feeling tired
Poor work relationships	Lack of energy/apathy
Family illness	Poor judgement in work
Problems with children	Irregular attendance
Problems with parents	Inadequate time keeping
Alchohol/drug-related problems	Unacceptable appearance

Note: There are no direct correlations between one list and its opposite; indeed one cause may result in several different indicators. Further, another individual may not display the same indicators even where the cause is similar. There is no order of priority intended in either list; nor is either list exhaustive.

SHOULD MANAGERS COUNSEL?

Managers can make effective use of counselling skills to identify, through discussion with an employee, potential areas of concern in a more sensitive and thorough manner and this may enable the employee to find solutions. However, it is necessary for the manager to be trained in the professional use of counselling if he intends to take interaction with an employee further and therefore confront adequately the types of areas mentioned above. In both circumstances it is necessary for the person in the counselling role to first recognise and second work to, specific key factors:

- The counsellor needs to be aware of the limitations in his own personal areas of competence and experience. Attempts to go beyond such areas may have adverse affects on the outcome of manager–employee interaction.
- Unrealistic or unchangeable expectations on the part of the employee may give rise to problems (particularly if the counsellor is perceived to be part of the employing organisation since this may encourage the employee to seek solutions through the manager rather than through his own efforts and insight).

- The counsellor needs to avoid encouraging feelings of dependency from the employee, the aim being that the employee should be independent.
- The ability to establish appropriate boundaries at the commencement of a counselling relationship is an important element, e.g. time spent in discussion, personal relationship boss *v.* counsellor etc.
- The counsellor needs to be able to call upon a range of resources available for referral purposes and know at what stage these are appropriate, means of contact, fees, etc.
- There should be precise guidelines concerning confidentiality. The employee must be certain that information revealed during an interview will not be divulged and if it is considered necessary or beneficial to the employee to break confidentiality then this should occur with the person's knowledge and where possible approval. The person his or herself should also be encouraged to bring the matter out into the open. Managers may experience problems of dual loyalty.

Whilst suitably trained managers would be able to undertake the range of potential difficulties that arise in the course of a person's life to the depth required in counselling they may find it difficult to be totally effective due to role conflict problems originating from organisational factors, e.g. role ambiguity, dual loyalty, time etc. Added to which the employees' perception of a manager in the counselling role may not be conducive to the openness and honesty required before solutions can be sought. Managers not directly responsible for the employee or staff roles such as personnel or welfare would also be subject to these difficulties although possibly to a lesser extent.

INDEPENDENT COUNSELLING RESOURCES

An independent counselling resource would potentially overcome many of the problems originating from organisational factors. It could remain totally independent; meet the employee's expectations of total confidentiality, and not threaten future career progression or job security; achieve a non-judgemental environment; provide counselling for the potential range of employees' concerns including work-related problems; and it would be able to assess and develop a range of suitable referral resources.

The negative aspects from an employee's perspective might be that the counsellor would have little or no authority to institute organisational changes. Communication goes from the employee to the counsellor but external action comes from the manager to employee; therefore the value of the counselling resource depends on its ability to help an employee understand his own emotional problems and work out an effective solution to them, rather than implement changes on behalf of the employee. Employee-initiated solutions would be more likely to be adhered to and therefore enable them again to be fully productive not only in the work place but also at home.

Functions external to a counselling resource, e.g. line managers, personnel, trade unions etc. may draw upon its expertise in recognising the extent of their limitations and that common objectives are shared; those of a healthy, productive and happier employee and consequently organisation.

THE OVERLAP OF COUNSELLING AND COUNSELLING SKILLS

We have discussed the use of counselling skills and the point at which counselling is more appropriate. The interrelationship of these aspects needs to be clarified to take into account the various permutations that may arise if an employee, for whatever reason, is not performing to the extent of his expected abilities. Figure 16.5 attempts to clarify these aspects and is based on the belief that work or personal-related problems may eventually affect a person's ability to maintain a fully productive position at work (or at home).

Once an employee becomes concerned about a particular area there are a number of ways in which the person may respond. The type of response depends on the person's own coping mechanisms (*vis-à-vis* the type of problem) and the knowledge of suitable and available resources. The resources reflected in Figure 16.5 are taken to be: managers who are able to use counselling skills appropriately to facilitate the emergence, identification and potential resolution of the problem; an independent counselling resource which may be in-house or external, referred to by the manager or contacted directly by the employee; a sympathetic friend or colleague who can provide a shoulder to lean on; the person himself, who may be able to cope alone without any form of support; and lastly the manager who does not employ counselling skills, becomes aware of declining work performance, and initiates directive action such as suggesting leave, proposing training, or even implementing disciplinary action which if followed to its conclusion could result in dismissal.

In other areas of concern, counselling may combine effectively

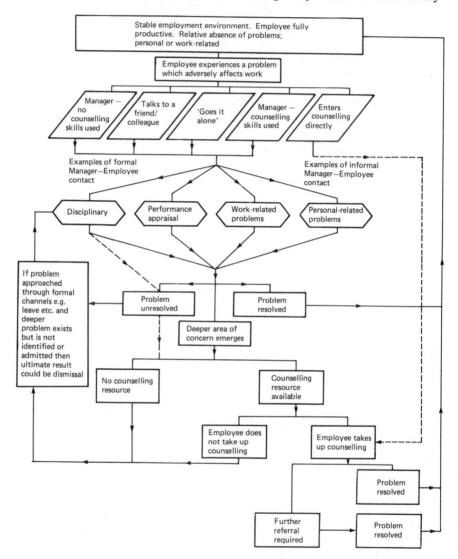

Figure 16.5   Interrelationship of counselling skills and counselling

with the range of other helping strategies to resolve difficulties. Redundancy is an example where the loss of a job may have repercussions which require a variety of coping mechanisms to be supported by different helping strategies as shown below.

Financial planning
Pension questions } information giving and advice
Statutory benefits

CV compilation
Application form filling } teaching and guidance

Interview training
Job search activities } coaching

Domestic problems
Personal stress and anxiety } counselling

CONCLUSION

The benefits from the use of counselling and counselling skills cannot be easily translated into neat, tangible ratios. Many of the benefits are preventive which may appear in aspects such as reduced turnover (and associated recruitment costs) and absenteeism, and improved communication. These factors in turn would be reflected in improved productivity and quality, plus better morale and job satisfaction. The contribution of counselling to the working environment and employee wellbeing is an aspect which may be 'felt' by the whole organisation but not easily measured. Counselling, it needs to be remembered, is distinct from counselling skills and the two should not be confused.

FURTHER READING

Kennedy, E, *Crisis Counselling. The essential guide for non-professional counsellors,* Gill and Macmillan, 1981
de Board, R, *Counselling People at Work,* Gower, 1983
Nelson-Jones, R, *Practical Counselling Skills,* Holt, Rinehart & Winston, 1983

The Counselling at Work Division of the British Association for Counselling provides an information and support network for people who use counselling or counselling skills in work or work related settings.

For further information please contact:
Dinah Wheeler
Secretary CAWD
82 Shepherds Hill
Harold Wood
Essex RM3 0NJ

17

Team building

Pauline Barrett

This chapter will explore the nature of teams, how to recognise them, how they are formed, why they are necessary, what they do and how they operate; it is about the realities of team life, the signs of a good team, and about ways of building teams from inside the unit or with help from outside.

It invites the manager, with some practical exercises, to pull everything out of the hat and to get the act together. The successful team may look as if it happened by magic but you can be sure that it did not. The winning team is the result of hard work and sound judgement and it is within any manager's grasp. Team building is challenging, exciting and rewarding; it is never dull and it is never ended.

WHY BUILD A TEAM?

Is team building just the flavour of the month? Is is really more than just good leadership? Does it have its own unique characteristics? I hope to be able to illustrate that there is something special about having a team (see Figure 17.1), and that a team building effort will give you a new base from which to leap to a higher level of success in both personal and business terms. If you have the feeling that 'things could be better round here' then you will find some ideas in the pages that follow.

The theoretical reasons for team building given in this chapter are supported by evidence from team leaders and their team members who have undertaken a team building exercise with outside help; the quotations come from participants who have engaged in team building events once, twice or three times over the past four years. I will be considering team building both as an event aided by outside intervention, and as those management skills and practices which can be instituted by managers without outside assistance. In either event the task of building and maintaining the team belongs to the manager.

TASK

GROUP INDIVIDUAL

Figure 17.1 The mysterious 'team'

So why should you devote time and energy to team building? Perhaps you have worries about your work group, or you are under external pressures which are causing you a headache. Your group/ team is not performing well and there is criticism from influential 'others'. You are aware that you have some square pegs in round holes, that internal tensions are inhibiting progress, and that there are people out there gunning for you. Inside or out there are powerful individuals or groups who could help you into oblivion. There is plenty of evidence to show that the well established team is in a strong position to survive when the weak go to the wall, so if you are under pressure from internal or external sources then this chapter will be of interest and use to you.

Why others bothered

The following quotations give a variety of reasons why other groups have taken the necessary steps to turn themselves into better teams. The reasons include the need for survival, members' unclear or conflicting goals, personal difficulties, or the pressing need for improved performance. Managers on recent team building exercises say they did it because:

● We were not pulling together as a group, we needed improved morale and output.
● The senior managers were a group of individuals and rarely thought or acted as a group.
● A new management team was created by reorganisation.
● We had rumblings of unrest between members, a lack of

understanding of each other's burdens and no real sense of
corporate direction.

- Ours was a new team and although individually able they were
not working well enough as a team. To the outside world they
did not have a team approach.
- To be effective in new markets we needed a team approach
which matched aptitudes to needs.
- Team building was to build confidence in each other, to agree
mutually acceptable objectives and ensure the best possible use
of team members.

WHAT IS A TEAM?

Time and again the question 'what is a team?' evokes answers in the
realm of feelings and perceptions. When asked to explain 'teamness'
both team members and team leaders fall back on what they *felt*
rather than what they *did* to explain the need for team building. There
is plenty of speculation about when a team is not a team, and many
attempts at the ultimate definition, but for any work group it comes
down to knowing that this work group feels and acts like a team.

To define the team it may be helpful first to say what a team is not:

- a collection of individuals who happen to have the same work
place;
- a collection of individuals who happen to have the same
director or line manager; or
- a collection of individuals who do the same job in the same
department.

It is a group which shares, and says that it shares, a common purpose
and recognises that it needs the efforts of every one of its members to
achieve this. A team is a team when it sees itself as a team, is going in
the team direction, and has worked out its own team ways.

There is nothing in this definition which speaks of permanence, or
the inability of members to be independent, or anything about living
in each other's pockets. Teams do not need continual meetings or
total involvement in every decision. Teams do not diminish the
leader, or the leader's authority. They do, however, banish hurt
feelings over exclusion, and stifle that paranoia which makes people
go to meetings they have no need to attend for fear of missing out, or
being overlooked. Teams do not do everything together; they are not

a hunting pack; they are more like members of the relay team which passes the baton accurately and swiftly at exactly the right moment.

Why teams are necessary

The evidence is that teams are much more than the sum of the individual parts. The existence of a team is liberating and enabling. When a work group is a team the leader gains in confidence, each member sees his/her own contribution in a realistic light, and there is a release from the fears and mistrusts which are so often part of work life. Team building gives a new perspective on the leader, the members and the task in hand.

One team member lists the benefits of a quiet weekend in the country, where his group set about team building, as:

> Clearer recognition of mutual responsibility in establishing and fulfilling common objectives.
> A breakdown of some of the barriers of rivalry/jealousy which were a legacy of the previous structure.
> An improved climate for debate by the team of important (and less important) issues.
> Greater willingness to contribute/participate in discussion and mutual support.
> Reduced preoccupation with the risk of making a fool of oneself before fellow team members.
> Greater awareness of other team members' pressures and problems.

If you think your team has solved all those problems of working life then go no further. If, however, you still think that your team has some distance to go then stay with these ideas and reflect upon your next steps to develop and build your team.

WHAT TEAMS DO

Any book with a chapter on team building will give its own list, so for busy managers I give a checklist on the winning team. Ask yourself whether, on these criteria, yours is a winning team which:

- knows where it is going
- sets realistic targets
- uses all its resources in energetic and imaginative ways

- has a wide range of alternatives for action
- instigates coping strategies as needed
- trusts its members to pursue their part of the common task
- has a confident yet realistic self-image
- handles its relationships with the outside world sensitively and assertively.

Teams do just what any work group does but they do it differently and more productively. They:

- plan
- have agreed goals
- make decisions
- solve problems
- succeed and fail
- agree, or agree to differ and get on with the job
- resolve conflict
- consult inside the team and out
- collect, sift and distribute information
- use known, understood and effective communication channels
- lose and gain members
- meet the outside world
- manage change.

Successful teams have seen themselves operating in the following ways:

- More planning, relating individual events to the total objective, less defensiveness in meeting or group discussions.
- Greater involvement in projects of individuals who had previously been consulted at too late a stage.
- Paying more attention to looking at short- and long-term objectives in our meetings.
- Greater reliance can be put upon each other, and there is a common view of objectives. Much more can be achieved by way of productivity, confidence of others (outsiders) in us, and adaptability to changing circumstances and pressures.

HOW CAN TEAMS BE DEVELOPED?

There are two areas of team building operation. There is team building as a routine activity of any manager, and there are team building events designed and used by external agencies acting as catalysts. In each case the principles of building the team are the same, and many successful teams are built without any outside help. We will look at the necessary ingredients for any team building activity and relate the different methods of development, comparing and contrasting their strengths and weaknesses. There is a logical process to the practice of team building as shown in Figure 17.2.

Figure 17.2   The process diagram for team building

The diagnosis

Before anything can be built there has to be an analysis of the present position, a collection of the facts. The groundwork has to be done to see the nature of the foundation for the building. Often the diagnosis itself can carry a team forward most productively for they have not previously given their 'teamness' much thought.

This section includes an array of suggested exercises for you to carry out on your own team; they will begin the process of team building for you.

So ask yourself some stock-taking questions to measure the state of your team now.

The style of the team

This is the first area for diagnosis. Look at the 'THIS' or 'THIS'

Figure 17.3 **A series of pictures for team analysis. Which pictures illustrate your team now?**

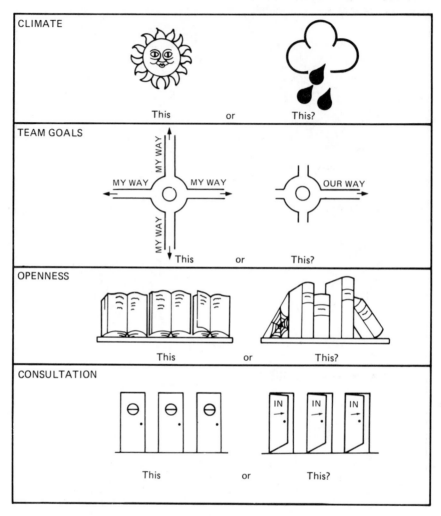

Figure 17.3 *(concluded)*

pictures in Figure 17.3. What are your conclusions about the state of your group?

If that gave you a few ideas but an inadequate picture try a descriptive exercise. Below is a list of adjectives which can be used to describe either the whole work place, or a small group within it. Go through the list ticking those words which describe your team and then write a descriptive paragraph using those words.

Heavy	Interesting	Soft	Traditional
Innovative	Tired	Energetic	Colourful
Respected	Closed	Learned	Outdoors
Reflective	Driven	Harmless	Feeble
Despondent	Changeable	Nervous	Solid
Polished	Fun	Open	Gloomy
Rich	Experienced	Promising	Young
Driving	Pro-active	Sheltered	Genteel
Attacked	Pressurised	Muddled	Past it
Narrow	Threatened	Inscrutable	Childish
Winning	Naive	Complex	Expanding
Dreary	Dynamic	Worthy	Worried
Distinguished	Jumpy	Fantastic	Competent
Trusting	Excitable	Confused	Belligerent
Patient	Losing	Anxious	Motivated
Supportive	Clueless	Treacherous	Threatened
Negative	Unhappy	Cheerful	Optimistic
Battling	Approachable	Reactive	Skilled
Nice	Divided	Organised	Creative
Boring	Practical	Talkative	Purposeful
Visionary	Academic	Businesslike	Influential

This is how you see your team. Read on to diagnose more.

The people in your team

These people are the lifeblood of your operation. Where has your team come from and what are you all like? The team building aspect of work life concerns itself not with the professional/technical competence of you all but with the match and mismatch of your styles and personalities. It is not about whether you have about you good engineers, accountants, lawyers or planners. It is about your separate and collective hopes and fears, your ambitions and past experiences. It is concerned with building team energy levels, team productivity, and the team's confidence in itself in the organisation or the market place.

So where has your team come from? Did you inherit? Did you choose? Or have you a mixture? Think about each of your team members and answer the following questions:

- Was this person your choice?
- If so, on what grounds did you choose him/her?
- Did you make the right choice?

- On what have you based that judgement?
- If you did not choose this person what did you think when you found him/her in your team?
- Has s/he matched up to your expectations?
- Does this person perform his/her own role adequately? Or well?
- Has s/he grown in the job?
- Does s/he fit well into the slot s/he now occupies?
- Is s/he stretched?
- Is s/he happy?
- When did you last have a conversation that lasted longer than a few minutes, and what was it about?
- What are the development needs of this individual?
- Are you in danger of losing this person for any reason? If so what?
- Do you wish you could lose this person? Why?
- What are your plans for this individual's future?
- How does this person relate to all the others?
- Are you satisfied with performance in all areas?

For the total team answer these questions:

- Are they the right mix of abilities and interests for your needs?
- What is this mix that you need?
- Do they pull together?
- Are there easy and accepted ways of dealing with conflict and disagreement?
- Are there any misfits?
- Is your present team up to future demands, individually and collectively?
- Are you happy with your team leader position?
- Do all your team members come to you for help when necessary?

Your answers may indicate areas of concern or the need for team building; this diagnosis is the first step of the team building activity. You have already started if you have come up with some rueful thoughts about your present situation.

Current team issues

These form the focal point for your team building. Write down some of those aspects of your group which you know could be better, together with some of the things which would help you all to achieve more and, in hard times, to survive.

Whether you are working on your own to develop your team or using external help, this diagnosis of issues and needs is a vital step. It is important to realise and remember that in the field of human relationships many issues remain hidden while insidiously affecting the course and the outcome of any event. It is in this area that checklists or other instrumentation can be used to provide a common base from which team members can discuss the way they see things. They can identify their similarities and differences of view and feeling. There are useful books with diagnostic instruments, including the *Team Development Manual* by Mike Woodcock, published by Gower.

One team leader illustrated the extra value of an external agent when he was shown the list of problems, needs and issues of his team. He said that none of these was a surprise to him but that now they had been 'named' they could not be ignored.

Getting started

If you have thoughtfully and honestly answered the questions above you will know that there is always scope for improvement. For the manager who has a product or service which relies on individuals and the group working well, and who is wishing to improve the performance of the unit/organisation then it is pretty certain that there is a team waiting to be built.

Asking the team members how they see the team is a good way to start. If you are serious about wanting to build your own team you could do a lot worse than find one, two, or all of your team members and show them the exercises on these pages. Taking them through these, preferably in a relaxed environment, could be your first step. Of course it is a risk; most of us have a work culture which is not open to the true expression of views, and which suppresses discontents until they develop into boiling cauldrons of frustration. It is these which the team can handle and the run-of-the-mill work group cannot.

If any of your own answers to the exercises give you cause for concern then start your team building by selected conversations to find out how the ground really lies. This may be quite tricky if your team is not used to this approach, and you may have to be reassuring about your motives for such uncharacteristic behaviour. You may also need to refer to other chapters in the book for tips on how to do it.

Working on team meetings is another good place to start your team building. Team meetings are often the only time when all team members come together and frequently they are deemed to be unsatisfactory for one reason or another. A recent comment was 'they're so boring'; many are worse: they are time wasters, battlegrounds, ego trips, and pointless. For the next exercise think back to your last team meeting and answer the following questions:

- Were you satisfied with the results?
- Did every group member make his/her contribution appropriately?
- Was it worth the time it took?
- Does everybody know what they should do now, and will they do it?
- Were there any undercurrents? If so, what were they about?
- Are you confident in your skill in the chairing role?
- Are you looking forward to the next meeting? And are the others?

Answers to those questions may give you some clues about making the team more productive and cohesive. If you would really like to build a team, type out those questions plus the next few and get each team member to answer them for discussion at your next team meeting. It is worth giving up an agenda item now and again to review how you are operating in your meetings. The additional questions could be:

- Did you have any difficulty in getting your ideas listened to?
- Were you happy with the agenda?
- Did you have enough information before the meeting?
- Were the environment and the timing right?
- What could have improved the meeting?

Team building tools

Whether team building is pursued as a routine activity within management, or as a special event with outside help, it is an art, a science and a skill. Working as a facilitator to other people's teams I find it difficult to explain what I do; and when I can explain, it sounds so much like common sense that it seems unlikely that everyone isn't doing it for themselves. But that view overlooks our management culture of keeping stiff upper lips, taking the medicine, not rocking the boat, and many more individual messages that are carried around in our heads.

You could already have done a great deal of team building if you have read the earlier pages and had a go. If you haven't, you might feel happier knowing a bit more of the theory. But eventually it isn't the theory that will build your team; it is the recognition of need and the determination to take on board something of the unknown.

The art of team building is to have an armoury of understanding about people, singly and in groups. Although a knowledge of the business/service and detailed work assists credibility, this is not what the team builder is there to develop. Indeed the art of team building is concerned with talking through needs, differences, and individual contributions, and not about the details of the business. The closeness of the team builder to the balance sheets, market demands and production difficulties can often make it extremely difficult to achieve the amount of detachment needed to help a team to achieve its deeper needs. In any team development there comes the moment when the team is ready to address itself fully to business plans and the future programme, but it is important that these details do not figure too much too early. In the team builder's art is the ability to see the team as a whole, and to release the energies of the members towards the solution of joint problems and away from the petty differences which can inhabit the work place. If the team builder is the manager then keeping the art going is harder, particularly when the manager may be threatened or uneasy about what is going on in the group.

The science of team building is the collection of the facts. Building a team will entail the investigation not only of what has happened and what it is perceived will happen, but also of how people behave, and how they feel about what is happening. Within the walls of British institutions fact finding is well developed in areas which can be seen to be measurable. There is, however, less investigation into the underlying workings of the greatest industrial, commercial and service resource – people.

There are now plenty of theories and practical instruments which can measure personality, ability and performance; and these provide both valuable diagnostic information and a wealth of discussion material. But the team builder will always use diagnosis as a guide, data as a tool, and instrumentation as an additional asset. The scientific approach of listening intently, collecting facts and testing assumptions is the key to the enabling skills of the team builder.

Understanding team life, its characteristics and its dynamics, is an essential part of the team building process. In recent years much interesting work has been done on teams and a knowledge of this work and its application to your own group can help in the building of the team through understanding and planned development.

The great strength of a team lies in the differences between members, and yet these same differences can be the source of so much conflict and misunderstanding that strength is rapidly turned to weakness. Meredith Belbin has described in his book, *Why Management Teams Succeed or Fail* how people are different, and how these differences play a vital role in their working lives. His studies show how individuals make their unique contribution in groups; he defines the characteristics of eight team roles; and illustrates how people with very different (or very similar) ways of working will not work well together. This has opened the door for a new look at work groups.

Charles Margerison and Dick McCann in their Team Management Wheel model have developed a scheme for mapping differences. They have researched into the work that groups have to do to have a fully successful operating unit. From their research into the necessary work functions (Figure 17.4(i)) and their analysis of personality, they have devised a comprehensive model (Figure 17.4(ii)) of the work *preferences* of individuals. There is, in their model, a link between personal preferences for style of working and the function needs of the job. By using the identification of these preferences and building up a team profile it is possible to see how balanced and finely tuned the team is to tackle the task in hand. It also opens up discussion between team members of their own preferred way of working which has been previously misunderstood, ignored, or undervalued.

The team management resource, built around the team management wheel, is a computerised analysis of team members' preferences backed up by exercises which help the group to identify its preferences and assess performance. It is a most useful tool for the selection and the creation of balanced teams and project groups; but is also most productively used for already existing teams, offering them a tool for diagnosis and, perhaps even more valuably, a focus for discussion which can cover every area of the team's activity from individual relationships to work allocation.

A good team is a balanced team, but even the existing unbalanced team can better understand its difficulties and take steps to ease them by co-opting new members or redistributing tasks and responsibilities. The team management resource offers a method of both analysing and developing team working and team skills. It provides a

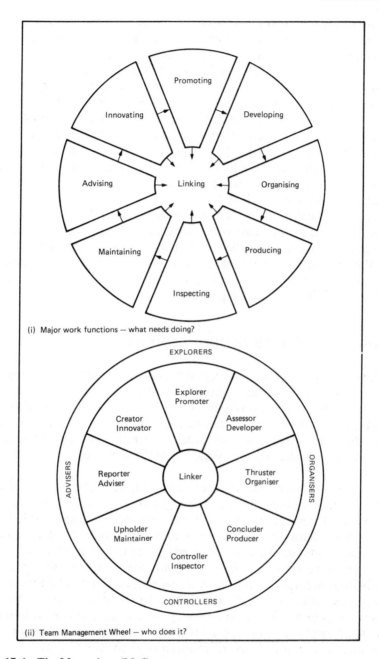

(i) Major work functions — what needs doing?

(ii) Team Management Wheel — who does it?

Figure 17.4 The Margerison/McCann team management resource

basis from which team members can understand themselves and their colleagues in a new way which opens doors for the renegotiation of work practices to the benefit of the organisation.

The skill of the team builder is that of the juggler. The juggler knows what the act is, knows the price of failure and against that balances the excitement of the risk and the likelihood of success. The juggler understands the environment and the essential resources, has many balls in the air, and plans strategies and practices to perfection. There aren't so many jugglers around these days and it seems there aren't enough team builders either. Practice and confidence in assessing situations and making interventions are the real skills for juggling and team building.

The practical skills which one sees a successful team using are nothing more or less than good management practices; the alarming thing is that so many work groups (not teams) do not achieve them. So the team builder's crucial skill is to open new doors, to unfreeze attitudes, and to reassure team leaders and members that this effort is one which will continue to pay off.

WHAT HAS TEAM BUILDING ACHEIVED?

It has to be said that not every work group is capable of being built into a great fighting force. Sometimes the ingredients are all wrong and the only thing to do is to go back to the drawing board. But going back to the drawing board can be a premature (and costly) business, and there are plenty of team leaders around who are amazed and delighted with the changes which have been wrought in an unlikely crew.

Teams which have been successfully built have been surprised at the improvements which they have brought about, and delighted with the unexpected results of their efforts. For those teams which have addressed themselves to the issue and have taken the path to team building, sometimes the accelerated one of external intervention, the changes have been felt in three main areas: the team leader, the individual members, and the work practices. These changes have in every case made a significant change to the organisation. In some cases it has been an insurance policy for future survival. It has given the team the tools and the confidence to face often overwhelming odds in the cut and thrust of modern organisational life.

For team leaders

Once a team leader is considering team building seriously there is a very good chance that the outcome will be successful. Many managers will see no need for team building and many others would be so threatened by the whole idea that they would never start. If you have stayed this far you are probably interested in the benefits which others, team leaders and team members, have seen for the team leader:

- The team leader became stronger, more dogmatic and decisive and more effective.
- The leader changed his style, individuals took responsibility for the group and not just for themselves.
- There was an appreciation by the team leader that he needed to show positive interest in team members and their departments.
- It emphasised the leader's difficulty in being a leader.
- I was more able to speak 'directly' to the team. I have slowed down my thoughts/actions ... as I have realised through getting to know them better that it is better for them to move one step at a time.
- Made more personal contact with some team members, felt that some (but not all) of the status and hierarchy had been got rid of. Greater commitment to the team and its objectives, great expectations had been generated, worried that they could not be fulfilled.

For individual team members

For the individual team members the benefits of team building have most frequently concerned receiving information from colleagues on personal and sectional matters. This has led to the unravelling of unsatisfactory relationships, the identification of further training needs, the challenge of colleagues' expectations, and frequently the growing confidence which comes from understanding self, others and the situation. The following quotes confirm:

- Individuals softened or amended their approach (although some did not). I felt I was able to be more tolerant of others and more free to approach superiors without feeling hidebound by hierarchy.
- Earlier problems with a particular colleague getting better, still disagree but we do debate the problems and listen to each other.

- Training needs were identified, some individuals had more confidence in colleagues and themselves and more issues were raised. One member realised that he did not fit in and could not make the grade so resigned.
- Less forthright and less confident members of the team subsequently blossomed into very effective managers and have revealed the potential that was stifled under the previous regime.
- I sensed a greater freedom and ability to communicate and to have dialogue with colleagues where previously I wouldn't have bothered.

For work practices

A team building event is often the first real look at collective responsibilities. It is a fresh look at the work group as a team and is a thorough reappraisal of the strengths, weaknesses and interactions of group members. And it can provide a new direction and drive which permeates other parts of the organisation or institution.

For the team it can increase understanding, and acceptance of their need for one another; it gives a new awareness of what motivates other people, and it is an opportunity to sit back together and think of the issues facing the group.

Work practices are seen to have changed in various ways, including:

- Team meetings more structured and effective.
- Chaired meetings better, ensured minutes circulated within five days.
- Improvement in working to objectives, reviewing and evaluating individual and group inputs in a more professional manner.
- Communication now more comprehensive and effective, even where the network is quite elaborate. Strong commitment to new goals.
- Greater autonomy for line managers but also more corporate management when called for.
- Greater use made of colleagues and working together at the top has affected work practices further down the line. Old dividing lines much more blurred.

In short, 'better results'.

ACTION FOR TEAM BUILDING

At this point it is appropriate to discuss the practice of team building using the external approach.

While there is an immense amount any manager can do to develop and maintain the team working strength of the group there can be a good case for outside intervention, and there are many consultants, facilitators, enablers, trainers and developers in the market place. There are instruments and packages, and there are people with skills. Some of them can really help you with your team building. In their book, *Organisation Development through Teambuilding*, Woodcock and Francis give some advice on choosing a consultant. Every manager has a choice and there are ways of finding the contacts. The Association of Teachers of Management has a directory of consultants who engage in team building activities and will supply information. Acquiring a consultant/trainer/developer/team builder needs some care for it is your group (and maybe neck) that is at risk. However, after those words of caution, it has to be said that you can progress faster and further with professional help than without it.

Of course 'she would say that, wouldn't she?' But years of experience of management development, with a focus over the last five years on team building, has given me the confidence and conviction that there is certainly a place for the fast lane to improved team performance.

My personal preferred style of working is to engage in an investigative stage with team leader and team members, to analyse the issues emerging from this investigation and design a programme of team activity which will address these issues, and plan future action.

It is possible to start in a small way on team building and to start today. Starting from inside or outside, with or without help, team building activities can be routine and gradual, or swift and accelerated. But before deciding about whether and how you should be proceeding to build a team you had better think about yourself, for there is no more exposed position than the one you hold. There are plenty of analogies about leaving the kitchen if you find the heat too much, but heading up a section, department or organisation is more like the chill at the top of the mountain. It is extremely cold, the winds blow strongly and there are few people to share the view. Team building is a demanding activity; your team members may resist the idea that things could be improved and may need persuading; you may meet some defensive behaviour and be tempted to give up. But if you do decide to work along these principles you will be climbing the mountain in congenial company, and others will smooth the road. One team which had a particularly bad experience after its team building exercise has said that its members could not have coped without the new foundations which they had built.

Another team leader wrote: 'Team building, like all sound structural engineering, should make sure foundations are right, that the structure has stability with flexibility, and also integrity.' Could you wish for more for your team?

Getting on with it

Collect the facts about your team; what does each member do, think, feel? What are the group dynamics and what needs improving? Which areas of the business are shaky? What is happening to the setting and the achieving of targets? Is all right with the group/team world?

Analyse the issues; those which everybody knows about and talks about, *and* those which everybody knows about and doesn't talk about. Take one or two which you have been avoiding over the past months and find a route by which you can approach them with the people or person concerned.

Choose the route by looking ahead to your destination. Let yourself daydream a little to see your ideal team. Then come down to earth and imagine the small changes which would make such a difference to you, to the team members concerned, and to the climate of success in your group.

The reading list will give you lots of starting points. But your greatest asset and tool for success will be the realisation that there is work to be done in the field of team development, and the determination to do it. Set yourself short targets which will indicate your success. Your journey will have no end; people and situations will be constantly changing, but it will be interesting and it will be productive.

Start now!

Open your own team building parcel (Figure 17.5) and discover for yourself that there is something new in there, that teambuilding is *not* a passing fancy but a positive way forward to the results which you want for yourself, your team and your organisation.

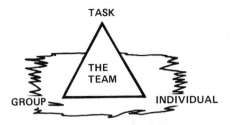

Figure 17.5   The team unites the task, the group and the individual

FURTHER READING

Belbin, R Meredith, *Management Teams, why they succeed or fail*, Heinemann, 1981

Margerison, Charles and McCann, Dick, *How to lead a winning team*, MCB University Press, 1985

Margerison, Charles and McCann, Dick, *Team Management Resource*, Details from IMCB, Castle Street, Buckingham MK18 1BS

Woodcock, Mike, *Team Development Manual*, Gower, 1979

Francis, Dave, and Young, Don, *Improving Work Groups*, University Associates, 1979

Woodcock, Mike, and Francis, Dave, *Organisation Development through Teambuilding*, Gower, 1981

Patten, Thomas H, *Organizational Development Through Teambuilding*, John Wiley & Sons, 1981

Adair, John, *Effective Teambuilding*, Gower, 1986

Hastings, Colin, Bixby, Peter, and Chaudhry Lawton, Rani, *The Superteam Solution*, Gower, 1986

18

Making the most of your support staff*

Corinne Devery

There are hundreds of books written on management, and many different training courses. Yet very few books or courses provide practical training or even basic information on how to use support staff, usually called 'secretaries'. Most managers learn through trial and error, i.e. by being trained (or not) by the secretaries they encounter in the course of their careers.

THE NATURE OF THE BEAST

There is a reason for my inverted commas above. To most people, the word 'secretary' conjures up a mental picture of either a pretty 'dollybird' sitting on the (male) boss's knee, or a ferocious old dragon, zealously guarding the entrance to the boss's office!

The truth, of course, is *not* to be found half-way between the two. A secretary, in modern terms, is an assistant to management, who helps managers achieve objectives by coping with routine administration and anything else that a manager chooses to delegate.

Nowadays, the word 'secretary' is almost synonymous with 'typist', so a variety of other job titles have been created: personal assistant, coordinator, executive secretary, and so on. But, whatever the job title, as a manager you will one day acquire the services of an assistant.

* Corinne Devery wrote this chapter while at the Industrial Society.

WHAT DO SECRETARIES DO?

In addition to processing text — the modern equivalent of typing — on a word processor or typewriter, the secretary's actual job falls into four main functions: information, coordination, organisation, communication. A secretary also needs certain skills and qualities such as initiative, tact, loyalty, a sense of humour, and an understanding of the manager's job. Let us hope that your secretary possesses all of these admirable traits, and more. However, as a manager you have certain responsibilities too. Within each of those four basic functions, there are actions that managers must take to ensure that the secretary is able to do the job properly.

INFORMATION

The use of initiative and the ability to think ahead depends entirely on knowledge and experience. Much of that is provided by you. *You* must tell your secretary about: the organisation — what it does, who's who, structure, policies and plans; your own job, where it fits in to the overall structure, main internal and external contacts; the secretary's job itself — standards expected, working method, office systems.

This last point may provoke a cry of 'It's the secretary's job to do the filing . . .' and this is a good example of how the boss/secretary partnership should operate. You should *both* decide on a system that works, and leave the monitoring and maintenance to the secretary.

Strange as it may seem there are managers who like filing, or rather, they like hoarding bits of paper, or keeping everything under lock and key! Trust is a vital factor in the boss/secretary partnership — remember that the word 'secretary' implies confidentiality.

Never underestimate the secretary's intelligence when it comes to filing — I have felt rather disgusted when a manager has said 'my filing system is very technical, and I really couldn't expect my secretary to understand it!' Remember, you are paid to get on with the job of managing, not to spend valuable time doing things your secretary should be taking off your hands! Some help from you may be needed, especially at first, but familiarity with the papers that appear daily on a desk usually helps decide what goes where.

Often, a good filing system becomes unwieldy because it is not 'weeded' regularly. You must be ruthless with paper, and discard unnecessary items that will never be required again. (Chapter 3 offers guidelines and ideas.)

COMMUNICATION

The key to a successful boss/secretary partnership is communication. Indeed, the primary complaint by secretaries is that managers fail to communicate. They may have meetings regularly with other staff, but assume that as they have walked past the secretary's desk several times in a day, sufficient communication has taken place!

There is the problem of the 'disappearing boss' who leaves the office without telling the secretary and is nowhere to be found when needed. There is also the problem of managers who realise subordinates need to know why some jobs must be done as well as how, but forget that secretaries need information to function properly. Many secretaries work in a vacuum, carrying out instructions but afraid to use their own initiative or judgement because they lack necessary background knowledge. A shamefully large number of bosses never actually *talk* to their secretaries, other than social chat, or when giving dictation.

You, of course, will not make any of these mistakes! You will make a habit of a regular briefing meeting, apart from dictation sessions. One every two weeks is the minimum. (Lack of time is no excuse because the meeting need last only ten minutes and will probably save more time than it occupies.) The following could be discussed at such a meeting:

- the results of any meetings you attended;
- future plans affecting your, and therefore the secretary's workload;
- reassessment of your priorities to help the secretary organise time so that important things are done first;
- checking diaries to see that the same appointments appear in both;
- telephone calls received, action taken and advice needed on future action;
- potential office problems, e.g. a discontented member of staff who does not want to speak to the boss personally.

Once this routine is established, suitable subject matter will suggest itself. The idea is to improve communication between you and your secretary so that you get used to talking fairly formally (and therefore seriously) about work. Often, secretaries have useful suggestions for improving an office system or solving a problem but they never pluck up courage to approach the boss. I am sure you would hate to have such an effect on *your* secretary but there are some intimidating bosses around!

A possible source of irritation is the telephone. If you repeatedly fail to ring somebody back (perhaps because you do not wish to talk to them) your secretary may be blamed for not informing you of the calls. Another telephone 'sin' is failure to listen when a secretary briefs you about the caller. You then pick up the phone, and say 'Bloggs here, what would you like to speak to me about?' This will exasperate the caller who then has to go through the entire story again. Notice that I have suggested filtering calls via the secretary. Modern telephone systems often bypass secretaries but they learn about your contacts by intercepting calls, and can save you time by dealing with many of them. It is, I feel, somewhat arrogant to assume that you are the only person who can deal with a call; it may well be a particularly technical, or political, matter, but often a caller simply wants help and a secretary can as easily provide that as you.

ORGANISATION

As I have mentioned, much of the secretary's time is spent saving management time, and dealing with routine administration. To put things another way, managers plan; secretaries process plans. However, to enable this to happen, you must let the secretary deal with certain aspects of your work. The diary is a good example and you should let your secretary take charge of the main diary. If you also like to keep a pocket, or duplicate, diary then make sure you liaise frequently to avoid double booking.

If your secretary has actually made the appointment then changes become easier − it is frustrating and difficult to be half-involved in any project. It will also be the secretary who is asked of your whereabouts and if the answer is 'I don't know, and I'm not sure when he/she is back . . .', you will *both* look inefficient. Communication and information both come into the successful running of the diary. If you have kept your secretary informed, then it is easy to estimate accurately the amount of time needed for an appointment or meeting. You will not have to rush from one thing to another, inadequately prepared. Your secretary can organise relevant papers, and save *you* the worry of remembering.

The post is another delegated responsibility. If your secretary gets to it before you, it can be sorted and prioritised, and thus save your valuable time. You may well say, 'but I like getting my letters first to see what comes in'. Remember, management is concerned with giving others a chance to develop their skills (delegation) and showing your confidence in their abilities (motivation). Also, your secretary will be kept informed, and be able to anticipate the resulting workload.

Do let your secretary write as many letters as possible, on your behalf. This saves time spent dictating and gives your secretary the opportunity to develop a valuable skill. On the subject of dictation, it is true that shorthand is less used nowadays but if your secretary can take shorthand, and wants to make use of it, then do practise dictation. Practice makes perfect, and secretaries welcome the chance to ask questions and clarify any points. That, of course, is the real benefit of shorthand, as audio is much quicker and cheaper in terms of time spent. Ideally, both should be used but the slowest and most irritating method of transferring your thoughts to a typewritten text is to write it all out in manuscript. You speak much faster than you write and it really is a question of practice. Yes, I know you like to 'see things written down' but a draft copy, done on the word processor, will enable you to see how the text is shaping up.

By the way, please do not get carried away by the correction facility on word processors. You may find that a document takes far longer on the word processor because you have overdone the number of drafts, when you would have thought twice if a typewriter was used.

MEETINGS

If you are fairly typical of managers today, you will be expected to attend and arrange meetings. (You may say 'far too many, in fact' but that is another story, dealt with in Chapter 20 of this book.) When you need to attend a meeting, your secretary can collate any relevant information, such as minutes, reports etc. and make sure you get there on time.

If *you* have to hold one, just tell your secretary who needs to be there, what it's all about (*very* important) and how long you need — an hour, a morning etc. This gives your secretary an opportunity to use initiative in anticipating refreshments, equipment etc. and saves you all the ringing around to find a suitable day. In fact, if you exclude your secretary from arrangements of this kind, you will eventually find it causes resentment. You probably will want to rely on your secretary sometimes to make the excuse, 'in a meeting . . .' so it makes sense to delegate this task. It is much more efficient to let secretaries liaise with each other about meetings, and provide bosses with details of time, venue and purpose (if known).

EFFICIENT SYSTEMS

Secretaries are trained to create and maintain efficient systems in their offices. It may help if you know about one or two that may help you to organise yourself better.

The bring forward system is designed to remind you of something to be done at a future date and avoid putting too much of a strain on the memory, or littering the desk with reminder notes. For example, today is 8 January and a letter arrives, from Smith and Bloggs, to which you reply. Smith and Bloggs should send another letter within ten days, and if none arrives, a telephone call is needed to chase it up. The original letter and reply go on the appropriate file, and another copy in the bring forward file under 18.

Every morning your secretary looks under that day's date and takes appropriate action on each document. Thus, on 18 January, the Smith and Bloggs letter will emerge, and you or your secretary can finish dealing with it. If it is necessary to chase up the company again in March, put a note into the March file.

On the last day of each month, the current month's file should be empty, and all the papers from the next month should be sorted into date order and placed in the 1−31 current file; you can either use suspension files in a filing cabinet, or buy an expanding file, marked 1−31.

A bring forward system has many uses:

- letters requiring an answer
- reminders for deadlines
- due dates for reports and papers
- telephone calls to be made and returned
- papers for meetings
- follow-up action reminders from meetings
- reminders about appointments and anniversaries
- items for the agenda of meetings
- monitoring delegated work to team members.

It is *not* a good idea to put the original papers in the bring forward file, as this means the file is not up to date. It is better to use copies, or bring forward slips. The system must also be checked daily or will be useless.

Your secretary is responsible for helping you to sort out priorities. It helps if your mail (excluding all items that the secretary can deal with straight away) arrives on your desk already sorted into three piles – action, information and reading. This ensures that you can make the best use of your time, and know what needs attention first.

A final system worth mentioning refers to our old friend the filing! Whichever classification system you and your secretary have chosen, there should be an index, or list, of files contained within the system. This must be kept up to date by your secretary and will prove very useful when you need to find something and your secretary has disappeared (unlikely, of course!).

COORDINATION

As a manager, you will probably have responsibility for other subordinates as well as a secretary. You may even have to share your secretary with others, a common practice in offices nowadays. Then, communication becomes even more important. Your secretary should keep a 'movement sheet' on a weekly basis, informing you of your staff's whereabouts. You must tell your staff to liaise with each other and you via the secretary and monitor that this happens. Otherwise, your secretary will not be part of the team.

Obviously, a secretary who works for several bosses cannot provide the same level of assistance as on a 1:1 or 1:2 ratio. But too many managers fail to take note of this and constantly blame the secretary for not spending enough time on one individual, or misunderstanding priorities.

Here are some points worth noting if you have to share a secretary:

- Consult frequently other team members so you are aware of each others' workload.
- Work out priorities amongst the team so that the secretary is not 'pig in the middle'.
- Involve the secretary in team meetings.
- Understand that some of the personal assistant's functions will not be possible with a large typing workload.
- Ensure all your staff (if you are in charge) know and understand the office systems too.
- Avoid 'pulling rank' to get more attention.

- Always keep the secretary informed of movements and appointments.

If you stick to these simple rules you will make the best of what can be a difficult situation

MOTIVATION

In the preceding sections I have talked about what you as a manager should do to work well with your secretary. I have not mentioned motivation or, in other words, what will make your secretary want to work for you willingly and well. The following comments give examples of what motivates a secretary:

- 'He never takes me for granted. His thanks are always genuine and not just empty or insincere words for courtesy's sake.'
- 'My boss takes me into her confidence over problem issues and gives me the chance to put my views forward. She makes me feel that my presence is of value − I like that.'
- 'I get a warm glow when he rings up to say that he'll be out of the office all day but he knows I can cope. Other bosses I've worked for have thought they were indispensable.'
- 'It is flattering to work for a boss who is not too proud to ask my advice on office matters.'
- 'Other secretaries in the company pity me. They think my boss is a Tartar because she demands perfection. But they don't see her good side − and I appreciate that my own standards have risen since I came to work for her.'
- 'If my boss asks me to carry out any private jobs for him (shopping, booking theatre seats, and so forth), he makes it clear that I am doing him a personal favour and doesn't expect it as a right.'
- 'However busy he may be, my boss always takes the trouble to explain the background to any project we may be working on. It makes my job so much more interesting.'

In addition to all this, a secretary will respond to the same motivators as your other subordinates, i.e. thanks, praise, encouragement. Aim to become a 'gardener boss', one who grows and develops people to their full potential. You will benefit in the end although it is very tempting to hang on to someone who is good and tell yourself you cannot manage without that person.

The aim of management is to achieve results through others, and your secretary is the one person whose job exists purely to help you achieve *your* objectives. Remember, a good secretary can make an inefficient or downright bad manager look good whereas a bad secretary will make a good manager seem ineffective!

When you recruit a secretary, sit down and discuss how you are going to work together, and make a good start on your working partnership. Secretaries are an overlooked resource in many offices and it makes economic sense to encourage their contribution. Those who feel their work and ideas are valued, and who realise the important part they play in obtaining results will work harder and more willingly than those who are made to feel very small cogs in a huge machine.

Of course, all the above applies to clerical and administrative assistants too. They all come under the umbrella heading of support staff and should be treated exactly the same way as other members of your team.

If you bear all this in mind and act upon it your performance as a manager will be enhanced.

FURTHER READING

Devery, C, *Working with management − a secretary's guide*, The Industrial Society, 1985

Devery, C, *Working with a secretary − a manager's guide*, The Industrial Society, 1986

Garnett, J, *The manager's responsibility for communication − notes for managers*, The Industrial Society, rev. 1971

Forrest, A, *Delegation − notes for managers*, The Industrial Society, 1971

Pernet, R, *Effective use of time − notes for managers*, The Industrial Society, 1978

Simpson, W.A., *Motivation − notes for managers*, The Industrial Society

19

Managing communication

John Adair

> Communication and consultation are essential in all establishments. They are necessary to promote operational efficiency and mutual understanding, as well as the individual employee's sense of satisfaction and involvement in his job.
>
> Industrial Relations Code of Practice

Many social changes during recent years have highlighted the need for better communication. The increased complexity and pace of life, the rising standards of education, ever larger organisations, rising personal expectations in the work situation and the impact of television: these are some of the factors creating the greater need for communication. But meeting that need is not an easy matter. Although communication among humans is potentially so much more rich, varied and important than that of our nearest relatives in the animal world, yet it is more prone to error, breakdown and disaster. Those who climb high must risk the worst accidents. Only by understanding and practising good communication can we hope to win the rewards and avoid the penalties.

FACTORS WHICH INFLUENCE COMMUNICATION

First it is worth setting the scene by outlining three factors which have a direct bearing on the content of communication in organisations: *size, change* and *expectation*.

Size

For a variety of reasons, predominantly economic, the prevailing tendency towards the growth in size of human organisations in almost every sector of life looks like continuing. Indeed some prophets have forecast that by the turn of the century we shall all be working for about 300 universal giants. Be that as it may, the speed towards corporate bigness has certainly accelerated in the last decade.

But what is a 'large' organisation? Would you call a firm of 3000 employees large, small or medium? Experience suggests that people have very different internal scales for measuring 'small' and 'large' in human groupings. To put my own cards on the table, I regard any organisation of more than about 500 people as large, for that number is already getting beyond the maximum that any one leader can hope to know by name.

Although it solves many problems by the well-known 'economies of size', the increased bulk of organisational life creates other ones no less thorny. Foremost among these is the problem of communication. In the group or small organisation this can be done simply by word of mouth. In the modern corporation even communication has to be organised and managed.

Moreover it should not be lightly assumed that the problem of communication afflicts or troubles only the industrial giants, such as General Motors, Ford, Imperial Chemicals or Unilever. The Civil Service and the Churches encounter the same difficulty, as do the larger trade unions.

The larger an organisation grows the more time and energy it must devote to communication among its parts. Matters concerned with creating or maintaining the spirit and practices of unity must occupy a bigger share of the communication content. The rules, procedures or meetings which ensure coordinated effort will inevitably take up more time in the communications within larger organisations than in very small ones. The result is that issues like human relations, work on problems of communication and of people understanding one another, which we used to think of as the frills of a business organisation, now become absolutely central.

Change

Communication and consultation are particularly important in times of change. The achievement of change is a joint concern of management and employees and should be carried out in a way which pays regard both to the efficiency of the undertaking and to the interests of employees. Major changes in working arrangements should not be made by management without prior discussion with employees or their representatives.

When changes in management take place, for example, following a merger or take-over, the new managers should make prompt contact with employee representatives and take steps to explain changes in policy affecting employees.

These sentences from the Industrial Relations Code of Practice highlight the importance of good communication in times of change. Change means the intrusion of the new, the unfamiliar or the unknown into the ordered working world; as such it can produce the symptoms of fear, anxiety or insecurity. But the pace and scope of change has accelerated: we all have to live with it and cope with the consequences. Whether or not it is perceived and accepted as progress or rejected as a loss of a way of life will depend as much on the integrity and trust which has been built up in the relationships within the organisation, and the presence of good communications as on the intrinsic merits of the change.

Expectation

In the Second World War more than one commander noted that intelligent soldiers fought much better when they were told what was going to happen. The conditions of modern warfare made close control impossible, and the soldier who knew the plan could use his initiative in carrying it out, even though he was separated from his officers. Moreover it was noted that the simple act of telling men what was the task, and the problems involved in it, had a profound motivational effect.

A major difference now is that an ever-growing majority of men and women at work expect not only to be told what they are doing but also why it has to be done that way. In addition they expect to be consulted much more often, if not about the aims at least about the objectives and methods of their daily work. Managers, supervisors, foremen, shop stewards and work people expect their leaders to communicate with them on a regular and thorough basis, just as they recognise the increasing demands made on them to communicate with others both within and without the organisation. But *any* communication will not suffice. There are certain areas or topics that people want to hear about and discuss.

TOPICS FOR COMMUNICATION

In contrast to families, working organisations have a *purpose* to serve, which they break down into the more concrete *aims* and attainable *objectives*.

In social terms to 'organise' means to form into a whole or to create a definite and orderly structure, *for a definite purpose*.

In small teams the characteristics of organisation are there in embryo, although it may take the sharp eyes of a social psychologist to discern them. In particular there are some kinds of tasks and allocations of roles which may be single functions or a few functions associated together. In part these roles (made up from functional actions) meet the need to achieve the common *task*, in part they serve to *maintain* and build up the common life of the group; and lastly, they include responses to the recurring needs of individuals, as persons who are both ends in themselves and means towards the common success.

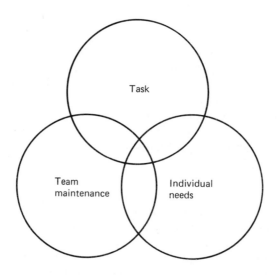

Figure 19.1 **Model of the interrelation among the three areas of need present in working groups**

The interrelations among three areas of need present in working groups can be portrayed by the model of three overlapping circles (see Figure 19.1). Success or failure in the *Task* circle helps to build up or break down group unity (the *Team Maintenance* need). Also it affects the *Individual* for good or ill, because in a large part his own higher needs (physical, social, esteem, achievement and self-actualisation) and values are bound up with the common advance or corporate progress, as well as the quality of the common life. Yet performance rests on the knowledge and skill of individual members, just as the social life of the team rests upon the humour and courage which individuals export into it. The circles are thus interacting. But there is also a tension between them, which is important for the understanding of organisations.

The purpose of communication in organisations is usefully defined by the three circles: to achieve the common task, maintain the unity of the whole body and to meet individual needs. Thus the *content* of communication falls into the three (overlapping) areas:

- Purpose, aims, objectives, plans and policies.
- Procedures, rules and normal standards.
- Conditions of service, performance, progress and prospects.

This conclusion is supported by some classic research which suggests that these are the subjects people at work want to hear about. A study of two big American firms made by Princeton University in 1949 showed the employees could put to best use these three types of information:

- Anything which gave them a better insight into their work, and its relation to the work of others in the firm.
- Anything which gave them a sense of belonging to the firm.
- Any information which improved their sense of status and importance as individuals in the firm.

PRIORITIES FOR COMMUNICATION

All managers have to think in terms of priorities, not least when it comes to communications. The three general topics outlined – matters concerned with the common task, team (or organisational) relations and individual needs – have to be constantly scanned in order to select the priorities, which must then be matched by the best-grade methods of communication available. The less important matters can be married off to the less effective communication methods. The manager or management may find it useful to bear in mind three concentric circles of priority to balance the three overlapping ones (see Figure 19.2).

There will be a mass of material which deserves to be communi-

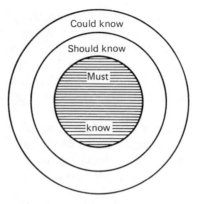

Figure 19.2   The three concentric circles of priority

cated in any organisation so it is important at a given time to break it down into:

MUST KNOWS: vital points necessary to achieve the common aim.

SHOULD KNOWS: desirable but not essential.

COULD KNOWS: relatively unimportant.

In industrial organisations there is room for debate on what should fall into the MUST, SHOULD and COULD circles in a specific situation, but generally speaking there is wide agreement on the areas which have to be constantly considered for such priority decisions. Peter Masefield, a former chief executive of British European Airways, has listed – and commented on – these important main categories of key information to the effect that an effective two-way process within a company should deal with this type of information under seven main headings:

1   The policy and objectives of the company, both in broad terms and in their detailed components right down to floor level.
2   The results and achievements – both financial and general – gained already from the application of the company's policy, together with such modifications of policy as are suggested by experience.
3   Plans and prospects for the future and the basic assumptions on which forward estimates are based.
4   Aspects of conditions of service and improvements which are desirable and can be attained.

5 Ways and means by which efficiency and productivity can be improved.

6 Problems of industrial safety, health and welfare among staff.

7 Education – general and specialised.

Under each of these headings we can ask ourselves 'What do the men – and the women – on the shop floor want to know about this aspect of the business?' And we can also ask ourselves, in addition, 'What do we want to know about their reactions on this subject?' If we are wise, we shall want to know a lot.

In the case of policy in my experience the important thing is 'Why'. The 'why' of the business can range from commercial policy dictating why prices are set at the figures they are, down to such items as why re-equipment is being pressed forward or postponed, why a competitor may have established a particular lead, why advertising is concentrated on certain lines and why profits are ploughed back.

On policy matters above all else, one thing inevitably leads to another. In my experience a full and free discussion can work wonders in improving morale. Such an exchange alone can bring to light facts that lead to a proper understanding of the reasons for given action. Without this background, our decisions may very easily be misunderstood. 'To know all is to support all' – provided management is sound and knows how to express itself.

The ability to communicate implies the equal ability *not* to communicate. There are good reasons as well as bad ones why certain information cannot be briefed or spread throughout an organisation. The words 'good' and 'bad' bring us back to the realm of moral judgements. It is important to consider these value dimensions, because they are bound up with the creation and maintenance of trust. If anyone wishes to create good communication in organisations the first essential for consideration is the line of relationship which joins the potential senders and receivers. If that line is strong in trust it will have the necessary reserves to overcome the occasional necessary non-disclosure of information to avoid industrial espionage, for instance. It also will cope with the odd distortion or failure in communications, such as we fallible humans are prone to commit.

But 'bad' reasons, for example withholding financial information to prevent wage claims, breed mistrust and impugn the integrity of management. And integrity is the foundation of good communication; techniques are only its servants.

METHODS OF COMMUNICATION

Methods are ways of doing things, especially according to regular plans or procedures. A system is a group, set or aggregate of things, natural or artificial, forming a connected or complex whole. Thus any organisation has a system of communications, although few managers may be aware of all its ramifications. In order to understand the system in a given organisation it is necessary to study it objectively. This kind of research is still the exception rather than the rule. Once the profile of the system has been established its strengths can be confirmed and its deficiencies made good. To achieve these improvements, however, it is important to grasp the characteristics and functions of the main methods which form strands in many contemporary organisational systems.

We must first distinguish between the method and the people who are involved in it. A railway network may be judged a good one, even though the diesel engines are slow, the train drivers incompetent and the buffet-car food bad. But the remedies for these ills would not include tearing up the tracks.

The six sections below deal with some of the main methods or systems which many larger organisations have evolved or adopted for handling the increased load of communication that contemporary business and the rising expectations of employees require. Doubtless the reader will be able to add other systems to the list, such as the regular meetings of trade union representatives and management, or annual general meetings.

Line management

An obvious line of communication in any organisation follows the structure of roles or the hierarchy. The pyramid or tree structure persists, despite the undermining activities of recent years, simply because large organisations need it for their work. It is true that the degree of participation in policy decisions has increased, and will do so much more in the coming years. But, if nothing more, the implementation of decisions does require a structure of roles with a definition of accountability. Nor should we imagine that a measure of clarity in such matters is antagonistic to human values. Professor D S Pugh and his University of Aston colleagues drew this conclusion from their extensive research into organisations:

Most important of all is the finding that work groups having many standard procedures and rules do not necessarily become dissatisfied and disunited. . . This supports the view that a reasonable amount of job definition and control by procedures does not lessen readiness to innovate. (See Further reading for details.)

Thus, despite its military overtones, the 'chain of command' allows for essential information to flow downwards or upwards in any kind of organisation. Moreover this exchange can happen in a series of personal interviews or conversations, which may or may not be formalised. In an age which rather favours group meetings and group discussions it is important to retain the centrality of the one-to-one transmission of instructions, information or ideas. In vital matters there is often a tendency in organisations to revert to fundamentals: to communicate directly to the individual, supporting the spoken word with a letter, memo or report as necessary.

One source of confusion in communication is a lack of understanding of the distinction between *line* and *staff* management. Line authority is exercised by any manager over his immediate subordinates, and carries the right to direct their work. Staff authority is exercised by a staff manager only over other managers who report to a line manager in common with him, and carries with it the right to advise on how previously agreed policies, plans or procedures should be carried out. Thus the line of authority can be shown in Figure 19.3, though of course the staff manager in it will have a direct line of communication with line manager (B) as well.

Briefing groups

The personal one-to-one link works well, but in large organisations it needs to be supplemented by briefing groups, just as the modern university has had to introduce seminars to augment the traditional one-to-one tutorial system. Briefing groups are the method whereby one communicator passes on orally some instructions or information to a small number of communicants (i.e. not less than two, not more than about 30). It is usually assumed that the communicator will be of a senior status to the group – their leader, manager, supervisor, foreman or chargehand. Such meetings may be ad hoc briefings or they may be formalised so that everyone belongs to a briefing group which meets regularly.

The word 'briefing' comes from the legal world. A brief (from the Latin *breve*) was originally a writing issued by an official or legal

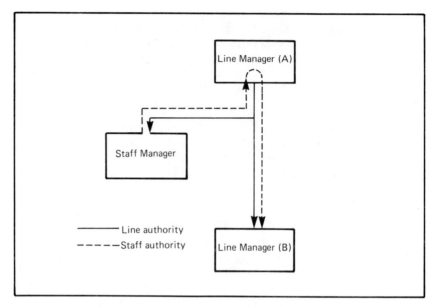

Figure 19.3   Line and staff authority

authority, such as king or pope. The term survived in the legal profession to mean a summary of facts and points of law, drawn up by a solicitor for a counsel in charge of a case. Thus paradoxically 'to brief' originally meant to put something down on paper. It has always included the notion of brevity, for the ancient documents or letters were comparatively short and terse.

Such is the triumph of oral communication that briefing now stands for a spoken passing on or interpretation of instructions. The Industrial Society has played a leading part in advocating the introduction of such purposeful meetings. In his booklet *The Manager's Responsibility for Communication* (1964, revised 1971), the Society's Director John Garnett proposed the following 'drill':

> Each department will organise its systems of face to face communication differently depending on the number of levels and the work arrangements, numbers involved and whether on shifts or days. The system for each department should be written down and made known to all concerned. A typical arrangement would be for a works manager to see his deputies and section heads together; they in their turn would see their plant managers and foremen together, and the foremen would then see the men and act as management's spokesmen.

In this way five levels of management would be covered in three steps. It might be possible to get the whole management team together at one time but the groups should not be larger than 18. *Understanding* of policies and decisions is only achieved if the group is small enough to allow questions and discussion. Eighteen is normally the maximum.

On many occasions the manager or supervisor will need a written brief to guide him, which may be an abstract of a much larger and complicated administrative document. How often should briefing groups meet? John Garnett suggested these guidelines:

> Briefing sessions should ideally only be held when there is something important to communicate. If it is merely left to this, however, there is a danger that in practice sessions will be held only when there is something to tell which is to the employees' disadvantage such as the coming of redundancy or the tightening of an incentive scheme. It is therefore essential to stipulate that a minimum number of meetings are held – at least four a year which, because of holidays, are not necessarily spread equally through the year. Down to the level of supervisor the minimum frequency is eleven times a year.

Lastly, the Industrial Society has emphasised the importance of brevity, proposing 30 minutes as an ideal. Two-thirds of this time should be spent on covering the decisions and policies which affect the work – the nature of the job and the conditions of employment – leaving one-third for questions and points which the working group may want to raise.

The evidence suggests that briefing groups are a most valuable practice.

Joint consultation

Decisions in any group or organisation must be taken by the leader and the members in varying proportions amongst themselves, depending on the situation, the knowledge of the subordinates, the nature of the decision and the philosophy of the organisation. The more people share in decisions which affect their working lives the more they are inwardly moved to carry them out. Enthusiasm, involvement, commitment, a sense of responsibility: all these are strengthened by participating in the process of decision making. Athough the final decision may rest elsewhere, and may turn out to be other than an individual member would have desired, the fact that his voice has been heard and listened to is a positive incentive in itself.

Consequently there is a solid case for meetings where the main emphasis is on upwards communication. Three possible aims for such consultative or representative meetings have been succinctly defined in the booklet by John Garnett:

- to give employees a chance to improve decisions by contributing comments before decisions are made;
- to make the fullest possible use of their experience and ideas in the efficient running of the enterprise;
- to give management and employees the opportunity to understand each other's views and objectives. (p.16.)

Characteristically these are meetings where discussion takes place on any matter influencing the effectiveness or efficiency of the enterprise before decisions are made. Sometimes the group's views will be passed upwards; sometimes the decision will be made by the manager or supervisor on the spot and in the presence of those who have contributed to his judgement.

Consultative meetings may be distinguished from formal management/union discussions on such topics as wage systems, job evaluation, hours of work, holidays and holiday pay. In the latter instance elected representatives of work people in trade unions are seeking to reach formal agreement on matters relating to the 'individual needs' circle in the trefoil or three-circles model on p.358. In consultations the active working members of an organisation are being asked to contribute towards decisions mainly in the field of the common purpose, aims and objectives, and the shape of the structural organisation necessary to achieve those short and long term ends. As the circles overlap it is not always possible in practice to separate matters of concern for trade unions from those which belong to the individual as a member of a particular organisation. But there is a distinction, and it is worth bearing in mind.

It is usually assumed that a consultative group, formalised into a consultative committee, should exist on a factory or plant basis, although in very large organisations there may be a case for regional, national or international councils. Normally one might find one joint consultation committee, consisting of representatives from management and shop floor, in a factory employing perhaps 1000 men and women or more. Thus it would act as a forum of debate, rather than as a cabinet for decision. Except in schemes for industrial democracy, where the committee becomes the governing council, the final decisions and the ultimate accountability will still rest with the board of directors.

Personally I think that the formally elected 'constitutional' consultative system needs to be supplemented by the flexible use of briefing groups in a secondary role as consultative groups, engaging in such activities as discussion, problem solving and creative thinking. So that at some briefing meetings as much as two-thirds of the time might be reserved for *upwards* consultation in all the various degrees or shades of that word. The formal consultative meeting or committee has a 'safety net' role to play, especially where for some reason there is a majority or significant minority of non-union members. But we should expect to see its importance declining as the quality of leadership in working groups improves, the membership of white-collar unions grows, and the actual concerns of trade unions reach out beyond their present preoccupations with pay, hours, safety and job security.

Committees

Committees have come under such heavy fire in recent years that it is worth recalling that in their heyday between 1900 and 1939 they were hailed by industry with as much enthusiasm as briefing groups are today. From the turn of the century they have inspired much faith as a method for running large organisations with the maximum involvement of individuals and departments.

The reasons for their present disfavour include the identification of committees with a particular method of making decisions by majority vote or consensus. They are associated with the institutions of democracy, in that Parliament does much of its work through committees, such as the Committee of Ways and Means, and has done so for centuries. Bodies which set out to copy Parliament, such as church synods and county councils, also adopted the committee method as one means of bridging the gap between the legislative and executive functions.

The emphasis upon individual accountability and the growing appreciation of the necessarily undemocratic (but not anti-democratic) nature of most working organisations, have drastically affected the image of committees. They are seen often as time-consuming chores. Yet the board of directors is a committee, and it often needs to appoint sub-committees. Contrary to the prevailing orthodoxy it is necessary to assert with Albert Sloan that large organisations cannot run without committees, in the general defined sense of 'a body of persons appointed or elected for some special business or function'.

The part played by committees in the total decision making activity of an organisation depends upon the purpose, structure and ethos of that organisation, and discussion of it lies outside the scope of this chapter. But committees do have an important function in communication which is neither primarily downwards (briefing) nor upwards (consultative) but *sideways* or lateral.

This aspect of communication becomes especially important in large organisations, where individuals, departments or divisions are separated by large distances. Upwards and downwards communication may be taking place perfectly well, but it is also necessary for lateral discussions to happen as well.

House journals and surveys

Letters, memoranda, reports and the like, follow the main trade routes of communication — upwards, downwards and sideways. Sometimes they travel the channels alone; at other times they act in concert with the spoken word. Their contents do not concern us here. For, to revert to the railway analogy, it is the network of tracks that we are considering, not the type of train which is travelling on them. Company magazines, bulletins or newsletters, however, providing they appear at regular intervals, do merit attention, because they form another distinct line of communication.

Usually companies pay for most of the costs of their magazines and it is therefore not surprising that in the past they should be seen mainly as promoting downwards and sideways communication. In terms of the priority circles, the MUST and the better part of the SHOULD areas ought to be covered by personal encounters or small group meetings along the 'chain of command'. But that leaves the SHOULD–MIGHT shades to be conveyed by such means as bulletins, notice boards, newsletters or house journals. This paperwork will be enhanced by illustrations, photographs and diagrams. In the future they may be increasingly supplemented by films or closed-circuit television programmes. We cannot help being interested by the people we work with or for, and such methods help us to understand the personal and social nature of our organisation, however vast. Fortunately there are plenty of examples of good company journals and much sound advice on producing them.

Magazines are much less good at present as lines of communication for 'up' trains. Some journalists have hinted at Machiavellian (in the worst sense) practices by management to prevent or smother letters of complaint.

On the other hand it could be argued that correspondence columns are an inefficient method of righting grievances. First, it is a slow process. There is nothing so sapping in interest as watching a slow-motion debate about the price of British Rail tea conducted in the correspondence columns of the daily newspapers, let alone in monthly journals. Second, a minor point becomes a great *cause celèbre* by publicising it to perhaps 300,000 employees, and the spirit of discontent is contagious. The pen may be mightier than the sword, but the printed letter is as slow and cumbersome as a medieval battering ram.

There are other methods of uncovering complaints as well as positive suggestions. The consultative meeting should be the place where people feel free enough to raise what appear to be critical points. Such a setting has the advantage that others present can confirm or refute the universality of the complaint – are *all* washrooms dirty, or only those in the painting shop?

The correspondence column does give the opportunity for anonymous letters. These are the cousins of 'poison pen' letters, and frequently suggest a lack of moral courage. On the other hand, a natural reticence at hurting people's feelings or jeopardising a working relationship may drive us to take refuge behind a pseudonym. One more effective method of locating and releasing these critical but unassertive opinions is the *survey*.

The method of running surveys usually follows three stages: announcement; group interviews to establish the subject matter uppermost in employees' minds; similar interviews to list the concerns of management. The consultant develops the questionnaire, which may be in the form of choosing one of four possible answers to each question – this is to simplify analysis, but, as it may also frustrate, there should be spare pages for any who wish to raise other subjects. All reports should be voluntary and anonymous, with the results fed back to all concerned.

Although expensive in terms of time and money, surveys do have a part to play in the life of large organisations, e.g. they may be useful:

- to identify matters requiring attention;
- to establish some way of measuring morale and its *trend* (this is difficult to quantify but trends can be measured positively or negatively);
- to provide vital data for personnel planning;

- to provide information for management training to illustrate what employees expect;
- as a positive morale builder in that it indicates that the management takes the subject seriously;
- to provide powerful justification for management's action;
- to provide a measure of management performance. Employees are asked for opinions on their managers and the trends of these opinions are of great interest; they can lead to improvement in performance as a result of the objective advice of a behavioural scientist.

But, like all public opinion polls, their interpretation requires specialist knowledge – and some pinches of salt.

The grape-vine

Informality is one of the keynotes of our age. It conjures up a picture of relaxed ease, and a brave dispensing with all pompous and rigid formalities. But its history cannot support this edifice of value judgement. Unflatteringly, the dictionary defines *informal* as, 'not done or made according to a regular or prescribed form, not observing forms, not according to order; irregular; unofficial, disorderly'.

It is common knowledge that alongside the network of official or regular lines and junctions of communication there exists an unofficial or informal exchange of ideas or information. The unreliability of this method is notorious. Indeed, during the American Civil War a 'despatch by grape-vine telegraph' – later shortened to 'grape-vine' – meant an extravagant or absurd story circulated as a hoax or a false report.

Passing any message from person to person is liable to lead to distortion, even if only two people are involved, as the following examples of secretarial errors illustrate:

WHAT THE MANAGER SAID	WHAT THE SECRETARY TYPED
I can *heartily* reciprocate your good wishes.	I can *hardly* reciprocate your good wishes.
It is not wise to *mix* type *faces*.	It is not wise to *skip* type *spaces*.
He *acceded to* these restrictions.	He *exceeded* these restrictions.
Archimedes said . . .	*Our committees* said . . .
This will *enable* us to close the contract	This will *unable* us to close the contract.

The more people in the lines of communication the more the content tends to lose its shape.

Thus informal communication allows rumours to grow especially if they contain threats to individual needs and hopes. Bad news travels fast. For these reasons managers have traditionally looked upon the factory grape-vine with a suspicion amounting to hostility, overlooking the fact that they have their own grape-vines and 'old boy networks'. But these informal contacts should be positively welcomed as a valuable 'alternative system' to the formal system of communications. In other words, the grape-vine ought to give upwards feedback on how well the main channels of communication are working, and whether or not they are carrying the information which is necessary in the situation.

Second, the grape-vine can bear good news as well as bad. Truth can leap along its branches, especially when the 'official channels' are clogged thick with green slime and mud. Sometimes leaders can choose to send messages along the grape-vine, or relay them through those who use that medium most. Only good coins will drive out a debased money. Rumour originally meant a widespread report of a *favourable* or *complimentary* nature, and it only came later to have its more neutral tone, as general talk or hearsay not based upon definite knowledge or clear evidence circulating in a community. Obviously the better rumours are those which act as advance guards preparing the way for good news. The only way to scotch or control bad rumours is to produce the knowledge or evidence, or the reasons why they are not available, and explain the general policies of the organisation in that field. But this work should be done through the normal and formal system, not through a series of 'crisis' meetings.

Any organisation needs much informal exchange of ideas and opinions upwards and downwards, and no system of communication has yet been invented which can bear all the growing volume of that legitimate traffic. We shall always need the coffee breaks, lunch meetings and conversations on the train. What we hear between the words, and what we project non-verbally in confidence or anxiety is as much part of the total communications in an organisation as the briefing group or the company telephone system.

These informal contacts are especially important for lateral communication. It is perhaps salutary for those of us engaged in management training to reflect on the fact that a major value for the participants in staff college courses, and in-company and in-service programmes lies precisely in the opportunity such get-togethers provide for the exchange of ideas and attitudes, names and jobs on the sideways or lateral communication dual carriageway. Relationships forged at such times facilitate the intercourse of information by hook or by crook. Of course bad leaders always fear their subordinates getting together to compare notes, because they fear the exposure of their own incompetence and because they entertain a low view of human nature anyway. Fortunately the number of organisations with such helmsmen at the tiller is dwindling rapidly.

FURTHER READING

Adair, John *Training for Communication*, Gower, 1984, from which this chapter draws heavily

Aurner, R and Wolf, M P, *Effective Communication in Business*, South-Western Publishing Co., (5th edition) 1967

Garnett, John, *The Manager's Responsibility for Communication*, The Industrial Society, 1971

Pugh, D S (et al.), 'Organisation structure, organisational climate, and group structure: an exploratory study of their relationships', *Occupational Psychology*, vol. 45, no. 1, 1971

Thayer, L, *Communication and Communication Systems in Organisations, Management and Interpersonal Relations*, Irwin, 1968

Stanton, Nicki, *What do you mean 'Communication'*, Pan, 1986

Stanton, Nicki, *The Business of Communicating*, Pan, 1986

20

Making meetings work

John Gregory

Managers spend a great deal of time in meetings, often ineffectively and often with a growing sense of frustration. This chapter looks at meetings and at why they often do not work, and suggests some steps to be taken to make them more effective. The chapter concludes with a simple seven-point guideline for the chairman and the meeting member.

GOOD MEETINGS MEAN MORE PROFIT

It is popular to grumble about meetings; indeed this pastime can become a dangerous obsession so that, in some organisations, the climate is such that managers find it very difficult to conduct effective meetings. Jokes and 'laws' about meetings proliferate and the well known video *Meetings bloody meetings*, although admirable, may have unwittingly contributed to the myth that meetings are a nuisance. Perhaps the typical management attitude to meetings is best summed up by a story told to me by a financial manager. He recounted the final act of a long and difficult meeting when after 2½ hours little had been achieved and the only decision that they were about to make was a time for the next meeting so that they could continue their fruitless endeavours. After much diary searching the chairman thought he had found a consensus and announced 'How about next Wednesday?' To which one of those present replied with a groan, 'Oh no not *Wednesday* – that ruins two weekends!'

So what is the message? It is that senior management should encourage and cultivate a 'good meetings climate' because in doing so they will improve:

- *Communication.* A business organisation is, by definition, two or more people engaged in commercial pursuit. Organisations cannot cohere or achieve goals without communicating and effective meetings play an essential part in this process.
- *Policy formulation and planning.* These activities require ideas, discussion and debate on key issues and on alternatives. They benefit from the collective wisdom of the management team and carefully considered proposals and options. This process can only take place in meetings.
- *Decision making.* Some decisions have to be made in formal meetings (or endorsed by them) because of constitutional or statutory requirements; for example Cabinet, council and boardroom decisions. But there are many circumstances in which the quality or durability of a decision will be enhanced if it is subjected to careful (and urgent!) consideration in a meeting at which those responsible for implementation or affected are present.

Better communication, better planning and improved decision making will have a positive effect on the bottom line and this is a justification for giving thought and energy to improving meetings.

Do we need a meeting?

If so many managers express the view that they spend too much time in meetings, perhaps they should not be there in the first place. It is undoubtedly the case that some meetings should never have been called so it is worth exercising the discipline of asking 'Do we need a meeting?' before setting one up. Figure 20.1 is a useful checklist which can be used to determine whether there is a need for a meeting.

A positive answer to one of the questions in the checklist suggests that a meeting is needed – but just by calling a meeting you don't communicate better, build teams, make good decisions or solve problems. Many meetings which undoubtedly should have been held fail. Let us now consider why this happens.

WHY DO MEETINGS FAIL?

Meetings can be broadly classified into formal and informal. The formal category embraces all those meetings that are required by some written constitution, Articles of Association or Statute. The

Do the rules require a meeting?

So many formal meetings are required by statute or constitution and they have to be called and held in accordance with the rules. Although they often seem tedious and pointless, such meetings are consistent with open, democratic administration and provide some reassurance to those with an interest in the organisation concerned.

Is there a need to communicate?

How often do you hear the complaint 'nobody tells us anything'? When a business is proposing change there may be a strong case for holding briefing meetings in order that a positive attitude can be encouraged. The great advantage of a meeting over a written briefing is the two-way nature of the communication. So if you want to avoid rumour and distortion, you want to change attitudes or you want to take people with you, consider the case for a meeting or series of meetings.

Is there a need for team building?

Well conducted meetings can do much to build a good team. Leaders of the best sports teams, and winning generals, have recognised the benefits of the 'here's how we win' meeting and the same thing can work in business.

Do I need advice and guidance before making a decision?

It doesn't follow that if the answer is yes, a meeting is required since a few phone calls or a one-to-one discussion may achieve the desired result. However, collective advice reviewed and weighed in a meeting will often lead to a better decision. It has to be recognised, though, that some managers who are poor decision makers use meetings as a device for delaying or compromising when they would have been better to take speedy action.

Have we got a problem or crisis which can be better dealt with by a group solution?

Not quite the same as the last point because in this instance there is a crisis and a need for urgent action — but there are many circumstances in which a 'war cabinet' approach is needed. For example, an unexpected take-over bid, a lightning strike, a serious accident. The crisis may involve several departments or call for a range of specialist views or skills; the sooner they are all brought together in a meeting the better.

Figure 20.1   Checklist — do we need a meeting?

conduct of formal meetings is usually governed by rules or custom and the membership controlled by election or some form of qualification.

By far the more frequent and managerially important meeting is the informal type which may be a regular or ad hoc problem solving type of meeting. Whatever the type the chances are that they fail from time to time or, in some cases, all the time! But why?

People problems

Since a meeting is a social group it is not surprising that they reflect the weaknesses and idiosyncracies of their members, for example:

- an incompetent chairman;
- an idle committee secretary;
- interpersonal conflict between members or departmental rivalries (the 'point scoring' syndrome);
- an anti-meeting culture (the 'this is going to be a waste of time' syndrome);
- mistrust or envy by those outside the meeting (the 'what are they up to' syndrome);
- ill conceived membership – for example vertical or diagonal slice when a peer group is demanded.

Planning problems

The varied and awkward nature of human beings does not mean that meetings are always going to be difficult and ineffective provided someone gives some thought to the structure and content. More typically what happens is that there is:

- insufficient notice of a meeting or silly timing;
- no understanding of the aim: 'Why are we here?'
- no agenda or a badly structured agenda;
- poor paperwork: 'These figures don't add up!'
- a feeling that 'we've discussed all this before'.

Progress

It is a common complaint that after a meeting, even productive meetings, nothing happens. For example there is no:

- record or minute circulated;
- action or follow-up on decisions taken;
- continuity between meetings;
- upward reporting.

It follows, therefore, that to achieve better meetings something has to be done to change managers' attitudes towards meetings and this can be achieved with attention to the three 'P's: people, planning and progress.

PEOPLE

It is worth giving attention to three 'people' factors, attitude, selection and training. Let me explain.

Attitude

Much damage is done because managers lack a positive approach to meetings. To encourage a positive view:

- *Avoid the word 'committee'.* Bureaucracy and inactivity are too closely associated with the word committee so where possible stop using it. Consider alternatives, using active descriptions such as working party, task force, and action group or using descriptions which emphasise efficiency or excellence like quality circle, profit improvement group etc.
- *Emphasise importance and urgency.* Senior managers have a key role to play in emphasising the importance of the work done in meetings, and by encouraging their own staff to take a positive attitude by, for example, arriving at meetings on time, by preparing for meetings and by constructive contribution.

Selection

We rightly take time and care to recruit managers but rather less concern is shown when assembling a group to perform some managerial task. It seems that the 'least busy' or 'buggin's turn' principle is often applied. When forming a meeting group such matters as intellectual ability, experience, seniority, need for confidentiality, representational and personality factors all need to be considered. The group will have an aim similar to a manager's job description and there is, therefore, a case for preparing a 'group specification'. Obviously, in some circumstances, the group task preselects the group but there will be many occasions when members of a working party or task force should be carefully selected.

If care in picking members is important, the choice of chairman is often critical to the effectiveness of a meeting. There are occasions when seniority or status leave no room for consideration but when there is a choice, personality and skills such as listening, managing time, prioritising, summing up, fairness, firmness, impartiality etc. must be taken into account.

Training

Once the importance of meetings is recognised the need for modest but effective training follows. There are short courses on effective meetings, training films and videos, and useful booklets. Any training aimed at improving the effectiveness of meetings will also help change the attitude to them. Don't overlook the special training needs of the chairman and of the secretary (preparing agendas, taking notes, writing action reports).

PLANNING

Once management attitudes are positive, the climate is right for effective meetings but this won't happen unless the chairman and the secretary give some thought to what they want to achieve and how they intend to set about it — in other words, planning. Specifically they will need to:

- time meetings to be cost effective and acceptable to the members;
- fix the location to be convenient and free of interruption and distraction;
- clarify their terms of reference or aim;
- plan and prepare an agenda. Some informal meetings may not need a written agenda as long as everyone knows why they are there and what is to be covered;
- consider the need for supporting papers which should be well written, up to date and accurate;
- consider the need for prior consultation and discussion on difficult issues in order to prepare the ground and save valuable time at the meeting.

In crises, meetings have to be called at short notice and little preparation is possible. In these circumstances the chairman's role becomes even more significant as does the post meeting progress of which more below.

PROGRESS

If I had to nominate one single factor which has contributed to the 'bad press' which meetings enjoy it would not be easy but post

For the chairman

1 Know your committee (terms, rules, members)

2 Prepare (compile agenda, plan meeting)

3 Consult before the meeting (i.e. prepare the ground)

4 Be firm but fair

5 Convey sense of urgency/importance

6 Listen

7 Seek consensus/agree the action

For the member

1 Prepare/know your facts; consult subordinates before the meeting

2 Don't be late

3 Accept the chair

4 Be constructive

5 Don't lose your cool

6 Question if in doubt

7 Fight your corner — but don't waste time

Figure 20.2 Checklists for better meetings practice

meeting inactivity would be high on my list. Nothing will have a greater potential for convincing managers that they are wasting their time if they can see no cause and effect relationship or if they are continually covering old ground. If something positive happens they will soon begin to change their attitudes to meetings. What needs to be done?

- *Circulate a record of the meeting.* Call them minutes if you like but, if you are free of procedural requirements, it might be better to describe them as an 'Action and information report'. In any event it is a good thing to have an 'action column' in the record so that the names of those responsible for carrying out the agreed decisions can be noted. This puts the action manager on the spot and goes some way towards avoiding the 'I didn't realise I was supposed to do anything' reaction.

- *Take managerial action.* This means taking an interest in what happens post meeting − asking for a progress report and generally encouraging and prodding to ensure that matters are progressed.
- *Report post meeting progress.* Let those at the meeting and others know what has happened. This may encourage others and it will enhance the status of meetings.

SEVEN WAYS TO BETTER MEETINGS

Given that the priority is to produce a better meetings climate by encouraging a positive attitude there is much that the individual manager can do to improve his own performance in meetings be he the chairman or just a member. As a reminder and as a guide to better practice two checklists (Figure 20.2) are provided, one for the chairman and one for the member. Use these lists as a reminder. A bit more thought and some effort could do much to improve the effectiveness of your meetings.

FURTHER READING

Carnes, William T, *Effective Meetings for Busy People − let's decide it and go home*, McGraw-Hill, 1983

Fletcher, Winston, *Meetings, Meetings: how to manipulate them and make them more fun*, Hodder, 1985

Janner, Greville, *Janner on Meetings*, Gower, 1986

Jay, Antony, *How to Run a Meeting*, Video Arts, 1980

21

The politics of management

Andrew Kakabadse

Politics in organisations is ever present. No matter who you are, or what you do, it is impossible to escape the power/political interactions that take place between people at work.

Men and women *say* they find the politics in organisations distasteful, sometimes downright stressful. Politics can, however, be quite motivating, stimulating and exhilarating. Politics doesn't arise for negative reasons, but for powerful and all-pervading organisational and personal reasons. Once people come to terms with these factors, it's possible to become more effective at managing politics.

Though this is the time of large companies, you need political flair in small ones – to deal with suppliers and customers, for instance.

Simply doing a good job is not sufficient. Professional competence is only the first step. High office achieved quickly requires negotiating skills, an ability to look ahead, the determination to make projects work and the ability to get on with people.

Many people spend much of their time managing conflict, competition and the formation of alliances as an everyday part of their workload. There are frictions and difficulties that arise between top management, who are involved with strategic change, and middle management who are concerned with making the existing systems work.

UNDERSTANDING THE PEOPLE WHO PLAY POLITICS

To understand the processes of politics, it is necessary to understand the people who play politics.

A number of well known psychologists and philosophers have

come to similar conclusions as to why people develop particular personalities. They concluded:

- By using their experiences from the past, people learn how to cope with the world around them.
- Athough this learning process is never ending, people, quite naturally, reject the more unsuccessful ways of coping.
- After a while, people develop a repertoire of thoughts, feelings, behaviours and skills which is their best way of coping with their world.
- The more successful the repertoire, the more fixed it becomes, the more people develop and form their personality.

The behavioural scientist, Erving Goffman (1974), called this repertoire *frames of reference*, a now commonly used phrase to indicate how an individual subjectively interprets the world around him. Other writers on psychology and philosophy suggest that we all structure our experiences to form a map (like a geographical map) which shows boundaries, hills, mountains, valleys, difficult routes and easy routes to follow. Just as we would use a geographical map to find the easiest or most difficult routes to follow, so we use a *mental map* to drive our behaviour. How then are mental maps and the politics of management related? The hypothesis offered is that politics constitutes an influence process which can be perceived as positive or negative, depending on whether one's own mental map is being supported or threatened.

Let us explore further this notion of a mental map being supported or threatened. In my capacity as an academic consultant, many managers have said to me:

> I get on fine with my subordinates. It is just that my boss keeps on interfering with everything I do. I am getting sick of him.

In many people's minds, there seems to be a split between legitimate and illegitimate attempts at influence. In dealing downwards with subordinates, the manager feels comfortable. Managers seem to influence downwards on the basis of their knowledge of particular individuals and groups. A good manager is one whose subordinates state: 'My boss knows how to handle me!' The good manager is someone who helps subordinates feel comfortable.

Yet, in managing upwards, so many middle managers seem to use a different approach. They are so used to leading downwards that they forget that relations upwards are also a mutual dependence process. So many managers seem to stereotype people in a top–down way so that their mental map is not sufficiently flexible to cope with upward influence. They forget that bosses are people. The boss is no longer a person but a stereotype in the person's mind. Should the boss do something to break the stereotype, then the individual believes that politics is being played. Note that under such circumstances, politics is linked with negative influence.

Stereotypes of people will sooner or later be broken. Hence, is there any way of giving people insights into the width and breadth of their mental map and the mental map of others to help them understand why people do things the way they do?

I believe there is. From my observation of people, as an academic and a consultant, I can identify two fundamental drives which lead to the formation of mental maps – people's perceptions and their actions.

THE PERCEPTION/ACTION MODEL

Figure 21.1 represents the perception/action model. The model shows the dominant values people hold and the attitudes they adopt.

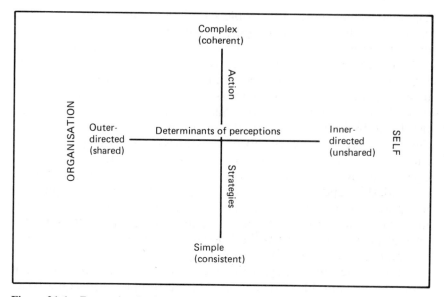

Figure 21.1   Perception/action model

Perceptions

In Figure 21.1, the horizontal axis represents the determinants of people's perceptions, i.e. their values or beliefs, probably the most powerful factors in personality.

The two extreme ends of the continuum are *inner-directedness* and *outer-directedness*. People who are inner-directed develop their perceptions and views with little reference to the outside world. Those who are outer-directed feel a need to comply with the perceived attitudes and behaviour that others seem to exhibit in that situation.

Complying with the perceived norms of the situation is termed shared meaning. People who need to operate under conditions of shared meaning adhere to the values of the organisation, the structure in the organisation, the power dependencies in the system and the monetary and status rewards the organisation offers.

People who generate their own values of life and norms of behaviour are self-dependent. They live with unshared meaning. They appreciate that a number of the people with whom they will interact feel differently from themselves, but see no need to adapt their particular views to suit others.

Actions

The vertical axis represents people's abilities to put into practice their views and values, i.e. their repertoire of action strategies. There are two alternative types of action strategies: simple and complex.

Those who practise strategies classed as simple aim for consistency. Irrespective of whether the people in the situation work on shared or unshared meaning, the behaviours they feel they should adopt are predictable, commonly recognised and probably previously practised. In this way, individuals and groups are seen to be *consistent* and previous experience of those behaviours reduces the degree of felt threat. For example, simple action strategies could involve being open, trusting and sharing with others in one's group. Sharing comradeship and only adopting those behaviours that would be acceptable to the other members of the department, team or unit does not involve any original thought, for one draws on previous experience of positive interactions. The key point is to behave in a manner acceptable to all others in the situation.

Complex action strategies involve people behaving in ways that they consider suitable to meet only their needs in the situation. To an outsider, the individual may exhibit no consistent pattern of behaviour. Only by possessing knowledge of the individual's objectives or by observing his behaviour for some time, will some sort of picture emerge. The pattern of behaviour may be inconsistent but *coherent*, i.e. it makes sense once one knows the individual and/or his desired objectives. For example, complex action strategies would involve planning a campaign to have a particular policy adopted in the organisation, identifying key people who would support the policy, influencing others who are less committed and isolating those who are against one's own ideas. Complex action strategies do involve new and original ideas and actions and possibly taking risks.

The combination of the inner/outer-directed axis and the simple/complex action strategies axis forms the individual's mental map. It is inevitable that people will interact with others who hold a different map from their own, even if the difference is slight. It is equally inevitable that people will experience elation or threat by interacting with other people. It all depends on the state of your map and the other party's map on meeting each other.

On this basis, politics in organisations is inevitable.

As a result of having observed managers at work, four particular behavioural patterns emerged: traditionalist, team coach, company baron, and visionary. This is illustrated in Figure 21.2.

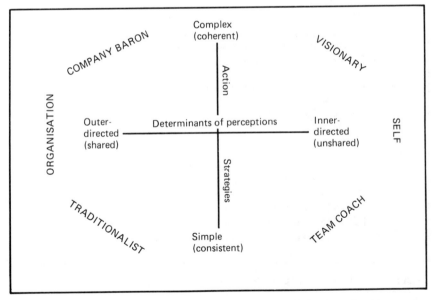

Figure 21.2 Perception/action model showing the four behavioural patterns.

---

1   A GOOD BOSS

   (a) ☐ avoids the use of power for its own sake,
   (b) ☐ is impersonal and sticks to the formal channels of communication,
   (c) ☐ is someone who lets me get on with the job,
   (d) ☐ keeps his distance.

2   A GOOD SUBORDINATE

   (a) ☐ is responsible and reliable,
   (b) ☐ complies with the duties of his job,
   (c) ☐ should be treated as a co-worker, contributing
        particular skills and abilities to the total team effort,
   (d) ☐ is someone who sticks with his team mates
        through thick and thin.

3   AT WORK

   (a) ☐ before I do something, I make sure my boss agrees,
   (b) ☐ I like to be with people who are creative and seem
        to be doing something new,
   (c) ☐ I feel I am able to stimulate good working relationships,
   (d) ☐ I feel it is important that senior management
        maintain their distance by sending directives from
        the top down, and in turn assess information that
        is fed up to them. In this way life is fair for everyone.

4   AT WORK

   (a) ☐ if the truth be known, I only really reward those
        people who like my ideas or suggestions,
   (b) ☐ I lose interest when projects get bogged down by
        lengthy decision making processes,
   (c) ☐ I often find it easier to do a job myself than to get
        others to do it right,
   (d) ☐ in order to work effectively with people it is
        important to get to know them personally.

5   AT WORK

   (a) ☐ any form of change or disruption is acceptable when it
        comes to improving the standards of goods or services,
   (b) ☐ I am fed up with people who seem to know little
        about my job and yet try to get me to do things differently,
   (c) ☐ I do not mind changes as long as they are not too disruptive,
   (d) ☐ changes are acceptable as long as they are planned and orderly.

Figure 21.3   The self-perception inventory

6 AT WORK

(a) ☐ people work well together when the systems and procedures define the way they should work,

(b) ☐ I tend to get annoyed with people who don't do things by the established procedures,

(c) ☐ rules and regulations should be interpreted so as to accommodate different people's needs,

(d) ☐ if I want something done, I take little notice of the rules and procedures and do what I want.

7 AT MEETINGS

(a) ☐ I tend to keep quiet if I seem to be the only one who supports a particular idea or action,

(b) ☐ I can't be bothered trying to convince people of something they don't want to accept,

(c) ☐ I try to make sure that people don't lose sight of the main objectives,

(d) ☐ I try to stimulate warm and friendly relationships with others.

8 FOR ME

(a) ☐ large scale organisational changes are an opportunity for advancement,

(b) ☐ improving my status in the organisation is as important as being paid more money,

(c) ☐ going to work is important because of the people I meet,

(d) ☐ things should be kept the way they are.

9 I DISLIKE

(a) ☐ people who pursue personal power. They make me feel uneasy,

(b) ☐ people who question my suggestions or decisions,

(c) ☐ discussing and handling details,

(d) ☐ people who always seem to want to do something new.

10 AND FINALLY

(a) ☐ becoming part of the 'old boy' network is a good way of getting to the top,

(b) ☐ to take a risk and do something new, even though it may harm my position in the organisation, really turns me on,

(c) ☐ when all is said and done the only person I safely depend on is myself,

(d) ☐ I really don't mind what people think, as long as they don't upset others around them.

Figure 21.3 *(concluded)*

Managing other people

Statement	Traditionalist		Team coach		Company baron		Visionary	
1	d		a		b		c	
2	b		d		a		c	
3	a		c		d		b	
4	c		d		a		b	
5	b		c		d		a	
6	b		c		a		d	
7	a		d		c		b	
8	d		c		b		a	
9	b		a		d		c	
10	c		d		a		b	
Total score								

Figure 21.4 Statement chart

WHO ARE YOU?

As an exercise in self-perception and awareness, complete the checklist (Figure 21.3). For each section, distribute a total of seven points which you think best describe you and your behaviour. You may wish to spread the seven points amongst some or all of the four statements, or you may wish to place all seven points on one statement. Once you have completed this procedure, enter the points in the statement chart (Figure 21.4).

388

The column with the highest score represents your most used style. The second highest score represents your back-up style, and so on.

Examine the spread of scores. If the difference in scores between your most preferred style and back-up style is high (i.e. greater than 6), that indicates that you prefer to use that style most of the time. If the differences in scores are low between your most preferred style, back-up style or even a third style, it indicates you have a range of styles to call on to suit different circumstances.

THE FOUR TYPES OF POLITICIAN

Traditionalist

Traditionalists wish to fit in with the rest of the organisation. They accept the fact that they are dependent on the objectives provided by others. They accept the way resources are allocated, even if it is detrimental to their interests. If resources were allocated in the past in a particular way, then that is the way it ought to continue.

By sticking so much to the past, traditionalist-oriented people are concerned that others do likewise. Hence, they emphasise control of group membership, especially new people entering the group. Considerable time will be spent discussing other people's suitability to enter the group. Are they the right sort of person? Will they rock the boat? Do they dress appropriately? Most of all, do they look right? Once in the group, how do they behave? Traditionalist people will ensure that their group's identity and prevailing attitudes are not threatened with change or extinction for they pay particular attention to the way new members interact with the more established group members. If someone is seen to misbehave or try to act above his station, then some form of retribution will follow, usually a reprimand. In extreme cases, the erring individual would be threatened with expulsion from the group.

Despite their group orientation, traditionalists do not like warm, friendly relations. Their dominant concern is their role and status in their group. They strive to be 'top dog' over others. They would prefer to maintain superior/subordinate distance especially with subordinates. Becoming too close to people might mean losing status.

As far as work is concerned, traditionalists prefer to work on details and be closely supervised by someone they trust and respect. That someone should have been a member of the organisation for some time and not be too young. Young people coming up the organisation are considered a threat and disliked.

Not only does the traditionalist want his group/unit/department to stay the same, but also wants it to stay the same in its status and position to the rest of the organisation. Any reorganisation that takes place could be seen as threatening, even if it does not directly affect the traditionalist's group. His concern is — when will it be us?

Although traditionalists are conservative, inflexible and fearful of change (especially changes of group leadership), they do play a vital role in organisations. Their preference to work on detailed tasks is of great advantage for they will complete all the tiresome jobs others would not wish to do.

Further, their link with the past provides for stability in the organisation. They tend to be loyal to each other and to the organisation. It is ironic that when changes occur, their loyalty and hard work are not rewarded. The very people previously in demand are now no longer needed. No wonder they are fearful of changes of situation and leadership.

Traditionalists can tolerate each other. As stated, what they cannot tolerate is dramatic or unexpected change or people who are very different from themselves (i.e. company barons and visionaries). When confronted with one or either, traditionalists show a high concern that the organisation could deteriorate. They hold a pathological attitude: 'why is it that things were always better in the past?'

Team coach

The team coach develops his own ideas and beliefs as to how he would wish to conduct his life and affairs. However, independence of thought is not matched by independence of action. The team coach does need to belong to a group of like-minded people and may spend some time searching for a group with which he wishes to associate. On becoming members of a group, team coaches may see themselves as missionaries, whose calling is to shift the predominant values of the organisation nearer to the values of the group. The team coach would be sincere in his attempts to help others in the organisation experience the same degree of work satisfaction as he does with his team/group or unit.

In contrast to the traditionalist, the team coach pays substantial attention to nurturing warm, informal, personal relationships, especially to newcomers in the group. They would be made to feel welcome and their induction to the group would be a comfortable experience. Relationships in the group are likely to be conducted on a first-name basis.

The team coach would try to ensure that his group is satisfied and content. Anyone who indicated dissatisfaction would be given plenty of attention in an attempt to improve their situation. Anyone who was constantly disruptive within the group would probably be asked, politely, to leave. If the person did not leave, then the others in the group would be urged to ignore them.

A group of bright, energetic team coaches can together make for an innovative team. They do have the capacity for independent thinking and generating new ideas. Team coaches do seek a task orientation to their work. Rather than being concerned with their personal role or status, team coaches would aim to provide goods, products or services of high quality. Their role position in the organisation would be considered a relatively unimportant concern. They would find it acceptable to see their role altered if it led to product or service improvement. Team coaches take pleasure in applying their skills to certain new and exciting areas of work.

Hence, the team coach is far more flexible than the traditionalist. He can accept changes of role or status, job content and even changes of resource allocation as long as there are no significant upsets in his group/unit as a result. As long as the group remains intact, change can be seen as a challenge. Once changes upset the structure of the group or its position in the organisation, team coaches would act together to prevent any further changes taking place. Team coaches are flexible to the extent that they are stimulated by interacting with people who think and feel differently from them. However, their need for consistency of behaviour prevents any real change of group opinion and hence any substantial innovation in tasks. Task accomplishment amounts to doing what you were good at before but always a little better.

Similar to the traditionalists, team coaches can become over-concerned about changes that take place in the organisation. Unlike traditionalists, team coaches are unlikely to display the same loyalty to the organisation. They are likely to display far greater loyalty to their group. If sufficiently threatened, they may leave the organisation *en masse* or shortly after one another, to seek another job.

The team coach got his name from interviews conducted with soccer coaches. It was recognised that certain people can cope with unshared meaning but insist on consistency of behaviour.

Company baron

The company baron has two dominant characteristics: an ability to see the total organisation as it really is; and a continuous strong drive to enhance his position and, if need be, emphasise and amplify his role at the expense of others.

Both the company baron and the visionary share one strong characteristic; the insight to develop a 'bird's eye view' of their organisation. The skill of both types is their capacity to think and conceptualise in whole organisational terms. They seem to be able to foresee potential problems in the organisation. For example, if the organisation were to market new services or products, the company baron and the visionary would attempt to predict the repercussions such moves would have on the organisation. Hence, both types seem to be able to recognise quickly how resources are really allocated in the organisation, who to influence to get what they want and what are the unspoken norms and values in the organisation that should never be challenged.

However, that is where the similarities between the two types cease. Although the company baron has considerable insight into how things are really done and why, what he finds difficult is to disengage or become separate from the majority in the organisation. As a result, the company baron rarely attempts to introduce large scale changes into the organisation which would involve shifts of organisational values and changes of structure. More than likely, he would examine the performance of particular divisions/departments/units/work systems in order to make any necessary alterations. One fact is sure: the company baron would never do something unless it suited his purposes.

The company baron is likely to practise two political styles in the organisation. On one side, he would constantly manoeuvre to ensure he had the upper hand whilst on the other, he would support the traditionalists of the organisation and champion values such as loyalty, hard work and patronage.

The self-oriented style would mean the company baron would be conscious of his status in the organisation. He would attempt to enhance his role and become involved in the various power struggles in the organisation as long as his role and position are not harmed. The company baron makes an excellent committee politician.

The fact that he is outer-directed and shares the values and norms of the organisation is a good measure of his commitment to work within the existing systems. He is likely to be efficient at working on the smallest details as well as tackling larger issues and organising the necessary parties to make their contribution to any project. His style is to collaborate with others and usually seek their opinion before making his move. He needs others on his side before action is taken. His working towards gathering support from others could be misinterpreted as sitting on the fence.

The company baron plays an important role in the organisation. He has the ability to gather together various individuals and groups of differing vested interests and help them work towards particular objectives. Some may dislike his self-centred role and status orientation but that is outweighed by his capacity to work at the pace of others who are not united in their objectives, without leaving any stones unturned. In achieving medium and long term strategy plans, the company baron is a vital link.

Despite his administrative skills, the company baron will only seek to introduce evolutionary change. Typically, he has probably been part of the organisation for some time. He may even have 'grown up' in the system. He will have identified with the old values of the organisation. He would have known many of the people who have stayed there for any length of time. Hence, his commitment to the established values of the organisation and his personal knowledge of the people in it makes it psychologically impossible for him to introduce dramatic change. He is unable to distance himself from the past.

As indicated, the company baron shares the values of maintaining traditions, patronage, honesty and hard work. He could easily dislike people who would 'rock the boat' with too many bright ideas or too many demands for change. He may be in favour of conducting more intellectual discussions as long as they do not become intense and they do not result in active demands for change and reorganisation.

The company baron is a difficult individual to handle. On the one side, his need for power and self-gain makes it difficult to control him or even to predict his next move. On the other, his capacity for loyalty to the organisation makes him a valuable asset. He provides a fatherly stability, coupled with a good appreciation of present and future problems.

In a sense, a number of company barons together cancel each other out. One is unlikely to let any other become king. In addition, with their sense of oneness with the organisation, they are unlikely to destroy the kingdom if they do not get what they want.

Visionary

As stated, the visionary, similar to the company baron, possesses an ability to see the organisation in total. Although he can think and conceptualise in whole organisational terms, the visionary does not feel the same need for loyalty to the organisation. Hence, not only can the visionary question and examine the way resources are allocated in the organisation and explore what are suitable structures for the organisation, but he can also stand back from the values, views and stereotypes held by the majority in the organisation. Such independence of mind is invaluable if faced with reorganisation and restructuring.

Visionary-oriented people tend to operate from their visions of the future concerning the organisation and the world outside. They have particular, personal values as to how things ought to be done and beliefs about what will happen in the future. Coupled with their ability to conceptualise organisations in whole terms, they are able to predict which parts of the organisation require alteration and adjustment in order to achieve certain long term objectives. Sir Geoffrey Vickers (1968) described such people as possessing 'systemic wisdom' – having a clear insight into how long term trends in the world outside will affect the organisation.

As visionary people develop their own personalised visions and beliefs about the future, and their own philosophies about work and strategies for action, they tend to operate in relative isolation from others. Such philosophies tend to be a personal expression of self; their identity, what they stand for, all which have been generated in isolation from others and hence are difficult to share with others. Sharing personal values is difficult. It is hard to cooperate with someone who has the ability to develop equally well formed ideas that are different (or even similar) but stem from separate personal values. In-fighting between board members of companies can be the result of such fundamental differences of opinion. Usually, there is little room for compromise unless one party surrenders. Often, battles amongst visionaries are conducted in an undercover, cloak and dagger way with little animosity shown on the surface. If such battles go on for too long, it is possible that the organisation may suffer in terms of forward planning. Usually one of the warring parties has to leave. It is the visionary's ability to interpret current events, predict future trends and generate an alternative identity that makes his view of the world unique. It is a matter of 'two into one won't go'.

However, it is to the advantage of the visionary to share with others how fundamental strategies, once decided, should be implemented. The involvement of others not only ensures that strategies are put into practice but allows them to identify with the new values, attitudes and norms of behaviour in the restructured organisation.

Whether others approve of the new changes or not, the visionary would seek to introduce more dramatic change. He would not value planned, step-by-step change as he is not committed to the previous values and structure of the organisation. In his day-to-day style, the visionary would be far less cautious than the company baron in playing politics and introducing changes. He will 'test the water' before making his move but will not be too dependent on the support of others. Rather, he would use his influencing skills to state his case. He would use his interpersonal skills to influence individuals before and after meetings. During meetings, he would probably be more assertive than the company baron and be prepared to handle any conflict that is directed towards him. On the whole, the visionary is more prepared to risk.

Visionaries are a valuable asset in any organisation. Their drive, energy and flamboyance makes them attractive to others. Their new ideas, if properly harnessed, make an invaluable contribution to the development and growth of the organisation. However, visionaries are not easy to manage. If they are not doing something challenging, they could become bored, critical of management and the organisation and possibly leave. They may also feel constrained by the systems in the organisation and again be over-critical of management.

There tend to be few visionaries. Not unexpectedly, their skills are much in demand. Their capacity to rationalise in whole organisational terms and create fundamental, realistic and at times adventurous strategies for change and then work towards developing a series of interrelated tasks to match the original strategy, is unlikely to be developed through management training. They train themselves on the job.

Visionaries have been used as action men brought in at the top to revitalise an ailing organisation.

Behaviours the four types will find comfortable and uncomfortable:

TRADITIONALIST

Comfortable with

Maintenance of superior/
subordinate distance.
Small recognisable group of
acquaintances that have
developed over time.

TEAM COACH

Comfortable with

Introduction of new people to the
group.
Helping to develop potential in
the group.
Consensual decision making

TRADITIONALIST

Comfortable with

Being given directions on standards required for tasks.
Supervision of well structured tasks.
Administrative tasks.
Routine, established procedures and detail.
Keeping to the status quo.

Uncomfortable with

Changes of work pattern, boss or organisation structure.
Confrontation.
Too much discussion about ideas and developments for the future.
Involvement in major decision making.
Supervising poorly structured tasks.

COMPANY BARON

Comfortable with

Established procedures and rules.
Lengthy decision making processes.
Change within the existing system.
Compromise, tradition and patronage.
Manoeuvres for increased power.
Long periods in one organisation.

Uncomfortable with

Acting in isolation.
Criticism and confrontation.

TEAM COACH

Comfortable with

patterns.
Changes of work patterns.
Small changes in resource allocation and task activities.

Uncomfortable with

People who dramatically threaten the status quo.
Large scale changes that threaten the unity of the group.
Non-consensual patterns of decision making.
Being personally criticised.
Arguing for changes of resource allocation.
Representing the group on key policy matters to other groups

VISIONARY

Comfortable with

Criticism, confrontation and conflict.
Using personal influencing skills.
Low affiliation with people.
New, innovative and risky ideas.
Working in poorly structured situations.
Working on large scale change.
Controlling people and projects.

Uncomfortable with

Detail and routine.
Working within role constraints and established procedures.

COMPANY BARON

Uncomfortable with

Sharing with others.
People who generate too many innovative ideas.
Ideas or policies that are considered new, unpopular or risky.
Displays of openness and warmth by others.
Dramatic change.
People who display little loyalty to tradition.

VISIONARY

Uncomfortable with

Displays of warmth from others.
Lengthy decision making processes.
Maintaining group cohesion for its own sake.
Remaining within one job, organisation or well developed career hierarchy, for too long.

MANAGING THE POLITICS

Politics is a process, that of influencing individuals and groups of people to your point of view. You may wish others to accept your ideas, do what you want them to or simply get them to re-examine what they are doing so that they can improve their performance. Being in a position of formal authority is not sufficient. All too often an unacceptable boss finds that he is blocked, out-manoeuvred or even out-talked by smarter subordinates. What is required is to influence others sufficiently to accept your particular ideas and efforts.

There are seven approaches to effective interpersonal influence:

1 identify the stakeholders;
2 keep the stakeholders comfortable;
3 fit the image;
4 use the network;
5 make deals;
6 withhold and withdraw;
7 if all else fails ...

Identify the stakeholders

The stakeholders are the people who have a commitment to act in particular ways. They have invested time, effort and resources to ensure that their objectives are adopted by the others. The stake-

397

holders are the ones who are likely to influence what should be done and how it should be done. The only way to understand the pressures and strains is to identify the stakeholders. How influential they can be depends on their own skills of interpersonal influence and their determination to pursue certain issues. It is not important that the stakeholders have formal role authority, for pursuing particular objectives is a matter of influence and not command. Further, it may be difficult to identify the stakeholders. They may take refuge behind others, especially those with formal role authority. People who wish to have their view adopted do not necessarily have to make themselves visible to show their hand.

Keep the stakeholders comfortable

To be effective at interpersonal influence, help the stakeholders to feel comfortable, unless it is absolutely necessary to do otherwise.

Helping an individual to feel comfortable involves concentrating on those behaviours, values, attitudes, drives and ideas that the person in question can accept, tolerate and manage, i.e. their comfort zones. The reason the 'comfort zones' are emphasised is that every person has developed a range of values and behaviours which they find acceptable and wish to put into practice. The range of values and behaviours is their identity.

Hence, people will pay attention to the concerns of others as long as their own are not threatened. Once an interaction with another concentrates on the issues important to only one party, and is threatening to the other party, that interaction is likely to be terminated. And why not? People only communicate when they have sufficient interest in a situation. They are concerned with the final objective, i.e. what is in it for them, and the manner in which the final objective is achieved, i.e. the process. By managing the interactions so that the process feels comfortable to the receiving party, the outcome can satisfy both parties.

Working on the 'comfort zones' is synonymous with motivating people and gaining their trust and confidence. The point is that different people require a different approach. Each person should develop some idea as to what other individuals can and cannot accept. Otherwise a sincere attempt to motivate may be interpreted as manipulation by the receiving party.

A word of warning: by all means work on the comfort zones of the stakeholders, but there is always the danger that meeting the needs, whims and fancies of others means relegating your needs to second place.

There is a fine dividing line between working on the comfort zone of the other and ensuring that others recognise and reward your contribution.

Fit the image

By working on the comfort zones, it is possible to influence the stake-holders to one's own way of thinking. However, to gain the recognition and acceptance of superiors or individuals considered powerful and influential, it is necessary to work continuously on their comfort zones. As a result, one becomes aligned to the powerful other; one fits his image.

Once one has fitted into the image of the powerful other, then maintaining that image is no simple task. With the traditionalist and team coach, accepting group norms is sufficient to fit the image. With the company baron and the visionary, however, fitting the image for any length of time will be difficult, for lack of sharing is their norm. Rather than become a fallen star, it is important to consider what one requires from the powerful other, how long it would take to get it, and if necessary, whether realigning with another powerful individual may be required.

Working on the comfort zones and fitting the image of an influential person is likely to be effective in the short to medium term. Plan ahead for when the relationship ceases to be fruitful.

Use the network

Most people in organisations have a number of identities. First, all employees have a job or role. All job holders are held accountable for certain tasks and responsibilities inherent in their role.

In addition, most individuals belong to certain interest groups which are formed for non-organisational reasons and may attract members from a number of separate organisations. These interest groups are termed networks.

The network is determined by the values and objectives of its members. Like-minded people gather to debate, exchange information and achieve consensus over issues that concern them. Depending on the prevailing issues and the dominant personalities in the network, a network can be a more powerful determinant of the objectives to be pursued and how they are to be acted upon, than the formal organisation.

Consequently, attempting to influence people who belong to networks is as necessary as attempting to influence particular individuals in an organisation. The principle of working on the comfort zones has to be extended to influencing individuals and groups. The key to networking is to identify the dominant core values of the network, and the individuals who are generally seen as upholding them, and influence them by working on their comfort zones.

There are four different types of networks: practitioner networks; privileged power networks; ideological networks; and person-oriented networks.

Entering the networks

Getting yourself known and becoming recognised as someone who has a worthwhile contribution to make, is achieved by entering one or more networks. The individual must be aware of the following processes.

Identify the gatekeepers. The gatekeepers are individuals who are influential in the network, trusted by the network members but spend as much time outside the network as within. Naturally, they meet with others who may wish to join the network or have a contribution to make. The gatekeepers will assess whether the individual is worthy of introduction. If a gatekeeper acts as a sponsor to an individual, then that person will have saved considerable time and effort for he will become acquainted with the senior network members.

Adhering to network norms. Once in the network, it is important to be aware that certain values and norms of behaviour should not be challenged as they are sacred to the network. Whether one's intentions are to sponsor one's own career through the network, or to introduce or even prevent changes in a particular profession or the community at large, one should not introduce too many issues too quickly. Each network has its own way of doing things. To raise too many issues in too short a time could upset the other members. It is as important to fit into the network as it is to do anything new.

Make deals

Making a deal with other individuals or groups is common practice in most large organisations. Whether resources are limited or not, different individuals or groups may agree to support each other to achieve a common purpose as long as there are benefits for them. It is realistic to expect individuals and groups in the organisation to wish to promote their own goals, which may be at the expense of others. Consequently, coming to some sort of agreement about common policies, or at least not disturbing each other's aims, may be necessary.

The way deals are made is as important as the actual deal itself. Making a deal with a traditionalist or team coach is somewhat different from making a deal with a company baron or visionary. Making deals with traditionalists could be perceived by them as a threatening process. They may feel unable to control the events around them and may not even be able to understand the issues at hand. Consequently, if a deal is to be made with traditionalists or team coaches, it has to be seen more as a gentleman's agreement which is to be kept and honoured.

Making deals with company barons and visionaries is a different matter. Whatever agreements are reached between the parties, they may not be adhered to in the future. The agreements may be willingly broken by either party if this is seen to be to their advantage. More likely, however, is that as circumstances change, so people's needs alter and new agreements need to be negotiated. Time brings about change. People wish to alter previous agreements. If both parties are aware of the new developments, then change can be negotiated openly. If, however, one of the parties is unaware of new developments or finds that change of circumstances is not in his favour, he may then attempt to hold the other party to the agreed arrangement. Even if the other party is willing to stand by the agreed arrangements, it is unlikely he will do so for long. Changes take place and previous arrangements are unlikely to be adhered to, but such developments will be underhand and hidden from the other party.

Whenever deals are struck between two or more parties, it is worth considering the true intentions of the other party and for how long one could realistically expect the arrangement to stand as agreed.

Withhold and withdraw

It is impossible to satisfy the needs of all parties in any diverse organisation. One way of ensuring that certain groups do not over-react to issues which they recognise as important is to withhold information. By doing this, the manager can achieve whatever objectives he has identified without facing opposition that could destroy his plan. In such circumstances, the manager should be fairly convinced that his plan is valuable, even if others have not, or will not recognise its worth. However, constantly to withhold information is not recommended, for such behaviour is indicative of a manager who cannot confront certain problems. Continuously withholding information is a means of protecting the manager and not the policy.

Withdrawing from a situation is sometimes necessary. There are times when the presence of a manager in a dispute or negotiations is of no help. To withdraw and allow the different factions to negotiate their own terms, or for management to withdraw an unpopular policy and shelve it for the time being, are common practices. The larger and more diverse an organisation becomes, the more important is the timing of actions. When to introduce or withdraw plans and information is an important consideration for policy implementation.

When all else fails

Just because certain strategies to increase one's personal influence have been practised, these do not guarantee success. Things do go wrong and situations can get out of hand. What to do then, when all else fails?

The range of options is limited. The most obvious solution is to leave the job, situation or organisation. However, suitable alternative employment may not be easy to find. Job searches take time. Further, any individual would require a reference from his previous boss for any potential new employer. If the interactions between boss and individual have not been successful, then obtaining a worthwhile reference may not be possible. In fact, it may be more difficult to leave than to stay.

The second alternative is stick it out. Living and working in an unpleasant environment is, however, not easy. It is both distasteful and demoralising to continue interacting with others who do not appreciate one's contribution and who may wish to prevent one's further growth and development. The only real advantage in trying to stick it out is that the individual can reassess his own values, beliefs and action strategies. Was he trying to do too much too quickly? Were the underlying issues that important? Is constant action necessary? Certain uncomfortable experiences simply have to be lived with and accommodated. It is possible to use the time to re-examine one's own purpose and objectives, if for no other reason than that similar uncomfortable experiences should not recur in the future.

The third alternative, if adopted, is a high risk strategy. It involves getting rid of the stakeholder. A superior putting pressure on one person in the hope that he leaves makes others uncomfortable. They wonder when it will be their turn. Trust, respect and work performance is likely to drop sharply.

For a subordinate to try to get rid of his boss is equally dangerous. The only realistic way is to conspire with the boss's boss in order to remove the troublesome superior. However, the boss's boss may feel uncomfortable for he is having to relate to a subordinate who is operating outside his role boundary. You may be successful in getting rid of your boss, but there is always the danger that you may be next to go!

DON'T BE AFRAID OF BEING POLITICAL!

Understandably, many people may fear the politics played in their organisation. Equally, many people may not wish to play politics. Whatever each individual decides, at least he should not be afraid of being political. Politics is not all negative and bad.

What is the difference between motivation and manipulation? The answer is the interpretation the receiver puts on attempts to influence him. If he is influenced in a positive and favourable way, the person may consider himself as motivated. If, however, attempts at influence are not well planned or well conducted, the other party may feel himself manipulated. Undoubtedly, most people at work will experience situations where stress, discomfort and manipulation are a common occurrence. Such situations can be managed and turned into positive experiences.

Politics is nothing more than getting what you want done, preferably with the full permission and approval of the others around you.

FURTHER READING

The material in this chapter was drawn from Andrew Kakabadse's book, *The Politics of Management,* Gower, 1983, and 'Playing for power', by Andrew Kakabadse, *Working Woman,* November 1984, pp. 86–88.

A number of behavioural scientists have worked on the concept of mental mapping.

Goffman, E, *Frame Analysis. An Essay on the Organisation of Experience,* Penguin, 1974

Bandura, A, *Learning Theory,* Prentice-Hall, 1977

Mischel, W, 'Self Control and the Self' in Mischel, T (ed.), *The Self: Psychological and Philosophical Issues,* Rowman and Littlefield, 1977

Vickers, Sir Geoffrey, *Value Systems and Social Processes,* Tavistock, 1968

For recent work on how people learn to cope with the culture of organisations see:

Cole, D, *Professional Suicide: A Survival Kit For You and Your Job,* McGraw-Hill, 1981

Argyris, C and Schon, D A, *Organisational Learning: A Theory of Action Perspective,* Addison-Wesley, 1981

Kakabadse, A, *Culture of the Social Services,* Gower, 1982

Part III
MANAGING THE BUSINESS

Introduction: Understanding the business

Last but not least, you need to understand the business. There are enormous differences between industries and between individual businesses within an industry, but there are also skills and knowledge held in common. The secret of success as a manager is to broaden your skills and knowledge base to include something of all these, instead of sticking narrowly to your technical specialism, accounting, production, marketing etc., which earned you your promotion to management. Great managers are generalists.

Understanding the business provides answers to such fundamental questions as: why are we here? what do we think we are doing? what should we be doing? how do we do it? If you feel these questions are perhaps a little metaphysical for a manager, consider how even the great seat-of-the-pants operators can also come unstuck. Prevention *is* better than cure.

In Part III we offer ways of thinking about these matters as well as guidelines for developing your own business skills. It begins with an introduction to strategic planning, and the way to answer those questions. We follow with a review of two main functions: accounting (written to dispel the non-accountant's bafflement), and marketing, which is demystified and given a salutary critique. A chapter on the whole process of project management, from project concept to post-completion audit, applies to every function of management, but may perhaps be seen to add a production viewpoint.

Three techniques chapters follow in areas which are crucial to the business: creativity and innovation (and not just for new product development); decision making and problem solving; and negotiating. We conclude with your role as ambassador for your organisation, both unconsciously and deliberately. The author would encourage you to make sure that your contribution to your organisation's PR is both helpful and considered.

22

Strategic planning

Bruce Lloyd

> If you don't think about the future you won't have one.
>
> Anon

The key to corporate survival and growth is the ability to innovate successfully. To manage change in an age of turbulence, organisations must have a clear idea of both what they want to be — objectives and strategy — and how they will get there — planning and operational decision taking.

CORPORATE NEEDS

All organisations need a well formulated strategy, as well as the means to implement it and monitor its success, in order to operate effectively today. This applies to organisations irrespective of whether they are large or small, simple or complex, in the public or private sectors.

These requirements exist regardless of the external economic, political or industrial climate and they must be continually addressed by senior management, if success is to be achieved and maintained.

Strategy must be developed and set by the top team. It must provide a framework for decisions relating to an organisation's products or services, its markets, key capabilities, growth, return on capital, and allocation of resources. It is only once this framework is established that an organisation can begin to develop operational plans.

Over the past 20 years some ideas on strategic planning for private and public sector organisations have changed, while others have remained the same. The conditions under which management has to plan have also changed. The 1950s and 1960s were full of growth-oriented confidence, while the 1970s were dominated by a combination of high technology expectations and the upheavals created by the oil price rises.

Today, management must take for granted that we live in a world that is economically, politically, socially and technologically turbulent, ambiguous, changing and unpredictable.

In addition there have been changes in the way top managements approach creating the future for their businesses. This chapter describes the evolution of the elements of strategic planning – each of them relevant to circumstances. To flourish in today's turbulent world the top management of large or small organisations – in particular large ones – must be able increasingly to think and act strategically.

THE EARLY STAGES

In the initial entrepreneurial stage of most corporate development, planning is carried out by owner managers, usually in their heads. They do not have – and could not afford – the expertise of planning staff. Instead owner managers operate by personal contact, getting information through direct observation and then integrating that information into operating decisions.

The price of success in the initial stage is growth and its attendant demands for more delegation of decision and formalisation of plans in order to integrate the various aspects of the business. This process leads to an immediate need for budgets and control.

BUDGETS AND CONTROL

The systematic use of annual plans as a basis for budgetary control is usually introduced by a finance director.

Under this system the various managers with responsibility for functional departments or divisions in the organisation prepare their budget estimates for the forthcoming accounting year. Expected levels of activity are assessed and the budgets are coordinated by the accounting department as a basis for the management's annual plan.

Top management may refer back budgets for improvement before agreeing the overall plan, and participation in the budgetary process is widely held to encourage commitment to achieving the planned results.

Variations between planned and actual results form the basis for management control. In times of uncertainty these variations can be marked. Budgetary control is a fundamental management tool; however, it is essentially short term and rarely has a strategy component.

LONG TERM PLANS

It is widely accepted that the further organisations look ahead the more uncertain the future becomes and so the idea of rolling over annual reviews is used. In addition, increasingly, organisations try to push the budget process further forward for two, three or even five years – at least in outline. The appropriate budgeting time horizon depends on the industry, the specific position of the company, and the nature of the investment decisions or other long term commitments it is making.

However, these modifications do not alter the fact that the basis of the plan is still dominated by the accounting approach, although the planning staff are incorporating views on economic expectations and the level of business activity. The completed plan is likely to contain income statements and funds flow expectations for the period. Top management then modifies and/or approves these plans and budget expectations.

The above approach has its limitations. Preparing plans takes time and money. Also projecting activities and prices a long way forward in a period of significant uncertainty can be hazardous. Consequently there is a risk that in becoming committed to a plan, management may not respond to new information which requires action because it affects some of the underlying assumptions. As a result of these problems long range planning that uses the roll forward approach can inhibit initiatives in strategic thinking and it can end up extrapolating the present rather than generating new strategies.

FUTURE PLANS

The next stage in the evolution of strategic planning usually involves the creation of a planning group, a staff function which undertakes studies about the future of markets, products, economies, technology and other factors relevant to the future of the enterprise. This unit provides information, ideas and support management.

The elements in this approach to planning are:

- identifying aspects of the company's situation in which future changes would significantly affect the business;
- building up a picture of possible alternatives;
- considering whether action is necessary in the short term to change the organisation to meet future needs.

This future-oriented planning is in effect an information system providing an additional resource for top management.

A critical factor in this approach is the business objectives. 'What business are we really in?' has become a widely accepted phrase. A new emphasis on marketing, that emerged first in the 1960s, is symptomatic of the orientation. Products and markets were evaluated to find new opportunities within the framework shown in Figure 22.1. The idea of synergy arose out of this approach, encouraging one part of a business to attempt to build on the strengths of another.

	Existing products	New products
New customers	Market development (existing products into new markets)	Diversification (new markets and new products)
Existing customers	Growth of existing business	Product development and extension (new products for existing customers)

Figure 22.1 What business are we in? And where are we going?

Various other techniques were developed to help planners predict the future. Simulation models were built to help forecast market trends. Data bases were created. Unfortunately in a world of accelerating change and uncertainty, the ability of forecasters to do more than speculate has been called into question. Most of the forecasts made in the later 1960s of the likely world in the 1980s make amusing reading. Nevertheless the need for large organisations to think systematically about the likely nature of the world a decade or more ahead cannot be overestimated. It is often useful to incorporate this thinking into scenario planning exercises, which essentially take a 'what if?' approach.

The questioning of objectives, together with explorations of 'what business are we in?' is a useful part of the strategic planning process. However, the main constraint on this approach occurs when the future predicted for the enterprise or organisation is in conflict with top management's 'beliefs', values or culture. Challenging the basic culture, value system, orientation and thinking of a business can be an extremely difficult and threatening experience. It can only be initiated and implemented effectively if there is commitment to it at the top.

CORPORATE PLANNING

The economic pressures and commercial facts of life in recent years have forced managers to take a more active interest in planning. No longer can it be assumed that existing products and markets provide a basis for continuing success. In reality it never could, but in recent years competition has increased dramatically in almost every sector; profit margins have been squeezed; product life cycles shortened; new technologies have reduced market entry barriers and traditional industrial sectors have been broken down.

In many cases top management has had to think radically about its corporate plans for the first time: which had sound cash flows; which had products with high market share; which had significant potential; what were the organisation's real strengths and weaknesses; where were significant economies and diseconomies of scale; what were the future capital and manpower requirements; where was value really being added in the business? What was the organisation's unique selling proposition (USP)? Many of these issues have arisen because of the rapid growth in merger and acquisition activity.

Today product groups, divisions and companies in the portfolio of the enterprise are increasingly analysed for their actual and potential synergy and contribution to the 'bottom line' of the parent. The use of the Boston Consulting Group business analysis of cash flow, market growth and profitability can be valuable (Figure 22.2).

This approach can be refined and developed in many ways. (See Chapter 24 for a critique of the approach.) However, despite the use of these and other techniques, companies found their position of

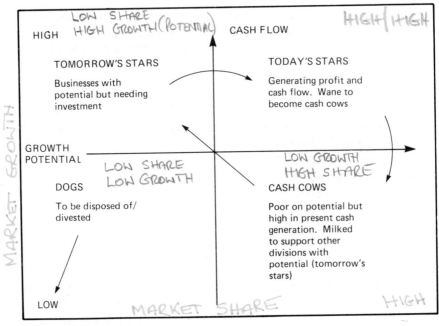

Figure 22.2   The Boston Consulting Group's analysis of business

market leadership continually being challenged by more innovative, usually smaller, competitors. This reflected the reality that to combine people and information effectively into a coherent corporate strategy becomes a progressively more difficult as organisations get larger and more mature.

Critics of corporate planning questioned its flexibility and power to both adapt itself and change its corporate vehicle to meet the new needs of the rapidly changing external environment. It became apparent that those responsible for the direction of the business had to take ultimate responsibility for the formulation and implementation. It was the prime board responsibility.

STRATEGIC PLANNING

The expertise, advice and information of a staff group can be valuable but the board must ultimately take responsibility for the strategy and direction of the organisation. Hence the basic role of directors is the formulation and implementation of strategy. To do this the directors need to understand all the issues, opportunities and threats in their changing environment; they need to identify, and be clear about, their objectives; they need to understand the organisation's strengths and weaknesses; and they need to establish processes that lead to effective strategic action.

The whole process is time-consuming but it is also a challenging and creative task. The process can be summarised as follows:

- Review and/or establish the company's objectives – this is the key element.
- Assess past and present performance against these objectives.
- Produce clear instructions for the preparation of the plan to ensure that a consistent approach is maintained at all levels.
- Consolidate the plan and examine the short term needs within the context of longer term objectives.
- Test the plan for errors and omissions, and against existing or projected resources.
- Refine the plan through recycling the document through the same management structure where it originated.
- Agree and adopt the plan and assign accountable action tasks to individuals.
- Incorporate the plan into management information routines and ensure that progress can be monitored.
- Set up a reporting system that enables progress to be reviewed and the plan to be revised where necessary.

The process can be represented diagrammatically by Figure 22.3. Invariably it is the rigour of the process itself, rather than the correctness of any one set of answers, that will be the critical factor in determining the long term value of strategic planning.

But achieving effective results is not easy. Often, strategic planning produces a call for change in what is done, who does what, and how things are done. However, unless the bridges are there, no amount of strategic thinking or exhortation will bring operational changes about – at least not the changes intended, in the smooth, effective way expected. Often, strategy setting is an exercise in frustration which fails to win commitment because it is dominated by people too high in the organisation to understand the realities of the changes required in the operational areas. On the other hand, if strategy flows from the bottom up, the originators can fail to rise above their parochial concerns to view the total corporate picture.

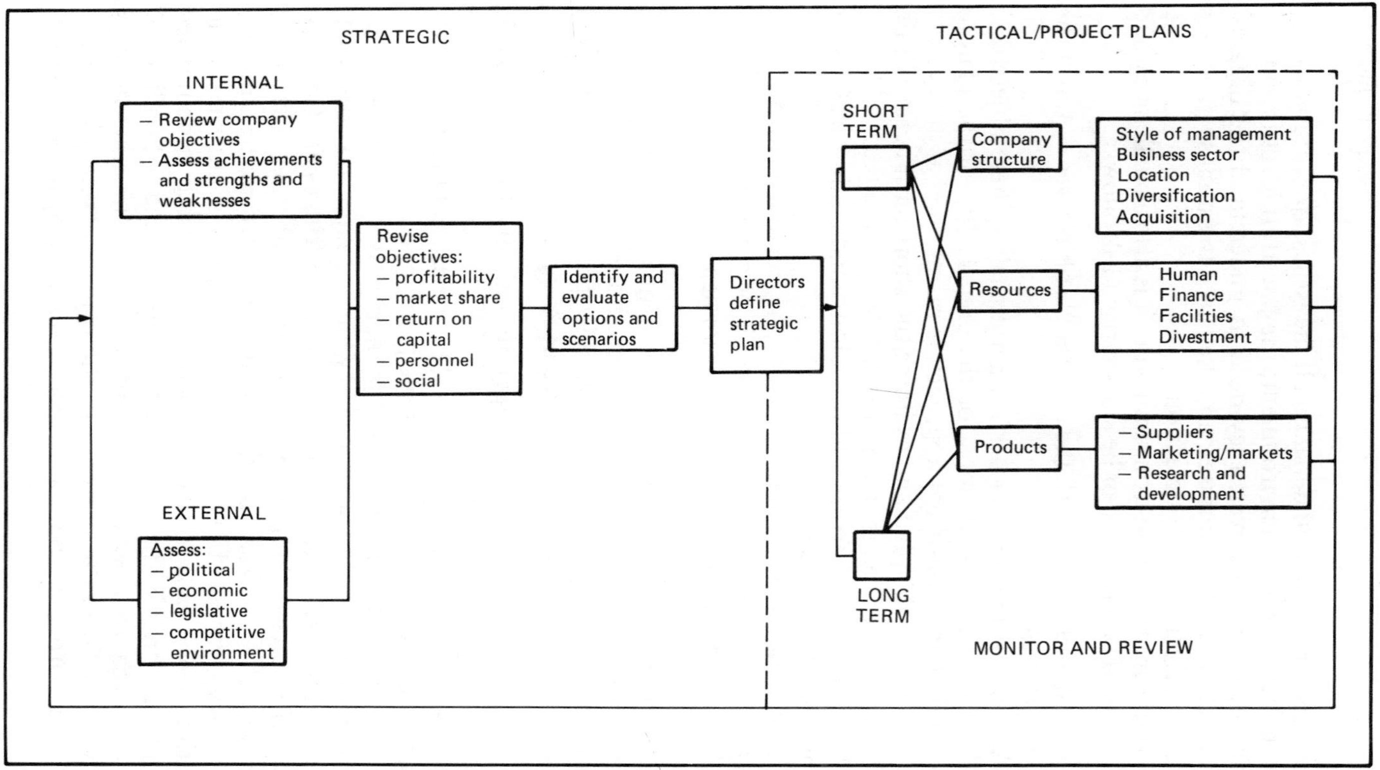

Figure 22.3   The planning system

The board, staff functions and operational management must all work together for strategic planning to be effective.

While new ways of pinpointing strategic potential are emerging which must be part of the process of strategy formulation, the key element in success is the extent to which the board accepts responsibility for thinking and acting strategically. Ultimate effectiveness, however, depends on total organisational commitment.

But effective strategic planning is not a bureaucratic process; quite the opposite. It aims to make organisations more creative, encouraging them to have more good ideas and helping to make them work.

Within this process the position of the corporate planner is always precarious. As someone once remarked, 'the main requirement of a corporate planner is for them to have a private income'. The importance of people in this whole process cannot be overstressed.

A final caution is that strategic thinking and planning cannot work by being left to a system. It is a tool managers have at their disposal to overturn traditions and challenge historic commitments, to question deeply held assumptions, and to think and perform 'the impossible'. At its core is vision, creative thinking and the management of change and innovation. This should be, but rarely is, the substance of management. This is why strategic planning is never easy to do effectively but it has to be done if any organisation wishes to survive and flourish in today's world. Figure 22.4 provides a checklist for senior management and the board.

FURTHER READING

Long Range Planning, editor Bernard Taylor, Strategic Planning Society, 15 Belgrave Square, London SW1

Harvard Business Review, Graduate School of Business Administration, Soldiers Field Road, Boston, Massachusetts 02163, USA

Ansoff, H Igor, *From Strategic Planning to Strategic Thinking*, Wiley, 1976

Taylor, Bernard and Sparks, John R, *Corporate Strategy and Planning*, Heinemann, 1977

Gluck, F W et al., 'The Evolution of Strategic Management', *Harvard Business Review*, July/August 1980

- Which stage is the organisation at in its strategic thinking?

- Where and how is strategy formulated?
    In the finance function?
    By the main board?
    In a staff planning function?
    Through executive teams?

- Is the board bogged down by routine, operational activities, and consequently spending insufficient time on strategic matters?

- How can strategic thinking be stimulated?
    By use of non-executive directors?
    Through existing directors?
    Are directors adequately informed?

- How is strategy formulated and how can the process be improved?
    New inputs to strategy discussions?
    Use of outsiders?
    Use of strategy seminars or think tanks?
    Position papers and presentations to the board?

- How does the organisation respond to emerging issues, threats and opportunities?

- Where are the pressures for, and sources of, innovation?

- Does the board have a shared vision about the future of the organisation and its environment? If not, why not? And what can be done about it?

Figure 22.4   Board checklist

Argenti, John, *Practical Corporate Planning*, George Allen and Unwin, 1980

Linneman, Robert E, *Shirt-Sleeve Approach to Long-Range Planning*, Prentice-Hall, 1980

Lorange, Peter, *Corporate Planning: An Executive Viewpoint*, Prentice-Hall, 1980

Shaw, W C, *How to do a Company Plan and put it into action*, Business Books, 1981

Miles, Robert H, *Coffin Nails and Corporate Strategies,* Prentice-Hall, 1982

Hussey, D E, *Corporate Planning: Theory and Practice*, Pergamon, 1982

Albert, Kenneth J (ed.), *The Strategic Management Handbook*, McGraw-Hill, 1983

Ansoff, H Igor, *Implanting Strategic Management*, Prentice-Hall, 1984

Rosenberg, Larry J, and Schewe, Charles D, 'Strategic Planning: Fulfilling the Promise', *Business Horizons*, July/August 1985

Fawn, John and Fox, Bernard (eds.), *Corporate Planning in Practice*, ICMA/Strategic Planning Society, 1986

Iacocca, Lee, *Iacocca: An Autobiography*, Bantam Books, 1986

23

Accounting and business decisions

William P Rees

A survey of investment analysts by Arnold and Mozier, published in 1984, showed that among their most influential sources of information were the income statement (first), the balance sheet (second), interim earnings announcements (third), and source and application of funds statements (fifth). (Direct contact with company personnel was ranked fourth whilst many of the remaining twelve categories were accounting based.) This dominance of accounting information as inputs into the decisions of these sophisticated specialists rather encourages the accountant whose faith in his product can be sorely tested by his awareness of its subjectivity and irrationality. Yet many have rejected the usefulness of accounting data after examining the difficulties of producing meaningful financial reports. However, the converse of the sceptics' rejection of accounting information is the arguably more dangerous reliance that the uninitiated may place on the apparent numeric exactitude of accounting statements, coupled with a reverential awe of the alchemy employed by the fiscal wizards who produce them.

It is the purpose of this chapter to give those uninitiated in the use of accounting information a balanced view of the reliability of the information produced by accountants, to convince them that a knowledge of the detailed methods of accountancy is unnecessary to its understanding, to explain and illustrate the techniques of financial interpretation, and to show how accounting information is used in management decision making. Throughout, the level of technical explanation is elementary, whereas a relatively sophisticated discussion of the implications is considered important to business managers. Jargon is kept to a minimum but the occasional technical term cannot be avoided.

The chapter is divided into four sections. In the first the process used by accountants to distil measures of income and wealth from a vast array of transactions is examined. The explicit focus is on the formal reporting system for the preparation of published accounts but in most organisations the same principles are employed for the internal reporting system. The second section examines the accounting statements of two competing organisations to illustrate the information that can be extracted from these data and the degree of reliance that can be placed on them. The later part of this section concentrates on the technique of ratio analysis. The third section drops the emphasis on external reporting and considers the managerial uses of accounting data, either for evaluating decisions or for monitoring progress. Although in many instances the accounting system will be part of this managerial process the information used is less formal or prescribed. The final section concludes the discussion.

THE ACCOUNTING PROCESS

Accounting attempts to measure two interrelated concepts, income and wealth. It should be emphasised that as concepts these are not directly observable phenomena. Consequently a set of rules has become generally accepted or enforced to try to impose some measure of standardisation on the assessment of these two ephemera. This is best illustrated by an example, focusing on one of the many transactions which might make up the activities of an organisation.

In this example a contract for the sale of a 'stegdiw' is won in month 1, and the raw material is immediately ordered and received. In month 2 the supplier is paid £500 in full settlement and the labour force completes and is paid for £500 worth of work. The 'stegdiw' is delivered in month 3, and full payment of £1500 is received in month 4. In addition monthly overheads of £150 are incurred and an asset costing £2400 with an expected life of 24 months is being utilised.

The transactions involved, together with the conventional accounting representation of these transactions, are shown in Figure 23.1.

Whilst this is a naive example it does illustrate most of the problems involved in accounting.

- Notice that there is no correlation between profit and cash flows. In the long run there is a usual but not necessary link.

	Month 1	Month 2	Month 3	Month 4
CASH FLOWS				
Purchases		(500)		
Labour		(500)		
Payment				1500
Overheads	(150)	(150)	(150)	(150)
	(150)	(1150)	(150)	1350
PROFIT AND LOSS				
Sales			1500	
Labour		(500)		
Purchases	(500)			
Stock adj.	500	500	1000	
Gross profit			500	—
Overheads	(150)	(150)	(150)	(150)
Depreciation	(100)	(100)	(100)	(100)
Net profit	(250)	(250)	250	(250)
BALANCE SHEET				
Fixed assets	2300	2200	2100	2000
Stock	500	1000		
Debtors			1500	
Bank	(150)	(1300)	(1450)	(100)
Creditors	(150)			
	2150	1900	2150	1900
Opening capital	2400	2150	1900	2150
Profit/loss	(250)	(250)	250	(250)
Closing capital	2150	1900	2150	1900

Figure 23.1 Example accounting transaction

This difference, or time lag, has been the downfall of many a profitable and expanding company.

- The income is taken to profit and loss account not when the order is received, nor when cash payment is made, but (usually) when the product is delivered.
- Expenses are taken to the profit and loss account, either when incurred, in the case of general expenses, or when the revenue for the product they have created is accounted for. Thus expenses are matched to the relevant income.

This point is especially significant in the case of the

depreciation charge for the asset purchased. The expense is gradually accounted for over the expected life of the asset. Thus the balance sheet item is not an assessment of the declining value of an ageing asset but the residual value of an expense not yet written off. Strictly speaking depreciation costs incurred in producing the asset should be added to the stock value in a similar manner to the labour costs.

- There is no necessary link between accounting measures of income and wealth and the underlying economic values. The asset values in the balance sheet are neither an assessment of the realisable value nor the replacement cost of the asset. Even if they were, the value of the firm as a whole may well be very different from the value of its constituent parts. In our example a valuation of the firm would have recognised the impact of the contract when it was won, not as it was completed.

This dichotomy between accounting and economic values can be shown by example if we accept stock market capitalisation of a company's shares as their economic value and compare this with the accounting measure of shareholders' equity (see Figure 23.2). It can be seen that the accounting measure of value is very different from the market's. More crucially the relationship between the two is unstable.

- Because there is a difference between the date at which inputs are purchased, notably fixed assets and stock, the date at which they are used in the production process and the date at which the product is sold, the original measure of the cost of these expenses is no longer accurate. This is due to the change in the purchasing power of sterling due to general price level inflation; and the change in the value of these costs in relation to other items. Both these items will tend to distort and, in the case of productive as opposed to financial companies, usually overstate any traditional accounting measure of income. Furthermore, if assets or liabilities are held which are measured in monetary amounts, such as debtors, creditors, loans, and bank balances, a company can incur a holding gain or loss during inflationary times. This distortion is not measured by traditional accounting systems.

- When accounts are prepared for any company there will be a great many transactions in various stages of completion at the accounting date and many more that will have been completed during the period under review. The sheer magnitude of the task involved in collating and valuing the myriad transactions presents a serious

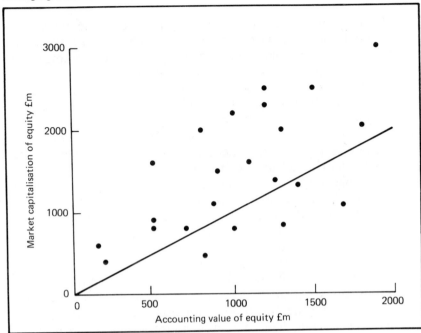

Figure 23.2 Accounting value of equity vs stock market capitalisation
The data refer to a cross-section of companies from the FT 100. Companies whose accounting value is equal to the market capitalisation would lie on the line shown.

practical problem in measurement for the accountant and the degree of subjectivity involved complicates the auditor's task of verification.

We can see that accounting tries to measure income and wealth by applying a set of procedures. For the UK these are laid down in the Companies Acts, by the Stock Exchange for quoted companies, and in Statements of Standard Accounting Practice prepared by the accounting profession. These requirements attempt to standardise a vast range of accounting practices but they must leave room for sufficient flexibility to accommodate differing circumstances. Whilst the detail is uninteresting there are certain general conventions which would bear examination.

- The accruals (or matching) convention. This refers to the attempt to account for expenses in the same period in which related revenues are treated and results in profit measurement differing from cash flows.

- The prudence convention. This governs the timing of the realisation of income, and hence expenses, in the accounts. As prospective losses are more readily allowed than future profits a pessimistic bias is reflected in the accounts.
- The consistency convention. Given the choices available from a wide spectrum of accounting practices it is desirable that a company should be restrained from switching between alternatives to suit its own convenience.
- The going concern convention. This assumes that the company will persist for the foreseeable future and that the value of assets on liquidation is thereby not normally relevant.

Further to those specified, a number of implicit but not necessarily trivial conventions apply. First we measure and aggregate diverse items in monetary amounts though the value of money is not stable. Second, we define and report on an entity but the specification of that entity can be problematical when groups of companies are involved. Finally we define and report on a specified period of time and it is the attempt to allocate transactions to particular periods that creates many of our problems.

It is interesting to speculate why these conventions and the multiplicity of more detailed rules have come into being. We have seen that they fail to produce measures that are consistent with economic reality, that they fail to cope with the distorting effects of inflation and that flexibility in the accounting rules, together with the subjectivity required in applying them, allows considerable scope for 'creative accounting'. This does not sound like a strong recommendation. However, the source of these conventions lies not in any deep and consistent theory, but in a pragmatic trade-off between economic relevance and practicality. These accounting rules were adopted as standard practice because they were, rather more flexibly, general practice. As such they represent the distillation of experience.

A renowned academic, David Solomons, reviewed this dichotomy between the practicality of accounting conventions and the irrelevance of their output to economic decisions and concluded that 'so far as the history of accounting is concerned, the next twenty-five years may subsequently be seen to have been the twilight of income measurement'. Unfortunately he made that prognosis in 1960. Why was he wrong and why do analysts pay more regard to accounting rather than any other source of information? I suspect that if one is aware of the shortcomings of accounting statements and knows what to trust and how far to trust it, such statements contain a vast range of useful data relevant to many decisions. That is not to say that improved methods of accounting for inflation, or alternatives to income measurement-based statements, could not perform much the same, or even complementary functions. But it is conventional historic cost statements which are currently understood and utilised, though not necessarily at the same time, by the business world for external reporting, and crucially within an organisation for decision making and control procedures.

UNDERSTANDING ACCOUNTING INFORMATION

It can be seen from the preceding section that accounting is not only an imprecise language, but it is not always sure what it is trying to say, let alone how to say it. Under these circumstances the value of the accounting numbers comes not from their absolute value but from the comparison with others. The problem here is to find valid comparisons. The measurement difficulties and the instability of any bias mean that the performance for one company in any year cannot easily be compared with the results of a different company or year. To give some insight into the information that can be drawn from accounting statements, this section will describe and compare the accounts of two typical companies.

A further difficulty is the mass of data presented and the awkwardness involved in making comparisons between organisations of differing size. Both of these problems can be countered to some extent by the use of ratio analysis which concentrates the information contained in accounting statements into summary statistics and in doing so attempts to standardise the ratio for size.

The accounting statements

The exhibits here are simplified and adjusted data from two large quoted companies operating across a diversified range of activities (see Figure 23.3). The accounts are prepared for the group as a whole with subsidiaries (at least 50 per cent owned) 'consolidated' into the totals. Other partly owned companies, associated companies or investments are accounted for by a variety of methods which only take account of the relevant proportion of the investment.

According to the accounting profession's discussion document,

CONSOLIDATED BALANCE SHEETS (£m)	Alpha 1986	Alpha 1985	Beta 1986	Beta 1985
Capital employed:				
Fixed assets				
Tangible	122.2	114.7	158.5	135.0
Investments	27.8	25.0	50.0	39.7
	150.0	139.7	208.5	174.7
Current assets				
Stock (inventory)	94.2	84.3	62.8	68.3
Debtors (accounts receivable)	111.7	100.2	49.7	54.3
Investments	3.3	12.3	0.7	0.0
Cash	16.7	11.0	21.0	18.2
	225.9	207.8	134.2	140.8
Creditors due within one year	−153.3	−142.5	−120.8	−126.2
Net current assets	72.6	65.3	13.4	14.6
Total assets less current liabilities	222.6	205.0	221.9	189.3
Creditors due after one year	−69.9	−80.3	−89.5	−79.0
Provisions for liabilities and charges	−5.2	−3.5	−1.2	−0.5
	147.5	121.2	131.2	109.8
Financed by:				
Capital and reserves				
Called up share capital	22.2	22.0	11.0	11.0
Share premium account	69.0	68.5	18.5	18.5
Revaluation reserves	22.7	10.0	72.2	48.3
Profit and loss account (retained profit)	27.5	14.7	4.3	9.0
Shareholders' funds (equity)	141.4	115.2	106.0	86.8
Minority interests	6.1	6.0	25.2	23.0
	147.5	121.2	131.2	109.8

NOTES TO THE ACCOUNTS (£m)	Alpha 1986	Alpha 1985	Beta 1986	Beta 1985
Creditors payable within one year				
Loans and overdrafts	42.7	45.2	32.0	38.4
Trade creditors	60.8	54.3	29.8	27.0
Other creditors	23.5	23.0	31.7	33.2
Taxation and social security	17.7	12.7	16.0	16.3
Bills of exchange	2.3	3.3	7.0	7.3
Proposed dividends	6.3	4.0	4.3	4.0
	153.3	142.5	120.8	126.2
Creditors payable after one year				
Loans	67.0	75.0	88.5	77.8
Taxation	1.7	1.5	0.5	0.7
Other	1.2	3.8	0.5	0.5
	69.9	80.3	89.5	79.0
Provisions				
Pensions	2.6	3.5	0.0	0.0
Taxation	2.6	0.0	1.2	0.5
	5.2	3.5	1.2	0.5

Figure 23.3   The balance sheet
Note. There would be many further notes to the accounts relating to other items, giving further detail or explanations, but as these are not necessary for this explanation they have been omitted for the sake of clarity.

427

The Corporate Report, 'Financial position statements (balance sheets) should be concerned with disclosing the amount and sources of capital employed and an appropriate analysis of its disposition'. The format shown here is prescribed by the Companies Act 1981 and most categories would be supported by notes to the accounts expanding on the detailed composition of the entries or their method of computation. It is by far the easiest way to think of a balance sheet as a list of the values of the assets and liabilities of a company with the net difference represented by the shareholders' investment in a company. We already know this to be a naive approach as the valuations attached to each category have little to do with their cost of replacement or their disposable value. Furthermore, even if the individual asset and liability values were accurate the value of the company as a whole could be very different from the component parts. However, bearing in mind the limitations of the valuations used, we can examine the individual items to discover what deductions can be drawn from the information contained therein.

The assets of the companies suggest that whilst Beta has slightly less invested in assets ($208.5 + 134.2 = 342.7$ as opposed to $150.0 + 225.9 = 375.9$) it apparently has a much higher percentage in fixed assets than Alpha ($100*208.5/342.7 = 61\%$ against $100*150.0/375.9 = 39\%$). The fixed assets are either tangible, such as plant or property, or intangible, usually investments in other companies. The distinction between fixed and current rests on the intention to maintain fixed assets as part of the company's strategy for earning future profits whilst current assets either rise as part of the trading cycle or are incidental stores of surplus funds such as short term investments.

Overall growth in assets is much the same for both organisations at around 8 per cent but whilst growth is a natural objective for management it ties up capital and is therefore only beneficial if productive. Note, however, that in Beta's case fixed assets apparently increased by £33.8m whilst current assets fell by £6.6m. We will see that this growth may be illusory. Fixed assets are originally valued at cost and for most assets this cost is gradually written off as depreciation. However at the same time inflation may well be increasing the net value of the asset and the unexpired cost becomes increasingly outdated as a surrogate measure of value. Both Alpha and Beta have tried to adjust for this by revaluing property, in Alpha's case by £22.7m and Beta's by £72.2m (see revaluation reserves). The amount of this uprating which occurred in the year under review accounts for much of Beta's fixed asset increase. Thus the difference in asset structure could be explained, either by differing enthusiasm for revaluation, or genuine differences in asset structure.

The liabilities of the companies are not readily identifiable from the balance sheets as they are revealed as summary statistics elaborated on in notes to the accounts. From the notes it can clearly be seen that a large section of creditors comprises sources of finance. Even using a narrow definition of finance, loans and overdrafts amount to £109.7m in Alpha's case and £120.5m for Beta (loans and overdrafts payable within one year plus loans payable after one year). The remaining creditors are either short term debts due for expenses incurred, trade and other creditors, demands upon the profits of the company not yet discharged (tax and dividends) or bills of exchange.

Provisions represent distant liabilities which are expected to fall due in the foreseeable future as a result of the current activities of the company though there is no present legal obligation.

The finance provided by the shareholders is divided into four sections. The nominal value of the shares sold is 'called up share capital' and any excess over the nominal value charged for those shares is 'share premium'. There is no significant difference between these two and together they represent the funds input into the firm by shareholders. The 'revaluation reserve' has already been discussed and represents the write-up of assets, normally property, though as no profit has yet been realised this adjustment is not taken through the profit and loss account. The 'profit and loss account' is the residual value of all profits earned on behalf of the shareholders which has not yet been distributed to them in the form of dividends. Minority interests represent the shares of subsidiaries not owned by the group.

The profit and loss account (or income statement) should, according to *The Corporate Report*, 'be concerned with the measurement of performance although they may also be used in the measurement of capital maintenance and income distributability'. Here we will consider only the performance measurement aspect of income statements. From the example accounts (Figure 23.4) it can be seen that the revenue realised by Alpha soared by 77 per cent whilst Beta's was relatively stable. In both cases some allowance should be made for the effects of inflation. No detail is provided on the operating costs incurred in earning the revenue but a full set of published accounts would give a crude breakdown and the statements used by management would be much more detailed. The operating profit percentage earned by Alpha has dropped slightly (10.2 per cent from

Consolidated profit and loss accounts (£m)	Alpha		Beta	
	1986	1985	1986	1985
Turnover	581.2	328.2	394.7	392.8
Operating expenses	521.7	291.2	352.9	357.3
Operating profit	59.5	37.0	41.8	35.5
Share of associated companies' profits	1.5	1.3	7.8	11.0
Investment income	4.0	3.3	2.7	3.2
Finance costs	−14.7	−10.5	−14.2	−14.3
Profit on ordinary activities before taxation	50.3	31.1	38.1	35.4
Taxation	−14.0	−9.0	−11.0	−9.3
Minority interests	−1.0	−0.5	−2.3	−2.8
Extraordinary items	−4.3	−2.2	−0.5	−1.8
Dividends	−11.5	−7.5	−4.8	−4.0
Retained profit	19.5	11.9	19.5	17.5

Figure 23.4 The profit and loss account

11.3 per cent). Meantime Beta's margin rose (10.6 per cent from 9.0 per cent), leaving them with a modest increase in income. The remaining costs and revenues allocated to this period are not dissimilar apart from the higher income earned by Beta's greater investment in associated companies (classified as fixed asset investment on the balance sheet) and the considerably higher proportion of income paid out by Alpha as dividends.

Flow of funds statements (statements of source and application of funds) 'should be concerned with distinguishing between funds generated or released by different means and the uses to which such funds are put' (*The Corporate Report*). Whilst these statements are the third main financial statement, and could be extremely informative, the methods of computation and presentation are not yet sufficiently standardised to make them readily accessible to the non-specialist. They are not dealt with further.

Ratio analysis

Ratio analysis is a technique which has built up something of a mystique and yet it is a simple attempt to produce summary statistics to save time in the perusal of a large number of accounting statements and to facilitate comparability by standardising the results for size.

Thus our two companies have reported profits on ordinary activities in 1986 of £50.3m and £38.1m respectively. Yet these results are not comparable because of the different scale of the two operations. It would be possible to standardise the results using a number of different scaling factors, for example turnover, capital, or employees.

	Profit margin	Return on capital	Profit per employee
Alpha	50.3*100/581.2 = 8.65%	50.3*100/147.5 = 34.1%	50.3m/10,050 = £5005/emp
Beta	38.1*100/394.7 = 9.65%	38.1*100/131.2 = 29.0%	38.1m/15,453 = £2466/emp

Which of the many scaling factors to use and which of the multitudinous possible combinations of ratios to compute rather depends on the focus of the study in hand, but some general guidance can be given. A study by Taffler and Sudarsanam analysed 80 financial ratios for 525 quoted manufacturing companies to determine which ratios told essentially the same story and which conveyed new information. Their results suggested that nine aspects of accounting ratios could be identified and that looking at one ratio which largely explains those factors precludes the need for further examination. These factors explain some 93 per cent of the variation in the total data set and the five most significant explain 81 per cent. The five main factors, which are examined in more detail below, are profitability, financial leverage, working capital position, asset turnover, and liquidity. It must be emphasised that whilst these categories were distinctive in the study it does not follow that they are universally applicable or necessarily significant. For instance whilst the inventory/current assets ratio was found to contain most of the available information about short term liquidity, liquidity is not necessarily a useful indicator for the analysis in hand. Nevertheless the five ratios indicated above would form a good starting point for a general review of corporate performance.

As with other accounting data, ratios must find a point of comparison. The ratio statistic in itself is uninformative and supposed benchmarks, such as a working capital ratio of 1.5, are misleading. I would suggest that a convenient way of obtaining both a time series and cross-sectional perspective would be to lay out the statistics as follows:

Sales growth %	1981	1982	1983	1984	1985	1986
Alpha (examined company)	23	16	25	13	171	77
Beta (competitor 1)	5	38	13	19	1	0
Gamma (competitor 2)	15	25	17	12	4	12
Industry average	12	21	14	12	5	8

This information could also be presented graphically. Some caution should be employed as inflation would tend to result in overstated growth rates and some expansion may not be generated internally but bought via take-overs.

It seems necessary to compare corporate performance with the closest competitors directly as industry groupings cover such a wide range of products and organisational sizes.

When using ratio analysis or attempting to interpret accounting statements it must be left to the individual's experience of the industry, coupled with the information that can be drawn from time series or cross-sectional trends, to arrive at informed conclusions.

One exception where a more general approach has become accepted is in the use of Z scores to try to predict corporate bankruptcy. This statistic is an amalgam of various ratios which have been found to have a significant relationship with impending failure. Thus commercial organisations publish the Z score trends for companies in comparison with sector averages. It should be noted that some commentators are sceptical of this approach and more subjective attempts to identify corporate difficulties or managerial incompetence have been suggested. Argenti's monograph (see Further reading) is a useful summary of the failure prediction techniques.

The key ratios identified are now examined and explained using the sample accounts for illustrative purposes. Alternative specifications of these ratios are often used.

Profitability:
Alpha 25.3% (17.2%) Beta 20.8% (22.0%)

Return on capital is profit before interest and taxation, expressed as a percentage of total capital employed, e.g.

$$100*(59.5 + 1.5 + 4.0)/(147.5 + 42.7 + 67.0) = 25.3\%.$$

As such this is a crucial ratio which measures a company's efficiency in earning a return on capital employed. In the example used, Beta's return suffered a marginal decline due largely to the revaluation of capital invested in fixed assets whereas Alpha showed a marked improvement due to the remarkable increase in reported profits. Further evidence on these trends would be informative.

However, this ratio, using the final accounting computations of capital and profit, incorporates and exaggerates any measurement errors involved. In inflationary times profit is often overstated and capital understated.

Financial leverage (gearing):

Alpha 60.8% (65.1%) Beta 61.7% (65.2%)

A complex ratio calculated as total liabilities expressed as a percentage of total assets, e.g.

$$100*(153.3 + 69.9 + 5.2)/(150.0 + 225.9) = 60.8\%$$

The higher the proportion of relatively cheap capital in the form of liabilities the greater the average return shareholders can expect, but the risk of large fluctuations in that return also increases. It is a moot point as to whether leverage is beneficial or not even when there are apparently tax advantages. This ratio is heavily dependent on the dubious valuation of shareholders' equity in the balance sheet and is more reliable when the stock market valuation of equity is used.

The competitors here show little difference though both have slightly increased their reliance on equity capital.

Working capital position:

Alpha 0.60 (0.60) Beta 0.39 (0.45)

This ratio is calculated as current assets divided by total assets e.g.

$$225.9/(225.9 + 150.0) = 0.60$$

and illustrates the relative importance of flexible and liquid current assets compared to long term assets. A high level of current assets does imply the possibility of inefficient asset management. The fall in Beta's ratio is due to the revaluation, but there is still a substantial difference between our two competitors.

Liquidity:

Alpha 0.42 (0.41) Beta 0.47 (0.49)

A slightly unusual method of computation is used here as inventory is divided by current assets e.g.

$$94.2/225.9 = 0.42.$$

However, the influence of current liabilities was examined in the leverage ratio and the statistic used here was influential in the cited study. Our example shows Beta with a marginally higher proportion of relatively illiquid stock but there is little evidence of any unhappy trends.

433

Asset turnover:

Alpha 1.55 (0.94) Beta 1.15 (1.25)

This statistic measures how effectively an organisation uses its assets to produce output and is calculated as turnover divided by total assets, e.g.

$$581.2/(150.0+225.9)=1.55.$$

Beta maintains a fairly stable level of output per unit of assets though there appears to be a marginal decline. However, the increase in assets is largely accounted for by the revaluations which pushed up the reserve by £23.9m. Alpha again shows a startling increase in asset turnover. Something is going on!

The ratios examined are not definitive and many alternatives are available but they are illustrative of the techniques that can be used to elicit information from formal accounting statements.

ACCOUNTING INFORMATION AND MANAGERIAL DECISION MAKING

The information produced by the accounting system is not only of importance to outsiders via the medium of financial reports. Management use accounting data to evaluate current performance to establish whether or not corporate objectives are being met, to assess the contribution that alternative decisions are likely to make towards reaching those objectives, and to monitor the progress of previous decisions. This managerial decision making process and the role of accounting information is best illustrated diagramatically as shown in Figure 23.5.

The two areas that we will focus on here are the decision making process and monitoring the effects of the decision via the budgetary control process. Brief mention is also made of the technique of financial modelling which is a valuable aid to both of these functions.

Managerial decision making

Although accounts are a measure of past events, they are important for what they tell us about the future. The presumption is that the results and trends identified by the accounting statements of the last few years can be suitably modified by management's appreciation of

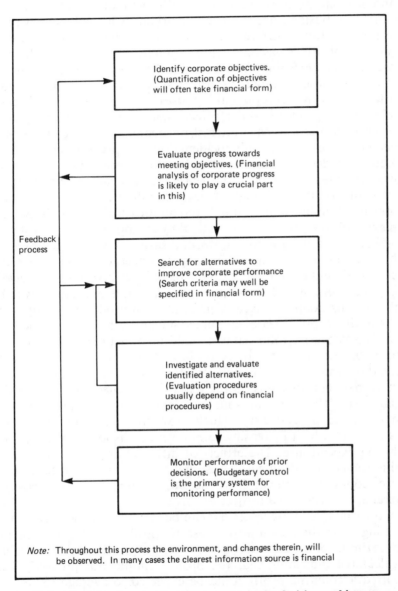

The diagram contains the following boxes and notes:

Identify corporate objectives. (Quantification of objectives will often take financial form)

Evaluate progress towards meeting objectives. (Financial analysis of corporate progress is likely to play a crucial part in this)

Feedback process

Search for alternatives to improve corporate performance (Search criteria may well be specified in financial form)

Investigate and evaluate identified alternatives. (Evaluation procedures usually depend on financial procedures)

Monitor performance of prior decisions. (Budgetary control is the primary system for monitoring performance)

Note: Throughout this process the environment, and changes therein, will be observed. In many cases the clearest information source is financial

Figure 23.5   The role of accounting information in the decision making process
Note. Throughout this process the environment, and changes therein, will be observed. In many cases the clearest information source is financial.

changing circumstances to give a useful forecast of the future. This is important as business decisions should primarily be evaluated by their effect on 'the future differential cash flows' of the company. *Future*, as we cannot affect past cash flows though we must live with their consequences. *Differential*, because it is the expected change induced by a decision when compared to the next best alternative that should be the focus of the decision making process. *Cash flows*, as it is cash receipts and expenditure which affect a company's ability to invest in alternative projects to earn interest or income. Thus the effect of a decision on the profit is only incidental to the cash flows generated.

Long term decisions require consideration of the timing of the cash flows generated by the decision. Early receipts can be reinvested to earn further returns whilst later receipts are still tied up in the project. Under these circumstances the differential cash flows, both income and expenditure, must be 'discounted' by an appropriate interest rate to adjust the cash flows to a uniform measure. This is a 'net present value' computation and any manager concerned with long term decisions should be familiar with the techniques involved. The detail is beyond the scope of this chapter but a simple example is worthwhile. In this example the early investment in productive equipment and working capital creates an immediate net cash outflow. The first year is also negative followed by a build-up of net receipts before the returns on the product start to decline. A terminal cash outflow is created by taxation residues and cessation cost. The discounting rate, here 15 per cent, depends on the risk of the project and not on the actual cost of the particular source of capital utilised. This technique can be applied to any decision which is expected to alter the cash flows of a company, be it increasing sales revenue, disposing of assets, or reducing expenditure. The effects of inflation and tax can be confusing and are best dealt with by estimating after tax actual cash flows and discounting by the after tax actual, as opposed to real, cost of capital appropriate to a project of this risk.

In the example in Figure 23.6 it can be seen that the net cash flows resulting from the decision to invest are positive. After adjustment for the timing of the cash flows, however, a negative net present value is calculated indicating that the project should not proceed. The reported accounting profit could be expected to average £3333 per year with higher profits in the years where sales peak. It would appear that profitability of a long term decision is not a suitable assessment criterion.

It is also apparent that management must be concerned with

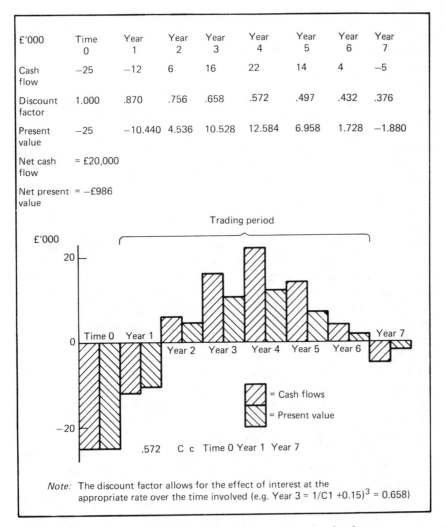

£'000	Time 0	Year 1	Year 2	Year 3	Year 4	Year 5	Year 6	Year 7
Cash flow	−25	−12	6	16	22	14	4	−5
Discount factor	1.000	.870	.756	.658	.572	.497	.432	.376
Present value	−25	−10.440	4.536	10.528	12.584	6.958	1.728	−1.880
Net cash flow	= £20,000							
Net present value	= −£986							

Note: The discount factor allows for the effect of interest at the appropriate rate over the time involved (e.g. Year 3 = 1/C1 +0.15)^3 = 0.658)

Figure 23.6 Actual and discounted cash flows for project evaluation
Note. The discount factor allows for the effect of interest at the appropriate rate over the time involved (e.g. Year $3 = 1/(1 + 0.15)^3 = 0.658$).

financing decisions but it is assumed that anyone involved in this is likely to be familiar with the contents of this chapter and therefore beyond its purview. Suffice it to say that whilst financing decisions might affect the value of a company they are insignificant in comparison to investment decisions where the viability of a company is determined. Good products will find good finance but poor products cannot be saved by efficient financing.

Short term decisions often drop the emphasis on cash flows in order to focus on the contribution to profit of a particular decision. This is an approximation as it is still the cash flows that are crucial, but where the timing differences are minimal the contribution towards profit is an acceptable compromise. The essential requirement is to separate out the costs and revenues that affect contribution from those that are fixed costs for the purposes of the decision under review. Many costs appearing as relevant to a product on traditional accounting statements are, in fact, beyond the influence of the decision maker and are therefore irrelevant to the decision. Crudely speaking those costs which require arbitrary allocation to different products or are unaffected by the volume of output of a product are uninteresting for short term decisions. Examples are depreciation charges, administration and overhead expenses, production costs unaffected by volume, even that proportion of production wages that is fixed in the short term. All costs are variable in the long term and most are at least sticky if not fixed in the short term. It should also be noted that just because a cost is allocated by the accounting system on the basis of some output measure does not mean that it is a variable cost.

When variable costs and revenues have been separated from the irrelevant clutter of accounting statements, decisions can be based on the maximisation of contribution towards fixed costs and profit. The example here is based on a pricing and advertising decision for a product whose fixed costs are thought to be £5000 per month and variable costs £15 per unit. Alternative prices under consideration are £18, £20, £22 and £24 for which demand figures are estimated at 3000, 2000, 1500 and 1000 respectively. The demand could be increased by 20 per cent by an advertising campaign costing £1000.

It can be seen from Figure 23.7 that the option of selling at £22 each, supported by the advertising campaign, is the preferred decision. The graph includes the fixed cost element for illustrative purposes but it is apparent that the same decision would be arrived at whether the fixed costs were £0, £5000 or £50,000, assuming that the costs are genuinely fixed and the option of closing down is not available.

Two points arise from the above example. First, the graphical presentation is unnecessary as the result can easily be calculated but the presentational benefits and the ease with which changes in expectations can be evaluated make the graph useful. Second, the

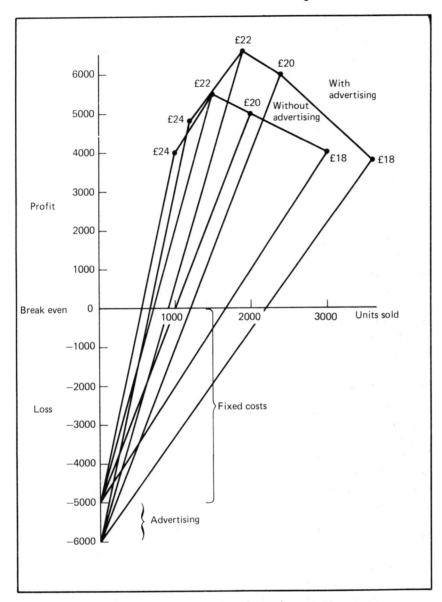

Figure 23.7   Graphical representation of contribution analysis

decision was arrived at after considering the total contribution which requires incorporation of the effects on demand of the alternatives. The traditional approach of pricing at cost plus is deficient where demand depends on price.

Financial modelling

Financial modelling is a use of accounting data that is closely related to the internal decision making of a company. A computer-based replication of the accounting statements is produced, usually utilising 'spreadsheet' software. The relationships between inputs, outputs, costs and revenues are carefully specified and the forecasts and decision variables obtained from management. The expected results from this complex set of interrelationships are then produced by the computer, allowing management to investigate readily the effect of changes in forecasts, decision variables, and the environment, and react accordingly. Whilst it will normally require a financial specialist to produce a sensible computer-based model, once it is completed, non-specialists should be able to alter parameters such as prices, costs, product mix, growth and inflation forecasts, and tax regulations, and immediately examine the results occasioned by such alterations.

Budgetary control

The budgetary control system is one of the key methods used by management to try to ensure that the decisions previously made are being carried out effectively and are having the desired result. Significant deviation from budget should instigate an investigation and remedial action, whilst providing feedback to the decision makers. The budgetary system is also sometimes seen as part of the (de)motivational process and it probably represents the non-financial specialist's most common brush with accounting data. Budget statements are usually produced by the financial accounting system and as such are similar in appearance and concept, though often only show a subsection of the full results. The clearest difference from normal accounts is the three categories of information reported: the results for the period; the intended results for the period; and the variance between the two.

Some crucial points need to be borne in mind when dealing with budget statements either as perpetrator or victim.

The reporting entity is often a subsection of the company and this resents troublesome allocations. Costs applicable to the whole organisation are allocated to budget centres, often on arbitrary bases, and as these are beyond the control of the centre manager they are irrelevant to the budgetary and decision making process. The inputs and outputs of goods and services by the centre require pricing if the profit or loss is to be computed, yet when this is not an arm's-length transaction the transfer price used can often be misleading.

The responsibility for the results of a budget centre must be matched by the power to affect those results. Thus a cost centre manager can often affect the volume but not always the price of the costs; profit centre managers may find aspects of the revenue generating process beyond their control, and investment centre managers would often have to live with the actions of their predecessors.

The budgetary regime which is designed to induce a congruence of goals and coordination within the organisation can often promote sub-optimal behaviour by managers. There is many an apocryphal story, but in general short term remedies to meet budget constraints can have a damaging long term effect, though cunning operators will ensure that they are long gone before the problem is realised.

The setting of budget targets can be a useful short term planning process and provides a motivational tool but this will not come cheap. If a budget is set easily it has probably been done improperly. It is essential that the managers who will have to meet budgets have been consulted about, and preferably have agreed to, their targets. It is also necessary to ensure coordination between the budgets of different centres and this can be aided by the use of financial models as previously discussed.

It is apparent that budgets are not popular but that they are essential both as an aid to planning and as an early warning system when those plans start to fail.

CONCLUSION

In one brief chapter it is impossible to give more than a flavour of the accounting process and its uses. However, it will be apparent to most managers or investors that financial data provide some of the most important sources of information available, the misreading of which can be fatal for a company's progress or a manager's career prospects. It is hoped that this chapter has illustrated that ignorance of accounting systems does not preclude a general understanding of accounting reports. Perhaps the most subtle insight is the required balance between unfounded faith in the numeric exactitude of accounting and sceptical rejection of its relevance to decision making.

Some examples of the uses of financial information have been alluded to. Although rather more experience would be required before one would feel confident applying these techniques perhaps the reader will have a greater understanding when subjected to them. Indeed there may be opportunity to point out to the perpetrators some errors in their ways.

FURTHER READING

Argenti, J, 'Predicting Corporate Failure', *Accountants Digest*, no. 138, ICAEW, 1983

Arnold, J, Carsberg, G, and Scapens, R (eds), *Topics in Management Accounting*, Philip Allen, 1980

Arnold, J and Hope, A, *Accounting for Management Decisions*, Prentice-Hall International, 1984

Arnold, J and Mozier, P, 'A Survey of the Methods used by UK Investment Analysts to Appraise Investments in Ordinary Shares', *Accounting & Business Research*, Autumn, 1984

Taffler, R and Sundarsanam, P, 'Auditing the Board', *Managerial Finance*, S.2, 1980

Walton, P and Bond, M, *Corporate Reports: Their Interpretation and Use in Business*, Hutchinson, 1986

In addition to the above, the manager interested in improving his knowledge of finance and accounting may find the six videos produced by Video Arts in the series *Finance for the Non-Financial Manager* a useful and relatively painless introduction. A more thorough understanding may be helped by using the computer aided learning series known as *Plato* and produced by Control Data in association with CAET.

24

Marketing

Peter Woodcock

One of the biggest problems of marketing is that the whole idea is so essentially simple: what we are really talking about is nothing more or less than putting the customer first. Now, the sad thing to have to report is that, protest as they may, too few firms actually do this. Too many are still in the position of 'having a good idea', and expecting a fortune to flow from it.

Odd as it may seem, an American, Ralph Waldo Emerson, is credited with having written the following: 'If a man write a better book, preach a better sermon, or make a better mouse-trap than his neighbour, tho' he build his house in the woods, the world will make a beaten path to his door.' Emerson died in 1882, and it is conceivable that what he wrote was true then, but it certainly isn't now. And it is probably poetic justice that it was in Emerson's native land that the ideas of marketing first prospered.

If, then, we put the customer first, what does this mean for our firm? The answer is that it changes things round radically. What we are doing is moving from the philosophy of making things and selling them to one where our first action is to enquire what the world out there needs, wants, or might need or want, and then set about producing this product or service to satisfy that need whilst ensuring that the financial returns are such that our enterprise continues to prosper. For, whether profit is one of our goals or not, clearly, we cannot continue to serve our customers unless we are financially sound.

And there are other implications. If we are setting out to serve, then we will see to it, as a matter of course, that our quality is right, and that where required, our after-sales service is adequate. One key idea is that of offering value for money, and the success of firms like

Marks & Spencer illustrates this point. Nobody would suggest that their goods were the cheapest on the market, but the combination of value for money, together with the attitude to customer problems – the ease of changing articles, or returning items which are not satisfactory – shows what can be done in terms of serving the customer. And a look at the financial results shows that this attitude has done absolutely no harm.

What this amounts to is that the *whole firm* has to play its part: marketing and the philosophy it implies is the responsibility of everybody. And this does not lead to a quiet life. It is so easy for accountants to concentrate only on the details of accounting, and for production engineers to become fascinated by the possibilities of computer aided manufacture – in fact there are so many enthralling things going on inside the firm that it is all too easy to forget that, at the end of the day, there are people called customers out there, and that you neglect them at your peril.

Let us move on to analyse the functional operations of our firm. We can place all of them under five headings:

- *production* – including the purchase of raw materials, equipment, and other items such as packaging which are needed in the manufacture of the product;
- *research and development* – from the product concept through to pilot plant samples of our new product;
- *personnel* – including the design of the organisation, all recruitment, selection and training, and industrial relations;
- *finance* – the raising of temporary and permanent finance, and the accounting for day-to-day inflows and outflows of money;
- *marketing* – discovering what people 'out there' need and want, deciding which of them we can serve, and how to go about it.

THE FOUR 'P's

To help in the analytical process, marketing itself has been further sub-divided into four areas, often referred to as the four 'P's – *product, price, promotion and place.*

Product

This is concerned not only with the item itself, but more and more with all the bits and pieces which ensure that the customer receives it in first class order. So packaging is a primary concern, and it is not unusual for the packaging to have cost more than the contents. A second role of packaging is to ensure that the customer recognises 'our' product.

But the concept of product is more complex still. Most firms have a product range, and it is important to ensure that this range is coherent − that there are no 'oddballs' in it. The reason for having a range is that the markets we serve are likely to be heterogeneous. If we are Ford, we have Fiestas, Escorts, Sierras, Capris and Granadas, and variations inside these five main groups. So, quite deliberately, Ford has designed this product range to appeal to the range of people it has set out to serve.

At this point, it is worthwhile detailing those sorts of people it has *not* set out to serve. For example, it has no cars at the extremes of price: it is making no attempt to serve either the market for very basic vehicles or to cater for those wanting luxury vehicles. Though Ford itself might disagree, there is no serious attack on the sports car market. One could support this comment by reference to Lotus Cars, recently bought by General Motors. Had Ford been interested in serving that part of the market, one might have expected them to have put in a bid for Lotus.

Price

This is often seen as being another part of the product. Indeed, as this analysis goes on, it will become clear that it is no more than a convenient label, for a product or service is actually the sum of the various parts, and if one part is missing or weak, then the whole product suffers.

Price is very often where the customer starts. He may want a new car, or a dishwasher or a holiday, and he often starts off by asking himself what he can afford, and then what is available in his price range.

Price is intimately bound up with ideas of quality. For many people, it is the only guide to quality, for few of us are qualified to assess whatever it is that we intend buying. Sayings like 'you get what you pay for' reinforce this attitude. And just as you will probably need a product range which is coherent, so this range must have a coherent set of prices. If there are obvious 'bargains' or apparently overpriced items, these must arise from deliberate policy rather than from oversight.

Promotion

This is another aspect of the product, for if we want a recognisable package as part of the product, then that idea of recognition must integrate with our promotion. Anything that tells people about our firm and its products is promotion. To help with analysis, promotion is split up into the promotional mix. The simplest approach is to define two members of this mix.

Personal promotion and sales people of every sort come under this classification. Whether they appear in the guise of the milkman, the person on the phone trying to sell you advertising space, or those you meet face to face in shops, offices and at home, all are concerned with personal promotion, and the costly business of human interaction.

Impersonal promotion. The most obvious and visible form of this is advertising. However, in terms of the money spent on them, what are called promotions are of similar importance. These include all sorts of competitions (not least *The Times* Portfolio Gold) for customers, for intermediaries, and for your own staff, as well as brochures, catalogues, mailshots, taking stands at exhibitions, and so forth. The range of promotions is enormous, and it is a nearly impossible task to try to produce a definitive list.

PR. A third area which is usually included under the general heading of promotion is public relations. Most people equate PR with press relations, or, slightly more widely, with media relations. Any firm ought to recognise that it has a range of publics, and that it needs to keep in contact with all of them. Apart from its customers, it probably needs to keep in contact with suppliers, shareholders, government at both national and local level, employees, and those who live in the neighbourhood of its offices and factories. (Much more on this is in Chapter 29.)

Each of these aspects of the promotional mix has its own role to play, and needs thought. Most of the alternatives are expensive, and some are very expensive. Because of its high profile, promotional mistakes become obvious and very visible. Nevertheless, this is no reason for abstaining, for promotion in all its aspects is a key part of the marketing mix.

Place

More often called distribution, place is no less important because it is the last part of the mix to receive mention. There is a school of thought that would propose that this is the most important part of the mix, not least because it is so often neglected. The saga of Land Rover underlines the problem of an excellent product which has not been developed to its potential largely as a result of indifferent distribution. Regrettably, Land Rover is not alone — two further examples from very different backgrounds underline the problem.

The first concerns Zantac, an effective product for the treatment of peptic ulcers developed in the UK by Glaxo, for whom the product now generates high returns (a good example of a *cash cow*). In spite of having tried very hard to be independent Glaxo was unable to obtain adequate distribution in the USA. It eventually entered into an agreement with the American subsidiary of the Swiss pharmaceutical company, Hoffmann La Roche, to take care of distribution in the USA.

The second example is bicycle lamps developed by Ever Ready, and now marketed under the brand name of Night Rider. The products now on the market are significantly different from those originally designed. This resulted from the proposed main distributor refusing to handle the original product. Whilst the manufacturers had carried out research with potential customers, they had failed to think in marketing terms, and had thus failed to bring the distributor into the development of the product.

Both of these stories underline not only the importance of the distribution chain, but of the ultimate power of its members.

Two other items come under the general heading of distribution. The first is warehousing. As soon as a firm obtains more than local distribution for its products, the question arises as to how it will deal with buyers outside its immediate neighbourhood. There are mathematical models to help in coming to a decision when faced with this type of problem, and with the advent of cheap computing power, alert marketing managers will ensure that they have this facility at their elbow. The immediate consequence of warehousing is the question of how best to arrange distribution to the final customer, or to the next member of the distribution chain. Here again mathematical models can help. One of the earliest problems solved that way was concerned with the routeing of delivery lorries where each would have to make several drops per journey. Over a period, it was found that these models were about 25 per cent more economical than the best human lorry routers.

The second item which is usually part of distribution is after-sales service. So often, you as the manufacturer have to rely on the distribution chain to service your product. Indeed, the legal situation in the UK is now such that the consumer returns to the retailer who is formally responsible for the quality of the goods sold. No longer can the retailer hide behind the manufacturer − and it is in both of their interests to ensure as few complaints as possible, and as expeditious a dealing with those which arise as can be devised.

To sum up, the four 'P's are all vital to successful marketing. No one is more important than the others, for all are essential. There is a tendency to dismiss them as mere nuts and bolts, but unless they are right, the whole structure is jeopardised.

Let us now move on to some of the theories which inform marketing.

MARKETING THEORIES

Before embarking on describing some of the theories in marketing, two generalities need to be stated. The first is that most marketing theories are intuitively attractive: they appeal to our common sense. The second is that they are exceedingly difficult to apply − putting them into practice is a distinct challenge.

Market segmentation

The first theory we will examine appears to be almost self-evident. It says that markets are heterogeneous, made up of lots of little bits which differ from each other. And the whole idea of market segmentation is that you identify one or more of these bits or segments and set out to serve it or them. Now this idea is intuitively appealing. Common sense tells us that there are the young and the old, male and female, rich and poor, and that it is likely that each of these segments will not only want, but need, products and services which are different from those which another segment might use. And if you look around the market place, very few products or services are aimed at the whole market. So it would seem that we are on course with the idea of market segmentation.

Two problems arise. The first is the stability of the segment you have identified. So that is what it looked like when you did your marketing research, but how long is it going to look like that? Suppose you are looking at 'the teenage market', whatever it is. For how long can you rely on your findings? The answer is 'not long', so if you wish to keep serving that market, you have to undertake marketing research on a continuous basis to keep your finger continually on the pulse, so that you can keep your offerings in line with what the market wants.

The second problem arises in terms of how far your marketing research findings are applicable. The research was done, let us say, in England and Wales. Are these findings applicable to Scotland or Ireland or France or Germany, or Western Europe?

This question identifies a series of marketing problems about policy. When you aim for a segment, are you looking for the things which make its members the same as, or different from, other people? Should we be like Coca Cola, with essentially one product and one advertising theme, or should we look for the differences? This question is of considerable importance both to production and to promotion. If we can reduce the product range, and thus reduce the range of advertising, we will automatically reduce costs. One of the criticisms of British Leyland is that they had simply too wide a range of cars, and they have since removed such well known names as MG, Wolseley, Riley from their product range.

Finally, you might think that financial success would tell us whether market segmentation was essential, but we get no help. As you might expect, there are successful firms who segment, and others, equally successful, who hardly segment at all.

Product life cycle

The PLC theory says that the sales of products go through four phases between birth and death. These four phases are: introduction, growth, maturity and decline. Yet again, this anthropomorphic view is appealing: this is how things are, isn't it? Rather like market segmentation, there are two main problems.

The first is what to do with this idea. How can you use it? If you look in almost any standard marketing text (a couple are mentioned at the end of this chapter), you will see a diagram similar to Figure 24.1.

The authors will have explained that, as time goes on, you will have to spend more on promotion to maintain sales as the competition

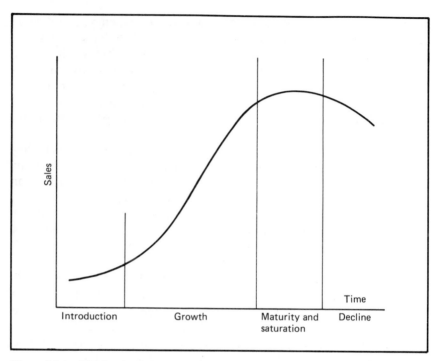

Figure 24.1 The 'typical' product life cycle

increases. The problem is that, somewhere along the line, someone will have had to identify a decline in sales as having arisen from the efforts of the competition. The real problem is to decide whether the decline in sales has come from competition or has happened for other reasons – the weather, the political situation, a substitute product now being available, or the distribution network (or important parts of it) have decided to reduce stock levels by x per cent. The key problem here is to identify a *real* decline in sales as against variations which occur for 101 reasons, but which are temporary.

The second problem is that many products continue for a very long time – often far outliving their inventors. This must obviously be true of commodities – bricks or cement or steel or sulphuric acid. But there are quite a few branded products which are over 100 years old, like Bovril or Guinness, and which show little sign of dying.

The defenders of the PLC idea explain that there are at least three different life cycles. To start with, there is the generic – cigarettes, for example. Then there is the form – king size. Third, there is the brand – Players or Embassy. By this time the whole concept has become so complex that one might well wonder how helpful it is. Indeed, in 1976, there appeared an article in the *Harvard Business Review* entitled 'Forget the Product Life Cycle concept' (see Further reading at the end of this chapter for details). The authors argued that a whole range of perfectly good products had been killed off 'because management, on the basis of the PLC theory, believes the brand has entered a dying stage'. Perhaps we would be wise to accept their advice.

The Boston matrix

Developed in the late 1960s by the Boston Consulting Group (BCG), the matrix classifies products in a firm's product range according to its share of that market, and the rate at which that particular market is growing (Figure 24.2). This is yet another concept which is intuitively appealing. *Cash cows* are the financial engine of the firm, and give support to the development of new products on which the future of the firm is going to depend. Clearly, we also need to identify

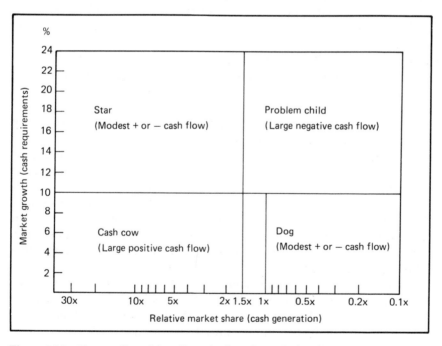

Figure 24.2 Boston Consulting Group's share/growth matrix

and eliminate the inevitable losers – the *dogs*. The *stars* should be more or less self-supporting and, as the rate of growth of their market slows down, they will become the *cash cows* of the future. Now, clearly, any firm wants and needs a balanced portfolio of products, and the Boston matrix is a useful analytical tool. Indeed, it draws attention to a number of important points.

The first is the need for the firm to analyse its product range. Attention has already been drawn to the need for developing and launching new products.

The second is that it draws attention to the need to 'milk' products at a certain stage in their development. Different management skills are required, and it can be difficult to persuade a manager who has been responsible for the development of the product thus far that a quite different approach is needed in the future. Nevil Shute, in his autobiography, *Slide Rule*, said that he believed that managers fell naturally into two categories, which he called 'starters' and 'runners'. Whether he was right or not, it is certain that very different skills are needed when developing and launching a product from those required to exploit to the full a well established line. So this matrix not only helps with the analysis of our product range, but should be useful in helping us to decide which of our management team ought to be running which products.

Third, the matrix helps to identify strengths and weaknesses, especially in terms of new product development. Lead times are often measured in years, and any scheme which helps us to focus on actual or potential gaps is useful.

One problem with the BCG matrix is how to define 'market'. Are we talking about the UK, or the EEC? Or should we be concerned solely with those segments of the market which we seek to serve? For clearly, one's market share is a function of how that market is defined, and can change a cash cow into a dog at a stroke!

A second problem arises during periods of economic stagnation. Originally, the dividing line between high and low growth was set at 10 per cent. But over the last ten years, such a rate of growth has been very unusual – indeed, at some times, any rate of growth has been a cause for celebration.

A third criticism is that the concept has encouraged firms to plunge headlong into areas that have been identified by those who ought to know as having high growth potential. At least two problems follow. First, too many firms plunge into these high growth areas, and profitless competition results. Second, the low growth areas are neglected. Too many potential cash cows are mis-identified as dogs. Rather like the product life cycle, the BCG matrix is seen as having been the cause of the premature death of products with plenty of life in them.

Diffusion of innovations

The last marketing theory we are going to look at is concerned with asking questions about how new products gain acceptance. Just who were the people who first bought fridges or washing machines or television sets, or the 101 things we now take for granted? For if we can identify those sorts of people who are most likely to buy novel products, then we shall be better able to direct our efforts to inform them of how we can supply their needs.

Yet again, research findings are intuitively right. There appear to be a small number of people who are opinion leaders. They are most likely to be young, well educated, and well enough off to be able to afford to make mistakes. If the product doesn't work, or is unreliable, they can afford to write it off. It isn't a disaster for them. Again, the sorts of products which are quickly accepted are often those which can easily be demonstrated.

The real problem about diffusion theory is that it draws on a rag-bag of enquiries. The overwhelming majority of these enquiries have little to do with marketing. Most of them come from rural sociology, enquiring how farmers come to adopt new farming processes. Equally, there have been several medical studies into such questions as how doctors come to prescribe new drugs, or to select new methods of treatment. Most of these studies have been of a non-marketing nature, quite unconcerned with any commercial outcome. One might well ask about the relevance of these studies to highly urbanised, highly commercial marketing problems. Rather like the other theories discussed, the answer seems to be that they are intuitively attractive and seem to make sense, but when it comes to hard facts, they are few and far between.

MARKETING RESEARCH

The task of marketing research is to answer these questions: *what* people want, *how much* of it they want, *where* they expect to find it – indeed, about answering any question implied in product, price, promotion and place.

Most research tries to answer two sorts of question. The first, and simplest, is the 'how many' – market size, market share, rates of growth or decline. The second is the 'who' and 'why' – what sorts of people are our customers, why do they buy (or why do they not buy)? And these are far more difficult to answer and, consequently, less often asked.

A key problem about any sort of research is that of classification and aggregation. What is needed are clearcut classes – like male and female, or age-based classifications – and easy ways of counting who falls into which class. And the most troublesome problems of research stem from these needs. Too often, classifications are used because they are convenient, rather than because they are appropriate to the problem. Aggregation brings its problems, too. As soon as one starts to use averages – even with measures of dispersion such as standard deviation – one loses information. This is the price you have to pay for the convenience you gain. Indeed, it would be quite impossible to describe every person individually, which is the reason we use concepts like averages. So we reach an *impasse*: we cannot handle disaggregated data because there are too many of them, but as soon as we try to aggregate, we introduce error because we lose the detail contained in the original data.

So, hard as you may try, you are not going to get error-free research findings. What needs to be considered is the accuracy required, and for the research to be directed in accordance with those needs. So, those commissioning researchers should ask themselves two questions: what do I need to know, and how accurate do the answers have to be to help me solve my problem? The answers to these two questions then dictate the amount of money which has to be spent.

One of the psychological problems associated with marketing is the general unwillingness of managers to spend on marketing research. They will happily spend on packaging, on advertising, or taking part in an exhibition, but seem quite unable to spend on research to try to find out whether that packaging is suitable, or that advertising is appearing in the best media. One can only assume that this is an aspect of their tepid acceptance of the whole idea of marketing.

Whatever the answer, the problem still remains that the first step towards marketing is marketing research. Despite its inherent weaknesses, its nebulous and almost ephemeral nature, this is the entry ticket to marketing. And like most entry tickets, the better seats cost more.

FURTHER READING

The literature of marketing is now voluminous, and is produced by many of the developed nations. Any business bookshop worth its salt ought to provide a wide choice, and the books and periodicals listed below represent only a tiny fraction of what is available.

Kotler, Philip, *Marketing Management*, Prentice-Hall, 5th edition, 1984. Kotler produced what turned out to be the standard text nearly 20 years ago. That it has now reached the fifth edition should speak for itself. For many, this book has become a standard by which others are judged.

Cannon, Tom, *Basic Marketing*, Holt, Rinehart & Winston, 2nd edition, 1986. Tom Cannon is Professor at Stirling University, and has made an important contribution to marketing thought in Britain.

For marketing research, two British authors spring immediately to mind. They look at the subject from different points of view and thus, used together, add a dimension to a subject which is too often treated as a routine.

Chisnall, Peter, *Marketing Research*, McGraw-Hill, 3rd edition, 1986
Crimp, Margaret, *The Marketing Research Process*, Prentice-Hall, 2nd edition, 1985

Many books have been published on special aspects of marketing such as advertising or sales management, but it is only recently that much has been published in this country about the marketing of services. The three volumes listed below help to fill the gap.

Naylor and McIver, *Marketing Financial Services*, Institute of Bankers, 1980
Silkin, S C ed., *Marketing Legal Services*, Waterlow Publishing, 1984
Lovelock, C H, *Services Marketing*, Prentice-Hall, 1984

Light is cast on the organisation of marketing by:

Piercy, Nigel, *Marketing Organisation,* George Allen & Unwin, 1985

Serious students of marketing should keep up to date by reading periodicals. Many general management publications have a quota of marketing articles in them. *Harvard Business Review, Management Today, Direction et Gestion, Revue Française de Gestion, Californian Management Review* all carry articles about marketing but are essentially general management publications.

The second range of periodicals is about general marketing topics. Publications such as *Marketing, Journal of Marketing* and *Revue Française* de Marketing fall into this category.

The third class of periodicals consists of those devoted to one aspect. For example, *Journal of Advertising Research, Journal of Marketing Research*, and the *Journal of the Market Research Society* are all concerned with aspects of marketing research. Other journals are even more narrowly focused – *Journal of International Physical Distribution* and the *International Journal of Advertising* are examples of these.

Marketing is now well catered for in terms of both books and journals from American, British and Continental sources. Anyone within range of a University or Polytechnic library should have little difficulty in obtaining what they need. Others who are less well placed should avail themselves of the superb services of the British Library which can almost always produce a copy of the book or periodical required.

Reading on marketing theories

Market segmentation

For a discussion of the key issues, see:

Wind, Y, 'Issues and advances in Segmentation Research', *Journal of Marketing Research*, vol. 15, pp. 137–337, August 1978

Product life cycle

Articles have been appearing for 30 years. One of the older references is:

Patton, A, 'Top management's stake in the Product Life Cycle', *Management Review*, June 1959

Many researchers have looked at wide ranges of products. Buzzell and Cook examined the sales histories of 192 consumer products, and in Britain, Cunningham investigated a range of industrial products.

Buzzell, R D and Cook, V, *Product Life Cycles*, Marketing Science Institute, 1969
Cunningham, M T, 'The application of Product Life Cycles to Corporate Strategy: some research findings', *British Journal of Marketing*, pp. 32–44, Spring 1969

More critical pieces have also appeared − Polli and Cook write in their conclusion '. . . we must register strong reservations about its general validity, even stated in its weakest, most flexible form.'

Polli, R and Cook, V, 'Validity of the Product Life Cycle', *Journal of Business*, vol. 42 pp. 385−400, October 1969

Dhalla, N K and Yuspeh, S, 'Forget the Product Life Cycle concept', *Harvard Business Review*, vol. 54, pp. 102−112, January/February 1976

The Boston matrix

The Boston Consulting Group, *The Product Portfolio*, 1970

Others have developed and modified the BCG concept. See, for example:

Day, G S, 'Diagnosing the Product Portfolio', *Journal of Marketing*, vol. 41, pp. 29−38, April 1977

Allen, M G, 'Diagnosing G.E.'s planning for What's Watt', in Allio, R J and Pennington, M W (eds), *Corporate Planning: Techniques and Applications,* AMACOM, 1979

Diffusion of innovations

The original book was

Rogers, E M, *Diffusion of Innovations*, Free Press, 1962

The third edition appeared in 1983 and contains an extensive bibliography.

25

Project management

John Lewington

Projects are the main mechanism used by management for coping with the introduction of new systems, products and processes, and any changes outside the normal day-to-day operations of the organisation. Projects inevitably bring about change to some facet of the organisation and often all of the skills embodied in this book will be necessary to complete a project successfully. A project may be as small as the implementation of a word processing system, or as large as the building and equipping of a new factory. Large organisations will have highly developed bureaucratic systems of project submission, appraisal, presentation, approval and resourcing. Small organisations with short communication chains will often have very simple decision making processes and informal systems of project appraisal.

This chapter will define the main phases of project management and show how a manager may tackle each phase in a professional manner (see Figure 25.1). All projects involve elements of risk. The level of risk can be very high if the size of the project is large in relation to the size of the organisation carrying it out. Successful projects should enhance a company's profitability, market position and self-esteem. However, projects often fail through poor appraisal of potential problems, inadequate organisation, lack of technical expertise and under-funding.

Good project management systems should embody the following aims:

- ensure that the organisation reacts to environmental pressures and changes in a rational manner;
- accurately estimate the resources required to complete the

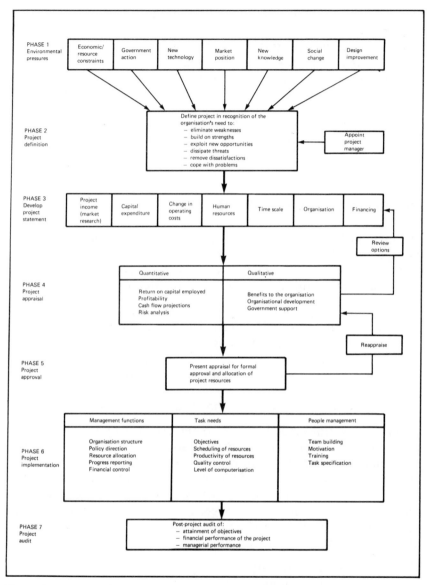

Figure 25.1   The main phases of project management
This diagram provides an overview of the main phases and components of project management.

project successfully, and ensure that no resource needs are hidden or
forgotten;

- fully appraise the total expenditure of resources in terms of the
  economic and organisational benefits;
- implement the project through a coordinated plan on a time
  scale appropriate to resources availability and organisational
  needs;
- develop the organisation's current systems and resources to be
  able to cope with the changes that the project will bring.

ENVIRONMENTAL PRESSURES

The main skills in this phase of project management are perceptual.
Change must be seen as possible or necessary due to internal or
external opportunities. The ability of the organisation to respond to
environmental stimuli will depend on a number of factors such as:

- attitude of mind of management to change;
- internal politics and management's perception of the relative
  importance of the problem or opportunity;
- organisation's size and structure;
- bureaucratic complexity and internal inertia in launching new
  ideas;
- perceived threats/risks of the change.

Small organisations may be quick to perceive new opportunities, but
will sometimes lack the financial resources to exploit fully the
environmental change. Large organisations will have the resources,
but internal politics, bureaucratic systems and organisational inertia
may stifle innovation. Most projects will be appraised on their
economic justification. The stronger the economic justification, the
more likely the project is to be raised to reality. The four main areas
likely to generate new projects are:

- increased productivity
- resource constraints
- new products, services and markets
- government action.

Increased productivity

Some projects may present obvious advantages and indisputable need through clear economic viability. Cost savings through increases in resource (labour, materials, space, equipment) productivity are vital to the survival of any organisation. The application of new knowledge and technology will provide the driving forces for change. Replacement of old facilities should also provide the opportunity to improve methods and implement new systems.

Resource constraints

Many projects are forced upon management through shortages of labour, raw materials, space and equipment. Successful products and services may outgrow their operational resource provisions. Therefore, projects are devised to provide additional capacity, the cost of which must be balanced by cost savings and additional revenue generation. Other projects will be developed to cope with physical shortages of raw materials and office/factory space that are constraining operations.

New products, services and markets

The introduction of new products, services and markets will generate projects which define the resources, timing and expenditures involved in the venture. The organisation will need to assess the impact of the new product on existing products in determining the possible viability of the project. The expenditures on R and D, new facilities and market launch must be matched by future forecasts of sales revenues.

Government action

New legislation often initiates new projects in order that an organisation's facilities and systems comply with government requirements. It is unlikely that these projects will generate cost savings or additional revenues. Therefore, organisations may use the project as a mechanism for controlling and minimising costs.

PROJECT DEFINITION

Projects must be accurately defined as the research involved in the development of a project statement may involve substantial investment of resources. Therefore, a project may be categorised under one of the following headings:

- cost savings
- new products and services
- replacement of plant, vehicles and buildings
- product research and development
- exploration for mineral reserves
- expansion of product/service capacity
- marketing campaign to increase sales
- organisational development/training programme to enhance an organisation's human resources
- environmental, health and safety enhancements.

All of the above categories would be expected to produce long term economic benefits, except for environmental projects which might be necessary to comply with legislation.

The initial sponsors of the project must clearly define its aims and objectives. This will require intense discussions about the 'fit' of the project with existing policies, resources and skills of the organisation. If the project is beyond the scope of the organisation's current skills, then it may be necessary to employ consultants or approach specialists to frame the project appropriately. The rationales and hypotheses should be submitted to senior management for formal approval before starting the next project phase.

DEVELOPING A PROJECT STATEMENT

When an idea, concept or suggestion seems worth considering then the approval of senior management will generally be sought. The data collection will involve considerable time in the compilation of a large project statement. Therefore, a presentation of the objectives, rationales and potential benefits may be necessary before starting the study. The technical and business research involved in this phase may involve several of the following activities in order to make accurate estimates of expenditures and revenues:

- Market research − estimates of selling price, market share, market size, selling costs.
- Technical research − experimental products and model plants.
- Patent surveys and searches.
- Development of synthetic time and work standards.

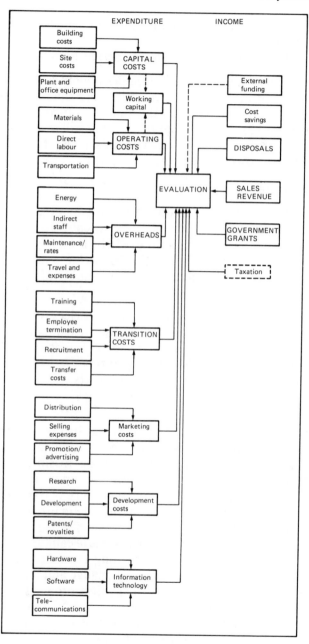

Figure 25.2 Factors of income and expenditure for project statements

- Preliminary negotiations with government, local government and unions.
- Computer simulations to aid the design of systems.

In many projects with a long gestation period and high technological uncertainty these estimates will be little more than guesstimates or 'ball park' figures. A diagram of the main cost factors that can arise is given in Figure 25.2. From Figure 25.1 you will see that there are a number of areas to be considered in this phase to ensure that a comprehensive project statement is compiled.

Project income

Most projects will stand or fall on their ability to increase the organisation's net income, either through new revenue generation or cost reduction. The increase in 'cash flow' will be the sole justification for the capital expenditure. Any of the following sources of income generation may be used individually or in combination to justify the project's capital expenditures:

- sales revenue from new products or services (or royalties)
- release of capital through disposals of existing assets
- increase in revenue from expansion of capacity
- reduction in costs of existing operations
- government grants and special contracts.

Capital expenditure

Every project statement will contain a listing of the capital expenditures (long term assets) necessary. A wide variety of funding methods (see Financing, page 467) may be feasible/desirable for different facets of the project depending upon the size of the expenditure, corporate policy and attitude to risk. Expenditures may be categorised according to their economic life in order to make some forecasts of depreciation.

There is always a tendency to *underestimate* capital expenditure on projects. This is particularly true of long term projects where the problems of delays, inflation, technical change and new factors (e.g. pollution control) may surface as the project progresses. Therefore, the inclusion of a 'contingency allowance' to cover unforeseen eventualities and problems may be justified. The main areas of project expenditure can be stated as follows:

- land and buildings

- plant and equipment
- tooling and storage facilities
- working capital
- vehicles and materials handling equipment
- computers (hardware and software) and telecommunications networks.

Changes in operating costs

Most projects will result in some changes in operating costs. The main focus of a project may be cost savings in materials or labour through increasing capital investment. The result of this is a higher risk situation in terms of changes in the level of activity.

Productivity increase projects can be focused upon the following areas:

- improved material utilisation
- increased labour productivity
- overhead reduction or faster absorption
- reduction in telecommunications or energy costs
- reduction in sales or distribution costs
- improved information systems and decision making.

Human resources

A project may require special technological or managerial skills to be completed successfully. These skills may be in short supply. Therefore, the utilisation of these skills will either be expensive in terms of their actual or opportunity (internal to the organisation) costs. The creators, innovators and entrepreneurs who will be crucial to the success of the project must be coordinated and scheduled carefully. The project manager must consider the task needs in selecting and blending an effective team to solve potential problems. The 'real' cost of the man hours that will be required for the project must be accurately assessed.

Time scale

Some consideration must be given to an outline plan of the main activities to establish an overall duration for the project. There may be a tendency to *underestimate* the time scale in order to encourage project selection. Judgements about time scale are always partly subjective and there is always senior management pressure to reduce the total time scale of the project to a minimum. This will encourage the 'crashing' of activities, that is, the pouring in of resources to reduce activity time scale. Conversely, the delay and late completion of activities will have harmful effects on a project. If the cumulative loss of benefits (financial) and the overall cost of the project on different time scales are considered together, then the sum of loss of benefits and project cost may provide an optimal time scale (see Figure 25.3). Ultimately, product life cycles and other environmental stimuli (competition) may have the most profound effects on management's perception of an appropriate time scale. If it is feasible, some consideration should be given to phasing the project in such a way that the first phase will generate funding for subsequent phases.

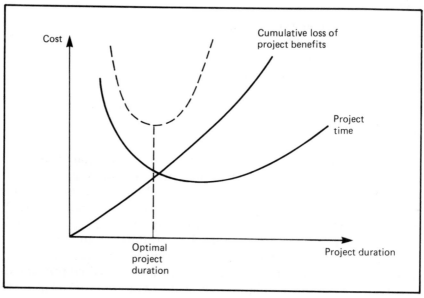

Figure 25.3   Total cost of project

Organisation

A preliminary assessment of organisational problems must be made. The way in which a project is organised and operated after completion will have cost implications in terms of expenditure and revenue. The person appointed as project manager will have to answer several key organisational questions:

- How should the personnel be organised in order to maximise communication, motivation and task completion?
- Should the whole project be handed over to a sub-contractor on a turnkey basis?
- What sort of organisation will be required to operate the new system in order to plan for training and staffing?
- What information and computer systems will be of benefit to the project team?

Financing

Most projects will be financed internally using current cash flow or borrowing capacity. However, large and/or high risk projects may require alternative funding strategies. One of the following alternatives may be used to reduce the impact of adverse risks on your organisation:

- venture capital funding
- joint projects in the form of partnerships or consortia
- royalty and licensing agreements
- locating to obtain government employment grants and subsidies
- leasing and renting buildings and equipment.

Once these issues have been decided the project is ready for appraisal. The estimates, guesstimates and 'ball park' figures will form the basic budget for the project. Some updating, review and changes will undoubtedly occur from feedback during the appraisal.

PROJECT APPRAISAL

In this phase management are concerned with appraising the information and rationales put forward in the project statement. Several alternative options should be appraised to allow for choice. However, this is not always practicable. The appraisal may result in feedback on management's attitude to facets of the project which will result in revisions of the project statement and reappraisal. As the project statement may have been gathered from a wide variety of sources the information must be screened for consistency.

Surveys reveal that great emphasis is placed on the quantitative factors in project appraisal. However, it should be remembered that these are only *estimates* and *forecasts*. In addition the qualitative factors expressed in the objectives, rationales and non-quantifiable benefits should fit with current strategies and business policies. Therefore, the main objectives of this phase are as follows:

- To determine whether the project meets the organisation's criteria for financial return on the investment.
- To ensure that the estimates present an accurate/practical/ realistic view of the project.
- To appraise the risks in relation to the economic returns.
- To determine the fit and effects of the project on the organisation's future strategies and policies.

Project appraisal may require considerable management accounting and computing skills; you should therefore consult Further reading at the end of the chapter for the detail behind these techniques.

Profitability

Most projects will be undertaken because they promise to improve the economic position (wealth) of the sponsoring organisation. One problem in selecting projects is to define an appropriate rate of return for any given risk. Many organisations ignore this problem and set one rate of return for all projects. Deciding on an appropriate rate of return can be affected by many factors such as the organisation's cost of capital, returns from other similar projects, or returns from other investments outside the organisation. Other factors such as inflation, current interest rates and taxation may have some bearing on the figure. Profitability criteria can be expressed in a number of ways, but payback period and rate of return on investment predominate.

Payback period

This is the time taken to repay the investment out of the cash flow from the investment.

Payback period (years)	1	3	5	7
Projects	Computers	Vehicles	Property	Government

The payback method is very easy to understand and is very widely used by all sorts of organisations.

Rate of return on investment

This is expressed as a percentage rate per annum.

Generally, organisations set a minimum rate (sometimes called cut-off rate) of return to be obtained from their projects.

Minimum rates of return (%)	10	20	30	40
Projects	Government Property	Vehicles	Pharmaceuticals	Computers

Several techniques are used for assessing rate of return, all of which give different answers. Some employ formulae (accounting rate of return); others attempt to forecast cash flows then apply discount factors (discounted cash flow DCF). There are two kinds of DCF technique: net present value (NPV) and internal rate of return (IRR). Net present value utilises the organisation's minimum rate of return and determines the result on a 'go' – 'no go' basis. Internal rate of return attempts to determine the exact compound rate of return for the project over its entire life. The result is then compared with the minimum rate of return. Both techniques lend themselves more to computer models of sensitivity then manual calculations.

Projects not meeting the organisation's criteria for profitability will rarely be progressed. If a project makes good basic business sense then it might be recycled through the statement and appraisal phases for investment trimming and re-thinking.

Cash flow projections

Expenditures, forecasts of income and time scale projections should be combined into a cash flow projection. This will provide management with an overall view of cash commitments and the rate at which loans might be paid off. Using a spreadsheet will enable a model of project cash flows to be developed. This will allow management to appraise the effects of inflation and taxation.

Risk analysis

A spreadsheet cash flow model will greatly ease the burden of examining the risk aspects of the project. The relative significance of the investment decision is dictated by the size of the investment in relation to an organisation's net assets. Failure of a small project can be absorbed, but failure of a large project could be disastrous. Therefore, risk analysis should make management aware of the 'downside' risks which might evolve under certain environmental conditions.

One technique of risk appraisal is *sensitivity analysis*. The approach is to take each main factor in the project (e.g. sales income, materials cost) and vary it by + 10 per cent and − 10 per cent, one at a time. This should give some indication of the most sensitive variables which will provide a concentration of attention. This awareness of potential problem areas may result in some reorganisation of the project or hedging of risks.

Another method is to examine the project through a variety of scenarios. This may provide some insights into how the project should be managed in different environments.

Generally, risk should be related to reward. If a project has high risks then a high rate of return should be expected. However, most organisations have one rate of return for all types of projects. This rate of return is set relatively high on the basis that those projects which work out will pay for those which fail.

Benefits to the organisation

In project appraisal the decision making process will undoubtedly be affected by some qualitative factors which cannot be expressed in economic terms. In cases where accurate estimating of costs and revenues is difficult then these may be the most important decision making variables. Any one or a combination of the following factors may be used to provide project justification:

- improvement of product/service market position
- stronger cost structure of products or services
- security of employment for the work force
- release of non-productive assets
- improvements in the organisation's financial structure
- implementation of new technology to meet competition
- establish technological lead over the competition
- establish a position in a high growth market
- development of new products or services
- comply with health and safety regulations
- improve corporate image
- develop new skills and expertise in the work force
- improve managerial control and decision making.

Organisational development

Projects may be the catalyst for organisational development. They may provide many new directions to the organisation's task systems, a focus for change, learning, conflict resolution and a new set of working relationships.

Government support

In most industrialised countries the government plays a significant role in providing financial support for high risk and economically marginal projects. This support may be through taxation relief, direct loans, grants or contracts. Intangible government support may make funding easier to obtain or provide an opening in export markets. The effect of government funding is to reduce risk and provide a market for products and services. In return the government will require job creation and stability of employment for a specific region.

PROJECT APPROVAL

In this phase the project statements and appraisals should be combined into one summary document for presentation to senior management. In large organisations this will involve the completion of standardised forms covering the factors to be considered by their specific type of organisation and business. The summary report may be accompanied by a presentation, 'selling' the project to senior management.

The report and/or presentation should contain the following elements:

- main objectives of the project
- main rationales supporting the project
- models, pictures and outline designs of new products or services
- market information – strategy, size, share, pricing, promotion and advertising
- proposals for the organisation and staffing of the new system
- outline of information systems and data processing support networks
- product/service cost data
- list/summary of main capital expenditures
- profitability statements
- cash flow forecasts
- financing proposals

- potential risks and environmental problems.

If the project is not approved then senior management should provide their reasons for rejection. This might then involve further research and appraisal before re-submission.

PROJECT IMPLEMENTATION

The implementation phase involves the planning, scheduling and coordination of a wide variety of resources. The physical activities must be paralleled by the development of appropriate human resources to implement and operate the new system. The integration of activities will involve the mobilisation of resources on both an internal and external basis. The organisation of the project must evolve around clear lines of responsibility and communication married to an integrated set of activities with a time phased plan.

Task objectives

In general, the aim is to minimise project duration. However, while this may be an important consideration in many projects it is not the sole criterion. Projects may be implemented using one or more of the following objectives as a guide to planning:

- minimise total project duration;
- minimise the total systems cost of the project;
- minimise cost for a given project duration;
- provide an even (steady) loading on scarce resources;
- minimise time for a given project cost;
- maximise the use of available resources.

Organisation structure

Project management requires both a vertical and horizontal flow of work which cannot be achieved through rigid formal authority. Three basic structures exist for managing projects. However, none provides a perfect solution and each has its strengths and weaknesses.

Functional structure

Where projects are confined to one specific function (e.g. production, marketing) in the organisation then this approach may be appropriate. Where projects cut across functions, control becomes difficult.

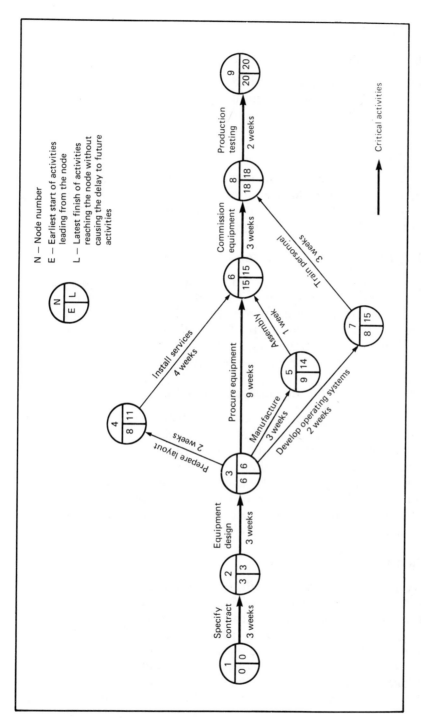

Figure 25.4 Example of a simple network

Project structure

Teams of specialists are formed to carry out a specific project. Responsibility and lines of communication are very clear in this type of organisation. However, the costs of maintaining this type of structure in a multi-project environment can be very high.

Matrix structure

In this structure the project manager maintains a team against a background of functional activities. This structure promotes learning and a strong technical base, but may sometimes evoke a conflict of priorities with functional managers.

Policy direction and resource allocation

Projects often create new operating systems, but managers have to maintain the existing systems. This will cause conflict between the project manager and functional managers if priorities are not clearly stated by senior management. Resource requirements should be identified, related to tasks, and provision made to ensure that the resources will be available at the required time.

Financial control and progress reporting

Most organisations will operate their main controls through the finance department. The simplest way is to plot a cumulative forecast of expenditure and then monitor the actual expenditure against it. The purpose of this is to highlight possible overspending before it gets out of control. Expenditure forecasts are generally broken down into spent (bills paid), committed (orders placed), and to be committed. Written reports and occasional presentations will be required on some projects.

Scheduling of resources

The scheduling of resources will be accomplished using a network to link activities logically (Figure 25.4). Organisations use a variety of names for this approach; critical path method (CPM) or analysis (CPA), precedence network or programme evaluation and review technique (PERT). Once the network has been drawn logically relating the completion of activities then a bar chart can be drawn or produced from a computer package (Figure 25.5).

First, management must make a decision on the detail in which they

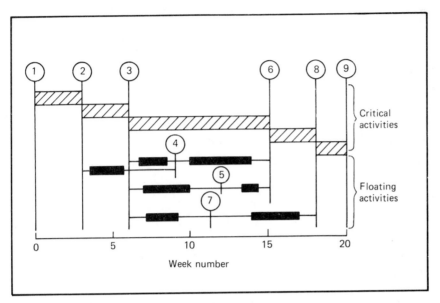

Figure 25.5   Example of a simple bar chart

plan to schedule each task. The basic information required on each task is:

- a brief description of the task
- a time duration of the task
- a responsibility for the task
- a list of tasks that must be complete before the task can start.

An arrow is used to represent a task in the project and this is most commonly known as an 'activity'. The activity is bounded at each end by a circle commonly known as an 'event' (or node). An example of a single activity such as 'write report' is shown in Figure 25.6. The length and orientation of the arrow is *not* related to the duration of the task. However, the arrow does point in the direction of the time flow for the task. After the activity 'write report', the next task may be 'typing' and this is represented as shown in Figure 25.7.

The numbers at the tail and head of the arrow are called 'event' numbers. Therefore, activity 1−2 is 'write report'. If the report were a long one then it might be worth commencing typing before it was completely finished. However, for this example we will assume that typing cannot start until the writing is finished. The cover of the report could be designed whilst the report is being written; and such

475

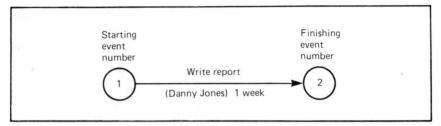

Figure 25.6 Example of a single activity network

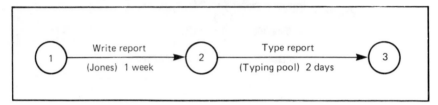

Figure 25.7 Two-activity network

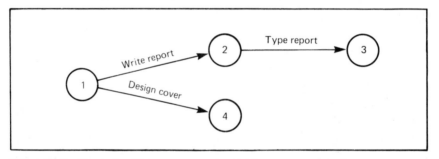

Figure 25.8 Example of how concurrent activities are represented

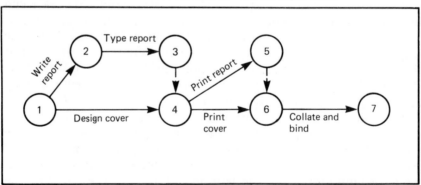

Figure 25.9 A complete network, showing logical order and unique numbering

concurrent (or parallel) activities are represented as shown in Figure 25.8.

Once the report and cover are ready then they may be printed, bound and distributed. Figure 25.9 shows the complete sequence. The dashed arrow connecting event 5 and event 6 is a 'dummy' activity with zero time duration and it is used to maintain proper logical order and unique numbering (for computer input purposes) within the network diagram.

The network is not only a plan, but is also a communication device for ensuring that all departments understand how their contribution fits into the whole picture. A main network may have to be broken down into a series of sub-networks to be used within individual departments.

Even small projects justify the drawing of a network and construction of a simple bar chart. Larger projects will justify the use of computers for control and updating purposes. If computers are to be used then schedules of resources associated with each activity may also be required. If activities are delayed or get ahead of schedule then the impact on later activities can clearly be seen. A wide variety of commercially manufactured aids for displaying projects and plans is also available.

Some activities will have to be completed to an exact time schedule; these are called the 'critical path' activities and set the shortest time in which the project can be completed. Activities not on the critical path will have some free time referred to as 'activity float'. This means that management will have some limited discretion on the start and finish of non-critical activities. This discretion may be used to level demands on scarce resources.

Level of computerisation

The level of computerisation depends very much on the size of organisation and systems available. The advent of microcomputers allied to low cost packages means that it is now economical to set up even a small network on a computer. The increased power of microcomputers allows for hundreds of activities to be handled and a wide variety of sophisticated features made available to the project manager.

Principally, these features are:

- calculation of start, finish and float times for all activities;
- development of bar charts for each activity;

- preparation of activity schedules by individual manager responsibility;
- production of calendar and milestone charts;
- sorting of reports according to need;
- incorporation of public holidays;
- tracking of multiple (5+) resource demands and cost per activity;
- modelling and 'what if?' facilities that provide trade-offs between manpower, cost and time; and the levelling of resource demands.

The use of other computer packages such as spreadsheets and data-bases should provide further modelling and control facilities for larger projects.

Productivity of resources

The use of computer models and packages will enable the project manager to devise schemes and schedules of implementation for any of the six task objectives stated earlier in this section. Therefore, by using computer packages to update and reschedule resources the trade-off between project completion, resource costs and resource productivity can be constantly updated.

One of the greatest problems facing the project manager is that of resource peaking (see Figure 25.10). Therefore, the manager may attempt to 'smooth' or 'level' resource requirement over a period of time.

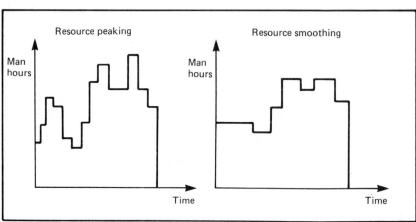

Figure 25.10   An example of resource smoothing

Quality control

This may present substantial problems particularly on large projects involving complex sub-contractor interrelationships. Therefore, the quality of work must be constantly monitored by designers, surveyors and architects. The information and reports should be stored using a database computer package for cross-referencing. This will enable project management to keep comprehensive control and records of all quality control reports. Quality circles can be set up to provide a constant dialogue on quality problems and project progress.

People management

Many aspects of personnel management are effectively dealt with in other chapters of this book. However, it is very easy to forget about human resource development when the task aspects (getting things finished) appear to predominate. But individuals and groups must be *motivated* to achieve project objectives. In technically complex projects there may be a high element of *training* taking place both formally and informally. Therefore, it is necessary to build effective *teams* capable of supporting and assisting each other (see Chapter 17 for team building). This involves good communications, mutual respect, and an ability to resolve conflict effectively. There is no such thing as delegation in the management of a project. Every activity must have an owner who is committed to resolving problems so that the task is completed successfully.

AUDITING PROJECT PERFORMANCE

To improve future performance it is not unusual to carry out a post-project audit. The main focus of an audit should be on the accuracy of the project statement, the adequacy of the project appraisal process, and finally the effectiveness of the implementation. All large projects should probably be audited one year after full implementation. Smaller projects may be sampled and appropriate examples of good and bad results examined. The results of the audit may assist management in formulating an effective organisational development programme aimed at greater effectiveness in project management for the future. The main areas of examination are listed below.

Objectives

Has the project achieved its objectives in terms of performance, resolving problems, exploiting opportunities and provided an appropriate return on investment?

Project statement

How accurate were the forecasts of costs, expenditure, income and time scale? Could/should more accurate estimates have been prepared?

Appraisal

Did the appraisal process properly consider all of the practical alternatives, risks and organisational implications? Were effective strategies developed for coping with potential problems and reorganisation?

Implementation

This will undoubtedly come in for the greatest scrutiny in the following areas:

- planning and scheduling of resources
- procedures for contracting and tendering
- labour, materials and equipment utilisation
- adequacy of financial control mechanisms
- progress reporting and communication systems
- analysis of delays and lost time
- organisation structures and personnel policies.

Use of the checklist

The checklist that follows is designed as an *aide memoire* for the busy manager and should be used in conjunction with Figures 25.1 and 25.2 to ensure the rounded consideration of a project. Most large organisations will have their own systems, procedures and project peculiarities; and it may be useful to develop an internal checklist of factors for your own organisation's environment.

PROJECT MANAGEMENT CHECKLIST

Environmental pressures

1 Does the organisation have sensing mechanisms and communication channels in order to:

- spot market changes;
- recognise new business/service opportunities;
- adopt new technology and systems;
- reduce costs and be more competitive;
- incorporate employee suggestions;
- resolve customer problems;
- respond to social change.

2 Who is responsible for project initiation?
3 How are potential projects formulated for project definition?

Project definition

1 Can the project be adequately categorised (i.e. R and D, cost saving, replacement, expansion etc.)?
2 Which person/group/department/committee is responsible for defining the terms of reference/objectives/constraints of the project?
3 Is the potential project consistent with the current policies of the organisation?
4 Is it likely that top management will support the project?
5 Are the technical expertise/skills requirements within the scope of the organisation or should consultants be employed?

Developing a project statement

1 Has the project been approved in principle by senior management?
2 Have the rationales/objectives/constraints/importance of the project been adequately defined for costing and estimating purposes?
3 Can the income/sources of revenue for the project be adequately defined/guesstimated/forecast?
4 Have all of the following items of expenditure been properly considered?

- land, new buildings and site facilities (roads etc.)
- machines, office equipment and computers (hardware and software)
- training costs for completion of the project and implementation of the new system
- employee recruitment and termination
- relocation of employees and facilities
- research and development costs
- marketing and sales.

5 What changes in annual operating costs will occur after the project is completed?

- materials and staffing
- transportation, distribution and energy costs
- rates, building and equipment maintenance
- computing and telecommunications costs
- staff travel and expenses
- marketing and sales.

6 Will any specialist scarce human resources be required to complete the project successfully?

7 Does the estimated time scale for the project conflict with the required completion date? If so, how can the two be reconciled?

8 Will a special organisation structure be needed to complete the project?

9 Will a new organisation structure be required after the completion of the project?

10 Can the project be financed internally? If not, where will the external financing come from?

11 Can appropriate measures of profitability be calculated from the information available?

Project appraisal – quantitative

1 Does the project meet the organisation's criteria for profitability in terms of payback and/or return on investment?

2 Will the project/investment enhance the long term profitability and security of the organisation?

3 Will the cash flow projections for the project affect other

projects and/or the normal operational requirements of the organisation? If yes, how can this problem be coped with?

4 Will the project involve cost savings and stronger market position?

5 Can any limits of accuracy be placed upon the market size, market share and product life?

6 Will inflation have a significant impact on the larger items of expenditure?

7 Can the relative risks be assessed in quantitative terms through 'sensitivity analysis'?

Project approval

1 At what level in the organisation can the project be approved (department manager/area manager/managing director/board)?

2 Are you satisfied that the project statement represents the 'best' solution to the problem?

3 If the project cannot be approved in present form what areas need changing to make the project viable?

4 Are the contingencies for cost overruns sufficient on large items of expenditure?

5 Can resources be allocated in step with the current time scale for the project?

6 Is the project too large/risky for the present organisation? If so, should a partner/venture capital be found to form the project as a separate venture?

Project implementation

1 Has an appropriate balance been defined between resources – time scale – projected expenditure?

2 Have responsibilities/organisation structures been defined to ensure successful completion of the project?

3 Has senior management provided appropriate policies for the conduct of the project?

4 What progress reporting will be required in terms of frequency/detail/format/expenditure?

5 What financial controls should be implemented to ensure successful completion of the project?

6 What mechanisms exist for coping with cost overruns and expenditures not originally forecast?

7 Have the main task activities been clearly defined and responsibilities allocated?
8 Are the milestone dates and activity completion times clear to the whole team?
9 Is the scheduling/rescheduling of resources and activities complex enough to justify computerisation?
10 Do the current plans maximise the productivity of project resources?
11 Who is responsible for controlling/monitoring the quality of the work completed?
12 What processes are planned into the organisation structure for developing the project team and/or the team to operate the new system?
13 What incentives exist to encourage the team/contractor to complete the project on time?
14 What training will be required for the project team members and/or the people operating the new system?
15 Have appropriate task specifications been prepared for individual members of the project team?

Project audit

1 Is the project sufficiently important to warrant an audit? If so, how long should elapse before an audit is meaningful?
2 To what extent has the project achieved its objectives?
3 Did the project attain its financial performance objectives in terms of return/project budget?
4 Was management of the project effective and were resources used efficiently?
5 What can be learned to improve future projects?

FURTHER READING

General

Stallworthy, E A and Kharbanda, O P, *Total Project Management: From Concept to Completion*, Gower, 1983
Harrison, F L, *Advanced Project Management*, Gower, 1985
Meredith, J and Mantel, S S, *Project Management: A Managerial Approach*, Wiley, 1985
Lock, D (ed.), *Project Management Handbook*, Gower, 1987

Project definitions and statements

Twiss, B, *Managing Technological Innovation*, Longman, 2nd edition, 1982

Bright, J, *Research, Development and Technological Innovation*, Irvin, 1964

Project appraisal

Souder, W E, *Project Selection and Economic Appraisal*, Van Nostrand Reinhold, 1983

UNESCO, *Project Evaluation*, HMSO, 1985

Franks, J R and Scholefield, H H, *Corporate Financial Management*, Gower, 1979

Project implementation

Dinsmore, P C, *Human Factors in Project Management*, American Management Association, 1986

Hoare, H R, *Project Management using Network Analysis*, McGraw-Hill, 1973

Lockyer, K G, *Critical Path Analysis*, Pitman, 1966

Project auditing

Turner, W S, *Project Auditing Methodology*, North-Holland, 1980

26

Creativity and innovation

Pauric McGowan

> 'Discontent is the first step in the progress of a man or nation.'
>
> Oscar Wilde

Managers need to recognise that continuous creative and innovative activity in their organisations must be as fundamental a part of their strategic thinking as the very definition of what business they are in or what environmental factors will have a bearing on future plans. The aims of this chapter, therefore, are:

- to increase the consciousness amongst managers of the creative and innovative forces already at work within their organisations;
- to increase their knowledge of the creative and innovative processes and their appreciation of the importance of a consistent commitment to them;
- to introduce managers to some of the important elements for generating a 'creative' environment, the most common sources of ideas, including a few of the simpler techniques for stimulating creative thinking and the innovative process itself.

It is hoped as a consequence that managers will be better placed to create such an environment within their organisations as will foster a general dissatisfacion with the status quo and positively encourage greater creative and innovative activity.

DEFINITIONS

Creativity is a talent or personal skill latent in most of us, dulled mostly by the environment in which we work or in which we have been brought up. It is a force, however, which, if sensitively handled, can be tapped, with real benefits for the organisation. It is an integral part of the innovation process (which we will look at later) and should not be seen as some sort of separate exercise. It is treated separately here only for the sake of simplicity.

There are degrees of creativity. *Pure creativity* is the identification or discovery of an idea or practice which is absolutely new or unique. Such activity is usually the focus of dedicated research and development departments in the larger organisations.

However, a new idea can be unique to an organisation. It may be an idea or practice which has been about for some time in some shape or form or in some other sufficiently unrelated market. However, in the case of *relative creativity* the organisation in question will not have known of it before. In adopting it or by introducing it into its markets it will be doing so for the very first time.

A variation of this last type of creativity is where a new idea or practice derives from something which has already been discovered. In such a case the result would be an extension of the existing idea or practice, perhaps because of an association of other more unrelated ideas. This is generally known as *informed creativity* because it has been derived from information already widely available.

Must creativity in an organisation always have a purpose or focus?

When Fleming discovered penicillin he had no idea what good it might do until ten years later. When the Wright brothers pioneered 'flight' in the early part of this century they could not have conceived the future implications of their invention.

Is there a case at all for unfettered or unplanned creative activity in a commercial enterprise? Many ideas are suggested in an organisation which initially may have no apparent application or potential use. Creative thinking, however, can help to give a number of different viewpoints which may subsequently help to spot otherwise unseen potential.

There is a danger, therefore, of rejecting even the most outlandish proposal too soon, though creative and exhaustive screening is essential.

Always at the back of management's mind is the need to keep the organisation commercially successful. Operational arrangements must be efficiently controlled if targets are to be met. Most writers on this subject acknowledge that an organisation which is geared essentially to efficiency is compromising its potential for creativity.

On the other hand too much freedom in the interests of encouraging the creative spirit may be wasteful and lead too often to grand solutions to the wrong problems.

Herein lies a particular management dilemma. A sensitive and imaginative management style is essential to striking the right balance between organisation for efficiency and freedom for creativity. We will return to this important matter when we discuss organisational structures for facilitating creativity.

THE CREATIVE PROCESS

This process is an intense mental activity where the creative thinking of members of some disciplinary project team is brought to bear on identifying new opportunities for an organisation and correctly defining the needs and problems associated with these new opportunities. It is the first step in the innovation process and will be repeated throughout until opportunities identified have been fully exploited.

The activity requires both a vivid imagination and considerable analytical skills. It involves a guided combination of a number of abilities and techniques in order to stimulate both.

The types of talent or skill that a person must have to participate effectively in the creative process are:

- an ability to transfer or apply knowledge or technology already in existence to the solution of more than one problem;
- an ability to associate ideas which at first might appear to have no relationship at all and thus gain a new perspective on an old problem;
- an ability to redefine an old problem in a different way in order to see new approaches or dimensions for further analysis and eventual solutions;
- an ability to fantasise or engage in unconstrained thinking and thus to go beyond conventional thought patterns to the unorthodox where many a novel solution may lie.

There are several problem solving or thought provoking techniques which may be used to ensure the maximum use of an individual's creative ability.

A most important one to mention here is the use of the multi-disciplinary team. (Other techniques considered later in the chapter use such teams as an essential base.) The multidisciplinary team will usually be made up of some twelve members of various professional backgrounds and levels of experience. Each will bring a different perspective on the problem to be solved and provide stimulation to each other's input.

However, it is recommended that some interested but neutral chairman always be involved to referee and guide the team's activities to ensure appropriate solutions. Properly guided, the interactions of the members of the project team will prove to be a considerable source of fertile thinking.

One barrier to effective creativity in the process is the 'wood for the trees' syndrome. All this intense mental activity often takes the participants too close to the problem to see all the possible answers. A period of detachment from the problem, perhaps to consider some other unrelated exercise, can lead to a subconscious mulling over of the issues raised by the original problem. Some of the results of this approach might be a reappraisal of these issues, perhaps a redefinition of the need or problem, or better still the *eureka* experience when the solution comes in all its clarity with unexpected spontaneity.

INNOVATION AND THE INNOVATION PROCESS

Innovation is a creative activity where the emphasis is not so much on identifying new ideas or production opportunities as on the adoption of those opportunities (let us call them inventions) and their subsequent development into either a finished article or useful practice. The innovation process is outlined in Figure 26.1.

As a consequence of the creative process (make sure you understand the relationship between the creative and innovation processes) an invention will have been discovered or a new practice identified. These opportunities bring with them associated problems and needs. The same creative processes will have an important contribution in ensuring that the new opportunity is fully exploited.

Importance of creativity and innovation to managers

In Chapter 24 of this Handbook (Marketing) Peter Woodcock introduced the product life cycle and the strategic implications of this concept, in particular the need for continuous new product

1	Identify an opportunity or need to be fulfilled, or problem to be resolved
2	Gather all information currently available on the opportunity or problem
3	Identify the dimensions of the opportunity/problem and classify the correct nature of same:
	• associated ideas/opportunities
	• additional problems arising
4	Propose alternative ideas/solutions to opportunity/problem for analysis
5	Evaluate proposals with respect to 2 and 3 above
6	Select the best idea/solution
7	Invest in, develop and implement idea/solution
8	Assess impact of idea/solution on target market
9	Revise if required

Figure 26.1   The innovation process

development. The product life cycle theory means that if a company fails to plot the market appeal of its existing product lines and to prepare for the timely launch of new additional products before those existing lines go into decline, it will seriously compromise its market position, its profitability, its potential for growth and perhaps, therefore, its very existence.

Business organisations need a constant flow of innovative ideas for continued growth. To find those ideas an organisation may either decide to acquire someone else's or to innovate for itself. In the former case it may do this by:

- buying patent rights to some novel idea;
- seeking to acquire some other company which has a portfolio of projects but no viable way of exploiting them;
- producing a new product under licence for someone else.

In the latter case the organisation will:

- retain control of its own portfolio of ideas instead of depending on the flow of ideas from outside sources, and eliminate the need to compete for those ideas with other 'idea-hungry' organisations;

● greatly enhance its own standing in respect of innovative and creative activity and positively affect the environment.

Other applications for creative and innovative processes

Creativity and innovation are not solely for new product development purposes. The same imaginative applications are required in the definition and introduction of new practices. Current practices or operational procedures require constant review, evaluation and revision in the interests of ongoing efficiency hopefully without compromising the value of flexibility and freedom for creativity within the organisation. Such revisions, often thoroughgoing and painful, lead to the introduction of change. Proper recognition must be given to the human element in any such change to minimise avoidable and wasteful resistance.

Resistance can never fully be avoided, however. The generation of an appropriate environment where creativity, innovation and change are seen as part of the organisation's very culture will do much to reduce this resistance.

WHY ONE ORGANISATION IS MORE INNOVATIVE THAN ANOTHER

An organisation's level of success as a creative and innovative operation depends on:

● the environment within the organisation and whether or not it is conducive to such activity and attractive to the people who have the potential for it;
● the imaginative and efficient application of the innovation process in developing the creative idea;
● the organisation's record of creative/innovative output, as reflected in the quantity and quality of ideas generated by its creative people;
● the effectiveness of screening the ideas for adoption and commercial exploitation.

Figure 26.2 gives a simple overview of the management of creativity and innovation.

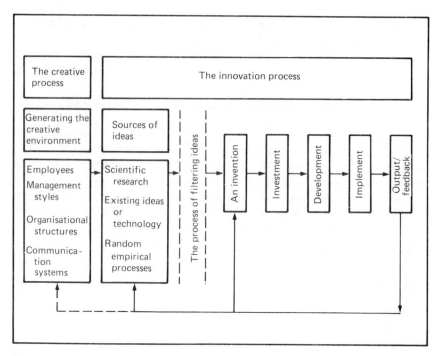

Figure 26.2   The management of creativity and innovation — an overview

Generating the creative environment

If the environment of an organisation is unsupportive or is at odds with those of its people who have a talent for creativity and innovation then it will soon lose those people who through frustration will move to other organisations where they are appreciated. The organisation will be the loser.

Such creative people include those engaged in new product development or with an ability to view issues, problems, or needs from a different perspective from that 'normally' taken. They are valuable assets to any organisation; they thrive in a creative environment and can infect it and the other people in it with their imagination. They must be retained and allowed to flourish. The environment must encourage them to stay and participate.

GENERATING A CREATIVE ENVIRONMENT

The successful generation of a creative environment depends on the type of employee, the style of management, the organisational structures, and the communication systems of the organisation. Let us consider each in turn and the contribution each can make to the generation of a creative and innovative environment.

The organisation's employees

An organisation is made up of people. Their personalities, interpersonal and professional skills and individual ambitions will determine the nature and character of the organisation in which they work, its objectives and its ability to fulfil those objectives.

Creative people within the organisation can influence their colleagues, helping to establish and develop an environment which is conducive to greater creative and innovative activity. It is important, therefore, for management to be able to:

- identify creative people already employed by their organisation;
- establish appropriate training and development programmes in the area of creativity and innovative techniques to highlight their value and application;
- recruit creative people into the organisation (see P T Humphrey's chapter on 'Recruitment and selection' (Chapter 12)).

Identifying creative people is not easy but can be made easier if the manager can at least obtain an idea of the approximate characteristics of such people (see Figure 26.3). Managers may see something of themselves in it as they read through.

Management styles

The management of creativity and innovation and, in particular, of creative employees requires a very different approach and style than would be needed for purely operational management issues.

Figure 26.4 outlines the approximate characteristics of the management style that would be appropriate for creative and innovative organisations. Management should comprise facilitators and guides of change within the organisation. Their role is fundamental if the organisation is to derive any real benefits from having generated a creative environment. How they approach the people and issues involved will determine just how successful the organisation will be in this area and activity.

- Actively seeks and prefers freedom of action. Flexibility is important to him/her. Resists the influences of traditional beliefs or prevailing value systems, is essentially open-minded.

- Is relatively detached as a personality (perhaps as a consequence of the above points), requiring sensitive management to encourage his/her participation.

- Is a critical evaluator of existing ideas and things.

- Is sensitive, therefore, to problems — seeking redefinition and originality, implying a fluency of thinking.

- Is a divergent thinker, seeking possible alternative solutions and rejecting, therefore, the *first* answer as a matter of course.

- Is a good, almost dramatic, communicator. Is a prolific generator of ideas — good and bad, with and without a purpose. Is often given to fanciful thought patterns which may, at first anyway, seem to have no particular focus or application.

- Is strong on presentations with perhaps a record of lectures, demonstrations or even publications.

- Is essentially self-contained.

- Is adventurous/curious/resourceful/speculative in nature.

- May sometimes be irrational, is certainly a complex character.

- Enjoys his/her work and is committed to it.

- Is responsive to opportunities to develop, especially into unplanned areas.

- Is particularly appreciative of recognition and peer interest.

- Is sensitive to criticism and creatively impotent in an environment which is constrictive, highly organised or ignorant of the value of such activity.

Figure 26.3   Checklist — appropriate characteristics of the creative and innovative person

The management style in *any* organisation is determined essentially by:

- what business the organisation is in;
- the training and experience of the management team themselves;

- Essentially creative (review Figure 26.3)and, therefore, sensitive to the creative character and able to recognise it.

- Frequent communicator with 'associates' throughout the organisation both laterally and vertically.

- Essentially non-authoritative, no bossing or threat of punishment or sanction. Rather more participative and collaborative, seeking consultation with associates, offering guidance, advice, encouragement and reward/recognition. Democratic, therefore, in nature, 'people-oriented' but without losing sight of the task.

- Receptive to new (even unplanned) ideas, actively seeking feedback from associates and using it, placing a primary emphasis on associates' continued commitment to the organisation's innovative development. Provokers, therefore, of focused change in the organisation.

- Pro-active in nature, anticipating change, patient, energetic and determined.

- Aware of own knowledge limitations but conscious of the need for an appropriate balance between freedom to innovate in the short term and for control and organisation to achieve long term economic goals.

- Control and organisation, therefore, through networks of project groups or a matrix structure.

Figure 26.4 Checklist – an appropriate style for managing a creative and innovative organisation

- the number and characteristics of the employees in the organisation;
- the type of work being done;
- the size, structure, and system of communications in the organisation – the degree to which employees feel they can participate in the development of the organisation and assume responsibilities themselves.

The creative organisation is different, however, in the way it deliberately seeks to stimulate the generation of useful and original ideas – what we will call *focused change* in the organisation.

Some of the more important factors, however, influencing the introduction of focused change within an organisation are:

- the constraints (actual/perceived) placed on the creative person by himself, and/or the environment within which he works and lives;
- the personal willingness of the innovative person to share

his/her ideas and the degree to which the environment in the organisation encourages him/her to participate in working with and sharing his/her opinions with colleagues;

- the degree to which dissatisfaction with the status quo is fostered within the organisational environment;
- the distribution and nature of authority and control throughout the organisation: centralised for efficiency, or decentralised for freedom and creativity;
- the existence of 'organisational slack' in the organisation (a margin of 'fat' in the organisation which allows opportunity for carrying on innovative activity with lower risk).

The organisation's structures

The structure of any organisation is the framework for management coordination of the relationships between the many diverse elements that make it up. It facilitates the executive decision making process.

The choice of structure by an organisation is an important strategic decision. The type of structure adopted is an important asset in itself to the organisation and is determined by:

- the need for efficiency (for the effective communication and implementation and timely revision of plans);
- the nature of the product (the method and scale of production);
- the span of control (centralised *vs* decentralised).

Any organisational structure has a formal aspect which reflects the hierarchical relations and channels of communications, and an informal aspect which reflects the unplanned associations and friendships that have emerged throughout the organisation. To generate a creative and innovative environment, however, requires that any structure adopted by the organisation should:

- allow the creative person flexibility or freedom to work in the area of greatest interest to him/her and where he/she can be most fruitful (this has implications for mobility across the organisational structure);
- facilitate contact and greater interaction between all creative people across the organisation, particularly on an informal basis, thus allowing a greater cross-fertilisation of ideas;
- encourage an open communication system throughout all levels of the organisation to ensure an optimum flow of information between creative people themselves and the management;

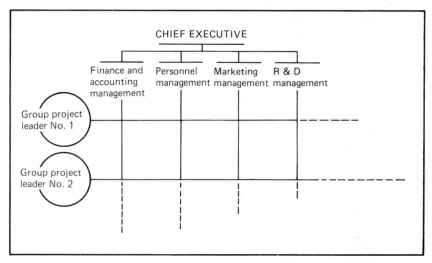

Separates the functional areas from the production or project areas.

When a new production is identified, a suitable team is established drawing the requisite skills from each of the functional areas.

Main advantage: rapid response to change, substantial personal involvement and interest generated.

Main disadvantage: breaks principle of unity of command. (Any one person has two bosses.) Requires, therefore, careful planning and introduction to ensure people understand the system and to minimise conflicts.

Figure 26.5   Example of a matrix structure

- provide scope for real recognition and appreciation of the efforts of creative people in the organisation in terms of both monetary reward and professional advancement;
- ensure the easy identification and access to that person who is responsible for and has the authority to make sure an idea is taken up and its potential explored without any demoralising delay.

A highly coordinated organisation structure, therefore, geared to efficient exploitation of scarce resources to manufacture products is less likely to be able to foster real creative spirit or to implement effectively the changes arising from such activity.

Management must decide what is the optimum mix between 'organisation for efficiency' and 'freedom for creativity' and adopt an appropriate structure.

One type of structure which offers scope for a balance between the two is a *matrix structure* (see Figure 26.5). This structure is based on the establishment of project teams formed for specific purposes or to address particular problems.

These teams traditionally draw their membership from across the functional divisions of the organisation (marketing, personnel, accounting) or wherever the talent required (especially creative) is to be found in the organisation. They are, therefore, multidisciplinary and offer a team-based approach to problem solving.

In addition a matrix structure allows for greater project management control and an opportunity to define 'what has to be done' as far as a specific project is concerned. Creative and innovative activity will then have some focus as a consequence.

It also offers an opportunity for the creative person to 'detach' him/herself from the current problem and to become involved in other project teams for a while. (Remember the 'woods for the trees' syndrome mentioned above.)

The approach has one main drawback which needs to be recognised. There is often a confusion of loyalty for team members to their project group on the one hand and their functional or specialist group on the other. Senior management have a role to play in resolving this confusion and ensuring a full commitment of team members to the project in hand until its completion.

Communication systems

In Chapter 19 (Managing communication) you were introduced to the communication process and the importance of an effective communication system.

The successful generation of an organisational environment for creativity will depend on how effective the communication system is within the organisation. This in turn will depend on how completely the barriers existing in the system have been identified and removed.

If the organisation fails to identify and remove barriers to open communication it will seriously undermine its potential for creative activity. The results will be misunderstanding, misinterpretation, and inaccurate, tardy, unhelpful feedback. See Figure 26.6 for a checklist on barriers to communication.

Overcoming these barriers to open communication will require a style of management and an organisational structure appropriate to the type of creative environment which the organisation seeks to establish.

- The intrapreneurs's fear of being perceived as stupid, irresponsible or wrong. This may be based on a personal anxiety about revealing plans, especially unplanned or outlandish ones which as yet have no immediately definable focus.

- Self-censorship by the intrapreneur because of fear of early criticism of his/her own ideas. As a consequence, ideas are not revealed to associates for assessment but rather bottled up and left unexploited. A loss to the organisation.

- Feelings of futility on the part of the intrapreneur in the face of management indifference or ignorance of his contribution. 'Nobody else cares so why should I?'

- A sense of inertia experienced by everybody in the organisation about mentioning ideas because time is short and the organisation's structures are geared to efficiency, not creativity. The very size of the organisation itself may be a barrier to open communications.

- A sense of suspicion on the part of intrapreneurs abour sharing their ideas with colleagues and management. This may be due to misplaced rivalry and internal competition or just an inability to communicate their ideas in terms that operating people can understand.

- Inability of operational people and management to understand the technicalities/language being used with respect to the project idea.

Figure 26.6   Checklist — barriers to open communication

SOURCES OF INNOVATIVE IDEAS

In the light of our earlier discussion on the product life cycle, we know that a company must be continually innovative if it is to remain competitive, selecting new products to supplement those which may or will inevitably lose their market appeal. The innovation process begins with the generation of these product ideas.

The market place

The market place itself is a very important source of innovative ideas, particularly for an organisation committed to the marketing concept. Given that its customers' needs and wants are central to its strategic planning, the organisation must endeavour to find out just what those are. Suggestion systems, point of sale interviews and group discussions, are ways of canvassing customers for their views on an organisation's products and in particular how the products might be improved.

The company's own people in the market (sales executives, company representatives, service engineers) are a ready source of feedback on customers' ideas, criticisms and suggestions. Indeed, they are often a fertile source of ideas themselves for product improvement and on gaps in the market which neither the organisation itself nor its competitors have yet appreciated. Regular communication with such field executives coupled with appropriate recognition and encouragement will reap its own rewards.

Competitors

Competitors are a source of creative ideas and as close a watch as legitimately possible must be kept on them and their research and development activity. Any new product launched needs to be assessed quickly so as to establish its likely success in the market, and identify its main characteristics with a view to developing an improved version. This is known as *creative imitation*. Remember always, of course, that your competitors are watching you.

The organisation's own product line

The development of new products from those already in the organisation's product mix is a possible source of ideas. A redefinition of an existing product or concept may suggest itself for different uses and lead to its introduction to wholly new markets. It is in this very area that the organisation stands to make its biggest return on its investment in generating a creative environment and for encouraging innovative activity among its personnel. The creative talents of such people will allow them to analyse and redefine the fundamental elements of an existing product or concept and to see in them possibilities which would otherwise have been missed by the casual observer.

Organisations' own research and development

Research and development is often dedicated to expensive basic research. It may be an essential requirement for large mature organisations, leaders in their own markets and determined to remain so. Such a dedication of scarce resources for the smaller to medium sized operations, however, may be rather too expensive. Once again, an early commitment to generating a creative environment throughout the organisation is more likely to pay greater dividends for less cost.

The universities

The new breed of technological university, the polytechnics and the advent of technological or science parks have done much to dissolve the 'ivory tower' image of academia. The mission now is to build greater contacts between industry and the universities, and the latter are eager to get involved. Industry pays the money and funds the professorships, and the universities carry out the research; and it is not *all* highly expensive and hi-tech.Most universities, also, actively promote the notion of student enterprise and many a project with real potential can be identified from this source. Even modest individual faculty research, if picked over, can offer a wealth of unexpected opportunity.

Miscellaneous sources of innovative ideas

These are:

- offices of patent agents;
- entrepreneurs with the ideas but not the business expertise or capital to exploit the ideas − can be contacted through enterprise agencies or regional development boards;
- marketing or advertisement journals or sundry publications, particularly those from outside the organisation's immediate geographical location or market.

TECHNIQUES FOR GENERATING CREATIVE THINKING

Identifying promising ideas is a start. An investigation must follow into their potential both technically and from the point of view of the market place, which will require an application of both imagination and creativity. There are a number of thought provoking problem solving techniques to help.

The importance of multidisciplinary project teams has been mentioned before. The contributions of a number of creative people from different backgrounds guarantee a greater diversity of input and a greater chance, therefore, of many different angles being suggested on a given problem to be solved or idea to be expanded.

Brainstorming

This is a technique for stimulating ideas by working in a multidisciplinary group. It is an experience in imagination and, therefore, requires careful managing. The role of group leader is extremely important in ensuring all group members have a chance to participate equally. The elements are as follows:

- Suspend judgement – no criticism.
- Freewheel – the odder the ideas the better.
- Quantity – the more ideas the better.
- Cross-fertilise – combine and improve on the ideas of others.

Running a brainstorming session back at work (not more than twelve people should be involved) should follow this procedure:

- Define the problem.
- Problem background – the leader must familiarise the participants with the nature of the problem, highlighting any background information and quoting a couple of examples of the type of idea required.
- Select a basic restatement: 'In how many ways can we . . . ?'
- Warm-up session.
- Brainstorm – 70 ideas in 20 minutes; flipchart, silent in-depth mind work.
- Group ideas ⎫
- Select criteria ⎬ best ideas.
- Reverse brainstorming: 'In how many ways can this idea fail?'

Not more than 40 minutes should be allocated to the actual session, but the participants are asked to go on considering the problem and send in any further suggestions. These are then added to the list already obtained and all ideas are classified into logical categories by the leader. These are handed to the person who submitted the problem initially. He then undertakes evaluation of the list, possibly processing ideas by combination, elaboration or additions of his own.

Synectics

This is a variation on the theme of generating ideas in a multidisciplinary framework. Derived from the Greek it means a joining together of apparently different elements. The concept which underlies the approach is that an individual's creative mental ability is part of his/her subconscious and it seeks, therefore, to bring these thoughts out into the open as it were for identification and exploration.

The process seeks by a number of different mechanisms to make 'the strange familiar' (to put group participants at ease with what they don't *at first* understand) and 'the familiar strange' (to assist group participants to take a new look at old ways/ideas/concepts).

For a fuller coverage of the technique the reader is referred to the author of this approach: W J J Gordon (see Further reading).

Repertory grid technique

This is a simple means of finding out what a person thinks about an issue. It is potentially very powerful because it elicits constructs or scales by a special method which encourages the person to think hard about how he/she views things.

It has numerous applications in business, particularly in identifying and screening innovative ideas, including:

- the analysis of markets to identify new opportunities;
- conducting quantitative marketing and advertising research;
- the selection of experimental locations for test marketing;
- quality control work for production and processes, involving reliance on systematic, subjective and/or expert judgement.

For further guidance in the applications of this technique see Stewart V and Stewart A; and Jankowicz A D (see Further reading for details).

The suggestion box

A very simple idea for giving even the lowest operative in the organisation an opportunity to submit ideas for consideration.

FILTERING IDEAS

The potential for generating ideas is unlimited. However, the number of products which eventually make it to the market place, out of the many originally proposed, will be a very small fraction of that number indeed. Even then, the product idea, however original, is not quite ready to be declared a 'winner'. The consumer is the ultimate judge. The process of filtering is represented very simply in Figure 26.7 At every stage the entrepreneurial project team may abandon a product idea (no go), proceed with the idea (on), or ultimately launch the idea (go).

Process 1	Many product ideas are identified from sundry sources (based on existing bank of knowledge)
Process 2	Screening — ideas are screened to identify and eliminate bad ones as early as possible and avoid costs of further processing
	Note: An organisation must take care not to drop or adopt product ideas too quickly lest potentially good ones be lost and bad ones retained
Process 3	Product concept development and testing — the creation of an *image or idea* of the product for consumer tests
Process 4	Product development — a prototype?
Process 5	Product testing — technical feasibility — does it do what it claims?
Process 6	Test marketing — introduction of product into selected markets — feedback on market's reaction
Process 7	Commercial launch — broader based marketing campaign based on results from market test
Process 8	Consumer acceptance?

Figure 26.7   Filtering product ideas

It is preferable from a cost point of view to filter out those products 'least likely to succeed' at the screening stage. The cost of processing an idea mounts with each successive stage and the need for a 'success' becomes even more urgent — such urgency can cloud judgement and lead to serious mistakes.

Whether to proceed with a particular product idea depends on:

- the characteristics of the target market for the product, for example:
  - its size, segments, demography
  - its growth potential
  - its accessibility
  - the competition
  - the organisation's current position in the market;
- the implications of producing the product, for example:
  - characteristics, size, raw materials, functions
  - can it be improved/does it work better?

- is technology in the area stable?
- can it be produced 'in house'?
- implications of producing 'in house'?
● the financial implications, for example:
  - costs of production: plant (expansion of, location of), equipment, raw materials, skilled personnel (recruitment and/or training of), operational overheads
  - return on investment – the value and time scale *vis-à-vis* the risk element.

Marshalling your subjective judgement

This is an elementary way of carrying out product screening in a simple framework. It can be applied as a means of filtering out very marginal product ideas. Much more exhaustive research would be needed before deciding to 'go' on a product idea. Figure 26.8 offers a framework for such screening.

Criteria	Weighting 1 to 5	Product X		Product Y	
		Rating	Score	Rating	Score

Figure 26.8   Framework for screening

How to carry out product screening

1 Decide what criteria are relevant to you in evaluating any business idea, i.e.
   - that the market should be growing
   - that the market should be free from seasonality or

- that the product should be produced 'in house'
- that the technology should be stable or
- that the capital investment be low
- that the payback be rapid.

2 Weight these criteria to show their relative importance (e.g. from a scale of 1 to 5).

3 Rate each product idea using your best judgement (e.g. on a scale from -3 to $+3$)

4 Multiply each *rating* by the appropriate weighing to produce a series of scores.

5 Sum the scores to produce a net score. This should help in a number of ways, e.g.
   - Has your idea a positive score? It should.
   - Which ideas score highest? Prioritise.
   - Have you identified gaps in your knowledge that you need to fill? List them.

CONCLUSION

The two most important aims of this chapter were: that managers should recognise that generating a creative and innovative environment throughout the organisation is an important element in their strategic planning activity; and that they should critically appraise their organisation's encouragement of and involvement in this activity to date in order to highlight the areas for improvement. They have been introduced to a few of the ways to do this throughout the chapter.

The environment of any organisation will influence the behaviour of people within it. If you enter a church the appropriate behaviour is one of reverence. On the other hand, if you enter a sports hall, the environment is one of competition, energy and excitement. How would you appraise the environment in your organisation? How does it influence the people who work within it?

A final thought; once a manager decides that 'he has made it at last' in terms of success, he's in trouble and, like the dinosaurs of old, his organisation will soon be extinct. Open communications, association and interaction in an environment which fosters dissatisfaction with the status quo is a recipe for continued creative growth.

FURTHER READING

Gordon, W J J, *Synectics, The Development of Creative Capacity*, Harper and Row, 1961

Stewart, V and Stewart, A, *Business Applications of Repertory Grid*, McGraw-Hill, 1982

Jankowicz, A D, *Gridmap Suite, Manual for the BBC Micro Computer Based Repertory Grid Counselling*, Shannon Software, Plassey Technological Park, Limerick, Ireland, 1985

Rawlinson, J Geoffrey, *Creative Thinking and Brainstorming*, Gower, 1981

27

Decision making and problem solving

Peter Walker

The fortunes of large corporations depend on the quality of decisions made by their management. Despite this, many managers have little formal training in decision making and little understanding of how they finally arrived at a decision and made a choice.

Certainly, literature is available on many specific techniques which can aid decision making, but to be useful these techniques must be applied within an overall framework. The purpose of this chapter is to look at such an overall framework which may be used to make any decision.

Effective decision making will often require inputs from problem solving and contingency planning and hence these processes are also discussed. Because creativity is required in all the other processes it is also referred to.

DECISION MAKING, PROBLEM SOLVING, CONTINGENCY PLANNING AND CREATIVITY

The purpose of decision making is to make the best possible choice, based on sound information. However, if the information is either inaccurate or incomplete, the decision may fail. The purpose of problem solving and contingency planning is to improve the quality of information being processed.

Problem solving looks at the past with the purpose of understanding the causes of any problem that needs correcting. Contingency planning looks to the future with the purpose of anticipating future problems.

Problem solving, when required, must precede decision making because the decision must be based on the best understanding of the past and present situation. In contrast, contingency planning will be conducted after a decision has been made in order to refine or improve the chosen course of action before implementation.

Thus decision making can be seen as the process of bridging from the past to the future when the manager wants to change the present (see Figure 27.1).

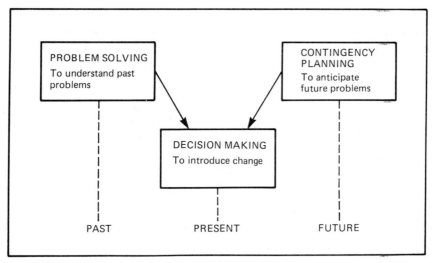

Figure 27.1 Relationship of decision making with problem solving and contingency planning
The causes of past problems and an understanding of possible future problems are information necessary for an effective decision.

CREATIVITY

Applied creativity is essential to each of the three processes outlined above. For example, creativity will be needed in problem solving to develop possible causes of problems. It may also be needed in decision making to develop new alternatives or solutions from which to choose. In contingency planning, creativity will be used to develop ideas about future problems which could occur and possible reasons for those problems.

There are several techniques to enhance creativity, of which brainstorming is the best known. However, one thing which is common to these techniques is that judgement is suspended while the new ideas are being generated. In other words, we should not try to both create and evaluate an idea simultaneously. Rather we should create first and evaluate second.

This is illustrated in Figure 27.2 where a concern is used to focus on creative generation of possible approaches to resolving that concern. Next, an analytical approach is used to select and implement the best approach to reach a solution.

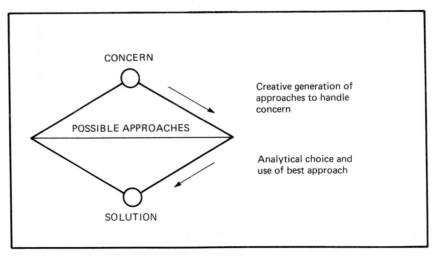

Figure 27.2   Separation of creativity and analysis

A simple example of this could be the situation in which you need to establish a rapid transport link between two towns. As a result of creative thinking the following 'possible approaches' might be generated:

- scheduled airlines
- private helicopter
- private car
- carrier company
- railway transport.

Evaluation of these ideas is delayed until after they have all been generated, when criteria such as cost, time, reliability etc. can be used to evaluate them and a detailed schedule established for the chosen means of transport.

Each of the processes of problem solving, decision making and contingency planning use this two-step approach where ideas are first generated and then analysed and it is this separation of creativity and analysis which helps to make the process so effective.

Where the phrase 'brainstorm ideas' is used in this chapter it means 'creatively generate new ideas without stopping to criticise or evaluate at this stage'.

PROBLEM SOLVING

The purpose of problem solving is to discover what caused a current situation, so that this knowledge may be used to decide how to handle it. If the causes are already fully understood, or there is no desire for change, there is no need for problem solving.

The formal use of problem solving is badly neglected for the simple reason that many managers fail to recognise that their problems require analysis. Rather, when something goes wrong they make an assumption about the cause and then act upon that assumption without checking it. If the assumption is correct then all is well, but too often the hoped-for improvement fails to occur and this triggers another idea on problem cause which is once again acted upon. In this way time, effort and resources may be wasted while the problem continues.

The definition of a problem

We have a problem when 'an object or a system has a defect and the cause of that defect is unknown'. In turn a defect can be defined as a deviation in performance from the required standard (see Figure 27.3). The first step in problem solving is to write down a problem statement. This is particularly important in group problem solving when agreement on the statement ensures a common understanding of the problem. A good problem statement will be a short sentence which specifies the object and its defect.

Thus, for example, if the floor in part of the factory becomes particularly dirty and the reason for this is unknown, then the problem statement could simply be: 'Floor in area B gets dirty'. Note that the required standard is that the floor should be 'clean'.

A common mistake is to phrase the problem statement in terms of the expected solution. Thus an incorrect problem statement would be: 'How to clean the floor in area B'.

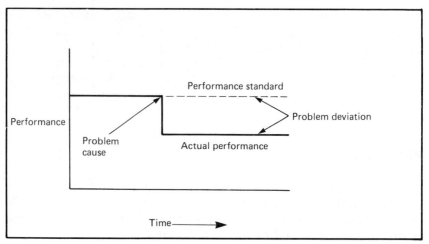

Figure 27.3   Deviation diagram
Note: The deviation could be a step function as shown or a gradual deterioration.

Use of the incorrect problem statement will focus people's thinking on solutions about how to clean the floor while at the same time tending to exclude the types of solutions aimed at preventing the floor becoming dirty in the first place. Certainly the group will give little thought to *why* the floor is getting dirty.

Getting to the root cause

Often problem solving will not stop when the immediate cause of the problem has been uncovered. Rather the cause of the immediate problem can become the focus of further problem solving to uncover the cause of the cause.

For example, the initial problem might be 'sales revenue below target'. Investigation shows the cause of this to be poor sales of product X. In turn, poor sales of product X are caused by a salesman leaving the company as the result of bad supervision. This can be illustrated in Figure 27.4.

Of course we can go further than 'bad supervision' and ask what caused the supervisor to perform poorly. The point at which we stop and cut the cause – effect chain is when we reach a cause where we can take effective action. For instance, if only one supervisor is performing badly we may choose to replace him while if a number of supervisors were inadequate we might need to go back further and find out why.

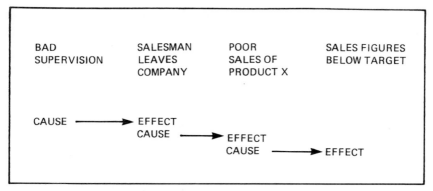

Figure 27.4 Cause/effect staircase

Methods of problem solving

Brainstorming

Used on its own this is the simplest technique for generating ideas on the cause of a problem. Here the problem solving group simply generates a list of possible causes which are written down without criticism by the group leader for all to see. Ideas from one person trigger other ideas from group members. In this way a very comprehensive list of possible causes can be generated which significantly increases the possibility that the true cause will be recognised.

The weakness of this approach is that it offers no way to test the ideas that are generated, and also there is no segregation of causes from causes-of-causes.

In the previous example, brainstorming would show 'bad supervision' and 'salesman leaves company' both as causes of 'below sales target' rather than 'bad supervision' as the cause of 'salesman leaving'. However, it is possible to reorganise the brainstormed list after it has been generated to identify causes-of-causes.

The Ishikawa Diagram

Sometimes called the 'Fishbone' or 'Cause and effect' diagram this is widely used in the quality circles movement.

It provides a simple way to structure brainstorming of problem causes in a manner which has a good visual impact and also segregates each level of cause from the preceding one, by introducing a branch in the diagram between each effect and its cause. It is common to start the diagram by assuming that all causes can be included under the headings of manpower, methods, machines and materials. This is

513

illustrated in Figure 27.5. The Ishikawa Diagram also has the weakness that it offers no way to test the ideas that are generated.

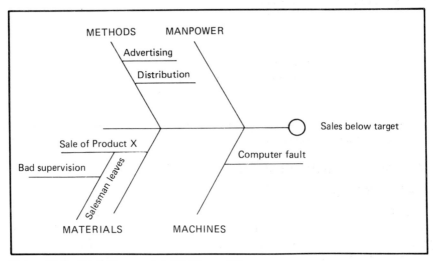

Figure 27.5   Partially completed Ishikawa Diagram

Difference analysis

This provides an analytical approach to problem solving which has a number of advantages compared with simple brainstorming and Ishikawa Diagrams. It provides a structured method for collecting information which:

- narrows the area within which the problem cause may lie and hence provides a focus for brainstorming possible causes;
- helps identify missing information which may be important;
- aids the process of disproving possible causes which are in fact incorrect.

However, while the method has significant advantages over other problem solving techniques, it is also more difficult to use and requires practice to become proficient. Working with a skilled consultant or attending a training course are probably the simplest ways to acquire the skill and get feedback on how to improve.

The principle behind difference analysis is however quite simple. If an object has a defect, then by definition it is not performing to the expected standard. The reason you believe the expected standard to be 'expected' or 'reasonable' is because somewhere, at some time, you have seen the problem object or something similar to the problem object meet the expected standard or a similar standard.

If you have a new and unique object that has never performed to the required standard then it is important to ask if the standard is reasonable and realistic. If you decide the standard is reasonable, the judgement will be based on your experience of the most similar object and situation you know. Thus if you have two identical objects in identical siuations, then by definition they must behave in an identical manner.

Hence the statement 'this object has a fault' means that it must in some way be *different* from a similar object without a fault, and further the difference provides us with a clue about why the fault exists.

Putting it another way, this means that when we are looking for the cause of a problem we can eliminate from consideration all those features of the faulty object which are identical with objects not having the fault.

This is exactly what the service engineer does when repairing faulty equipment. If when he looks at the faulty equipment he can see anything which is different from the way he knows good equipment to be then he will focus on that difference in looking for the cause of the fault.

The principle is obvious in the case of the service engineer, and when we are problem solving in a familiar situation we instinctively use the technique. We have a clear mental image of a non-defective object which we use to identify (and hence examine) differences which exist in the defective object compared to the non-defective object.

The principle may be illustrated by the following example. A hotel has purchased new cups and saucers. Afer a while the hotel manager notices that the new cups are getting chipped more frequently than the old ones used to, and also more frequently than the new saucers.

To learn more about the chipping he may compare the new cups with the old cups. Also he may compare the new cups with the new saucers. Dependent upon this comparison he may identify a number of things which are unique or different about the new cups, i.e. shape and decoration. Using 'shape and decoration' as a focus for further examination he may find that the new shape results in the cups knocking together in the dishwasher and hence chipping. Here a *change* (i.e. the dishwasher action) has acted on a *difference* (the cup shape) to cause the *problem effect* (cup chipping).

515

This is illustrated in Figure 27.6 where the 'set of objects with the problem' are the new cups and the 'set of objects without the problem' can be taken as the old cups. Then one of the 'differences unique to the problem set' is the new cup shape. Because the dishwasher action affects or acts upon the *difference* (i.e. the new cup shape) it may be the cause of the problem. Note that it is irrelevant whether or not the dishwasher action also affects features common to objects without the problem.

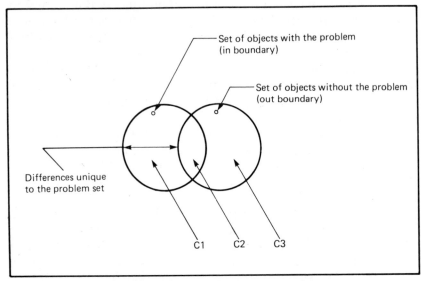

Figure 27.6   Differences unique to the problem set lead us to problem cause
C1 is a change that acts on a difference unique to the problem set, while C2 is a change acting on features common to both problem and non-problem sets and C3 is a change which acts on differences unique to the non-problem set. Here C1 is the only change which *may* be the cause of the problem because it is the only change acting on something which is *different* about those objects which exhibit the problem.

As a shorthand, we will talk about objects within the problem set as being 'in boundary' while any object not having the problem is 'out boundary', or outside the boundary of the problem set.

It will be clear from the above example that the technique of difference analysis is most obvious and easy to apply when we have very similar objects 'in boundary' compared to objects 'out boundary'. This is because the number of differences will be small and hence they should lead us quickly to the cause of the problem.

Thus the 'old cups' are probably a more useful 'out boundary' set than the 'new saucers' and both are clearly more useful than knives or forks, both of which are valid 'out boundary' sets but too far removed from the problem set (i.e. too many differences) to be really useful.

However, even when a close 'out boundary' set cannot be found, the method can be remarkably successful if systematic questioning is used to uncover the differences.

When looking for useful 'out boundary' sets look for the element of surprise. If you are surprised that the old cups chip less often than the new, then they are likely to be useful in the difference analysis. Because you are less surprised that the knives or forks don't chip then they are likely to be less useful.

Good questioning skills are crucial in the effective use of difference analysis. Rudyard Kipling summed it up in the following verse:

> I keep six honest serving men
> (They taught me all I knew);
> Their names are What and Why and When
> And How and Where and Who.

In order to uncover all the differences between the 'in boundary' problem and the 'out boundary' situation where the problem does not exist, questions must be asked systematically to cover all aspects of the case.

A common sequence in which to ask the questions is as follows:

- What − what is the object with which we are having difficulty?
  − what is the defect?
- Where − where is the object when the difficulty is first seen?
  − where on the object is the defect?
- When − when (time and date) does the problem occur?
  − when in the object's life cycle does the problem occur?
- How much − how much of the object is affected by the problem?
  − is there a pattern to the defects?

The full set of questions which must be asked is shown on the problem solving worksheet Figure 27.7. To explore the problem in sufficient depth, follow-up questions should also be asked to each of the questions shown.

For example, if we ask 'where are the chipped cups first seen?' the

PROBLEM SOLVING WORKSHEET			PROBLEM STATEMENT: *New cups chipping*	
	In boundary	Out boundary	What is different in the boundary?	Have any changes occurred related to these differences?
What object	What is the object with which you are having difficulty? *New cups*	With what other objects would you expect to have a similar problem, but are not? *Old cups* *New saucers*	Is there any feature which is common to the objects in boundary, which is in no way true of objects outside the boundary? *Shape* *Decoration*	*New shape and decoration on cups introduced one month ago*
What problem	What problem is occurring that should not be occurring? *Chipping*	What other problems might you expect to have with the object but have not? *Large cracks*	What is peculiar about the problem in boundary which doesn't apply to problems outside boundary?	
Where	Where geographically is the object when the problem is seen? *Preparation area for laying tables*	Where geographically might the problem be expected to occur but is not seen? *Laid tables*	Is there anything peculiar to the place in boundary which doesn't relate to other places outside boundary? *Washing and storage*	
	Where is the problem seen on the object? *Rim*	Where on the object might the problem be expected to occur but is not seen? *Handle* *Base*	Is there anything peculiar to the part of the object in boundary which doesn't relate to other parts outside boundary? *Thinnest part*	
When	When do these problems occur in calendar or clock time (not relative to events)? *Last month*	When might they occur but do not? *Before this*	Is there anything happening during the time in boundary which doesn't apply to any other stages outside boundary? *New cups introduced*	*Introduced one month ago*
	Within what stages (parts) of the life cycle do these problems occur? *After washing*	Within what stages might you have expected the problem but have not found it? *After evening clear up* *Before dishwasher loading*	What is peculiar about stages in boundary which doesn't apply to any other stages outside boundary? *Dishwasher action* *Dishwasher loading procedure*	*Dishwasher action* *Dishwasher loading procedure*
How much	How much of the object is affected by the problem? *10% of all new cups* *One or two chips per cup*	How much of the object might you expect to be affected but is not? *100% of all new cups* *Multiple chips*	What is peculiar to the affected area in boundary which does not apply to areas outside boundary?	
	How frequently do the problems occur? *One or two per day*	How frequently might the problems occur but do not? *Weekends only*	What is significant about the frequency in boundary which wouldn't apply to other frequencies outside boundary?	
	What is the trend of these occurrences? *Level at one or two per day*	What trend might normally have been expected but does not occur? *Varies with people on shift*	Is there anything significant about the trend in boundary which wouldn't apply to other trends outside boundary?	

Figure 27.7 Problem solving worksheet
A partially completed worksheet illustrating its use on the problem of the chipping cups.
Note: Everything changes with time. This means that any time differences (like dishwasher action) are automatically repeated in the changes column.

answer may be 'preparation area'. This leads us into the follow-up question of 'where in the preparation area are the chipped cups seen?' By narrowing down the area in which the problem is known to exist we eliminate equipment, personnel etc. not used in this more narrowly defined area.

At some point the follow-up questions will become so detailed that we don't have the requested information. If we still lack sufficient information to determine problem cause, then the follow-up questions point to the additional information required. When we have sufficient information, the 'differences' column will lead to a solution.

As we saw earlier the problem cause must be a 'change' acting on a 'difference'. Hence we can first identify 'changes' to the 'differences' and then identify which of those changes could be the problem cause. In practice people often find it helpful to simply use the 'differences' and 'changes' columns as a focus for brainstorming possible causes.

If we have an object that has always been defective, or defective over the time period that information has been available to us, then the 'changes' column will not help us and we must brainstorm problem cause from the 'differences' column only.

Disproving possible causes

Following brainstorming there will often be a significant list of possible problem causes with only one of them being the true or correct cause.

Typically people only try to verify theories about cause by checking to see if they can cause the problem in the defective objects. This is only half the story. Another key test is to see if the theory can also explain why the problem does not occur in all those objects in 'out boundary'.

For example, our theory may be that high humidity has caused the sudden outbreak of rusting on metal parts in stores. A key question to ask is, 'how does the high humidity theory also explain why other metal parts in stores are free from rust?'

In general most people try to prove their theories correct by looking for supporting evidence which can only make the theory more probable. However, if you look for evidence to prove your theory wrong but cannot disprove it, then there is a good chance you may be correct.

The method of trying to disprove possible causes is as follows. Each of the possible causes from the brainstormed list is examined in turn against the 'in boundary' and the 'out boundary' information. For each piece of 'in boundary' information we ask 'can the cause explain why we see that this problem exists in this way?' and for the 'out boundary' information we ask 'can this cause explain why this problem does not exist in this situation?' Any possible cause which cannot explain all the facts may be rejected, leaving perhaps one or two possible causes to be checked out through actual test.

Separation of individual problems is necessary in difference analysis because it is an analytical process designed to link a specific cause to a specific problem. This can be contrasted with simple brainstorming or Ishikawa Diagrams which may link a number of causes to a generalised problem.

For example, if you have an ongoing reject rate of 5 per cent in a production process (due to machine tolerances) which suddenly jumps to a total of 12 per cent (caused by a batch of faulty materials) then you have two problems.

Thus if you brainstormed the general problem of 12 per cent reject rate, both 'machine tolerances' and 'faulty materials' could appear on the list and be seen to contribute to the overall problem.

However, with difference analysis the problems of 5 per cent reject and 7 per cent reject should be treated separately or the information on one problem will blur the information on the other, i.e. it is more difficult to link the start of the 7 per cent problem to the receipt of the faulty materials, when our information also shows rejects occurring (due to the 5 per cent problem) before the faulty material was received.

While a simple problem may not require completion of a formal worksheet as shown in Figure 27.7, it is always worth checking what we believe to be problem cause by mentally checking if it explains all the 'in boundary' and 'out boundary' information we can think of.

DECISION MAKING

To be successful a decision must have:

- Rational quality – to the extent that there is a difference between the available choices it will be important that the alternative offering the most benefit is chosen.
- Commitment to implement – to the extent that the commitment of the people involved is necessary for effective implementation, it will be important to gain that commitment.

When choosing who to involve in a decision, you should consider who can contribute to requirements for quality and commitment. Although most managers give overriding consideration to achieving a high quality decision, more decisions probably fail through lack of a real commitment to follow them through and make them work.

The decision making process described here is ideal for use

individually or with a group. Because it offers a clear and logical approach to selecting a high quality decision while actively involving the group in the decision making process it is also excellent as a means of gaining group commitment.

Every decision will contain three elements:

- objectives – or the things we wish to achieve as a result of the decision;
- alternatives – or the choices available to us;
- risks – or the uncertainty that a particular alternative will actually deliver the objectives we want or has unplanned side effects.

The ideal decision maker will be someone who clearly identifies his objectives, creatively generates new choices or ways of meeting those objectives, and is prepared to make choices involving risk where the benefit/risk pay-off of a choice makes it the most appropriate solution.

However, our flesh and blood manager frequently behaves very differently from the ideal model. Typically he adopts an approach which may be called incremental analysis in which he moves a minimum distance from the existing situation when change is required.

First he may have no clear idea of his objectives. Rather he finds that something has gone wrong and he simply wishes to get out of trouble or make some improvement. Thus he is looking for an acceptable rather than the best solution.

Next he may have spent little time creatively generating new approaches with the result that the choices available to him only represent small changes to the existing situation.

Finally, he may not be working in an environment in which risk taking is encouraged. Too many people may have an investment in the current situation and be unwilling to exchange it for the uncertain future associated with a significantly different approach.

The process for decision making discussed helps to overcome these difficulties because it is structured in the following way. It starts with a discussion of the objectives (rather than an argument over the alternatives). By doing this we can:

- improve understanding of what an ideal solution could achieve;
- generate commitment to more than a minimum solution;
- avoid the politics of 'hidden objectives' because every individual knows that an undeclared objective will not be available to give weight to his choice at a later stage.

Following agreement on the objectives, a brainstorming session can take place to creatively generate new solutions or choices if this appears appropriate (i.e. existing choices appear lacking in some respect). The brainstorming can be creative and avoid criticism because it is understood that evaluation against objectives is the next step.

After alternatives have been generated they are scored against each objective in turn with the purpose of finding the maximum overall benefit (achievement of objectives). This avoids the 'information overload' and fruitless argument that can result from a direct overall comparison of alternatives against each other.

Having identified the alternative which offers the best overall benefit we then evaluate that alternative for risks. What are the unknowns and what could go wrong if that choice were adopted? If the alternative offering the best benefit also has significant risk, then other alternatives must be evaluated and the one offering the best risk/benefit pay-off chosen. This allows an open discussion on the level of risk people are prepared to accept.

Decision level

Decisions can occur at three levels and it is important to be clear at what level you are acting.

Decisions you can make are those decisions where you have the authority to act.

Decisions you can recommend are those decisions where you can only recommend to the person having the authority to act.

Decisions you must accept are those decisions made by others which will not be changed by any recommendation of yours. Here you can only make subsidiary decisions on how to come to terms with a situation which will not change.

If we try to act at too high a level then time is wasted in planning a decision that will not be acted upon. If we act at too low a level then we may be accepting unnecessary constraints which result in a sub-optimum choice.

The decision statement

The decision making process should start with a single-sentence decision statement to specify the decision to be made. Care should be taken to ensure that the decision level is correct and that there are no unnecessary modifiers. Take for example the decision statement, 'Buy a new car for my wife'. Is the word 'new' an unnecessary modifier and would you consider a second hand car? Do you really have the power to act or will your wife be unhappy if you choose a car for her, without her involvement?

Decision objectives

The extent to which an alternative meets an objective is the benefit that the alternative provides. In addition some objectives may have limits which must not be violated or the decision will have failed.

For example, if you can raise a maximum of £10,000 to buy a car but you would like to buy as cheaply as possible, then the benefit graph would look as in Figure 27.8.

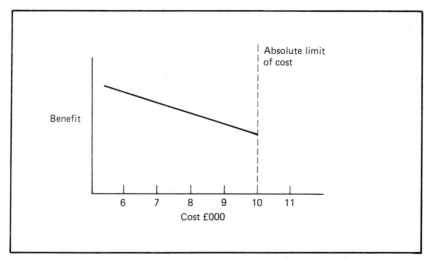

Figure 27.8   A benefit graph for car cost
Within a defined limit there is a relationship between cost and benefit. Beyond this limit the graph is discontinuous and no effective decision can be made.

By breaking the cost requirement into two parts it can be described as follows: essential objective − cost not to exceed £10,000; and desirable objective − cost to be as low as possible. However, not every requirement will have an essential and desirable objective within it.

For example, we order from a supplier a shipment of goods, but our plant is shut down until 10 August and our customer contract will be cancelled if the goods are not available by 20 August. Between 10–20 August it makes no difference when the goods are received. In this case we only need specify an essential objective, i.e. delivery must be between 10–20 August.

Note that if it were an advantage to have the goods early then there would also be a desirable objective – 'Goods delivered as soon as possible after 10 August'.

An example of a desirable only objective could be the plant colour scheme, i.e. – colour scheme liked by staff and promotes effective work practice. While it is possible to imagine a colour scheme so grotesque that people stop working or leave the company it is so unlikely that an essential objective need not be framed in these terms.

Setting objectives

The first step is to brainstorm all the possible objectives and examine them to ensure that all aspects of the decision are covered. Next examine the objectives for overlap and combine any objectives which are saying the same thing in different ways. Next, separate the objectives into those which are essential and those which are desirable.

Essential objectives should then be worded so that the limit is clear and measurable, because it will be important to know if an essential objective has been violated and that choice is a 'no go'.

Desirable objectives should be worded so that it is clear how alternatives can be measured against those objectives.

The achievement of some objectives will be more important than that of others and it will be necessary to weight the objectives so that the final choice will be focused on satisfying the most important objectives.

The method of weighting desirable objectives is chosen for two practical considerations:

- People are much better at making comparative than absolute judgements. For example few people have 'perfect pitch' and can tell you the frequency of a musical note. However most people can tell if one note is higher or lower than another.
- The ability to discriminate is limited and the weighting scale used must be comparable with our ability to use that scale. A scale of 1–10 appears practical and convenient.

In order to weight the desirable objectives, first identify the most important desirable objective and 'benchmark' it with a weighting of 10. Each of the other desirable objectives is then compared with the benchmark and given a weighting from 1 – 10 dependent upon how important it is seen compared with the benchmark.

It is quite acceptable to have two or more objectives with the same weighting. Be careful not to finish up with a large number of low weighted objectives which in total outweigh a single high weighted objected which is in fact more important.

Below is an example of what our objectives might be if we were considering a job offer.

Essential objectives
    Salary greater than £18,000
    House move not necessary

Desirable objectives	Wt
Offers interesting work	10
Salary as high as possible	8
Opportunities for advancement	4

Note that if you only have one job offer then you are faced with a binary decision so that you can either accept or refuse that offer. Your decision will depend upon how well your present job and the offer compare against the objectives.

Observe also how the essential objectives are clearly measurable, allowing a determination of whether an alternative meets the requirements and is a 'go' or 'no go'.

Generating alternatives

In some situations the alternatives are fixed and there is no need to pursue new, or attempt to improve existing ones. Choosing a new car might be an example where you are limited by what is available on the market within your price range, and generating additional alternatives will not be possible.

If none of the alternatives available meets your needs very well this is an indication that you should look for new ideas. Even if existing alternatives are satisfactory this should not blind you to the possibility of an even better alternative.

Brainstorming or other creativity techniques may be used to generate new alternatives, using your objectives as a focus for creating the new ideas.

525

Evaluating alternatives

Once alternative solutions have been identified they must be evaluated against the objectives to determine which one offers the most benefit. First, any alternative which fails to meet an essential objective can be eliminated. Second, all the alternatives should be scored against each objective in turn.

Say for example you have received four job offers and were evaluating the salary objective, then the evaluation might be as in Figure 27.9.

Objective	Job 1	Job 2	Job 3	Job 4
Salary as high as possible	Salary offer £17,500 Score N/A	Salary offer £18,500 Score 6	Salary offer £19,000 Score 8	Salary offer £20,000 Score 10

Figure 27.9 Evaluating job offers

Note that the job offering £17,500 has been eliminated because it does not achieve the minimum requirement of £18,000.

Note also that the score need not have a simple relationship to salary, i.e. because of current debts, house mortgage or other reasons, a salary of £19,000 might be much more valuable than a salary of £18,500, while a salary of £20,000 might be only marginally more useful than £19,000. The question the score should be answering is what does this (salary) mean to me? What is it worth?

Also be careful to ensure that what you measure is what you want. For example, if one job also offers a car, will you give that a cash value and add it to salary? If another job involves a long journey to work will you deduct travel costs to determine net salary?

Once the alternatives have been scored for an objective the weighted scores are calculated as a product of the objective weighting and the alternative score. Thus, where the salary objective has a weighting of 8 we get weighted scores for salaries in each job as in Figure 27.10

By summing up the weighted scores that an alternative has for each of the objectives we come up with an overall score which represents the 'benefit' delivered by that alternative.

Objectives	Job 2	Job 3	Job 4
Highest salary possible	Salary: £18,500 Score 6	Salary. £19,000 Score 8	Salary: £20,000 Score 10
Objective wt 8	Weighted score: 48	Weighted score: 64	Weighted score: 80

Figure 27.10   Weighted scores for salaries in each job

The alternative with the highest score is then the 'best initial choice'. This is illustrated in the case study which follows, 'Choosing an office copier' and the worksheet in Figure 27.11 which shows the Premiere copy machine being the initial choice with a score of 180.

Risks

When we make a decision, our initial choice is based on what we think is most likely to happen if the alternatives were implemented. However, making any choice involves some risk. The choice we make might not work out the way we expect, or its introduction may have unplanned side effects. Thus we have to make a final decision based on the benefits and the risks of the alternatives.

We all take some risks, and will for example cross a road without concern despite the risk of death associated with a car accident. When crossing the road the high seriousness of an accident is offset by the low probability of its occurrence.

As traffic builds up, accident probability increases and we delay crossing for a while. At the other extreme, people will risk a high probability loss (of cash) in a fruit machine because the seriousness of that loss is low.

Hence the size of a risk (and our willingness to accept it) is a function of probability (of occurrence) and seriousness (if it does occur).

When evaluating risk the elements of probability and seriousness may be conveniently evaluated on a three-point scale of high, medium and low. Risks with high probability and seriousness will be most significant, while those with a low probability or low seriousness will be the least significant. If the initial choice also has little risk then clearly it is the one to adopt.

DECISION MAKING WORKSHEET

Decision statement: Choose an office copier

OBJECTIVES	Wt.	Zenith MK 1 Info.	Go/No	Wt.Sc.	Premiere Info.	Go/No	Wt.Sc.	Alpha Copy King Info.	Go/No	Wt.Sc.
Essential										
Delivery by 1 June		Ex stock	Go		Promised 30 May	Go		Immediate delivery	Go	
Plain paper, judged acceptable by user for customer use		Yes	Go		Yes	Go		Zinc oxide paper	No Go	
Down time 2 days maximum		Contract available	Go		Contract available	Go				
Desirable	Wt.	Info.	Sc.	Wt.Sc.	Info.	Sc.	Wt.Sc.	Info.	Sc.	Wt.Sc.
Lowest cost	10	£2800	10	100	£3200	8	80			
Minimum down time	8	Replacement service	7	56	Good repair service	10	80			
Reduction capability	2	No	0	0	3 reductions	10	20			
INITIAL CHOICE (TOTAL)				156	Initial choice		180			
RISKS			Pr.	Se.		Pr.	Se.		Pr.	Se.
Probability/					Missed delivery date	M	H			
Seriousness					Dealer bankrupt	M	H			
FINAL CHOICE		Best overall choice								

Figure 27.11 A convenient format for information when making a decision

However, if the initial choice has significantly more benefit than the others but also has substantial risk, then the final choice is more difficult. Here we need to ask two questions: is this a level of risk I would be prepared to accept in any circumstances? and is this a level of risk which is justified by the superior benefits of this alternative?

If the risks associated with the first initial choice are too great then the next alternative must be evaluated, and so on.

Some people are temperamentally greater risk takers than others and there is no correct degree of risk to accept. Thus risk cannot be subtracted from benefit in a mathematical sense to arrive at the best overall choice. Rather the final choice is a matter of judgement.

While an effective manager may be a high risk taker he will also work to reduce risk to a minimum in a given situation and only take risks to achieve worthwile benefits.

An example of where risks may rule out an alternative is given in the case study which follows. In Figure 27.11 it can be seen that the Alpha Copy King has been eliminated because it does not use plain paper. The Premiere is the initial choice because it offers the best overall benefit (i.e. a score of 180). However the Premiere also has risks of missed delivery and bankrupt dealer which are both seen as medium probability with a high seriousness and which are not outweighted by its marginal advantage. Hence the Zenith Mk1 offers the best overall choice.

Case study – choosing an office copier

Imagine you have just opened a branch office and need to purchase a small copier which is essential to the operation. While cost is a major consideration you will have to pay what it takes to get one. The essential requirements are that it can be installed by 1 June, it must use plain paper and produce copies of a quality you believe can be sent to customers.

You require a minimum down time for repairs and it is essential that the copier is never unavailable for more than two days. Any down time will disrupt office routine to some extent.

While a reduction capability would be nice to have it would not be used very often; other special features are unnecessary as volume will be small. The following copy machines have been examined.

Zenith Mkl

This uses plain paper and is available ex stock at a price of £2,800. You have examined the copy quality and feel it is perfectly suitable to send to customers. From your past experience it is a reliable machine. However the manufacturer's service organisation can only offer you a next day repair service. However they have an excellent and reliable loan scheme which offers an immediate replacement machine if any repair exceeds 48 hours. This is a basic machine and offers no special features such as reduction capability.

The Premiere

This machine is new on the market and you are very impressed with the performance of the demonstration model which produces really first class plain paper copies. Because it is new, delivery is a problem and the dealer was very reluctant to commit to a 30 May delivery date. It will be repaired by an independent service organisation who can offer an excellent eight-hour repair time. However, you happen to know the service organisation is in financial difficulty and if it went bankrupt your repair contract with them would lapse. The machine has a number of features including three different reduction settings and looks good value at £3,200.

The Alpha Copy King

This produces clear, easily readable copies and at £1,600 it is by far the cheapest machine. The manufacturer has its own repair organis-ation and offers a 'guaranteed next day' repair service. Unfortunately the copier uses a special zinc oxide paper which is not of a quality suitable to send to customers. Immediate delivery is available.

CONTINGENCY PLANNING

When a choice is made the implementation of that choice can be seen as an action plan. Contingency planning is the process of protecting a plan against what might go wrong in future.

Without a plan, nothing can go wrong and hence contingency planning can only start once a plan has been developed (this is in contrast to problem solving which should occur first to provide the information needed to make a plan). Contingency planning may be needed because there is a weakness in a new plan or to protect an existing plan where the situation is changing . It can be seen as a number of brainstorming steps designed to uncover possible future problems which then become the focus of subsidiary plans to either prevent those problems occurring or to reduce their effects. Steps in contingency planning are as follows:

1   List all the steps in the plan and identify key areas which include unknowns or which are particularly critical to plan success.
2   Using 1 as a focus, brainstorm possible problems and then identify those on your list having a high seriousness and high probability of occurrence.
3   Using 2 as a focus, brainstorm possible causes of major problems and identify causes with a high probability of occurrence.
4   Develop plans aimed at preventing problem causes identified in 3 and which have a high probability of occurrence.
5   Using 2 as a focus identify problems still likely to occur (despite 3 and 4) and list the negative effects that would happen.
6   Develop plans to handle serious negative effects identified in 5. Ensure a warning mechanism if those effects could start suddenly or unexpectedly.

Because people are anxious for their plans to succeed, they often fail to examine them critically and hence miss flaws which could easily have been corrected. In the same way it is easy to be defensive about criticism of a plan rather than thinking how we can use the information to our advantage.

In contrast Napoleon is said to have mentally rehearsed every battle he fought weeks before the event. He would go over his own tactics, visualising the enemy defences, their reaction and the terrain.

In the same way we can significantly increase the success of our own plans by mentally rehearsing them both to eliminate possible problems and to prepare our defence should these problems arise.

FURTHER READING

Prince, George M, *The Practice of Creativity,* Macmillan, 1972

Kepner, Charles H and Tregoe, Benjamin B, *The Rational Manager,* McGraw-Hill, 1965

Yetton, P W and Vroom, V H, *Leadership and Decision Making,* University of Pittsburgh Press, 1973

Simon, H A, *The New Science of Decision Making,* Harper & Row, 1960

Buzan, Tony, *Use Your Head,* BBC Publications, 1974

Adair, John, *Management Decision Making,* Gower, 1985

28

Negotiating

Bill Scott

This chapter is in three parts. The first describes a style of negotiating designed to produce the greatest area of agreement in the joint interest of both parties. This is a pattern of negotiating in which the parties work together, creatively, *towards agreement*. The second pattern is one in which each party is concerned more with its own advantage than with the joint advantage. Goodwill and agreement are still important, but the overriding consideration is that which is *to independent advantage*. Third, when goodwill is not important, negotiations can sometimes deteriorate into a pattern of *fighting*.

NEGOTIATING TOWARDS AGREEMENT

When the parties are concerned to work together creatively towards agreement the key activities are exploration of each other's position, and creative recognition of what is in their joint interests.

Those phases of exploration and creativity, however, hinge on having first created a suitable climate and on having some procedure which helps the parties to work together. There is no cause for heavy use of negotiating tactics but there is a need for effective preparation.

The sequence in this section will therefore be:

- creating the climate
- opening procedure
- sequence in negotiations
- exploration
- creativity
- subsequent phases
- preparation.

Creating the climate

Negotiators usually operate best when the climate is brisk and businesslike. When negotiating towards agreement, they need a climate which is also cordial and cooperative.

The pace of a negotiation, be it brisk or lethargic, is set very early. Within seconds of the parties coming together, during the rituals of meeting and greeting, a pace is established which is durable. It should be a brisk pace — briskness established by the pace at which the parties are moving about and by the speed at which they are communicating.

The cordial character is established in an ice breaking phase. As the parties first meet and interact with one another, they need to adjust and to build their regard before getting into possibly controversial areas. The ice breaking, therefore, needs to be a period in which they focus on neutral topics — the football, the weather, the journey and so on.

The ice breaking is an essential preliminary, so important that it deserves possibly 5 per cent of the prospective negotiating time: a couple of minutes even at the outset of short negotiations; a preliminary dinner and evening out before protracted negotiations.

The brisk and cordial character is thus very soon established. The development of the businesslike and cooperative characteristics comes as the parties sit down and move towards business. Timing and the form of first remarks at the negotiating table should provide the right atmosphere: timing, by an immediate statement so that there is no long gap as members get seated; and the form of the opening remarks focusing on the business, towards agreement.

The cooperative character can be set too at this early stage. This depends on effectiveness in handling the opening procedure.

Opening procedure

There is nothing more likely to produce a cooperative atmosphere than the immediate question, on sitting down: 'Well gentlemen, can we first agree on procedure?'

Note that the word 'agree' is used at the outset. Note that the question is one which will most certainly produce the answer 'Yes'. Note that the two parties both establish the 'agree' mood from the outset.

There are four procedural items which should be explored and agreed in this opening stage — the four 'P's: pace, purpose, plan and personalities. The *pace* is the speed at which the parties need to move together. There needs to be harmony on this pace if parties are to work together effectively. There will not be such harmony if one believes that there is a whole afternoon available whereas the other has another engagement in half an hour.

The *purpose* is the reason why the parties are meeting. If one party thinks that the meeting is purely exploratory, while the other believes the purpose is to achieve a final settlement, then the parties are going to be working at cross-purposes.

Even when the purpose has been established in preliminary communication, it is still important at the outset to refresh the consciousness of that purpose. And to take the chance to emphasise that both parties *agree* on that purpose.

The *plan* should be in the form of a short agenda – some four main stages through which the meeting should move.

These first three 'P's – pace, purpose and plan – should be agreed at the outset of every negotiation. The fourth 'P' in the opening procedural stage is *personalities*: the introduction of members who do not know one another, their backgrounds, what they can contribute to the meeting. Skilfully used, this opening procedure has great advantages:

- The meeting can proceed with both parties recognising joint objectives and a joint means of moving forward.
- The plan gives a framework for control of the remainder of the meeting.
- The mood of agreement can be quickly stated and established.
- The groundwork is set for a smooth and cooperative entry into the later stages of the negotiation.

There is a consistent sequence in these later stages of any negotiation. The sequence is:

- exploration
- creativity
- shaping the deal
- bidding
- bargaining
- settling
- ratifying.

These phases are – or should be – found in any negotiation, even though they may sometimes become mixed and muddled. The importance of each phase varies a lot, however.

In negotiating towards agreement, the key phases are those of exploration and creativity.

Exploration

When two parties come together, each has its own distinctive view of the aims and possibilities for the negotiation. If the parties want to work together to bake the biggest possible cake, it is imperative that each should:

- recognise what both see in the same way;
- recognise and respect what others see in a different way; and
- be clear about the way in which their own interests are distinctive.

From such recognition can spring the creative spark of what is then most in their joint interests.

To achieve that recognition each party should independently make a broad statement of its own position, and give opportunity for the other to seek clarification. Then get a comparable 'broad picture' of the other party's position, and clarify that.

Each opening statement needs to cover:

- our understanding – the broad area within which we believe the negotiation will take place;
- our interests – what we would like to achieve through the negotiation;
- our priorities – what are the most important aspects for us;
- our contribution – the way in which we can help to our joint advantage;
- our attitudes – the consequence of our previous dealing with the other party; their reputation as it has come to us; any special hopes or fears which we may have for collaboration.

Characteristic of the opening statement are the following points:

- The opening statements of each party should be independent. Each should state its own position, and not attempt at this stage to state the joint interests of the two parties.
- They should not attempt to make assumptions about the position or interests of the other party. (The making of this assumption serves only to irritate, to confuse and to introduce disharmony.)
- The statements should be general, not detailed, not yet quantitative.

- The statements should be brief. Each should give the other party an opportunity to come into the discussion quickly, both so that the parties can quickly interact and so that others do not get a sense of being overwhelmed by either the duration or the complexity of an opening statement. Keep it short.

As one party makes its opening statement, the other party needs to listen, clarify and summarise.

Listen

Do not waste energy by thinking up counter-arguments.

Clarify

If in any doubt, question to get clear what he is trying to say. But note: question for clarification. Do not question for justification – that forces the other negotiator on to the defensive and runs counter to the creative climate being sought.

Summarise

Feed back the key points of what you understand him to be saying, so that he can check.

Having got clear the view of one party then comes the time for the other party to offer its own opening statement, and for first party's corresponding response – listen, clarify, summarise.

For really creative negotiations, there is a need for these opening exchanges to be carried through frankly in an environment of mutual trust and respect. For these reasons great attention has been paid to creating a positive climate and to underlining agreement and preparing minds in the opening process.

Skilled negotiators are skilled at giving and getting information. They are also conscious that some other parties will seek to exploit them. They therefore look out for danger signals which would suggest a need to change strategy.

If in the ice breaking, the other party insists on probing about business matters ('How's trade? cash flow? quality?') beware. Probably he is simply an unskilled negotiator, but possibly he is aggressive, seeking information that he can later use aggressively. If he is highly assertive in the phase of proposing and agreeing procedure – then again we must beware. An amber light is flashing.

If he is excessively anxious that we should be the first to make an opening statement, or in challenging that opening statement: then a further amber light is shown – indeed, this is virtually a red light.

Given a succession of amber lights, or just one red light, then the skilled negotiator will be prepared to change his strategy. He should seek a recess, even though it is still an early stage of the negotiation, reconsider the other party's behaviour and decide whether he needs to change to either of the strategies in later sections of this chapter.

But skilled negotiators practising this characteristic style of negotiating towards agreement can normally produce a positive response.

There is thus a great need for negotiators to develop the skills of creating a cooperative climate, of agreeing procedure, and of openness in the exploratory phase.

Creativity

Agreement-oriented negotiators now have a unique opportunity to achieve something to joint advantage, something bigger than either party could get when negotiating to independent advantage. This is the moment to be seeking together to bake the biggest possible cake.

To achieve that creativity they need first to be imaginative. Later they must impose the forces of reality, but the most productive of ideas may not be seen unless the parties are prepared to range as far as the borderline between reality and fantasy. Be imaginative.

Scandinavian negotiators have a special phrase to launch into this phase. Having summarised the respective positions of the parties as discussed in their opening statements, they say 'All right then – what are the creative possibilities?'

In looking for those creative possibilities there are a few guidelines:

- The pattern of generating the ideas must be broad in its sweep, and interdependent.
- It must be broad because immediately the parties focus on one suggestion (either criticising or exploring in depth), their minds cannot revert to broad and imaginative thinking.
- It must be interdependent, not only to sustain the cooperation between them but also because each fresh suggestion can kindle a new spark in the imagination of the other. The parties have great potential to be creative together.

This process on recognising creative possibilities should generate a number of different ideas. There then comes the need to form a bridge between the world in which the parties have been thinking imaginatively and the world of reality in which their performance must be measured by business criteria. They must decide which of their imaginative ideas offer realistic possibilities. They must then assess and agree on the action needed to turn possibility to mutual advantage.

Subsequent stages

The critical periods of negotiations towards agreement are the exploratory and creative phases. From them springs the recognition of mutual interest. There is, of course, need for the later realities to be foreseen, for agreement on the commercial conditions, and for the establishment of realistic plans to implement decisions. Given however the creative atmosphere, then views and possibilities for these commercial and planning discussions can be developed in a similarly open atmosphere.

The approach – 'Let us now explore together' – can be sustained through these later stages without the need to get into the tough bidding and bargaining encountered (and to be further discussed) in the context of other strategies.

However, before starting any negotiations, each party must arrive at the negotiating table well prepared.

Preparation

For any form of negotiation, the negotiator must have done his homework beforehand. He must know the facts, the figures, the arguments.

He needs also to have prepared in two other respects. First preparing for the procedure. He should think through the pace, purpose and plan which he will suggest for the meeting. And having thought them through, it is advisable to jot down the headlines of pace, purpose and plan on a postcard, to serve as a reminder during the meeting.

Second, he needs to have prepared his opening statement: his understanding of the matter for discussion, his interests, priorities, contribution, attitudes; and again, to jot the headlines on a postcard.

It is important, when negotiating towards agreement, not to over-prepare. The negotiator who has built a detailed framework of prices, deliveries and so on in his preparations is so mentally committed to those preparations that he obscures the possibilities for being creative in any wider sense.

To summarise, when their strategy is negotiating towards

agreement, the parties must first create a climate which is brisk, businesslike, cordial and cooperative. They must then establish and agree on a procedure helping them to work together effectively. From the opening procedural discussion they move into important exploratory and creative phases, and thereafter should be able to sustain the high cooperation already established. This must be founded on effective preparation by each party before the event.

NEGOTIATING TO INDEPENDENT ADVANTAGE

Different skills are needed when the negotiator is concerned with gaining special advantage for his party. In some ways these skills mirror those needed when negotiating towards agreement; in other ways, new and different skills are needed.

In particular bidding and bargaining become the crux of the negotiation. Early moves set the framework, and a different form of preparation is needed. The sequence of this section will therefore be:

- opening moves
- bidding
- bargaining
- preparation.

Opening moves

The negotiator working to independent advantage must approach the negotiation with a difference of attitude. No longer is his concern to work creatively together with the other party. Rather it is to establish the best deal in the interests of his own side.

Assuming however that the deal will need the other party's cooperation to be implemented, or that there will in due course be a need to negotiate some other deal with the same party, it is important that goodwill should be sustained. Aggressive tactics and power struggles should be avoided.

The negotiator's attitude should not be that he will work towards the other party's disadvantage. His attitude must be to find the best way to divide the cake to give satisfaction to both parties. If he likes icing more than fruit, and the other party likes fruit more than icing – there is no problem. Both sides can 'win'. The skilled negotiator thus works towards influencing the other party to value the fruit more than the icing.

The opening moves will again establish the climate for the meeting.

Because of the concern for sustaining goodwill it is again important that the climate should be brisk, businesslike, cordial and cooperative; and it is again important that procedure should be agreed at the outset.

Exploration now takes a different form. It becomes necessary quickly to identify the shape of the deal, rather than to look creatively for some new shape. In this process, both parties become more concerned with 'what our party wants'.

The response to the other party needs to be one of probing, to find out which issues or which ingredients are important to the others. Are they, for example, more concerned about price than delivery, quality, terms of settlement?

It is important in these exploratory stages to keep the dialogue on a broad front. If the move to discussion of a particular item (such as price) is taken too soon or too deeply, it is likely to lead to a premature conflict and also to erode some of the most effective possibilities for later bargaining.

Bidding

In negotiating to independent advantage, the guideline to bidding is to start with that which is the highest defensible. (For buyers, the corresponding phrase is of course 'lowest defensible offer'.)

The opening bid needs to be 'the highest' because:

- The opening bid sets a limit beyond which the party cannot aspire. Having once made it, no higher bid can reasonably be put at a later stage.
- The first bid influences others in their valuation of our offer.
- A high bid gives scope for manoeuvre during the later bargaining phases. It gives something in reserve with which to trade.
- The opening bid has a real influence on the final settlement level. The higher the level of aspiration, the greater the prospective achievement.

The opening bid needs to be high. At the same time it must be defensible. Putting forward a bid which cannot be defended does positive damage to the negotiating process. It is found to be offensive by the other party; and if it cannot be defended when challenged in subsequent bargaining, there is soon a loss of face, a loss of credibility, a forced retreat.

The content of the bid of course usually needs to cover a range of issues. The components of the opening bid in a commercial negotiation will not simply be price, but a combination of price, delivery, payment terms, quality specification and a dozen other items.

The 'highest defensible bid' is not an absolute figure; it is a figure which is relevant to the particular circumstances. It is specifically a figure which relates to the way in which others are operating. If they are pressing to their independent advantage, then we must open with a high bid; but if faced with a lot of competition, the bid must be tailored to the level at which it will at least enable us to be invited to continue the negotiations. If we have established cordial relationships with others, possibly over a long period of time, then we shall know the style in which they will operate and the degree of cooperation we can expect − we know the level at which it is prudent for us to make our bid.

On each individual item the opening bid needs to be the highest defensible. We are certain, when negotiating to independent advantage, to be pushed by others to compromise on one or two issues. We cannot be sure which until the bargaining process is under way; we must aspire high on all issues and keep room to manoeuvre.

The manner in which the bid is stated is important. It should be put firmly − without reservations, without hesitations − so that it may carry the conviction of a conscientious negotiating party.

It should be put clearly so that the other party recognises precisely what is being asked. The creation of a visual aid, i.e. taking a sheet of paper and writing figures on it, within the sight of the other party, whilst one is stating the bid − this is powerful reinforcement.

It should be put without apology or comment. There is no need to apologise for anything that can be defended. There is no need to comment since the other party can be expected to raise questions on matters which concern it. And voluntary comment (before others ask for it) simply makes them aware of concern about issues which they might never have considered.

Those then are three guidelines to the way in which a bid should be presented: firmly, clearly, without comment.

In responding to bids by the other party there is a need to distinguish between clarification and justification.

The competent negotiator first ensures that he knows what the other party is bidding. Precisely. He asks any questions which are needed to ensure that he gets the picture clear. He makes sure, in the process, that the other party recognises that these are questions for clarification and not demands to justify. And once satisfied, he summarises his understanding of the other party's bid, as a check on the effectiveness of communication between them.

The first party should at this stage deflect questions which demand that he justifies his position. He has put a bid and he has a perfect right to know what the other is prepared to offer in return.

Bargaining

The first two steps in the bargaining process should be: get it clear; and assess the situation. It is vital to establish a clear picture of other party's requirements at the outset. We should have got a clear picture of *what* he is bidding already. Now we need to know *why*.

The need is increasingly to build an understanding of what will give him satisfaction and of how to trade to advantage whilst giving him that satisfaction.

We must discover what for him are essentials and what else is desirable but not essential, and what aspects of his bid are really of fringe interest only – where he could readily give.

To achieve this clarity, the guidelines are:

- Check every item of his bid. Enquire why. Ask how important the item is and how much flexibility he could introduce.
- Never speculate on his opinions or on his motives. A speculation only irritates. Moreover it is often misconceived – it is out of our frame of reference, not his, and confuses the negotiations between the pair of us. Never put words into his mouth.
- Note his answers without comment. Reserve our position. Avoid deep diving or premature diving into any issue. Keep it on a broad front.

Assuming significant differences between the parties there are now three options for the negotiator: he can accept; he can reject; or he can carry on negotiating. If he decides on the latter he must be prepared for the next round. His options at this stage are:

- to make a new offer;
- to seek a new offer from the other party;
- to change the shape of the deal (vary the quantity or the quality or the use of third parties); or
- to embark on give-and-take bargaining.

The steps for preparing for that give-and-take are first to issue identification – list the issues in the package. Then prepare the bargaining position:

- an essential conditions list − those issues on which it is impossible to concede anything;
- a concessions list − those issues on which concession is conceivable. For each such issue, a progression stepped from that minimum which could be offered (against counter-concessions from the other party) in the next round of bargaining, to that ultimate limit which might be forced in successive rounds.

During the bargaining stages, each successive negotiation meeting should be opened with a new round of climate formation and with agreement on procedure. Each round should be concluded with the establishment of some means of resolving outstanding difficulties.

In between, the negotiations should be conducted laterally rather than vertically. That is to say, the aim should be to reach agreement in principle on a broad front, then to tackle more detailed negotiations, still on a broad front. A sequence of several successive moves across the broad front; not a succession of narrow penetrations.

When the time comes for compromise, neither party will readily 'lose face'. Neither party will readily concede on one issue without having some corresponding concession on another. It is thus important to solve difficulties on a broad front or, at the least, two at a time; not simply one at a time.

For example, when the parties have been exploring a difference between them in price and when they are reaching the stage of preparedness to make concessions, it is helpful to both parties if one of them interjects a comment such as 'Well, just before we finish that discussion on price, could we at the same time tie in this question about (e.g, the shipping risk) and who is to be responsible for that?'

And so sustaining goodwill and sustaining efforts to keep a cooperative climate even through tough bargaining − the negotiation should move towards settlement to independent advantage.

Preparation

As ever, preparation is of critical importance, and the general pattern of preparation should repeat that previously described, with one important difference. This is the need to be more specific during preparation processes. Whereas in creative negotiations it is important to keep one's preparations general and to preserve flexibility, in more divisive negotiations the negotiator needs to be protected from exploitation. He needs to have considered his bids at an early stage. There is this constant dichotomy between the need for flexibility and the need for precise preparations. The one is the enemy of the other. The choice should reflect the strategic situation which will be referred to at the end of this chapter.

To summarise: bidding and bargaining are the key phases in negotiating to independent advantage. It is a type of negotiation needing distinctive attitudes and skills. Bidding and bargaining become more important than exploration. Climate formation and procedural development remain important. So does preparation though it takes a slightly different form.

FIGHTING

Warfare is not a commendable form of negotiation. Nevertheless, negotiators do become involved in confrontations in which the aim has to be to 'win' — or, at any rate, to ensure that they do not 'lose' at the hands of an aggressive party.

This section will review:

- the use of fighting methods
- the pattern of a fighting negotiation
- fighting tactics
- counter-measures.

The use of fighting methods

The fighter's aim is to win and to make the other party the loser. This is a dangerous attitude to negotiations. It puts goodwill at risk; it obscures the possibility of creative cooperation; it naturally provokes the other party to fight back, causing delay and putting at risk the fighter's chances of success. Even when the fighter batters an 'opponent' into submission, he is not likely to find the deal implemented energetically.

The means which the fighter uses are powerful. Both by his personal behaviour and by the negotiating tactics which he uses, he seeks to reinforce the power of his position. His methods include:

- a constant search for gain at every opportunity;
- at each successive stage in the process of negotiating, he wants fresh advantage;

- any withdrawals must be deliberate, tactical withdrawals, designed only to promote greater advance;
- power methods; high in terms of the pace, size and forcefulness of demands, low in readiness to listen or to yield;
- task-centred, concern for his special advantage, not concerned with other party's pride or dignity nor with their feelings. Forcing them to 'accept or else'.

The pattern of a fighting negotiation

The central concern of the fighting negotiator is to win. This winning takes place in the fighting phase of the negotiation – a special version of the bargaining phase. A special version at which he is expert and best able to use his personal characteristics. Quickly he leads the negotiation to the point at which his form of bargaining becomes the dominant activity.

This leaves little time or interest for the early stages of negotiating; little time to get on the same wavelength as other party, or to agree on a plan; little time to explore mutual interests. Even issue identification is hastened and the negotiation quickly becomes focused on his first chosen issue.

The pattern of the negotiation is then 'vertical', deep diving on the first selected issue. He aspires high and pushes until he 'wins' on that and each successive issue.

Fighting tactics

He knows a lot of tactics and manoeuvres, and regularly uses a number. He has his own repertoire, and admires (and tries to emulate) tactics which have been used 'against' him by other negotiators. Here are some of them:

1 *Probing from the start*
   The fighter enters the negotiating room, shakes hands and wishes us 'Good morning' and immediately starts probing. Probing about our business situation, probing about the product or service in which he is interested, probing even about one's personal situation.

   The advantages he seeks are in getting information, in building a picture about other party and especially in recognising weaknesses and vulnerabilities. Additionally, he establishes a power position – a pattern of aggressive leadership.

2   *Get/give*

He is concerned to get something before he will give anything;
to get a small concession before he will give a small concession;
to get a big concession before he will give a big concession; to
get information before he will give information; to get the other
party's bid before he will give his own bid; to get the power of
being the first to make an opening statement.

Get/give tactics used by skilled negotiators can have positive
commercial advantages in the short term. They may well gain
ground during the early stages of a negotiation; but in the long
run, they lead to delay and deadlock (neither party being willing
always to give before it gets).

3   *Showing emotion* (anger, for example)

Loud and emotional statements, possibly banging the table: the
form of eye-contact, posture, gesture and voice, all displaying
emotions.

4   *Good guy/bad guy*

This is a tactic for use by a team of two negotiators. One takes
the role of the 'bad guy'; being aggressive, making excessive
demands, dominating, uncooperative. He holds the stage for a
long time whilst his colleague remains quiet. When he has
softened up the 'opposition' with his tactics, the 'good guy'
takes over the lead role constructively offering solutions,
quietly trying to reach a mutual understanding.

The tactic parallels the archetypal method by which prisoners
of war are cross-examined; the prisoner first ruthlessly interro-
gated by a tough investigator, then offered the sympathy of a
different personality to whom − with luck − he would open up.

5   *Poker-faced*

Giving away nothing by expression, tone, posture or gesture.
An important part of the fighting negotiator's armoury.

6   *Managing the minutes*

Taking responsibility at the end of each session for production
of the record. Slanting interpretations of what has been agreed
always to his advantage. Readiness to include the odd item
'which ought to have been agreed' even if there was insufficient
time to include it in the discussion − provided, of course, that
the odd item is favourable.

7   *Getting upstairs*

When unable to come to an agreement with the other negotiator, taking steps to contact his boss, or boss's boss's boss.

8   *PR*
Many fights are conducted by negotiators acting on behalf of other groupings. For example, the union negotiator representing the work force; the government negotiator representing his country. It is here important for the group which is represented to be kept informed and influenced so that they continue to give their backing to the negotiator. His ability at public relations is thus an important part of the fighter's armoury.

9   *Forcing moves*
There are, of course, yet other moves which some negotiators use — bribery, sex, blackmail, bugging. Most negotiators would see such devices as rankly unethical; but people negotiating very important deals are at risk and need to be on their guard.

Counter-measures

Counters to those who fight are in two forms: long term and short term measures. In the long term, where there is expectation of repeated rounds of negotiations, for example in labour negotiations, there is a need for the development of attitudes, skills and relationships.

This development takes place best when the parties can come together at a place remote from their normal battlefield, and at a time during the off-season for fighting. Especially fruitful is the practice, which has been well developed in Scandinavia, of holding joint working seminars for two or three days. The product of such seminars is not only the development of relationships but the planning of subsequent joint activities.

That is a long term approach. In the short term, measures to counter the fighter fall into three categories:

- head him off;
- control the battlefield;
- cope with his tactics.

The most satisfying way of coping with him is of course to head off the fight before it develops. If this is to be achieved it must be done in the critical opening seconds and minutes:

- deflect his opening questions;
- preserve a neutral ice breaking period;
- do not be drawn by his probing questions;

- do not let him assert leadership;
- do not let him dominate the early moments – what is being talked about, when to stand and when to sit, the seating arrangements.

We are able to control the skirmishing if we can somehow control the battlefield. In negotiating terms, this 'control of the battlefield' is control of the procedures of negotiating. Guidelines are:

- seek form and plan for the proceedings;
- seek opening discussion of purpose, plan and pace;
- keep bringing him back to the agreed plan;
- keep things fluid. Use the 'broad front' approach;
- seek for compromise. He will be impervious either to searches for creative resolution of differences, or to sensitive attempts to influence him. His metier is that of compromise. If his position is that he is asking £120 and ours is that it is only worth £100, then settlement is likely to be at the compromise point of £110. Bargain slowly until you get him down to at most £110.

Above all, keep control of the process – keep control of what is being negotiated and in which sequence – keep to the plan. It will irritate him. He much prefers to be able to run free, but do not worry. A caged fighter cannot do as much damage as one on the loose. To cope with some of the fighter's tactics: when he is using the 'get/give' tactic, we must not give too easily, for if we give before we get, he will regard this as a sign of weakness. He will want to get yet more and will change the tactic into 'get/get/give' and soon will be aspiring even higher to 'get/get/get'.

We must not give in. We must trade scrap of information for scrap of information, scrap of readiness for scrap of readiness, scrap of concession for scrap of concession.

The only counter to displays of anger is to suspend negotiations, either temporarily or permanently. The human brain is such that emotions (such as anger) are handled in one part of it, rational thinking in another part. Once the brain becomes focused on emotive thinking, then the rational part is cut off. The angry party cannot receive rational messages and it is no use other party trying to instil them. So the counter is to suspend operations.

It does not matter if first party's anger is simply a display rather than real anger. Second party has no way of being sure about the matter. First party has behaved in ways which are not acceptable and second party should immediately suspend.

The 'good guy/bad guy' tactic is difficult to recognise and difficult to counter. But, of course, if it has been recognised in one round of negotiating then the negotiator will be alert for it during later rounds and must hope either to be able to ignore the bad guy or to separate the two 'opponents'.

The counter to 'getting upstairs' is to state strong objection to the tactic and then to arrange for our own boss to come in and make it clear that theirs was a losing tactic.

Formality is, inevitably, a device used to try to bring order to such negotiations. However, the fighting negotiator becomes expert in framing and fighting for a rule book which is to his advantage. He is expert not only in drafting and amending rules but in interpreting and manipulating them. The effective negotiator from the other side therefore is forced to build his own corresponding expertise.

Preparation is, as ever, of critical importance for effectiveness in negotiating. When faced with a fight it is imperative to be well prepared procedurally and imperative also to have precise objectives, targets and prepared concession lists. There is special need to prepare options ('scenarios' in the current jargon), alternative approaches which could enable both parties to move forward whilst minimising loss of face.

The counter to his competence at public relations is to develop equal competence and to ensure that the relevant public is suitably influenced.

In meeting with a fighting 'opponent' then, the negotiator is operating in a world of power. He needs skill to control the battlefield and to prevent his being exploited.

But that is a short term approach. The longer term interest demands that he should work for some joint development of attitudes, skills and relationships with the other party.

SUMMARY

This chapter has been concerned with three distinct forms of negotiation: first, in which two parties seek to move forward cooperatively to create the best possible deal in their joint interests; second, in which both parties aim to preserve goodwill whilst at the same time trying to maximise their independent advantage; third and finally, with fights in which continuing goodwill is not treated as being important.

The choice amongst these approaches to negotiating will depend on a number of strategic issues:

- the extent to which the parties will need to come together again from time to time;
- the respective strength of the parties in the market place;
- the character and quality of their negotiators;
- the time scale and the importance of the prospective deal.

These strategic issues are considered at greater length in the last two books given in Further reading (below).

FURTHER READING

Karrass, C L, *Give and Take*, World Publishing Co., 1974. A good treatment of the tactics used by American negotiators.

Marsh, P D V, *Contract Negotiation Handbook*, Gower, 2nd edition, 1984. Excellent treatment of negotiating strategy of general interest. Preceded by a mathematical/economic analysis of bidding — also excellent, but demanding a reader with mathematical talents.

Scott, Bill, *The Skills of Negotiating*, Gower, 1981. A highly readable expansion of his ideas by the author of this chapter of the Handbook.

29

Being an ambassador for your organisation

Roger Haywood

There can be few areas in the running of an enterprise that can provide as much excitement and such returns as an investment in good communications. And, despite the sophisticated techniques that have been developed in recent years, nothing can improve on the effectiveness of face to face communications.

THE COMPANY SPEAKS

Everything in our society is paid for through the creation of added value by industry. Business leaders have a responsibility not just to their companies but to the communities in which we all work. You cannot be a silent leader ...

Make the boss the business voice

Every business manager has to be an ambassador for his organisation and this is particularly true of those with the most senior responsibilities. However, the principles apply to everyone in the organisation.

Whilst the chief executive may need to be chief ambassador, the supervisor needs to consider himself or herself as a deputy consul, whilst the lorry driver or machinist needs to understand that he or she has a role to play in the development of goodwill through acting as an information officer or PRO.

The chief executive must calculate how much of his or her time should be spent on ambassadorial activities. This could be 70 per cent or more. But even if it is only as little as 5 per cent — say a day a month — this time must be used to the maximum effect. If you want to manage your company communications from the top, ask yourself what is the most effective way to use the time available?

Why spend a day in briefing one local newspaper journalist when it could be used in hosting a factory visit by the editors of all the local papers plus relevant trade, technical and professional media?

Why take twelve days a year visiting all the factories when more might be achieved by spending three solid days at a management conference attended by all the heads of department?

Why deal only with those people who have the opportunity to enter your office when you could invest half a day every quarter featuring in a video programme that could be shown to every employee?

Why fritter away a couple of hours at the club with a friendly broker when the same time could be used hosting a private lunch for all the organisation's financial partners?

Why write to one or two shareholders when the time spent on a proper shareholder newsletter could keep all the investors properly informed?

Why make a speech to the local rotary club when a presentation to the Institute of Directors or your leading trade body would take no longer and would be reported to an audience a thousand times larger?

Why give your wisdom and wit only to those who attended when your speech could be reprinted as a paper and distributed to everyone who matters to the organisation?

Link your marketing and business communications

Two of the most significant changes in business practice in the last decade have an extremely close link; both depend upon the concept that business success comes from public consent not just management aspirations.

Marketing has revolutionised progressive business in recent years. Indeed, marketing is more than just a function, it is a way of business life. It is based upon the assumption that the customer is central to every organisation and decides whether that organisation will succeed or fail.

Similarly, *communications* recognises that the organisation prospers only through the support of the publics upon whom it is dependent. Goodwill can be created by both the actions and the communications of the organisation — but not by one of these alone. This has radically changed boardroom thinking; every company has to have an acceptable corporate personality if it is to achieve any substantial success. Today, the organisation not only has to be good; it has to be seen to be good.

It pays to create a good reputation

The managers of a successful business should remember that the goodwill they are creating may be as important to profitability as their product pricing or technical competence. This simple fact is easy to forget during the normal pressures of running the enterprise, but it becomes very clear whenever any business is being valued, for example, when it is being sold or seeking a public flotation. If goodwill can double or treble the value of the tangible assets, then it is worth spending a little time and effort on building this intangible asset – every pound spent on this activity will reap a dividend in better sales, employee motivation and profit.

The creation of such goodwill, with both short and long term benefits, is the work of the company ambassador. But goodwill is not created by accident. It requires thought, planning, positive effort and constant nurturing. Goodwill may take years to develop – and just moments to destroy.

Often, as business leader, you will need to undertake personally much of the work that will develop the goodwill. Even if you have a strong team to look after this management function, you will still need to *lead* the activity, decide the policy, the tone and direction of the efforts that are intended to build understanding and support.

Use public relations to build goodwill

In terms of modern business practice, this activity is effectively the management discipline of public relations. Frequently, PR is considered to be expensive, only relevant to very large companies or those that directly affect the man and woman in the street. Whilst PR is vital in this sector of business, it is an equally important activity across all areas of industry and commerce – no organisation can succeed without the understanding, the support and the goodwill of the many publics upon whom it depends.

As a simple example, the attitudes of customers are an essential factor in the buying decision – whether the organisation is selling boxes of matches or nuclear power stations. Sometimes managers lose sight of the fact that the customer pays for everything within the organisation. We all know what makes our products sell − their price, the performance, the service, the delivery, the back-up, the technology and many other elements. Those that sometimes get forgotten are the attitudes of the customer to the product and to the organisation.

Ask yourself the question, would you buy a Mexican watch? If not, why not? For all you know, the Mexicans may be excellent designers and manufacturers of watches. The product may be superb, the price attractive, delivery fine, service and back-up impeccable. Yet would you still question this purchasing decision?

The reason is your perceptions of Mexico − which do not seem to equate with a quality product like a watch. Perhaps you would buy Mexican foods, Mexican handicrafts, even Mexican clothes or shoes. But not a Mexican watch? The factor that makes you hesitate is not the product, its price, performance, service, back-up or what the manufacturer says (or even what the advertising says). The central factor is your attitude.

It can be seen from this simple example that attitudes can be critically important. However, you may well say this does not apply to *your* business − but the principle applies to *every* business. Consider a massive capital decision and the attitudes of the purchasing executives still matter. How would you like to negotiate the construction of a Union Carbide plant on an industrial site near *your* town — or how would you like the job of selling nuclear power stations on behalf of the constructors of the Three Mile Island plant?

Remember the striking success story of Barratt's the home builders? But look what happened to sales of timber-frame buildings when consumer confidence in the product had been undermined and public opinion turned sour. Damaging media coverage slashed millions from Barratt's share price.

Identify the company's personality

A one-word definition of public relations might be 'reputation'. The goodwill of the customer − or any other group − will only develop where an organisation has established a management style which is respected and trusted. The reputation is a reflection of the personality of the organisation. By having a clearly identified personality, your organisation will be able to behave in a consistent and acceptable way.

Small organisations tend to have strong personalities because of the nature of the managers and their central role in all policy decisions.

Large organisations can become erratic because of the influence of a group of diverse managers who are not all pulling in the same direction. Even worse, they can become bland where the personalities accept compromise on all issues.

One very sensible step towards consistent and acceptable behaviour is for the organisation to try to establish a code of conduct or a philosophy which is consistent with its personality. Many larger corporations develop a written statement of their ambitions or intentions which provides guidelines for management in handling any situation which might arise.

One of these corporate guidelines was an unseen factor behind a company crisis that hit the headlines some years ago. Johnson & Johnson, the US pharmaceuticals group, has a well planned corporate credo. One central element of this is that it defines its primary responsibility as being to its customers. When the company was unexpectedly hit by the Tylenol tragedy, this credo enabled it to react speedily, promptly and effectively.

Packets of the analgesic, Tylenol, had been maliciously poisoned in-store by a member of the public. As soon as the company was aware of what had happened, it was clear that the most immediate action to be taken was to protect the public regardless of the cost or consequences; the complete product was withdrawn and distribution stopped. This took precedence over any considerations related to the concerns of the pharmaceutical industry, retailers, wholesalers or shareholders, though, clearly, the overriding concern for the customer has to be in the best interests of all these groups.

Eventually, when the immediate crisis was over, the decision was taken to relaunch the product in secure packages. The public response to the company's prompt action to cope with a tragedy beyond its control generated such goodwill that sales of the relaunched Tylenol well exceeded the levels before it had been withdrawn. Good behaviour not only makes you feel good it makes you perform well too!

Therefore, the first step towards being an ambassador for your organisation is to define with your senior colleagues the personality of your organisation. For example, are you total-efficiency and high-technology − or informality and friendliness? Are you quality above everything − or value for money?

The agreed corporate code should become part of the business plan and well publicised. Some organisations produce this as a document and even have an inscribed version in the reception of their buildings. Others make it part of the induction programme for new employees.

THE COMPANY PREPARES

... and if you decide to speak then you must think about what needs to be said, where, when and how. That requires careful consideration and effective planning ...

Match the communications technique to the audience

An effective ambassador for an organisation creates the maximum goodwill when in face to face discussions; the most powerful means of communication is simply people talking to each other.

Plan your own workload in face to face communications. Identify the key audiences and those occasions on which there is no substitute for you talking to them. Sometimes this needs to be one-to-one or a small group. Often, the effectiveness of personal communication can be improved by the use of larger meetings, for example, talking to groups of wholesalers or key customers at sales conferences or shareholders at the annual general meeting.

Where the audiences may be spread across a large geographical area, it is possible to extend this personal presentation by the use of video or film. However, it is important to remember that all other forms of communication are substitutes for face to face discussion. Film, video, newsletters, reports, documents and leaflets may all have a role to play — but only within a planned framework and, ideally, with emphasis on the senior executive relating face to face with as many members of the important publics as possible.

Clearly, a coordinated programme of communications needs planning. In small organisations, it may be possible for the chief executive to undertake that personally. With larger companies, there may well be an executive to whom such planning responsibility can be delegated. Others use outside professional consultancies to help in both the planning and the implementation. Whichever route may be taken, it is essential to retain responsibility for policy. However, keep overtight control on all communications and you may create a vacuum in the information network: this can be extremely dangerous as (in the absence of proper information) rumour, gossip and speculation grow and these are always more damaging than the truth.

Combine the elements to build a campaign

There can be no rigid rules on the best way of carrying out a programme of communication but there are some useful guidelines. For example, it is important to allocate a budget for this activity. Once the importance has been appreciated, it is usually much easier to identify how much the company may be prepared to spend to achieve such objectives.

As a broad guideline, somewhere between 1 per cent and 2 per cent of turnover might be spent on those communications activities designed to develop the favourable reputation. Of course, if there is a substantial company marketing or sales effort, then a smaller percentage may be possible – and this may even be part of the responsibilities of the marketing communications function.

With small budgets, it may well be advisable to allocate the responsibility to an executive within the team. Above a certain level, it might be wise to consider the appointment of a full-time executive to handle this – though it is important to realise that any competent communications specialist would expect to have a budget available of at least three or four times his or her salary. At these sorts of level of expenditure an alternative might be to appoint a consultancy on a fee basis. Certainly, once the budgets exceed £50,000 to £100,000 then professional assistance becomes essential.

(There are books available on the management of professional PR resources and, at these sorts of level, it may well be worth consulting one of them. Alternatively, advice can be sought from the Institute of Public Relations on the recruitment of a staff professional or the Public Relations Consultants Association on the appointment of a professional consultancy.)

Whether the effort is to be tackled internally through an appointed professional or externally via consultants, the company still needs to be very clear on its communications policies. The three central questions that you need to be able to answer are: what are we trying to achieve? who are we trying to influence? how do we wish them to perceive us?

Indeed, one working definition of effective communications is: bridging the gap between how an organisation is perceived and how it would like to be perceived.

Set yourself some tough objectives

The only effective starting point for the planning of the campaign is to agree on the objectives. Ideally these should be quantified or they simply remain aims; but even broad aims will be more helpful than having no specific targets on which to focus the effort.

For example, one of the aims of a campaign may be to create goodwill amongst your wholesalers. Once this has been agreed, a complete range of options will then emerge on how this might be best established – quarterly discussions with the senior directors of the leading wholesalers, a wholesalers' newsletter, an annual conference and so on.

At the early stages of planning, such a broad aim may well be satisfactory. However, performance can better be monitored and budgets justified if the definition of what is to be achieved is made more specific. For example, it might become an objective within the first year to convince all your existing wholesalers that your company is a fair and ethical trading partner.

Or the objective may be to prove to all existing wholesalers, say, that the company is in the top three in terms of quality of service in your market sector.

A broad aim might be to improve awareness amongst wholesalers with whom you are not currently trading. This can be converted into a quantified objective by trying to put some measure on it; for example, the objective becomes: to ensure that all the top hundred wholesalers are fully aware of the products and services offered by your company.

Aims can be established for the communications programmes across all the audiences and, in most cases, these can also be converted into more easily measurable objectives.

Find out who matters in creating your success

The second central factor in the discipline behind the campaign will be clearly identifying those audiences that are important. In practice, this can best be agreed by discussions with senior managers in each of the operating disciplines of the company, for example, sales, marketing, production, personnel and so on. From these discussions you can build a list of groups upon whom the organisation depends for its success. These might include employees, prospective employees, local factory neighbours, trade associations, local authority officers, national government, civil service departments and statutory authorities, wholesalers, retailers, suppliers and so on.

When the communications programme has been developed, it must ensure that all of these groups are fully informed. This does not necessarily mean that individual efforts have to be directed at each section but it does mean that they do get exposed to company messages. In practical terms, this might mean that one part of the communications activity can be extended to cover other groups, for example, the annual report can be distributed to neighbours of the factory; key suppliers can be invited to the company open days; your more interesting trade or business news stories may well be relevant to the local papers; the actor in your expensive new commercial can be a guest at your trade dinner.

THE COMPANY ACTS

... as the voice of the company you must speak clearly and effectively. Your world wants to hear your views, needs to know your policies. The public will listen, reply and respond.

As ambassador for your organisation there will be some aspects of the communication that you can best tackle yourself, including key speeches and important media interviews.

Make your speeches really effective

The ability to make a persuasive speech, give a stimulating talk or perform a professional presentation can be learned. These skills come naturally to very few people. Indeed, those who believe they are natural public speakers are usually insensitive to their audience's reactions and rarely put the effort in to polish their technique.

Professional assistance is at hand in the form of publications on this subject and well established training courses. Ask your PR adviser or consultant for help in these areas. You will also find Chapter 5 in this Handbook helpful.

Learn the fundamentals and practise them. In the meantime, here are a few broad guidelines.

The audience

Never give a talk without knowing the nature of the audience. Who are they, how many are there, how were they invited, what do they expect, how have they been told about your appearance?

The venue

Where will you be talking, how large is the room, what is the lighting and sound system? The finance chief of a public company was invited to talk to the partners of a professional firm. He imagined a handful of greying directors in a panelled boardroom but was startled – and completely ill prepared – to find that he was talking to 65 young, bright and enthusiastic professionals seated in tiered ranks in a modern lecture theatre.

Content

Keep to the agreed length or, preferably, make it shorter. Be wary of humour unless you are experienced and confident. Make sure the content is strictly relevant to the audience. Avoid jargon or terminology peculiar to your profession. Work hard on getting the start right; you need to capture interest within 30 seconds. Have a plan for your talk and tell your audience what you are going to tell them. Build to a powerful conclusion; remember, this must include a very clear explanation of what you want them to do as a result of your talk. Above all, prepare thoroughly. Winston Churchill once revealed that each of his 'impromptu' speeches took an hour of preparation for every minute of presentation.

Handle the media like a professional

Projecting the organisation means reaching the people that matter. Very often the most effective way of doing this is through the media.

The organisation may have an official spokesman to deal with detailed enquiries from the media, but the chief executive is the figurehead and should be the voice of the company.

As it is never a good policy to make your mistakes in public, handling the media should not be learned by trial and error. It could cost your company dear. At one time, Freddie Laker was the darling of Fleet Street, the buccaneer of the airways – and they loved it when he embarrassed the big airlines.

Then one day, he stood on a table at Gatwick and thanked the media for their millions of pounds of free advertising. That became the turning point. Newspapers, radio and television covered his activities because his battles were exciting and newsworthy. They had not 'supported' him; nor were they aiding a campaign to make him rich. Editors were intensely irritated by this attitude; they felt used and many of the reporters following the story lost all sympathy for him. The tone of the media coverage abruptly shifted, though how that contributed to his subsequent problems is arguable.

What is unarguable is that if the reward for getting it right can be triumph, the penalty for getting it wrong can be disaster. No one should venture into this area unless they understand how the media work and have either received training or professional assistance.

There are several helpful books on the media interview and any reputable consultancy will assist in media relations or advise on training. But here are a few simple guidelines for talking to the press.

Journalists working for the print media have to translate what the company wants to say into what the readers want to know. He or she also has to translate your style into the publication's style. The possibility of error is considerable. It is worth preparing carefully for such interviews.

Homework

Before talking to any journalist, check what he or she wants to cover. What is the likely angle, where is the piece to be used, who else is contributing, how long is it likely to be?

Then do your homework on the subject areas. It will be no good having to turn to other colleagues for help on basic questions; this will undermine your credibility.

Professional support

If you have a public relations officer or consultancy, ask for their advice. Consider inviting your PR executive to handle the pre-briefing with the journalist and attend the interview. He or she may well spot problems that you would not recognise from your experience – and be able to correct these at the time.

Briefing sheet

Gather all the relevant facts together on one piece of paper and present this to the journalist. You may even include a prepared statement, to be expanded at the interview. In this way there can be no excuse for any of those irritating misunderstandings that creep into too many stories.

Tricky questions

Talk to your colleagues (particularly your professional PR adviser) and work out the nastiest questions that you could be asked. Then consider how you will deal with them. (The odds are you will never be asked more than a fraction of these but it will help your confidence to know you have an acceptable answer to every critical query.)

On or off the record

Sometimes (very rarely) you may need to talk off the record to explain some background, for example, some forthcoming redundancies that cannot yet be announced. Keep such comments to the barest minimum and avoid them completely if possible.

Even a journalist acting in good faith (and most are) can become confused about what he is allowed to report or not. The simplest rule is do not say anything unless you want it reported.

The competition

Be very careful with humour as jokes can look horrifying in print. 'Once we were small and chaotic, now we are large and chaotic ...' is a witty and self-mocking comment that UK managing director of Sodastream, Harry Hemens, once used to great effect in a speech. He would never have used it in an interview as it could look extremely damaging in print.

Equally, be very careful with criticism, particularly of your competitors. 'Everyone knows their products are a joke ... ' might be acceptable at the sales conference, but when used by a director of an electrical company briefing a key editor, it nearly resulted in a damaging and expensive legal action – and it certainly alienated both the editor and a large section of the wholesale trade. At the very best, talking about your competitors is little more than second-hand opinion and is giving them coverage that they should gain for themselves.

The use of the exclusive

An exclusive interview will generally result in a more favourable and substantial piece. Against this has to be offset the efficiency and the use of time. Sometimes a compromise can be reached where three or four journalists from non-competing publications can be briefed simultaneously, for example, one from your wholesale trade, one from marketing, one from export, personnel and so on.

Radio and television

Many of the points above apply when working with the broadcasting media. However, there are also some special considerations that need to be borne in mind.

Research

On radio and television programmes it is not unusual for the investigation to be carried out by specialised researchers rather than the interviewer. Do treat these research sessions seriously and ensure that the representative of the media is properly briefed. This can have a significant influence upon the eventual shape of the news story or feature.

Equally, remember it is your right to investigate the proposed programme. Before agreeing to participate, be sure that you know: how long the final piece will be; whether it will be live or edited; who else will be featured; whether your piece is to be used complete as an interview or divided to illustrate other points. One director of a water authority found that his interview had been edited into short sections and inserted into other material, which appeared to contradict everything he said. It was clever editing but an appalling communications job for his organisation.

The broadcast

The techniques for handling radio and television are specialised; no one should tackle these unprepared. The cost of professional familiarisation sessions will be nothing compared to the damage caused to your organisation through a poor performance. Radio and television interviewers are rarely as hostile as the public imagines. They are professional journalists looking for an interesting story. You can give them a good one which reflects well on your company – or allow them to develop an angle (just as interesting to the listeners or viewers) but which may not. Do not take the risk. Get professional help to develop your interview skill.

Know what you want people to know about you

The personality of the organisation can be best projected if the messages that are coming out are consistent. In our global communications village, there are no barriers to information and a small piece in the local newspaper of interest to factory neighbours can tomorrow be influencing city financiers through a headline in the *Financial Times*. Or, conversely, a sentence at the bottom of a column in the *Financial Times* can tomorrow create headlines in the local paper that throw the factory employees into turmoil, bring production to a halt and have the city councillors up in arms.

The messages must be consistent, though it is acceptable to project different facets of this message to different audiences. The way to get consistent messages is to ask senior managers to set down in writing how they would like the organisation to be perceived. Such messages should then influence and shape all activities of the organisation, particularly in the communications area. They will help ensure that the sales approach is consistent with advertising, personnel policy relates to community relations and so on.

An agreed set of messages for a manufacturing company might be that the organisation:

- manufactures durable, quality products that represent fair value for money;
- provides an effective back-up service to both present and previous customers for these products;
- behaves as a responsible, thoughtful and participating member of the local community;
- treats employees with respect, providing good working conditions with fair rewards;
- leads in the development of the best practices and acts as the authority in this business sector.

Say what you have to say in the best way possible

The effective programme to develop the reputation of the organisation is likely to include the three main elements of communications: face to face discussions, audio visual presentation and printed material. Often all three elements can be used together.

For example, in the wholesaler example earlier, the need to increase awareness might be met by a range of alternatives: a video documentary, a newsletter, regional meetings, an exhibition or conference, a media relations campaign or a sponsored sports event.

It requires considerable professional expertise to plan all such activities, calculate the costs and estimate the benefits that each might produce. Resist the temptation to become a very expensive (and probably very amateur) part-time PRO. A day of the chief executive's time must be better spent in running the business than in writing a brochure. External assistance may look expensive but is rarely so when compared with the real costs of the management time.

Professional communications assistance is normally available through two separate routes: the organisation can employ a staff communications expert or retain the services of an external consultancy (and sometimes both).

Use the staff route for depth of commitment

An adviser on the team has many advantages. He/she can become completely familiar with the operation of your organisation, its policies, its ethos, aims and ambitions; he can build strong relationships with other operating colleagues; and he is available full-time and often outside normal hours, usually without extra cost. The ideal candidate can be selected to match the temperament of the organisation and he brings his own personal aspirations, business ambitions and expertise to strengthen the management of the existing company team.

Some of the disadvantages are equally clear and need to be considered. He will need to be able to see a progressive career path and this might mean that your company is making a commitment to an ever-expanding promotional activity − or risking losing the staff specialist when he reaches the ceiling. In addition, he is one man and can only be tackling one job at a time and has limited physical capability; he may well wish to expand his department and create a bigger operation; he has to be paid for (but cannot work) when he is on holiday or sick; he requires training, motivating and the provision of health, pension and other costly facilities; his personality and style may not as closely match the organisation as it grows and changes.

Use the consultancy for breadth of skill

Again, there are several advantages in employing a consultancy. A firm can be selected that best suits the style of the organisation − and a number of alternative consultancies may well be persuaded to compete to win the business; the resource can be turned up and down as the requirements dictate; a wider range of expertise may be available as and when necessary; no office, overhead, establishment, training, holiday, pension or other employment costs will be incurred, although these will be incorporated in the fees paid; no commitment needs to be made to a long term career option; and if the chosen consultancy fails to perform, it can be dispensed with relatively painlessly, without disturbing other executives.

The disadvantages also need to be considered and evaluated. The consultancy cannot usually become totally immersed in the operations of its client and their politics; it is only available for a contractually agreed amount of time; hour-for-hour this may be fairly expensive time; and virtually everything undertaken will incur additional costs.

However, it has to be said that the intense competitive pressures within the consultancy industry do tend to ensure that high professional standards are being achieved by successful consultancies.

They will work extremely hard to win a piece of business and extremely hard to avoid losing it. There may be far less risk in appointing a consultancy; it will already have put a lot of work into its recommendations and in demonstrating its professionalism.

Be a leader of equals

The chief executive should see himself as an ambassador, but in common with all good ambassadors he must recognise that he is a figurehead and not personally responsible for *all* diplomatic relations. If you are adopting this role, you must set the tone but must delegate. You must decide policy but must encourage colleagues to pick up initiatives. You must stamp your own personality on activity but allow scope for other executives to add their own special skills and expertise. Above all, you must become the leader of a team, every one of which is equally committed to the development of a level of effective communication which will enhance the organisation's reputation.

THE COMPANY AMBASSADOR

A checklist to help the effective manager organise the role of the ambassador

1 Have we agreed the audiences, objectives and aims for this activity?

2 Have we advised our management colleagues of how we propose to tackle this responsibility?

3 Have we got their full support for the planned programme of activity?

4 What professional assistance can we call in to help us plan the campaign?

5 Should we consider the use of an outside consultancy or a staff communications specialist?

6 Do we have the support material to operate as an effective ambassador:

- literature
- audio visual aids
- prepared speeches or presentations
- a company film or corporate brochure?

7   Do we have a machinery for identifying speaking opportunities and handling the invitations or refusals?

8   Have we allocated an adequate budget to support this communications activity?

9   What steps have we taken to ensure that it is properly integrated with other company PR, promotional activities, advertising and presentations?

10   Have we defined the corporate personality to ensure that this is being consistently reflected across all activities?

11   Can we consider the publication of this as a corporate credo so that all employees will understand our aims and our stance?

12   Have we clearly identified the attitudes of each of the audiences with whom we wish to communicate?

13   Have we undertaken the necessary training to handle media interviews?

14   Is there any distinct difference between what the organisation says and what it does?

15   Could there be gaps between how the audiences see the organisation and the way it would like to be seen?

16   Do we always act to avoid any information vacuum which might allow rumour, gossip and speculation to grow?

17   Is it our policy to communicate regularly and consistently and not just when the circumstances demand?

18   Have we established procedures for feedback so that we can monitor attitudes and the effectiveness of these communications?

19   Are we ensuring that we always behave in the right way to build our reputation?

20   Are all other managers conscious of their communications responsibilities?

21   Are we sensitive to trends within the environment within which we work?

22   Are we able to handle the bad news as quickly and positively as we do the good news?

23   Are we proud of our identity and display it proudly, clearly, consistently, wherever we can?

24   Are our programmes using each technique to its best advantage and complementary way?

25   Have we agreed a method of assessing the cost effectiveness of these communications activities and ways that it might be further improved?

FURTHER READING

Howard, Wilfred, *The Practice of Public Relations*, 2nd edition, Heinemann, 1985. Published on behalf of the CAM Foundation and the Institute of Marketing, this book contains contributions by the editor and 15 others on various aspects of PR.
Institute of Public Relations, *Guide to the City for Professional Communicators*, new edition, 1986

Books with wide general coverage

Bowman, Pat and Ellis, Nigel, *Manual of Public Relations*, Heinemann, 1982
Thomas, Colin Coulson, *Public Relations is Your Business*, Business Books, 1983
Haywood, Roger, *All About PR*, McGraw-Hill, 1984
Jefkins, Frank, *Planned Press and Public Relations*, Blackie, 2nd edition, 1986
Mendes, Nicholas, *This Public Relations Consultancy Business*, Mendes, 1984

Journals

Public Relations, the Institute of Public Relations' own quarterly
PR Week

Reference sources

The PR practitioner has an array of excellent books from which to select for the reference shelf (in such a fast-changing scene, the only caveat must be not to rely on outdated volumes).
BBC Annual Report and Handbook
Benn's Media Directory (2 vols, UK, International)
Blue Book of British Broadcasting (Tellex Monitors)

British Institute of Professional Photography Members' Reference Book (Annual)
Director's Guide to Choosing and Using a PR Consultancy (IOD)
Editors (London Information News Distribution Agency, 5 vols)
Hollis Press and Public Relations Annual (17th edition, 1985/86)
Information, Press and Public Relations Officers in Government Departments and Public Corporations (COI)
NUJ Freelance Directory
PIMS Financial Directory/Media Directory/Media Townslist
PR Planner – UK/Europe: looseleaf, the former collated as *Media Information – UK*
PR Week Marketing and Public Relations Handbook (Kogan Page)
Public Relations Year Book (*Financial Times*, for PRCA)
Television and Radio (IBA, annual)
Willing's Press Guide
The Institute's own *Register of Members*
IPRA Members' Register
Who's Who in Financial Journalism (Dewe Rogerson)
Who's Who in Broadcasting (Carrick Publishing)
Who's Who in Public Relations (Carrick Publishing)
Who's Who in the Press (Carrick Publishing)

Useful addresses

The Institute of Public Relations
Gate House
St John's Square
London EC1M 4DH

Public Relations Consultants Association
10 Belgrave Square
London SW1X 8PH

Institute of Marketing
Moor Hall
Cookham
Maidenhead
Berkshire SL6 9QH

Hollis Press & Public Relations Annual
Contact House
Sunbury-on-Thames
Middlesex TW16 5HG

The Public Relations Register
AAR Services Limited
62 Shaftesbury Avenue
London W1V 7DE

Advertisers Annual
Thomas Skinner Directories
Windsor Court
East Grinstead
West Sussex RH19 1XE

Index